In 1875 Mother Mary of Jesus the Good Shepherd founded the Sisters of the Holy Family of Nazareth. Mother Mary recognized that a life devoted to religion is a "particular working of the Holy Spirit in the Church through individuals and communities," and her purpose, from the very start, was to integrate religion into the public, apostolic, and social life. In their day-to-day following of Christ, the order responded with love to the needs and problems of all. The services of the Sisters of Nazareth signified a kind of "evangelical immediacy."

Sister Mary DeChantal, herself a member of the Catholic order, presents a comprehensive account of the Sisters of Nazareth, relating the economic, educational, and religious situations which the order encountered, serving in times of war and peace, in prosperity and depression. Since its founding, the order's dedicated members have reached out to all levels of humanity—without discrimination—and with the full recognition of man's inalienable rights.

The congregation arose in an age overshadowed by social revolution and political unrest. A cloud of discontent hung heavy over nineteenth-century society: "God was shamefully left out of the affairs of men and men floundered disastrously."

The wo_____
came _____ it
times, fearlessly opposed the _____ical, and economic movements of the era.

The order lived and worked not only with the poor and the disadvantaged, but also with the oppressed and the rejected, bypassing popular acclaim in their efforts. In their vision of life and service, they sought to bring light, hope, and courage to all they served. Mother Mary and her congregation "aimed to encompass . . . the fullness of life, both human and divine." The foundress instructed the Sisters to use, as their model, the life of the first Christians: "One heart and one soul; holding all things in common; marked by simplicity, steadfast faith, and apostolic service as occasion presented itself—in the awareness of God's love and the intensity of true brotherhood with mankind."

ABOUT THE AUTHOR

Sister Mary DeChantal has earned graduate degrees from DePaul and Northwestern universities, and pursued advanced studies in other American and European centers. As a member of the Catholic Order of Sisters of the Holy Family of Nazareth, she served in the capacity of secretary to three major superiors.

The author's research for *Out of Nazareth* consisted of interviews with more than six hundred informed persons, the study of all available records on location at all convents, and nearly four years of study of the archival materials at the Order's general headquarters in Rome, Italy.

Out of Nazareth

Books by Sister M. DeChantal, C.S.F.N.

Out of Nazareth
The Healing Touch

Out of Nazareth

A Centenary of the Sisters of the Holy Family of Nazareth
in the Service of the Church

Sister M. DeChantal, C.S.F.N.

Foreword by John Cardinal Krol, D.D.
Archbishop of Philadelphia

 An Exposition-Testament Book
EXPOSITION PRESS   NEW YORK

13129

FIRST EDITION

ISBN 0-682-47820-2

Manufactured in the United States of America

To the Sisters of the

HOLY FAMILY OF NAZARETH

PAST

PRESENT

and

FUTURE

" 'Can any good come out of Nazareth?' "
. . . 'Come and see.' "—John 1:46

CONTENTS

LIST OF ILLUSTRATIONS

FOREWORD

One hundred years ago, the canonical status of the religious life of women in the Church was limited to Second Order contemplatives, a life pursued in enclosed monasteries in keeping with the spirit and Rule of a given monastic patriarch or mendicant founder. Any other organization, not represented in this sole category, was regarded as a pious society. Such were the conditions when Mother Mary of Jesus the Good Shepherd commenced the foundation of the Sisters of the Holy Family of Nazareth in 1875.

By decree of Pope Leo XIII in 1900, the canonical status in the Church was extended to those pious societies which sought such recognition and adapted their constitutions and way of life to specific requirements, whereupon they became designated as religious congregations.

The Foundress of the Nazareth Congregation, taking into account that religious life is a particular working of the Holy Spirit in the Church through individuals and through communities, aimed from the very outset to engraft her inspiration, embodied in the life of the Nazareth Sisters, onto the visible structure of the Church. With the blessing of the Church's pastoral authority, the Sisters of the Holy Family of Nazareth thus integrated their supernatural vocation into the ecclesial public, apostolic and social life.

What does it mean to be a true religious?

A true religious is an exemplary follower of Christ, identifiable by publicly vowed evangelical consecration, accepted in the name of the Church, and which conditions and disposes the totality of human existence to self-denial and sacrifice in the pursuit of the excellence of the Christian life.

To contemporary man the evangelical life proclaims a message that can be readily understandable. For society indicates in many ways its present disenchantment with affluence and its quest for an inner liberation to be found in detachment from material things.

Moreover, excessive preoccupation with sex and the sensuous has brought about a widespread and proportionate disrespect for the human person even to the total disregard for life, including the life of the unborn. Overcome by a sense of futility and morbid frustration, mankind craves the restoration of the joyful dignity of the children of God and a release of the spirit in integrity and purity of life. The modern world, too, plunged in an abyss of unhappiness and chaos, hopes for the healing of wounds inflicted by various forms of disobedience, revolt and willful self-seeking.

It is not simply for her own sanctification that a religious becomes poor, chaste and obedient, but for the glory of God and the sanctification of others as well. Consequently, chastity, poverty and obedience are lived

ix

out within the compass of the religious community, so that from within that religious community the fruits of religious consecration may radiate to the world at large.

The Congregation of the Sisters of the Holy Family of Nazareth produced a dramatic proof of sacrifice in the martyred execution of eleven of their sisters who offered their lives for the deliverance of prisoners condemned by the Nazis. The ordinary, daily summons to sacrifice, however, is less dramatic. It is the day-to-day exemplary following of Christ in a manner particularly typical of the Holy Family's hidden life at Nazareth, responding with love to the needs of time and place. In this light the service of the Sisters of Nazareth is indelibly marked with a kind of evangelical immediacy.

The reader may ask, "Of what value a history, a recounting of deeds long past and possibly irrelevant to our own situation?" But such a query would carry the peril of built-in indifference and superficiality. The only response can be the perennial one of St. Paul, "Stand firm . . . and hold fast to the traditions which you have learned from us by word or by letter" (2 Thes. 2, 16). A sense of history and the perspective it offers our life and work was rarely more urgent than today. A history such as this is, therefore, the timelier today.

May the consolation and appreciation of things past encourage the Sisters of the Holy Family of Nazareth—and all of us—that they can, with God's assistance, preserve the charismatic identity imparted to them by their saintly Foundress as they make Christ present in many lands, in season and out of season, without discrimination. On the threshold of the second century of their existence, their mission of extending God's Kingdom in the world is as fortunate and providential as it had ever been.

+ JOHN CARDINAL KROL
Archbishop of Philadelphia

June 26, 1973

INTRODUCTION

The decision to establish a religious congregation within the Catholic Church requires a supreme act of faith. Founders and foundresses of religious orders, of men and women alike, have been known to resist the inner voice prodding them to take up a mission involving the domain of the spirit of other individuals. Many were known to have advanced strong and sincere arguments against the counsels of spiritual directors, protesting their own unworthiness.

One hundred years ago, Mother Mary of Jesus the Good Shepherd was one of those souls who, in spite of herself, submitted at length to just such advice when she began to form the Congregation of the Sisters of the Holy Family of Nazareth. Like St. Jane Frances de Chantal, who—years after having founded the Visitation order—reflected that she had neither desired to initiate a community of nuns nor did she susbsequently plan to establish one like the Visitation, Mother Mary also, in the course of time, saw that the mold of the Nazareth Congregation acquired a design different from the idea she had herself at first begun to entertain. Hers, too, was a role of quest and discovery of the fine lines in God's blueprint for the way of life which she was called upon to introduce.

The centenary of the Congregation, falling due in 1975, is the occasion for a purview in retrospect, encompassing the rise, development and service of the Sisters of the Holy Family of Nazareth. The succession of events across the century, grouped in broad segments, coincides with the tenure of the respective superiors general who, in guiding the Congregation in its expanding apostolate, gave witness to the initial act of faith.

As is fitting, considerable space is devoted here to the person and activities of the Mother Foundress. This work, however, does not presume to be biographically complete. A distinct study of her life, *Francesca Siedliska,* by Antonio Ricciardi, O.F.M.Cap., was published in Italian in 1970, and was translated the following year into English by Prior Regis N. Barwig under the title, *His Will Alone.*

According to prevalent usage, the Congregation is frequently referred to briefly in this account as "Nazareth," similarly as the Carmelite order is often spoken of as "Carmel."

This work was commenced under the auspices of Mother M. Neomisia Rutkowska, superior general of the Sisters of the Holy Family of Nazareth, and progressed with her constant and generous support. Its completion was accomplished during the tenure of her successor, Mother M. Medarda Synakowska, who gave it continuing personal interest and encouragement.

The research, begun in 1962, was furthered significantly by the provincial and local superiors, who freely provided the time and the means necessary to conduct it on location. Moreover, the archival research at the generalate of the Congregation in Rome, was rendered eminently productive through the liberal assistance of Sister M. Christine Markiewicz, secretary general.

A wealth of information to the substance of this book was contributed by more than six hundred Nazareth sisters and other persons interviewed, while—in the course of its preparation—the manuscript benefited from the careful criticism and suggestions of numerous persons who displayed a sincere interest in the history traced upon its pages.

All these persons, by virtue of their association with this work, have a part in proclaiming the coming of the Kingdom out of Nazareth.

I

The Quest
1842-1873

1 YEARNINGS OF THE AGE

The nineteenth century may well be called a period of encounter with long-stifled yearnings of the human heart. In a degree heretofore unequalled, it brought out from the very depths of man's personality the tremendous craving for recognition of his individual humanity and of his prerogative to profess group loyalties, religious and civic. Volumes of written and spoken arguments, disputing these rights, were unable to stem the evolution of the spirit. Once the spirit was drawn toward the limitless horizons of its vast potential, it braved clash and conflict, force and persecution.

And so it was that, in an age overshadowed by political strife and social upheavals, the Congregation of the Sisters of the Holy Family of Nazareth arose unobtrusively, in quiet obscurity, after the preferred manner of the acts of God.

The cult of the Holy Family was then practically nonexistent. At an audience on June 10, 1878, Mother Mary of Jesus the Good Shepherd and several Sisters of her young Community were informed by Leo XIII that in the Catholic Church there is no approved devotion to the Holy Family as such. Obviously, the time was not yet ripe for the message which the life led at Nazareth by Jesus, Mary, and Joseph held for the panting world: the message of brotherhood in Christ, expressed in mutual charity that respects in others the dignity of the people of God. Like the mustard seed, the idea of the new Congregation had to germinate slowly drawing upon the lessons discreetly conveyed in the Gospels. For those lessons are charged with power to revolutionize, in the best sense of the term, the lives of all people.

But a cloud of unrest and revolution hung heavily over nineteenth-century society. Its intensity caused a ferment in thought as well as in the faith, and unleashed a misguided passion for human welfare, leaving in its wake devastation and despondency. On November 12, 1842, Frances Siedliska, the future foundress of the new congregation, was born into a bewildering era of stubborn individualities that, torn between cross-purposes, time after time disagreed, hesitated, and blundered. Already for over fifty years nations had been groping for solutions to gnawing problems. All along the quest for liberty, equality, and fraternity continued to be shrouded in oppression and unhappiness.[1] God, loving man infinitely, yields to his love and would bestow every good thing upon him; but God was shamefully left out of the affairs of men and men floundered disastrously. Such was the tenor of the age.

In the chain of Western Powers France was the weakest link. The turbulent consequences of her revolution inflamed the minds with unsettling ideologies. After the Napoleonic period of elation, the post-Napole-

onic debacle aroused conflicting trends throughout Europe. Within the
boundaries of France, repeated attempts to reconstruct her lost glory and
to reconcile it with popularized slogans collapsed with frequent changes
of regime.[2]

Liberal movements in Spain, which came alive in the hope of ridding
the country of corruption and despotism, met with severe persecution.
When repressions reached the proportions of a reign of terror, the
country was plunged into a revolution.[3]

The Belgians, again, forced by the Congress of Vienna into an untenable union with the Kingdom of the Netherlands, revolted and eventually
separated.[4] Soon thereafter Belgium suffered internal riots with demands
for equal suffrage that smouldered into bitter antagonisms.[5]

Only England, after the successes at Fontainebleau and Waterloo,
steered clear of serious involvements on the Continent. The pacts she
negotiated were either politely noncommittal or speculatively gainful in
order to protect her insular interests and her colonial development. Shrewd
statesmen, especially during the long reign of Queen Victoria, recognized
that unless domestic ills were promptly and effectively remedied, revolutionary activity could scarcely be prevented. A series of timely socio-
economic measures staved off the possible eruption of grievances in open
demonstration. In dominions abroad, however, the British had to contend
with waves of local nationalism that precipitated rebellion and mutiny.[6]

From the earliest days of her formative years, Frances absorbed at
her parents' estates an animated knowledge of world events, noting the
many distorted faces of liberty that moved in the shadows of low politics,
personal intrigue, and high policy. She was quick to capture the sad
nuances in the discussions of her elders and to ponder the dire hardness
of the heart of those who fettered the free spirit of man. In the so-called
Holy Alliance of Russia, Prussia, and Austria she perceived a disquieting
irony, for its unholy objective was to supress democratic movements in
Europe.[7]

In Central Europe, Hungary and related ethnic groups—rankled by
class, religious, and racial hatreds—sought autonomy from Austria, but
were crushed and again subjected to Austrian absolutism.[8] Austrian pressures likewise offended the national consciousness of petty Italian king-
doms and fomented armed resistance. Out of a long, unremitting struggle,
Italy emerged a unified constitutional monarchy, although for decades she
remained at the crossroads of shifting politics.[9]

Similarly, in the German Confederation, Prussia had usurped unbid-
den dominance, and the independent Germanic states repudiated her
vehemently. The chaos, which ensued, embroiled them in menacing street

fights, insurrection, and anarchy, until under Bismarck's iron hand the unification of Germany was achieved.[10]

Besides the hardships caused by strife, the ravaged countries fell victim to a distress of another nature, which added to their suffering. Crop failures, famine, epidemics of cholera and typhus swept across Germany, Holland, Belgium, and Ireland and occasioned a mass exodus to the new world across the Atlantic in quest of relief both political and economic.[11] To the consternation of the emigrants, acute differences in the United States over the question of slavery ultimately divided the nation against itself in the Civil War.

Meanwhile the imperialistic ambitions of Catherine, of the Nicholases and the Alexanders pushed Russia's frontiers south, west, and east, binding smaller nations under a rule of tyranny. Inside Russia a network of secret revolutionary societies, radically anti-czarist and in sympathy with the vanquished, undertook a terrorist program of organized redress. As a result they were hounded by surveillance, arbitrary arrests, and summary executions.[12]

Had Frances Siedliska been endowed with vigorous health, had she been drawn into the active games of childhood and the whirl of adolescent attractions common to her youthful companions, she would have been less wont to cultivate a soberly thoughtful mood. With the habit of reflection, her faculties of observation and introspection developed early to an exceptional degree. Herself born to the charm of life, she sensed some of its hardness. She was moved to compassion by the injustices inflicted by the mighty in the name of justice and felt a strange kinship with the dispossessed of the world.

Her native Poland, too, lay crumpled and despoiled, a prey to the aggression of Russia, Prussia, and Austria, accomplished jointly by partitioning the ill-fated country. These three neighboring Powers had perceived a threat in the dynamic nature of Poland's Third of May Constitution (1791) which aimed to establish a more realistic accommodation of the nation's governing groups to the contemporary mentality and needs of its people.[13] Because the document boldly proclaimed progressive principles of government, because it guaranteed to the peasants land ownership and liberation from serfdom, and granted universal enfranchisement to all classes, it tacitly discredited the autocratic systems maintained by the three potentates within their own domains.[14] It is easy to understand why they sought to bar the implementation of the Constitution; it is also easy to visualize how the formula "divide and conquer" could serve their ends.[15]

2 DARK NIGHT OF FAITH

In times of trial and peril the Church had always been to the Poles a moral stronghold; in fact, loyalty to the Church and national patriotism were so closely bound in their nature that they were identified psychologically: whatever endangered one implied a threat to the other.[16] To undermine their spiritual vigor, Russia and Prussia took recourse to religious persecution in those regions of Poland which they dominated.[17] But faith and patriotism glowed irrepressibly, fanned by secret meetings and organized devotions.

When the November Uprising of 1830 failed in an unequal combat with the adversaries, the Poles looked for assistance from abroad. As a matter of fact, the admiration and public praise, expressed for their cause in friendly diplomatic circles, kindled visionary hopes of support and help, but these hopes were soon to vanish with mere gestures of neutral courtesy that were accorded to Polish political émigrés.

Chafing under enemy oppressions, the nation sank into grim apathy. Its bruised spirit, moreover, suffered a crushing blow in the encyclical addressed to the Polish hierarchy, June 9, 1832.[18] Russian diplomacy, to serve its own political ends, had exploited the slow progress of information across Europe and succeeded to present to Pope Gregory XVI a distorted report of the conditions in Poland.[19] In the absence of authentic particulars, the Pope readily believed the Russian report, formally acknowledged the authority of the partitioning powers over Poland, and expressed disapproval of her efforts to regain independence.[20]

The impact of this action was felt most acutely in Poland. The clergy, the nobility, and the intellectuals, being the nation's natural leaders, now considered themselves forsaken by the Supreme Pontiff and defenseless against schismatic incursions. Czar Nicholas I added insult to injury when he prohibited direct communication with the Holy See, requiring all ecclesiastical matters of the Church in Poland to be channeled through the Russian capital.[21]

Ten long years elapsed before the Pope learned of the actual state of affairs that had been so grossly misrepresented to him. On July 2, 1842, in a conciliatory allocution he attempted to assuage the stricken nation with the intent of restoring its confidence in the good will of the papacy and reviving religious fortitude in spite of persecutions.[22]

Upon his accession to the Chair of Peter, June 18, 1846, Pope Pius IX showed genuine concern for the plight of Poland in his encyclicals and addresses, appealing to the Christian world for prayers in Poland's behalf,[23] and in the resumption of diplomatic relations with the Holy See through an accredited representative of Poland.[24] He also beatified the Jesuit Andrew Bobola and canonized Archbishop Josaphat Kuncewicz,

6

who, in an earlier period, had been cruelly martyred for the faith by Russian schismatics.

To offset the difficulties imposed upon aspirants to the priesthood in Poland, he founded the Pontifical Polish College in Rome and placed it under the direction of the Resurrectionist Fathers. Finally, in protest against the persecution of the Poles, he severed diplomatic relations with Russia and revoked the Concordat.[25]

The pontificate of Pius IX was a thirty-two-year long unbloody martyrdom, which at times placed his life in jeopardy. He was incessantly harassed by foreign tactics—political and military—which in a contest for supremacy on Italian soil, engaged in a drawn out conflict against the nationalist operations of Mazzini and Garibaldi. When the unification of Italy was at length accomplished, the Papal States became annexed to the Kingdom of Italy, thereby depriving the Roman Pontiff of the temporal power which had for centuries constituted a traditional heritage.[26]

The loss of temporal power was but one of the many trials of Pius IX's pontificate. Just as his outstanding achievements were of ecclesiastical and religious character, so, too, his most severe anguish was caused by anticlerical and irreligious movements. The dark genius of radical exponents infiltrated all levels of society in the Western World. It created a spiritual vacuum in the minds it affected and commenced to build a new order of things upon human weaknesses.

The Pope's spiritual martyrdom, however, was not without appreciable joys. There was evidence of honest search for true human and supernatural values in the rise of approximately a hundred new religious orders to tend to society's urgent needs and to spread the Catholic apostolate in missionary fields; there was an anticipation of unity in the restoration of Catholic hierarchy in England; there was merciful solace in the apparitions of the Holy Virgin at LaSalette and at Lourdes; there were glimpses of sanctity in numerous heroic souls who—in not too distant a future—would gain the honors of the altar.

3 IN THE GREAT TRADITION

Adolphe Adam Siedliski, father of the future foundress, began spinning visions of a grand and dazzling destiny for his daughter almost from the very day of her birth. She was his first child and, throughout his lifetime, he would lavish upon her his love and solicitude with an extravagance that had its source in his generous nature. He personally accompanied his infant daughter from his country estate at Roszkowa Wola, where she was born, to the church of St. Andrew in Warsaw to be baptized, November 20, 1842, and affixed his signature to the baptismal record.[27] The baptism was administered by Reverend Louis Zaleski and the child was named Frances Josephine Anne; her sponsors were Vincent Kozłowski, privy councilor and director of religious affairs in the National Commission of the Interior, and Anna Małowieska, her mother's sister.[28]

Her mother, Cecilia Marianna, was the daughter of Joseph Alexis Morawski, a statesman of irreproachable integrity and rare ability. By prudent negotiations with officials of foreign powers, Morawski rendered eminent services to his countrymen in the painful and critical period after 1830, in the years between the two major attempts to free Poland from foreign domination. He attained positions of trust and respect as chairman of the executive board of the Land Credit Association, as president of the National Treasury Commission, and as Minister of Finance.[29] Above all, he was a man of confirmed loyalty. Perhaps his very essence, his whole quality, was a shade too high for the commonplace values of the world about him and his vision far beyond that of most of his colleagues to be deterred by scarcity of plaudits in the fluctuating public opinion.[30]

To Cecilia he gave in dowry the beautiful manorial holdings of Żdżary,[31] consisting of extensive forest lands and a landscaped park, planned in the English fashion with flower and water gardens that surrounded the fine residence.[32] This estate lay in a serene valley, slightly southwest of Warsaw, in close proximity to the vast fertile farmlands of Roszkowa Wola[33] which Adolphe had inherited. Forking out of the Vistula, the Pilica River flowed through this region, contributing to the varied and abundant productivity of the soil.[34] Both estates were cultivated by village peasants after the manner generally practiced in nineteenth-century Europe. By comparison, however, the lot of Polish tenantry was lighter and their burdens fewer in number than elsewhere.[35] But due to foreign political interference, the enfranchisement of the peasants, including the right of ownership and the right to settle where they pleased, depended largely upon the particular dispositions and economics of landed gentry. Adolphe Siedliski, true to his expansive, liberal temperament, proceeded to implement the peasant manifesto with judicious fairness and

8

won the gratitude and devotion of the people who worked his lands.[36] Village schools, too, removed the barriers of illiteracy and for the more gifted of the peasant children opened opportunities to pursue further knowledge.

The villages, which constituted the Żdżary estate, alone formed a canonical parish, numbering 1,180 adults. The parish church of St. Nicholas, founded and endowed by Madame Siedliska's father,[37] is still in existence and is maintained as a place of worship. After the founder's death in 1855, a suitable memorial plaque was furnished by Adolphe Siedliski and is mounted near the entrance of the church.[38]

Four years after the birth of Frances, the Siedliskis greeted a son, Adam, on October 27, 1846.[39] Adolphe rejoiced in the arrival of an heir who would carry—he hoped—the family torch in honor and great deeds.

Adolphe[40] and his gentle spouse, Cecilia,[41] descended from time-honored nobility of Poland, were prominent among their peers. Cecilia, who for reasons of delicate health, reduced her social calendar to the minimum, preferred the quiet joys of family life and the works of charity for the improvement of the lot of peasant women and children. In directing household activities she was frequently relieved by Adolphe's widowed mother, Catherine (née Kulczycka), who resided with them.

Adolphe, in unswerving devotion to his wife,[42] deflected his exuberance to affairs of state and to patriotic and local interests. As a board member of the Land Credit Association,[43] he invested much time and material support in promoting the success of this project to help salvage the properties of landowners from the threat of expropriation. Through its widespread branch offices, the Association made loans available on easy terms, advocated the introduction of advanced methods and peasant reforms in agricultural management,[44] and furthered the growth of industry and commerce.[45] He was also active in the non-militant council of influential citizens whose aim was to build up the internal strength of the nation through educational and technological progress, rather than to dissipate it by rash and ill-advised revolutionary schemes.[46] To gratify his convivial bent, Adolphe occasionally gathered groups of intimates at the great country estate, or at the club in Warsaw, where he received them with princely gallantry.[47]

The Siedliskis bore the peculiar imprint of their age and environment, particularly in the outward reserve toward religious practices. For the wound heedlessly inflicted on the nation's sensibilities by Gregory XVI remained long unhealed and festered painfully, leaving many scars where faith could have blossomed in fervor. The seeds of rationalism found there a susceptible terrain. Similarly as in other countries, overt piety tended to be limited to attendance at Sunday Mass and the fulfillment of Easter duty; even the clergy looked askance at any noticeable frequency in the reception of the sacraments; children were not admitted to First Holy Communion before the age of twelve; cloistered nuns received Holy Communion at supervised intervals in deference to recognized virtue, as if it were within human capability to merit Christ's ineffable grace of the Eucharist. Active faith became eclipsed, but it was not obliterated; it retreated underground.[48]

News of the genuine sympathy and understanding of Pius IX traveled slowly to Poland. Gradually it penetrated the curtain of indifference and intensified the accord with the head of the Catholic Church; it also moved the people to religious ardor. In the period after 1850, Warsaw became the center of reawakened piety[49] chiefly due to the zeal of the Capuchins.[50] They were attached to the historic church of the Transfiguration, which was founded by King John Sobieski in gratitude to God for the victory at Vienna against the Turkish invasion. Their message had a special appeal to the upper classes;[51] under their guidance women devoted themselves to truly contemplative life; others engaged in positive works of social, moral, and educational rehabilitation of the needy, alike in urban and rural areas.[52]

Cecilia Siedliska and her sister, Anna Małowieska, readily placed themselves under the direction of the Capuchin, Father Leander Lendzian and frequently went to hear his exhortations during their seasonal stay in Warsaw. Usually, with the approach of winter, both families moved into the capital, occupying the spacious apartments of Minister Morawski in the fashionable section of the city, and remained there until after Pentecost.[53]

The Siedliskis passed their summer months interchangeably at one or the other of their estates, where they personally took part in the high point of the season, the harvest festivities,[54] to the undisguised pleasure of the people. The atmosphere of tender affection which pervaded the family relationships radiated, in turn, wholesome social attitudes and mutual respect within the ranks of the subordinates.[55]

4 DAUGHTER FRANCES

During the 1800's girls of the upper classes were generally educated at home. Of the several governesses and tutors who exerted a marked influence upon the childhood of Frances, the memory of her first teacher was preserved by her in lasting gratitude; from her Frances and her brother received the earliest instructions in the faith and its obligations.[56] After the premature death of this admirable woman, whom Frances mourned with sincere grief and affection, her parents engaged another young person, a Protestant from Dresden, brilliant and capable. Frances, intuitively perceptive of moral values, quickly noted this tutor's disdain for natural virtues, such as truth, justice, fidelity, and in consequence shunned her patronizing overtures. When on few occasions she indulged in spiteful ridicule of the Catholic Church, Frances informed her mother and succeeded to be freed of this person.[57]

There were also special instructors in music, singing, and other arts for which Frances displayed considerable talent and liking. While the Siedliskis sojourned in Warsaw through the winter, as was customary, her father proudly accompanied her to the theater, opera, concerts, and ballets. At first these performances fascinated and attracted her, but soon she wearied of them.[58]

Then the winter of 1853-1854 brought a turning point into her young life. Her aunt, Madame Małowieska, seriously regarding her own responsibility as godmother, advised that Frances be properly prepared for confession and First Holy Communion without further delay.[59] Canon John Dziubacki from St. John's Cathedral gave Frances a series of instructions which she attended eagerly and, on March 9, 1854, she made her first confession to Father Topolski at the church of St. Charles Borromeo.[60] Each successive confession evoked conscious efforts in pursuit of Christian perfection and a search for deeper spiritual insights.[61] She began to grasp the truth that God is always in the world and that it is the aim of Christian life to find God present in all things and in all activities. She also grew to realize that there are different ways by which his presence may be reached. It was at this time that she decided that dancing had no place in her life and determined to abandon her dancing lessons.[62]

During the following season, in November of 1854, Frances met the Capuchin Father Leander, who was invited to prepare her for Holy Communion.[63] As this entailed a departure from the precept of the monastic rule, her grandfather, Minister Morawski, enjoying friendly relations with the Capuchin commissioner general for the province of Poland, Bishop Benjamin Szymanski, had sought and obtained the necessary exemption for Father Leander to frequent his residence.[64]

On May 1, 1855, Frances arrived at the fulfillment of her great anti-

11

cipation. Together with a youthful friend, Hedwig Szymańska,[65] who had been taking religious instructions along with her, Frances was escorted through the monks' choir into the sanctuary of the Capuchin church. This day crowds filled the church to overflowing and a great number of people surrounded it, for May devotions were then being initiated in Warsaw by the Capuchins and an outdoor statue of the Virgin Mary was solemnly enthroned in the church square[66] to commemorate the dogma of the Immaculate Conception that had been proclaimed the previous December by Pius IX.

Kneeling at the foot of the altar throughout the entire service, the girls—two white-clad figures, wearing white hats trimmed with blue ribbons, as veils were not yet customary on the occasion of First Holy Communion[67]—Frances and Hedwig, received the Sacred Host at the hands of Father Leander. Frances was entranced; her joy increased on finding at home, among many gifts, a gold ring with the emblems of faith, hope, and charity from her father.[68] This compensated for his absence from Warsaw which was caused by the summons to the deathbed of his older brother, Amilkar, who died on April 29.[69]

Rapturously happy, Frances continued for days in prayerful absorption which nothing could distract—social visits, entertainments, or strolls in the exotic Saxon Gardens.[70] That same year, on the feast of the Most Blessed Trinity, June 8, she was confirmed at the church of St. Casimir by the venerable, heroic archbishop of Warsaw, Anthony Melchior Fijał-kowski. He was administering there the Sacrament of Confirmation to a group of girls from the private finishing school, conducted by the nuns of the Blessed Sacrament whose convent was attached to the church of St. Casimir. As her confirmation name Frances chose Mary.[71]

Because Minister Morawski was the nuns' constant and generous benefactor, Madame Siedliska and her daughter were readily accorded the privilege to enter the convent enclosure after the ceremonies in order to pay their respects to the Archbishop. Awe descended upon Frances as she passed the precincts of the convent; this, her first contact with nuns, drew her irresistibly. But in the subtle humility of her soul she deemed herself undeserving of so exalted a calling. She resolved then to strive for an ever greater degree of purity of heart and a closer union with God.[72]

Once again she had to struggle through an inner conflict, aroused by yet another teacher, an imprudent young person who, reveling in her own happiness, read her fiancé's letters to Frances and chatted indiscreetly about her plans for the future. For the peace of her conscience, Frances made these communications known to her mother for the purpose of securing her intervention.[73]

This memorable year held one other sad episode for the family, the death of Minister Morawski on August 17.[74] After the funeral in Warsaw, the Siedliskis acquired their own city residence, overlooking the beautiful Krasinski Gardens. A private chapel was arranged in their apartments and, with the Archbishop's consent, the Sacrifice of the Mass was celebrated there, in most instances, by Father Leander, under whose spiritual direction both mother and daughter remained.[75]

Aflame with a fervor that was incomprehensible to her environment, Frances had to be mitigated by her mother as well as by the confessor in the mortifications and practices of piety for which she felt a haunting need, as acts of atonement and of love toward God.[76] When the period of mourning for her grandfather was over, she was exposed to severe trials, heedlessly occasioned by her father, to whom she was attached with all the warmth of her filial affection and who—out of paternal ambition—desired her happiness, as he understood it, in a brilliant marriage.[77] Cecilia, on the other hand, submitted patiently to her husband's idea of life; she knew how to carry on with dignity and found the source of strength and peace in her faith.

Frances was a sensitive child, keen of intelligence, responsive to the goodness of God and man, compassionate and generous. She possessed rare personal charm that built up the pride of her father and in which her mother basked as in reflected glory. Adolphe, smitten with a secret dread lest he lose her to the cloister, leveled sharp criticisms against her piety, made unfair objections to Father Leander's guidance, demanded her presence at social functions and public entertainments when she neither had interest in them nor in the prospects of marriage for which these were intended to serve as a prelude.[78] But her will was a real match for her father's. While she deferred to his authority, she had no fear of dissenting, which she did with touching respect. She was an independent spirit, free and strong, with an astounding strength concealed under marvelous gentleness. There had to be compromises. When her father grudgingly condescended to her pleas against participating in dance receptions, he cajoled her into attending the widely acclaimed operas of Moniuszko and the concerts given by artists of international renown.[79] She, in turn, limited her association with Father Leander to occasional correspondence and chose as her regular confessor the Vicar General of Warsaw, Canon Paul Rzewuski of St. John's Cathedral.[80]

On presenting her difficulties to Father Leander, she received a letter in which he pointed out that the circumstances of her life are a test of her spirit to which she ought to submit, and added: "The spirit of God directs human life to an unmistakable destiny, just as in nature winds drive the clouds to where land must be watered. Yield to the touch of God, like a keyboard of a musical instrument, so that he might sound the tones and chords of his choice. Should you attempt to play as you want or feel, you will be out of tune; God will muffle his ears and say, 'Frances is a good child, but does not know her music.' "[81]

She sought to strengthen her moral reserves by penitential practices. When she wished to bind herself by the vow of chastity, Father Leander allowed it only for the extent of time from one feast of the Blessed Virgin to another with the possibility of renewal each time until the next feast.[82] However, by the time she was seventeen, her father plainly manoeuvered toward what he considered desirable marriage plans for Frances. He even took her piety into account, inviting and encouraging the visits of young gentlemen who were known to be devout and virtuous. To her troubled soul Father Leander addressed this sage advice: "As long as you are not seeking worldly pleasure or occasions to sin, you will not fall, for you are entering the world out of obedience. Remain faithful in prayer; have confidence in Our Lord; he and his immaculate Mother will support you."[83]

Although she maintained a kind of aloofness, she could not dissociate herself entirely from her environment and again complained to Father Leander about experiencing a certain amount of enjoyment in the round of social activities she had to attend. His reply contained a weighty statement: "Without hesitation would I willingly give my life to guard you against sin, so that you may be pleasing to God and his angels—innocent, upright, honest, humble, a true daughter of the immaculate Virgin Mary."[84]

To Frances this sounded a clear note which meant but one thing. Marriage was not for her. She decided to break with all uncertainty and announced her withdrawal from society. She declined invitations and braved the remonstrances of her parents. The cutting remarks of relatives and acquaintances led nowhere, except into a morass of hurt and humiliation, but left her unmoved.[85]

Distressed by the knowledge that she pained her parents and exhausted by the conflict to which their demands subjected her, she fell critically ill in the spring of 1860. By summer the physicians suspected lung involvement and declared Frances incapable of withstanding the rigors of the climate in Poland. They urged that she be taken to Meran, an idyllic mountain village with a mild climate, situated in the Tyrol in a spectacular setting among gaunt, dramatic peaks of the Dolomites. Under the circumstances, this siege of illness was her rescue.[86] In the future, Providence repeatedly sent her this strange ally, in the form of grave illness, to help her resolve the baffling problems that could have driven her into an untenable position.[87]

The threat to his daughter's life aroused in Adolphe Siedliski the stark realization of another threat. He had become so totally engrossed in meetings and plans for a new patriotic uprising against Russia that for the moment he was simply unaware of the implications. In principle he belonged to the moderates who—remembering the tragic aftermath of previous abortive uprisings—disagreed with the impatient young militants over a wide range of theoretical questions and, on practical grounds, with their espousal of armed revolution at this time. Their agitation interfered with the strategic efforts to establish peaceful diplomatic foreign relations, regardless of political complexities, in the interest of an assured emancipation of the country at a later date.[88] But, like so many others of his generation, Adolphe could not tolerate to have his national sentiments called in question and became inveigled in the preparations by providing financial support and offering protection to underground meetings at his country estates.[89]

Meanwhile, year after year in the last five years, Alexander II visited Warsaw for reasons that were obviously not friendly and proclaimed his views in no ambiguous terms.[90] It suddenly occurred to Adolphe that his patriotic collaboration, if discovered, should terribly endanger the safety of his family. Immediately he made arrangements for their departure from the country. His son Adam was sent to France to Collège Saint-Clément, conducted by the Jesuits at Metz,[91] while Cecilia and Frances, together with Mademoiselle Laurent, teacher and companion to Frances, became established in Meran.[92]

5 TOWARD A VEILED DESTINY

The methods prescribed in treating Frances were in large part responsible for the recurring bouts of lingering complications that forestalled her cure. Upon her arrival at Meran, the doctors recommended hiking excursions along the Tappeiner Promenade—a ribbon road, now and then growing steep, winding for two and a half miles through unique perspectives of snowy grandeur, through pine woods, and around little lakes. She delighted in the matchless beauty of her surroudings, but the exertion at increasing altitudes brought on mountain sickness, *mal di montagna,* with fierce headaches, blurring vision, dehydration, nausea, and stinging sunburn. For several months she was compelled to abandon all physical activity and to discontinue her studies. This incident justified her avoidance of the high social life that flourished in the Alpine resorts to which a sophisticated clientelle from European courts and elegant drawing rooms rallied the year round.[93]

In the quiet of her soul Frances turned more and more to contemplation. God was speaking to her heart, leading her toward a path that was still obscure. Convent life beckoned as the possible answer, the fullest gift of self in total consecration to Christ—she could not give less— though she felt no call to any particular order or rule. One thing was certain: she must guard the purity of her soul that she might keep herself entirely for God, awaiting the manifestation of his will.[94]

The following year, on medical advice, she left for Switzerland, dividing her stay between Interlaken—a panoramic strip glittering between Lakes Thun and Brienz, Einsiedeln—a cliffside town where the church of Notre Dames des Ermites is the object of numerous pilgrimages, honoring the famous image of the Holy Virgin, and Vevey—reposing placidly against the Jura mountains, with Lake Geneva at its feet.[95]

In the winter of 1862, when Frances returned to Meran with her mother and Mlle. Laurent, Adolphe Siedliski arrived to visit them. To allay their apprehensions, he gave enthusiastic accounts of the preparations for the uprising and appeared supremely confident.[96] He was just then on a secret mission to Italy,[97] where a school for Polish officers had been established under the patronage of Count Cavour.[98] It was necessary to contact military leaders at the post to maintain a communication lifeline with the home front on tactical matters.[99]

For a good part of the next year Frances remained at Einsiedeln in joyous communion with God. She had not the desire to appear conspicuous and little awareness of being so. Admired as few women were, she posed the problem of a woman's aloneness. With her mother and the governess who was also her companion, she lived apart in a small villa in the neighborhood of the ancient Benedictine monastery.[100]

She was tall and very slender. Her skin, which was extraordinarily delicate, had a golden glow in the intervals when her health returned, and her
bronze-colored eyes, with a quick intelligence about them, were as gentle
as satin. But more than most of her contemporaries, she had the courage
to speak without the slightest hypocrisy. However, what impressed the
resort guests were her musical improvisations, which were not only
beautiful, but unforgettable, each a masterpiece of technique and inspiration.[101]

The Siedliski ladies met Adolphe briefly at Reichenhall in Upper Ba-
varia on his homeward trip to Poland.[102] Foreign press had publicized the
outbreak of the uprising during his absence and its ultimate defeat. Suppressed with great ferocity, the venture resulted in the destruction of the
remnants of Polish autonomy. Single victories could not disguise the fact
that the nationalist forces were outnumbered; they fought heroically but
unavailingly.[103] Adolphe Siedliski was anxious to appraise the situation
in person.

Frances, having spent her youth among some of the most tragic turns
of fortune in the history of her country, knew and understood such things
as vast disagreements between well-intentioned parties, evolving trends in
political opinion, the glorification of might, and the reprisals of the vanquished. The Church in Poland was hampered in exercising its influence
for good, because it was suspected of identifying itself with resistance
against the aggressors and was looked upon with distrust by the Russian
occupants.

In spite of the unhappy news, Frances steadily sought to discover her
way, holding fast to God, longing to serve him in whatever work Providence should point out to her. Upon learning that eminent French preach-
ers were devoting themselves to the spiritual needs of resort guests at
Cannes, she proceeded there in the hope of finding light and guidance.[104]

At midwinter (1863-1864), when the entire family reunited at Cannes
for a Mediterranean holiday, Adolphe recounted his predicament.
Russian authorities held incriminating evidence against him: combatants
had been sheltered and discovered on his estates;[105] guerilla warfare had
been carried on in the Żdżary forests;[106] his support of the uprising was
known. He was subject to heavy penalties imposed either in the form of
payment of enormous fines or exile to Siberia.[107] Walking along the seaboard with Frances, he told her he had always intended to give her
Roszkowa Wola in dowry, but now he could not maintain the two estates
because his funds were depleted through the contributions he made to
the unsuccessful liberation effort.[108]

In this fateful hour she assured her father she would never marry and
had no need of Roszkowa Wola. She encouraged him to have no qualms

about selling the estate in order to procure the sum required for the political fine. Slow to yield to his daughter's attitude, Adolphe exacted from her the promise that she would not leave home as long as he lived. Nevertheless she gained an important point with her father in the stand she had taken and at once glimpsed more distinctly the direction of her life's course.[109]

As Adam was due to return to Metz, Frances and her parents accompanied him as far as Lyons. Here at Hotel Bellecour, the Siedliskis' rooms looked out onto the church of Notre Dame de Fourvières, famed for unusual favors received by the faithful who came to venerate the Blessed Virgin Mary.[110] Later in life Frances made a number of devotional visits to this hallowed shrine to implore assistance from the Mother of God.

When in the fall of 1864 the family went to Hyères in the south of France, they became acquainted with the learned Resurrectionist, Father Joseph Hube,[111] who had recently served as the second superior general of his order. He had a true understanding of the human nature, its inherent weaknesses and its spiritual needs. Frances gained greatly by every visit of his and came to realize definitely that she must embrace convent life. She had, however, the invincible conviction that the final word would come from Father Leander. Meanwhile the grace of God began to operate in Adolphe's soul through his friendly association with Father Hube who, with kindly patience, sincerity, and wisdom opened to Adolphe the treasures of divine mercy. On the eve of the Ascension, after years of neglect, Adolphe received the sacraments with touching piety to the unspeakable joy of his wife and daughter.[112]

That year, Adam, upon completing his studies in Metz, proceeded to the University of Montpellier to follow the specialized curriculum in agronomy. Since the city enjoyed a balmy Mediterranean climate, the family took residence there for a season.[113]

To Frances, at the age of twenty-two, it seemed she had already spanned a full cycle. She had voiced her irreversible decision to her father and had seen his return to the practices of the faith. She had met men of God who introduced her to dogmatic and ascetical literature. Under tutorship she mastered the French, Latin, and German languages, and became conversant with the world's literary and philosophical works; she acquired the knowledge of such sciences as were accessible outside the laboratories and lecture halls, while her own lively interest in human behavior found a rich field for the study of practical psychology in the manifold encounters with persons of diversified backgrounds.

She had traveled far and long, presumably in search of health; actually she was picking her way, groping, trying to detect the road marks to the will of God. Time and again she succumbed to protracted maladies because the state of her health had been inaccurately diagnosed and ineptly treated,[114] inducing toxic and painful conditions as side effects.[115] There had been the alarming process of disseminated neuritis that left her prostrated without surcease for weeks. There had been the incidence of what appeared to have been vertebral lesions[116] for which chemocautery was prescribed with the application of caustic Vienna powder.[117] Ineffectual therapy repeatedly confined her to suffering greater than the initial ailments.

All this she accepted on faith as fitting into the designs of God for her, by way of passive purification[118] and the dark night of the soul, leading to the renunciation of and detachment from those interests that might obstruct her progress toward her absolute commitment.[119] She was determined to remain open and available to the divine call. Convinced that nothing further was to be gained abroad, she readily complied with her father's plans to return to Poland at the turn of the year.[120]

6 THE MESSAGE

The religious superiors of Father Leander, in the meantime, transferred him from the monastery in Warsaw, from under the hostile eyes of prying Russian officials, first to Lublin, then to Nowe Miasto; the latter, a small town, situated near the Siedliski estate. As a former paroled prisoner, charged with nationalist activity, he was politically suspect. Even though he entered the Capuchin Order after his release from prison, his popularity and influence as a spiritual director excited distrust in the enemy camp and could easily make him liable to arrest, imprisonment, and exile or execution at the slightest inkling of political agitation. His removal from the capital was timed well in advance of the events of 1863.[121]

In an interview with Frances, upon her return, Father Leander explained that he had not been replying to her letters in order to give her freedom of choice and action. From his occasional visits, whenever his work brought him to Warsaw, and from the private chapel in her home she gathered the courage to patiently wait and suffer. For medical specialists here, too, fumbled but did not cure, while Father Leander, convinced though he was in his own mind about her future mission, had no indications as yet concerning its real nature.[122]

To complicate the difficulty, one of his penitents, Helen Aszperger, a woman of ambition and power, endeavored by unfavorable reports to discredit Frances to him. In his brusque, honest manner, Father Leander chided Frances for insincerity and affectation, threatening even to discontinue directing her soul. Frances endured harrowing anguish of mind under the strictures until, at length, Father Leander discovered the intrigue.[123]

The year 1867 was marked by Adolphe's loss of health. His usual vitality was rapidly deteriorating and he was becoming a helpless invalid. Neither the mineral springs at Aix-les-Bains nor the famed clinics of Dresden were able to restore his vigor. Back at his residence in Warsaw, seated in the wheelchair, he spent much time in the chapel, tranquil and resigned. Frances, grieving over the terrible change in her father, was suddenly stricken with a sorrow of another kind. In the middle of 1869, Mademoiselle Laurent, who for ten years was her devoted companion and instructor, died unexpectedly after a fulminating illness of but few days.[124]

Adolphe's downhill course continued without impairment of his mental faculties which enabled him to turn frequently to God in prayer and the sacraments. He died the day after Easter, April 18, 1870.[125] After the funeral, Frances and her mother retired to Żdżary. As soon as the family mausoleum was erected in the local cemetery, Adolphe's remains were transferred from Warsaw and entombed in the crypt in the presence of a multitude of villagers, lamenting the loss of their good master.[126] The remains of Adolphe's brother, Amilkar, and of Mlle. Laurent were also disinterred and placed in the same crypt.[127]

Under existing ordinances, legal and financial matters involving property title, patrimony, and investments were tedious and intricate. With her clear, logical mind, Frances lent reliable assistance to her mother and brother, since each one of them aimed to assure the welfare of the others before final arrangements would be undertaken affecting their personal lives respectively.[128]

Adolphe's passing left Frances free to consecrate herself to the service of God. This thought alone eased the poignancy of her bereavement. Since her mother also desired to embrace religious life, Frances saw her path open straight and undeterred by natural ties. Father Leander, however, advised against haste and recommended for the present that both, mother and daughter, become Franciscan tertiaries. On the day of her acceptance, Frances received Angela as her name in the Third Order of St. Francis.[129]

She and her mother concentrated on devout life, care of the needy, and embroidery of church vestments and altar linens. The amiable temperament of the young master, their son and brother Adam, allowed nothing to disturb the mode of life they adopted. Accommodating herself to the task of the moment, Frances knew full well that this was not what she was waiting for, this was not enough. But Father Leander, exerting stern guidance in the interior formation of his penitent, was still obliged to pursue his course as enigmatically as ever. He instructed her to cultivate the ecclesial spirit and to reflect upon the Gospels and scriptural passages from the Mass of each day.[130]

At this time she relapsed into an extended illness. Weakened by thirteen spinal apertures which were performed earlier according to accepted contemporary medical procedures,[131] she lingered on the brink of death. Worse than physical suffering, the agony of the spirit consumed her like a fever—nagging doubts, a sense of futility, utter desolation. She clung to dark faith as to the proverbial straw.[132]

Then one day, in a letter from Father Leander, she read these startling words: "I wish you would become a nun." Joy flooded her soul. The future, though remote, appeared promising. Later, on the eve of her baptismal patron's day, March 8, 1873, when Father Leander came to Żdżary to hear her confession, he said, "My child, I have something of great importance to tell you. Be prepared to receive it with a supernatural disposition. I must inform you that Our Lord revealed to a certain person that he loves you very much and that he is always with you. Do not question me to whom these words were spoken, because it is not expedient for you to know it at present. Suffice it now that you believe this." The following day, when he brought her Holy Communion, he declared emphatically, "It is the will of God that you become a nun."[133]

* * *

Some twelve years before that day when Frances felt the touch of destiny upon her, a number of Franciscan tertiaries had formed in Lublin the Society of Our Lady of Loreto. They were pious women of means and culture and free of family obligations, who divided their time between catechetical instruction of children, works of mercy, and the pursuit of higher Christian perfection. Living in common, they followed a pseudo-monastic pattern under the guidance of Father Leander who, in 1860, became the superior at the Capuchin monastery in Lublin.[134]

These Ladies of Loreto aimed to develop an essentially Marian spirituality. It consisted in the contemplation and practice of the virtues of the Mother of God as had been lived by her during her hidden years at Nazareth. For this reason they adopted the title that would honor her holy house now enshrined in the basilica at Loreto in Italy.[135]

In their worthy zeal they looked forward to other kindred souls whom they hoped Father Leander might inspire to join their Society in order to expand and invigorate its membership and, eventually, to gain for it the status of a full-fledged religious congregation. Realistically enough, they entrusted to him all their funds for the foundation purposes of the anticipated congregation.

Over the years—age, illness, and death continued to shrink the vigor and the numbers of the original group, but new members were not forthcoming. Meanwhile, Father Leander was again transferred—this time to the monastery in Nowe Miasto, midway between Warsaw and Lublin. This coincidence facilitated whatever contacts were necessary for the uninterrupted direction of his penitents at both points. Neither did he abandon the thriving hope of the Lublin Society, for he honestly wished to realize its idea and to assure its existence and growth for the service of the Church. Thus he considered placing over it a suitable superior from among his penitents to give it the vitality and leadership it needed.[136]

Years later it was learned that he had had three persons in mind for this position. One was Helen Aszperger, widow and Franciscan tertiary, possessed of certain natural qualifications, who at the moment was still committed to the upbringing of her teenage daughters, Michaeline and Marie. Another was Wanda Lubowidzka, one of three orphaned sisters who together conducted in Warsaw a private finishing school for girls; she, too, was a Franciscan tertiary and tentatively planned to enter one of the existing religious orders. The third possible choice, uppermost in his mind because of her edifying life, proven virtue, and outstanding intellectual gifts, pointed to Frances Siedliska; her precarious health, however, seemed to militate against such choice.[137]

He was still lost in the quandary when the little Society suffered the loss of its moral mainstay in the sudden death of Maria Wojewódzka. A woman of noble character and unflagging fervor, though blind, she was to the group a constant inspiration and exemplar. The need now to do something concrete about the prospective congregation forced Father Leander to petition heaven more earnestly for a discernible sign. He charged, therefore, Brother Stephen at the monastery of Nowe Miasto to pray for his intention that he might know the will of God, but made no mention of his reason for this request.

Brother Stephen,[138] born in 1843, was known in civilian life as Hippolyte Rembiszewski; he became a lay brother in the Capuchin Order where he pronounced perpetual vows on December 28, 1868. Of frail constitution and gentle demeanor, Brother Stephen's presence bore the calm dignity of a man who held frequent and intimate communion with God. For his innocence and sincere humility he enjoyed the esteem of Father Leander, who was his superior and confessor.

As the winter season began thawing into the springtime of 1873, Stephen had an astonishing message to convey. The youngest of the Ladies of Loreto, Theodosia Kobylańska, appeared to him at prayer. She told him she had just died and that Frances Siedliska shall be the superior of the new congregation which will arise from the Society of Our Lady of Loreto. Stephen at this time had not known Frances Siedliska. Although Theodosia's death was actually confirmed by a telegram from Lublin later in the day, Father Leander, prudent and discriminating in the matters of supernatural phenomena, took precautions against possible delusions and put the Brother to test. Brother Stephen subsequently related two more communications from Theodosia in which the latter gave the same information as the first time. In the last one she stated additionally that if Frances, in spite of ill health, accepts the work which God wants to entrust to her, she will recover and will receive the necessary light to realize it.[139]

As soon as Father Leander had sufficient evidence concerning the authenticity of the revelation, he gradually commenced to make the divine will known to Frances, preparing her from day to day for religious vows and for total surrender to God as his instrument in the accomplishment of his will. On March 21 he blessed a simple black dress of hers, saying that she should regard it for the present as her religious habit. In her diary Frances recorded under this date: "The history of my vocation begins here."[140]

The crucial trial of her faith occurred on Easter Sunday. Father Leander informed her that she shall organize a new congregation and disclosed that the communications about her mission were received not by him directly, but by Brother Stephen who rendered the reports to him. Brother Stephen, he explained, was also apprised of the spirit and purpose of the new congregation, its essential practices, and characteristic spirituality.[141]

Appalled by the idea that someone other than Father Leander should guide her along the precipitous road, which she was becoming conditioned to tread, Frances was dismayed at the prospect of a lay brother acting as her director. She was bewildered and apprehensive, questioning the reliability of the plan that had been placed before her.[142]

With infinite patience, Father Leander calmly demonstrated that the ways of God are different from the ways of men, for the Lord employs whomever he chooses to carry out his work, frequently selecting humble instruments the better to manifest the efficacy of his grace. Assuring Frances of her vocation and of her special destiny in that vocation, he encouraged her to accept in the light of faith all the circumstances associated with it, but—he added—the decision must be entirely her own, free and deliberate. She was impressed with his unruffled composure, a pervading calm voice and manner, contrasting with the burning jet black eyes. More than ever before, this encounter left upon her the impression of his vast self-control and implicit submission to a superior power—an iron restraint lest he encroach upon her liberty.[143]

She passed the day in prayer, pleading for light, for anchorage, for the gift of faith to believe the unseen, to be convinced without knowing the reason. The inner combat involved a tremendous spiritual crisis. By evening she was resolved to submit to the will of God as it had been revealed to her. She was ready for the complete holocaust of self, to be the instrument in God's inscrutable plans.[144]

On the following day Father Leander found her recovered. At his announcement that he had learned of her daylong struggle and her act of faith from Brother Stephen, the last vestiges of doubt disappeared. She had reached, she felt, the end of a phase. For this moment she had waited and prepared for half of her lifetime; now she was thirty years of age. From that point onward, until the day of her death, she had a sense of her life being ordered by a power outside of herself, and she surrendered herself to it, consciously and willingly. After the manner of the saints, Frances wrote in her own blood the pledge: "To Jesus forever."[145]

She wished for one thing only—the pope's explicit approval of this undertaking. In keeping with the dogma of papal infallibility, defined by the First Vatican Council (1869-1870), Frances looked to the Supreme Pontiff's authority as the Vicar of Christ, which conferred incontestable validity upon his pronouncements in matters of faith and morality. His word would be decisive for her.[146]

After a ten-day retreat Frances proceeded to Lublin in the company of her mother, who was determined to join the new congregation. The two surviving members of the little Society, Angela Nęcińska and Elizabeth Carolyn Załoziecka, welcomed them cordially, requested Frances to be their superior, discussed with her their work and their objectives, and offered to her disposal their funds and house. For practical reasons, they agreed, the foundation should be established abroad,[147] because flagrant persecution by Russian[148] and Prussian[149] occupation forces included the closing of convents and monasteries in Poland. They planned to sell the house after Frances shall have received the pope's approval for the new congregation.

Under continuing meticulous direction of Father Leander, Frances was prepared to make the vows of chastity, poverty and obedience. She pronounced them publicly on the feast of the Visitation of Our Lady, July 2, 1873, in the beautiful church of the Canonesses of St. Augustine in Warsaw,[150] taking the name of Mary as a religious. Her mother was named Rosalie. Frances entered into the habit of prayer without self-consciousness and with confidence; often drawn into her inward self, she had the experience as though her spirit, disembodied in space and transcending time, rose above ordinary intellectual processes to a momentary intuition of God and eternity. Without realizing it, she hovered on the verge of mystical experience. Her devotion to the Blessed Virgin, tender and personal from early childhood, expanded into a creative force in her interior growth and developed an oasis of sustaining hope.

On August 14, together with Angela Necińska, Frances arrived in Rome and took rooms at Hotel Minerva. Then at the Gesù church she met Father Joseph Laurençot of the Society of Jesus, vice-postulator for the beatification of Claude de la Colombière, S.J.,[151] to whom she presented the purpose of her visit. Angela, however, sweltering in Rome's midsummer heat, found the climate insupportable and returned to Poland without waiting for the outcome.[152]

Father Laurençot introduced Frances to Mother Marie of Jesus, foundress and superior general of the cloistered nuns of the Society of Mary Reparatrix,[153] commonly known as the Reparatrices, recommending that she reside in their convent while awaiting the audience with the Holy Father. The six weeks she spent there, in the atmosphere of perpetual adoration of the Blessed Sacrament uninterruptedly exposed in the chapel, opened to her a whole new world of the spirit, a vast contemplation of new perspectives.[154] She glimpsed the shaping of a pattern, not yet distinct, but revolving around the idea of reparation that captivated her generous soul. She saw in the doctrine of the mystical Christ a new dimension in spiritual relationships.

On the first day of October, Father Laurençot presented to Pius IX[155] the petition in which Frances stated the wish to establish the Society of Our Lady of Loreto whose members would model their lives on the hidden life and virtues of the Holy Family of Nazareth. Furthermore, moved by the difficulties which beset the Supreme Pontiff, she declared the chief purpose of the new congregation to be total self-immolation through prayer, work and suffering offered for the intentions of the Vicar of Christ and the Church. She understood that the trials which afflicted the pope were not private and personal, but—while they affected the head of the Church— by the same token they encompassed all the faithful and Christ himself. Pius IX was deeply touched. In his own handwriting he endorsed the petition, inscribing thereon the words: "May God bless you and enlighten your mind always that you might walk in the ways of the Lord."

The next day, on the feast of the Holy Guardian Angels, Frances was received in private audience by the Holy Father,[156] thanked him for the blessing, and unfolded the plan of the foundation. From this interview she gathered a stabilizing insight into the nature of the new Congregation and what its mission in the Church ought to be. Fortified by the Pope's advice, she preserved to the end of her life an unshaken certainty about the course the Congregation should follow, in spite of pressures and influences to the contrary.

For some time she continued to consult Father Laurençot, discussing details, principles, fundamental rules. This resolute, eager soul seemed to him to be marked for a special mission, but he could not discern its real character. To assist her better in realizing her vocation, he advised an interview with Father François-Xavier Gautrelet, former provincial superior of the Jesuit province of Lyons and currently rector of the College of St. Joseph in Lyons, who was highly regarded as retreatmaster and spiritual director.[157] Accordingly Frances left Rome on October 18.[158]

While in Lyons, she became acquainted with a young community of nuns, devoted to perpetual adoration, who under the direction of Father Gautrelet led edifying lives of exceptional fervor, but lacked adequate means of support. Father Gautrelet suggested to Frances to join this group and accept the position of a superior, whereby she would save the community from extinction and contribute to its eventual development. He was persuasive and convincing. The undeniable merits of the cause elicited from Frances instant sympathy to which she knew she could not yield. After an agonizing reappraisal, she conveyed her regrets to Father Gautrelet and a fortnight later returned to Poland.

II

Age of Formation
1873-1902

1 FIRST STEPS

As the golden autumn of 1873 yielded to a sudden and severe winter, Frances arrived home to Żdżary to set her affairs in order. For a whole year, she and her mother led a retired existence which Frances regarded as the first novitiate of the new congregation.[1] Under the guidance of Father Leander she found in Christ the purpose of her life and its fulfillment. She grasped the ideal which dominates the life of religious women consecrated to God, and endeavored to formulate the means by which it might be infused into her associates in order to animate their apostolate with distinctive features and enrich its effectiveness. Henceforth she professed, on a spiritual plane, the kind of undivided fidelity to and ardent love for God that has its counterpart in the personal devotion of the bride in a human relationship. Though she responded to the call into the unknown, ready to face whatever challenges would be thrust upon her, she wondered how God would step into her life to realize his mandate.

It so happened that the Capuchin monastery in Nowe Miasto was one of the few not affected by the imperial decree of suppression of November 8, 1864.[2] Nonetheless, the monks had no assurance of immunity from political harassment. Some, in fact, were forcibly evicted by Russian officers from their monastic quarters and placed under arrest for no apparent reason, except that their superior, Father Leander, stood under a cloud of disfavor. The menacing tactics of vigilance and search assumed such proportions that diocesan authorities decided to intervene for his safety and that of the monastery. For sooner or later they would be swept up, in ways not then envisioned, in the vortex of intolerance and russification.

At that time the administration of the archdiocese of Warsaw fell to Monsignor Stanislas Zwoliński[3] who—invoking the prerogative granted by the decree,[4] which removed all monks from under the jurisdiction of the major superiors of their orders and placed them under diocesan authority and police surveillance—ordered Father Leander to leave the country. As soon as he crossed the boundary, Father Leander notified his superior general in Rome of the events which compelled him to depart from his monastery. Upon reaching Paris in June of 1874, he received through the chancery office there the necessary permissions from his superior general.[5]

Brother Stephen, on the other hand, while a patient at the ophthalmic hospital in Warsaw, had become seriously implicated by trying to convert a schismatic, which act was in itself considered a crime subject to penal codes. Only with great difficulty was his departure processed in disguise, and he joined Father Leander in Paris during September of that year.[6]

With the assistance of Father Alexander Jełowicki, director of the Resurrectionist mission congregating about the church of the Assumption in Paris, Father Leander appraised the Polish colony as a promising locale for the new Congregation. In view of the full liberties which the Catholic Church enjoyed in France under the presidency of Marshal MacMahon,[7] Father Leander encouraged Frances to launch her work there and then. Furthermore, the French consul in Warsaw, Baron Finot, could be depended upon to facilitate official formalities. He was one of the most influential sympathizers with the Polish cause and, in a practical sense, more useful than others. By his reports to the Minister of Foreign Affairs in France he helped create a hospitable atmosphere for the Poles who sought temporary domicile in France.[8]

Thus, towards the end of the year, Frances with her mother and the two Ladies of Loreto arrived in Paris without undue inconvenience. They entered an old, graceful world, kept virtually at peace since the fall of the Second Empire, a world already dying, but with a splendid grace. The Polish colony lived here in an epoch of profound transformations, remarkably independent, set in its desire at once to mold new cultural patterns and to perpetuate its native mentality.

Frances was given a warm reception and was admitted into the inner circle of the colony where she surveyed its needs in the light of the services she yearned to give—religious instruction of children, visiting the sick and the poor, retreats for women. Instinctively aflame with enthusiasm to solve human problems, she realized she would have to first solve the problems in the hearts and minds of individuals. The prospect, displayed before her, exerted a powerful attraction,[9] but Frances—experiencing a definite sense of mission to establish a religious institute—was even more strongly motivated by a compelling sense of dependence upon God which led her to disregard purely material advantages in preference to his designs. To this unique quality of spirit she attributed, then as always, the preservation of her identity inviolate, never losing sight of her direction.

To find an unfailing answer she decided to spend some time in prayer at Lourdes where—but a brief seventeen years earlier—the apparitions of the Holy Virgin to the shepherdess Bernadette Soubirous impressed world's believers and unbelievers alike. After a satisfying interview with the affable bishop of Lourdes, Frances was inclined to settle with her companions in this place which bore the stamp of heaven's favor.[10] The choice seemed appropriate to the Marian character which was to mark the new congregation. In the solitary hours at the holy grotto she searched her heart and prayed for light. Rome was the answer. From childhood days, she recalled, she entertained a great love for the Church and its visible Head; in her studies Rome invariably captivated her interest as the center of Christendom.[11] No other place could adequately serve the ecumenical vision she nurtured in her soul.

At Eastertime, 1875, the pioneer group with one aspirant, a French girl,[12] came to Rome and took rooms at Piazza Minerva. They started life very obscurely for they had no friends and merely some passing acquaintances. But Frances had superb courage. Because from the outset she wished to adapt their mode of life to convent norms, they looked about for functional accommodations, which necessitated successive changes of residence at short intervals—to Via della Vite, Via Sistina, and Via Giulio Romano[13] to an apartment neighboring with the church of Santa Maria d'Aracoeli. The church, rising from the highest point of the Capitoline Hill, was famed for the charming image of the Holy Infant, venerated by the faithful with fond devotion; the adjoining monastery housed the Franciscan generalate.

Already then the founding group was known as Sisters of Loreto and Frances was referred to as Mother Mary or Sister Mary,[14] although occasionally in her correspondence she continued to use her civilian name. Assuming that Father Leander and Brother Stephen might have further communications for her and the Congregation, Mother Mary secured through the Capuchin superior general an indult for them to reside temporarily on the sisters' premises. Father Leander served as their chaplain and director, while Brother Stephen performed the duties of the sacristan and assisted with the external needs of the convent.

Soon after her arrival in the Eternal City, Mother Mary—upon the recommendation given her by Father Jełowicki—applied to Father Peter Semeneńko, C.R., requesting his advice for her work, especially in dealing with local matters, ecclesiastical and civil. During her first visit in Rome, Mother Mary met him, more or less casually, in the convent of the Reparatrices, which he frequented in the capacity of a director to their foundress, Mère Marie de Jésus. He was at the zenith of his public service and personal achievement in the Church as superior general of the Congregation of the Resurrection (1842-1845 and 1873-1886), as consultor to the Sacred Congregation of the Holy Office,[15] member of the Roman Academy of Catholic Doctrine, and first rector of the Pontifical Polish College. He distinguished himself as a writer of ascetical and learned works and as a fluent conference master. His many and varied activities included the direction of the Visitandines in Versailles; of the newly founded cloistered Sisters of St. Joseph in Boussu, Belgium, who later adopted the name of the Religious of the Consolation of the Sacred Heart of the co-foundress of the Sisters of the Immaculate Conception, Mother Marcelline Darowska; of Madame Celine Borzęcka and her daughter Hedwig, who later became co-foundress of the Sisters of the Resurrection; as also of several and sundry stigmatics and other persons claiming to experience supernatural phenomena.

As early as June 12, 1875, through the kind offices of Father Semeneńko, a small villa was located[16] in a peaceful, sparsely inhabited section of the city, at Via Merulana, No. 12, halfway between the two patriarchal basilicas of St. Mary Major and St. John Lateran. Mother Mary negotiated the actual purchase on September 19[17] and at once made arrangements to have the interiors remodeled to suit the purposes of convent living. The upper story was designed to accommodate a handsome chapel with stained glass windows and the statue of Our Lady of Lourdes in the altar niche. The sisters' rooms were also assigned to this floor. The dining room, kitchen, and other facilities were laid out to occupy the first floor. In the garden the caretaker's house was destined for the use of Father Leander and Brother Stephen.[18]

Meanwhile, the two Lublin ladies, notwithstanding their honest intent to participate in the foundation, became depressed by the season's interminable stifling weather in the city. Unlike the hardy Romans, who generally fled for a summer respite to the breezy hills or the placid seaside, they decided to leave Rome; Angela returned to Poland, while Carolyn traveled about for some time and three years later, at the age of fifty-nine, died piously in Rome without however again joining Mother Mary's company.[19]

On July 15, 1875 three candidates arrived from Poland—among them Eleonore Rembiszewska, the sister of Brother Stephen.[20] Even before Mother Mary's departure from Żdżary, Eleonore had indicated to her the desire to become a member of her Congregation. After several weeks two of the candidates failed to be convinced of their vocation and left. Since Eleonore, too, suffered qualms of misgivings and indecision, Mother Mary advised her to return to her mother until she should firmly settle upon her choice of life.[21]

And thus, young women came and went; some of them former penitents of Father Leander, others who were attracted by Mother Mary's exceptional personality, still others who had not found satisfaction in one of the older orders and ventured to try yet this one. Mother Mary received them with an open heart and gracious solicitude, careful lest an unguarded word or deed should deter the action of grace in their souls. But her humanity, at once tender and strong, carried no intimations of weakness. She instructed each newcomer as a God-entrusted charge, as if each life from then on and in the hereafter depended upon her. When they proved incapable or unwilling to scale the heights of sacrifice and love, patterned on the Holy Family, she would not detain them, for she understood that the outgrowth of sacrifice and love will be apostolic zeal and works of mercy and personal sanctification of individual members—a complete dedication. To expect less was unthinkable.

Father Semeneńko volunteered his assistance in the guidance of the candidates. On the way from the church of St. Claudius where he resided, to and from his occupations at the Vatican, he would often visit the "house of Loreto,"[22] as he referred to Mother Mary's apartment. A strong affinity of interests developed between him and Brother Stephen and a spiritual kinship with Father Leander,[23] who gradually withdrew his direction of Mother Mary, leaving it to Father Semeneñko.

The latter was undeniably a man of God, blessed with initiative and active zeal which enabled him to recognize in Mother Mary a rare magnanimity towards God, ready for whatever God might ask of her. Such generosity could be unusually useful to a priest who was eager to work for souls, when the whole society needed to be built up anew. The political and anticlerical movements had so shaken up the very foundations of religion that people were still adrift. It was not the time for idle groaning and Father Semeneñko set his mind to the rebuilding. Mother Mary, with her frank and confident determination, seemed to him to have been sent by God.

While he studied her closely, she was quick to perceive his delicate approaches and commented in a letter to him:

. . . Apart from sentiments of genuine friendliness, I had at no time intended that this little house, by virtue of our association, should come under the direction of the Resurrectionist Fathers. Such action would be entirely opposed to our objectives and to what we are committed in God. . . . Not only this house, but also my person, is in the hands of God. Once having submitted all to his care, I am at peace as long as my heart remains ever steadfast before him in truth and simplicity.[24]

The tone of her letter, as all the prolific correspondence of her lifetime, was couched with finesse in dignity and respect. It could not offend, yet its meaning was unmistakable. Father Semeneñko continued to offer his courtesies, introduced Mother Mary to ecclesiastical officials, and brought to the "house of Loreto" persons who wished to make her acquaintance and to experience an atmosphere of piety and culture.[25]

When his duties called him away from Rome or outside of Italy, he delegated other Resurrectionists to render whatever priestly services the sisters might need.[26] In this connection similarly, Mother Mary exercised sober judgment. On one occasion she wrote to Father Semeneñko:

. . . I regret I must admit, Father, that one of your expressions pained me somewhat, namely, your statement that I "found a treasure in Father Julian." I respect, esteem, and honor him and God's gifts in him, but he neither was nor is a treasure to me. God alone is my treasure and on him alone I learned to rely, in him I trust, and upon him I depend for everything. The best of people are helpful merely to the extent that God employs them.[27]

Early autumnal rains that year interfered with the progress of remodeling on the property at Via Merulana. Twice daily she went to inspect the details and encourage the workers.[28] Finally she and her companions occupied the new home, January 6, 1876, although much still remained to be accomplished by the sisters themselves. When on March 6 Father Semeneñko brought Canon Folchieri from the office of the Roman Vicariate to examine the chapel, the altar, and the appointments, everything was found to be in compliance with liturgical codes, and the Holy Sacrifice of the Mass was celebrated the following day for the first time in the house of the congregation.[29]

In the spring Eleanore Rembiszewska returned to Rome and to Mother Mary, and thereafter gained the distinction of being the first member who persevered until death, long after Mother Mary departed this life. Upon being permitted to commence the novitiate, she was named Josepha.[30] She was a childlike, joyous soul, fully dedicated to the love and glory of God, come what may, regarding difficulties as stepping-stones to the mountain of the Lord. She prayed and worked with zest, and learned the elements of religious life with an ever new wonder.[31]

The city about them was teeming with pride and activity in its rediscovered importance. It had become the capital of the unified Kingdom of Italy, and Italy had entered the family of nations. Projects for urban development sprouted everywhere. Energetic preparations were also underway in view of the expected multitudes of pilgrims and tourists who planned to pay their homage to Pius IX on the occasion of the fiftieth anniversary of his episcopal consecration. The jubilee was a year off, but its date was well noted on the agenda of the world. Ever since he became "prisoner of the Vatican," the Pope acquired supra-political stature as a spiritual leader with renewed and universal prestige.

Round about the convent at Via Merulana excavations for the construction of new buildings released noxious gases. Driven by the African sirocco, heavy vapors from the seas converged over the city and infiltrated into dwellings and ruins, valley fields and wall-enclosed gardens.

Cecilia Siedliska at fifty-five proved no match for the unfamiliar seasonal peculiarities of the climate. Physical health had been one of the unattainables for which she struggled all her life. Despite valiant efforts to collaborate with her daughter, she was compelled to abandon the undertaking when she collapsed irreparably.[32] Mother Mary placed her under medical care in a sanatorium at Kowanówko, near Posen, and instructed her brother to utilize the interest accruing from their mother's investments to defray the costs and fees.

On her journey back to Rome, Mother Mary tarried at Lyons[33] to pray and reflect at Notre Dame de Fourvières. The events of the past year left her with mixed feelings and she craved moments of uninvaded solitude to adjust her perspectives and to consult with the Jesuits whom she had previously come to know. From Lyons she proceeded to Paris, remaining there several weeks with the Augustinian nuns at St. Germain-en-Lay.[34] Her practical mind required the personal experience of actual contact with religious life under ordinary conditions. She has had sufficient opportunity to observe the life and spirit of the Reparatrices; she hoped to be permitted to make a similar study of other convents. She could readily obtain the principles in theory; what she desired was to see how these principles were lived in particular religious families to which they imparted distinct characteristics. One other object of her visits at this time was the grotto at Lourdes where she persisted in fervent prayer to the Immaculate Virgin.[35]

On arriving at her little convent in Rome with a French aspirant,[36] Mother Mary learned that Helen Aszperger was in Rome with her older daughter who was ill and that her younger daughter had died. She was accompanied by Wanda Lubowidzka whom Father Leander advised to come for the purpose of realizing her vocation.

Greatly encouraged by the encounter with Mother Mary and by what she saw and heard, Wanda notified her sisters, Laura and Felicia, of her decision to devote herself to Mother Mary's idea. They, in turn, wrote to the Foundress, requesting likewise to be accepted. Because the closing of their private school involved manifold technicalities, Wanda's presence in Warsaw was also necessary. She left, therefore, but the following year, May 13, 1877, her two sisters were the first to arrive at the convent; then, a month later, on June 16, Wanda came with three girls for private tutoring[37]—two of them cousins, Thecla Lubowidzka[38] and her sister Jane, with their friend, Sophia Rodziewicz. There was also with Wanda a young woman, Mathilda Sosinska,[39] who aspired to be a nun.

2 NAZARETH

The history of the house of Our Blessed Lady, preserved in Loreto, is rooted in pious tradition. It is said to have been the home of the Holy Family after their return to Nazareth from the self-imposed exile in Egypt. Before then, it was here that the angel of the Lord made the announcement to the Holy Virgin that she will become the mother of the Messiah, who was the Son of God.[40]

Installed into the unpretentious, one-room boxlike structure is an altar bearing the inscription "Hic Verbum Caro Factum Est" (Here the Word was made Flesh). All the days of the year the Mass of the Annunciation is celebrated there by countless pilgrim priests of various ranks from every quarter of the world.[41]

In her search for relevance, Mother Mary's contemplation carried her away from the idea of Loreto to Nazareth and—from the one admirable person of the Mother of God—to the unique adorable Family consisting of Jesus, Mary and Joseph. Since she aimed to encompass in the Congregation the fulness of life, both human and divine, her exceeding sensitiveness to the meaning of life brought out in her the concern for vitality and depth in whatever should affect the image of the Congregation.

She began to instill in her early associates the habit of reflecting upon the dispositions and virtues of the Holy Family of Nazareth to serve as an inspiration for their own interior lives. She instructed the sisters to model the external forms of their communal relationships on the life of the first Christians, which was one heart and one soul; holding all things in common; marked by simplicity, steadfast faith, and apostolic service as occasion presented itself—in the awareness of God's love and the intensity of true brotherhood with mankind.[42]

With the arrival of the three girls she commenced to realize the type of apostolate—Christian education of girls—which she recognized should be one of the functions of her Congregation in the Church.[43] In the occasional requests from laywomen for assistance in a private retreat or in an extended course of recollection she saw another field of service in which the sisters could effectively lead souls to dynamic encounters with Christ, to salvage a sincere faith from fading into indifference or from degenerating into superstition.

Of necessity she turned more and more frequently to Father Semeneñko for his expert advice in juridical matters, which she acknowledged as essential to the attainment of a formal status for her Congregation. The spirit of Nazareth and its purpose, visualized by her, lacked as yet the written framework of constitutions which should impart positive guidelines to the members and represent an authentic self-definition to ecclesiastical authorities. Her request for assistance placed her again in an ambiguous position, fraught with mental suffering, that challenged her stamina and tact against revived attempts at amalgamation. She had anticipated difficulties and slow progress, and these she accepted as a favorable sign of Providence; but she was acutely wary of deviating from the plan God expected her to carry out. At the risk of being rebuffed, she wrote with disarming frankness to Father Semeneñko, February 23, 1877:

> . . . It seems that the relationship between you and us, Father, is lacking in clarity. I should be pleased to remove whatever causes this, so that we might proceed in truth and sincerity as is fitting for souls whom the Lord approaches with love. Above all things, I desire to live by truth, I seek it, I aspire after it. Perhaps I have not recognized this truth in you, Father, whence comes the failure to achieve a mutual understanding. I earnestly hope this will cease as soon as possible so that our association in and for God may be radiant with truth and honesty.

Though her mission was pressed for time in the details of everyday activities, Mother Mary took responsibility not only for developing the religious personality of the sisters but also for their physical welfare. The experiences of past summers warned her against allowing newcomers to remain in the sun-drenched city during the peak season. She sent them all, candidates and girls, to Albano Laziale, east of Rome, to a villa in the Alban Hills. She also took steps to sell the property at Via Merulana since its location proved detrimental to the health of her group, but for a long time potential buyers were few and far between.

From this period there is extant a letter of hers to Laura Lubowidzka in which she offered with singular humility a terse critique of her own position:

> . . . Thousands of others would act by far better as instruments in the hands of the Lord, but since he condescended to grant me this grace and called me to accomplish his work, all my efforts are directed to promote the glory of God in this house, to coordinate everything according to his pleasure that our hearts may thereby tend to be so purified and disposed as to become acceptable to him for the establishment of his Nazareth in them.[44]

To utilize each day for consistent formation and progress, Mother Mary introduced a practical horarium.[45] Besides morning and evening prayers in common, the Little Office of the Blessed Virgin was recited and mental prayer was regularly scheduled. The time devoted to adoration of the Blessed Sacrament provided daily occasions for interior growth in a true personal relationship with Christ through deepening insights into his mysteries.[46] Periods of recreation and recollection enlarged the scope of pedagogical opportunities to inculcate the little virtues of happy family living and Christian companionship.

Mother Mary was the sisters' teacher and guide, leading them through the purgative way to the illuminative state and ultimately aiming to achieve union with God. She conducted group instruction about the nature and duties of religious life, and often held conferences with the sisters individually. Her dedication was equalled by their enthusiasm and eagerness. They carried her words with them throughout the day, pondering them while engaged at assigned chores.[47]

Classes planned for the three girls occupied the Lubowidzki sisters a part of each day. Thecla, fifteen years of age, eldest of the girls, soon displayed an inclination to the religious life and expressed her desire to enter Nazareth. Mother Mary prudently advised her to bide her time until she should be somewhat older and, in the meantime, to pursue her studies and develop her talents.[48]

Five days before the Christmas of 1877, Wanda, Laura and Felicia went into retreat and at Midnight Mass, celebrated in the convent chapel by Father Leander, they were admitted to the novitiate in the first formal ceremony of the Congregation. To signify their transition into the choice portion of Christ's vineyard, they received new names—after the examples recorded in the Old and the New Testament, when persons favored with a special vocation from God were given new names by him. The three sisters were named in honor of the archangels Michael, Gabriel and Raphael, respectively,[49] with the name of Mary prefixed to each; they were presented the religious habits, designed in the simple style of a priest's soutane, and veils of white tulle.[50]

While Father Leander continued their spiritual direction, gave them discourses on the Gospels, and prepared in writing a series of reflections for the liturgical year, he was thoroughly convinced that Mother Mary herself should attend to the formation of the future religious, for she alone had the inspiration to communicate to them the distinctive Nazareth spirituality.[51] She emphasized then the hidden life of the Holy Family, a life hidden with Christ in God, which required the self-discipline of humility and detachment, the shedding of affectation, conceit and smugness, the fostering of universality of charity in the bond of unity of the children of God.[52] Their vocation, she enlightened them, was a gift of God, and the vows which they aspired to profess would be their response of love for the sake of the Kingdom of God. She indoctrinated them in the practice of the evangelical counsels of chastity, poverty and obedience with the simplicity, fortitude and generosity of Jesus, Mary and Joseph.[53]

This was groundwork—exacting and unremitting, oriented to the creation of a new woman who, dying to self, would live solely for Christ, the One beloved by her above all. There were applicants who found such demands too arduous a task and, in their worldly sophistication—a folly. When informed that Nazareth will not have many external practices and austerities, common to the earlier orders, because its structure was meant to be adaptable to contemporary conditions, they regarded such departure from tradition a stumbling block and, entrenched in their skepticism, left disappointed.[54]

Persons given to spiritual complacency or eccentricity relinquished the ideals of Christian heroism for—what they called—the expediency of reasonable and moderate virtues. Their mediocrity being intolerable of a life of excellence, they deplored Mother Mary's exhortations to perfection, to total abandonment to the will of God, to renunciation of superfluities.

The cares, sorrows, and joys of the Church militant involved the sisters, at first prayerfully and, later, in various aspects of active participation. They revered the person of Pius IX for his good will which overflowed with the desire to cause the peace of Christ to reign everywhere. He had passed through crucial times and was wounded in his noblest sentiments. The sisters offered their spiritual tributes to God to alleviate the Pope's suffering and to restore the rightful position of the Church within the modern world.

They gloried in the news which—in January, 1878—reverberated throughout the city and beyond, that the Holy Father sent his own confessor to the dying Victor Emmanuel II, conveying his personal forgiveness and the Viaticum. Apart from politics, Pius had remained on courteous terms with the King of Italy and wished to lift the excommunication incurred by the monarch when he occupied the Papal States. Having asked pardon of the Pope, Victor Emmanuel died fully reconciled in conscience.[55] Scarcely a month had passed when Pius followed him to the grave. Two weeks later, on February 20, Leo XIII commenced his remarkable pontificate of twenty-five years' duration, concurrent with the remainder of Mother Mary's lifetime.

The constitutions of the Congregation increasingly absorbed her attention. Late into the night she remained contemplating and writing the points and principles which were to comprise Nazareth's rule of life; at times she was found kneeling at the desk before the crucifix while engaged in this labor of love.[56] The ideas she developed were subsequently studied and discussed with Father Semeneńko. On March 23 he presented to her a suggested outline of his own.[57] These initial steps were repeated innumerable times in collaboration and review, in consultation and continued search for a precise expression of the subtle inspirations that urged her on toward new horizons. In molding a distinct identity for the new Congregation that combined ascetic culture and contemplative formation with apostolic service, she wanted to assure it of a sense of belonging within every context of time and place in which it should find itself at the summons of the Church. This open approach was frequently unacceptable even to some of the forward looking religious leaders who still preferred to advocate the security of old and tried patterns of the existing orders.

Prominent among farsighted individuals who recognized the signs of an emerging new era for the Church and religious women were several outstanding members of the Roman Curia, notably the Cardinal Vicar of Rome Monaco la Valetta and Cardinal de Luca of the Sacred Congregation for Bishops and Regulars. Conflicting rumors about Nazareth aroused their practiced vigilance; but personal visits to the new Congregation for sessions of informal, confidential discussions with the Mother Foundress and her sisters gained for them a favorable appraisal with hopeful anticipation of things to come.[58]

Mother Mary was further encouraged in her work by Leo XIII when, June 10, 1878, at an audience, she and the little company of her first sisters approached him to render homage. A spirited conversation ensued in French in which the Supreme Pontiff questioned her extensively about the foundation, where it was located, its purpose and constitutions. He placed particular emphasis upon the drafting of the constitutions and imparted his special blessings for their successful development. He also commended his pontificate to the prayers of the young community.[59]

In its aim to engage in catechetical instruction of children and to work for the moral and religious renewal of families, it echoed the dominant chord of his long life. For even as Cardinal Archbishop of Perugia he opposed the vast conspiracy of atheism and communism which engendered vicious attacks against the indissolubility of the marriage bond, claiming to be purely a civil contract. Within ten months of his election to the papacy, on December 28, Leo issued the encyclical *Quod Apostolici Muneris,* calling for the preservation of the Christian family as essential to the preservation of social order, the state, and religion.[60]

The Pope was touched by Mother Mary's disclosure that the Holy Family is the Congregation's model of its life style. Although the Church had not hitherto seen fit to proclaim a separate solemnity in honor of the Holy Family,[61] the significance of such a possibility was not lost on Leo XIII, as his decree of later date revealed. This audience marked for Mother Mary the beginning of articulate relations with the Supreme Pontiff that proved providential to the survival of the Congregation in times of adversity.

With the advent of another summer abruptly descending upon the Via Merulana convent, Mother Mary felt grateful relief as she concluded the sale of the property, June 14, to Mother Augustine, superior general of the French Sisters of Charity of Our Lady of Perpetual Help, who declared with pleased earnestness that this was exactly what she had wanted for her group, convinced that it will satisfy all their requirements. One month later Nazareth was moved into a leased apartment at 44 Piazza Farnese. The accommodations were readily transformed into a convent, and one room—appropriately adorned—was converted into a devotional chapel, where Holy Mass was celebrated for the first time on the feast of the Nativity of Mary, September 8.[62]

It was Mother Mary's profound belief that the Congregation will grow and prosper to realize its mission, if it will have its basis and center in the Holy Eucharist. Through the years, whenever she opened a new house, her immediate concern was to provide a chapel for the sisters and to secure the requisite ecclesiastical permissions for the reservation of the Blessed Sacrament, as the constant, unfailing source for the sustenance of their spiritual vitality.

About this time the first Italian aspirant, Liberata Lanciotti, applied for admission; she became known as Sister Luigia and persevered in Nazareth to the end of her life.[63]

In carefully planned steps of guidance and formation, the prudent Foundress desired to lead the novices and postulants to a sound appreciation of Mary's role in the mystery of Redemption and to cultivate in them a filial confidence in her patronage. During the month of May, in 1879, she concentrated her efforts on this point with the assistance of Father Leander, who gave Marian instructions daily; the sisters then sang the Litany of Loreto, and benediction of the Blessed Sacrament followed. The month was impressively closed with an act of consecration to the Mother of God, pronounced by the whole community.[64]

By now, the three girls—Thecla, Jane and Sophia—were completing two years of studies in Rome; at the beginning of July they returned to their families in Poland. Thecla, growing certain of her vocation, was grieved at not being allowed to remain in the convent, but Mother Mary, aware of her parents' objections, persuaded her to submit to them for the present and promised to accept her at a later date.[65]

Once again Mother passed the summer mainly in recollection at the monastery of the Sisters of Perpetual Adoration in Lyons, retiring for prolonged intervals to Our Lady's shrine at Fourvières. The sisters' correspondence from Rome brought painful news of problems created by few unsettled characters, who by their unruly behavior disrupted the peaceful life of the convent. She took to heart these troubles and penned letters of extraordinary perception and sympathy, counseling the sisters in their attitudes under trial and difficulty. Dictated by unshaken faith, she wrote:

> ... How firm ought we to remain in our loyalty to Our Lord and how tenderly ought we cherish our Nazareth, since God leads it along the way of the cross. It is a visible sign that we are doing his work, when satan attacks it so vehemently.[66]
>
> ... May you find solace in the thought that all of you are helping me in this undertaking which is of so paramount an importance that I cannot withdraw from it, although the forces of evil raise obstacles to hinder it. Here, under the inspiration of Our Immaculate Mother, the spiritual structure of Nazareth is being fortified. Time will come when physical and moral afflictions will assail us, but the joy of Christ shall be our lot inevitably.[67]

Much as she was moved by compassion to join them in person in order to pacify and assure, to dispel doubts and resolve disagreements, her better judgment outweighed her sentiments. If the early sisters were to become future leaders and exemplars, they had to be tempered in the crucible of life's tribulations. While they had her full moral support, she wished them to test their faith and endurance in encounters with actual situations, to estimate their own resilience and clarity of vision under pressure. She guided them by direction and by indirection.[68]

Before returning to Rome she made an eight-day retreat in absolute seclusion. Back in her own convent, she proceeded to set matters aright and dismissed from Nazareth two recalcitrant novices[69] who had been the cause of discord. All the sisters then made an eight-day retreat in common and resumed their mode of life in fervor and peace.

Meanwhile another appalling task awaited Mother Mary. Prompted by a divine imperative which she had recognized during the sojourn at Lyons, she understood that the mission of Father Leander and Brother Stephen with respect to Nazareth has already come to an end. The gratitude she entertained for their dedication to the idea of Nazareth could in no way deter her from the inexorable duty in conscience which urged her to recommend that they return to the monastery of their order.[70]

Mother Mary had been under Father Leander's guidance since childhood; through him she discovered the path of grace and discerned the call of the elect. Her gentle soul shrank from inflicting pain upon anyone; so, to convey to this sixty-three-year-old saintly priest of God the decision which she knew she must, was psychologically a shattering experience. But Father Leander, true to his teachings, gave brilliant proof of his own supernatural motives and singleness of purpose which reposed in the accomplishment of God's holy will; he acquiesced without demur. The superior general of the Capuchins reassigned him to Poland, to the monastery in the archdiocese of Cracow, where the Austrian rule guaranteed religious freedom.[71] The last service which he performed for Nazareth was to accept the vows of the three Lubowidzki sisters on November 13, 1879. The vows were made privately, without ceremony, because their two years of novitiate were not yet completed; but the act itself clearly indicated the end of another epoch.[72]

Brother Stephen, on the other hand, was revoked to the Capuchin monastery in Rome. Soon he became desperately ill and, according to medical opinion, was doomed to a lingering death as a result of the demands which monastic observance placed upon him. The superior general expressed his willingness to dispense Brother Stephen from the obligations of the rule if Mother Mary would accept him in the capacity of a sacristan and commissary. This turned out to be an exchange of courtesies: originally the Capuchin superior general consented to Mother Mary's request for Brother Stephen; now she could not do less when he asked a reciprocal favor. After a brief absence, Brother Stephen again took up his former activities in Nazareth.[73]

3 LIGHT IN DARKNESS

By February 1, 1880 the convent quarters were transferred from Piazza Farnese onto the Slope of Montecavallo near the Quirinal. Housed in a substantial building, the sisters fairly expected to remain there until they should acquire a permanent site for their motherhouse.

Meanwhile new pressures kept obtruding themselves into Mother Mary's work on the Nazareth rules, distracting her efforts and disturbing her inner vision. Well-intentioned individuals offered assistance which was frequently at variance with her objectives and sometimes even motivated by ulterior interests. Notwithstanding her determination to the contrary, she was being hopefully prevailed upon at this time to adopt the rule of the Sisters of the Immaculate Conception. Though Mother Mary held in high esteem the foundress of these sisters,[74] she would not be induced to borrow from their constitutions in full or in part. Convinced that a community is a miniature cosmos in itself, and that whatever is written for it must come from the atmosphere it breathes, from the very blood coursing through the hearts of its members, she intuitively safeguarded Nazareth from becoming an anomaly.

Like the voice from the burning bush of Sinai, the addresses and encyclicals of Leo XIII resounded in Mother Mary's generous soul with creative intensity. Nazareth's prophetic significance in the economy of Redemption began to crystallize in view of the Pope's concern for the disturbed condition of the world. There was an overflowing of oppression of the Church and insult of the papacy, a contempt for God and outright impiety, and even a defiant worship of satan. To serve as a lever for moving the moral world, the Pope founded in Rome the Society of Catholic Nations for Reparatory Adoration, the object of which was to offer to Christ in the Eucharist a continuing tribute of homage and reparation.[75] Responding to his intents, Mother Mary enlisted her Community in the crusade of reparation which henceforth was to permeate all of its apostolic endeavors throughout the world, and the spirit of reparation would leave its imprint upon the interior life of every sister.

Despite the lack of a discriminating counselor, Mother Mary recognized the urgency of securing formal ecclesiastical sanctions. She committed her great need to God and with implicit confidence produced a schematic document which outlined the basic ideas for the future constitutions. She gave it the title *A Brief Plan of the Institute of Mary of Nazareth.*[76] It contained the following points:

    I. The object of this Institute is to glorify God and to respond to his love by total dedication to him through a life of prayer, immolation, and constant offering of oneself for the needs of the Church and the intentions of the Supreme Pontiff, for the eradication of errors and the conversion of the enemies of the Church, and for expiation—in union with Jesus and Mary—of the outrages committed against the Divine Majesty by secret societies condemned by the Church.

II. The Institute desires to be engaged in all works of zeal by means of which it may be able to guide souls to the truth and draw them to the knowledge and love of the Church of Christ. These works are:

    a. religious instruction of catechumens, Israelites, Protestants, and Schismatics;

    b. retreats for women;

    c. classes for girls in Christian doctrine and the history of the Church;

    d. preparation of children for the reception of First Holy Communion.

III. The model of its religious life is the hidden life of Jesus with Mary and Joseph in Nazareth, which the members practice through detachment and self-abnegation.

IV. The means which the Institute recommends to its members to assist them in cultivating the spirit of Christ are:

    a. adoration of the Blessed Sacrament in the tabernacle, to which the sisters devote one hour daily, praying principally for the needs of the Church;

    b. daily contemplation of Christ's Passion for the expiation of the sins of the world;

    c. praying in common the Little Office of the Blessed Virgin Mary according to Roman rubrics;

    d. deep reverence for and filial devotion to the holy Catholic Church, out of love for which they will sacrifice themselves and will constantly pray for her needs;

    e. unceasing openness to grace for the purpose of developing the supernatural life of faith, hope and charity and of union with Jesus Christ.

V. For admission to the Institute it is necessary to complete two years of novitiate, which period must be preceded by a postulancy of six months. Upon completing the novitiate, novices are admitted to the profession of temporary vows of obedience, poverty and chastity, dedicating themselves entirely to God in the interests of the Church. The vows are repeated annually for six years, following which the sisters are admitted to the profession of simple perpetual vows of obedience, poverty and chastity which bind them permanently with the Institute and, reciprocally, the Institute with them. For their final vows they prepare intensively during a period of six months in the manner of a second novitiate.

VI. The type of enclosure of this Institute is intermediate between the strict enclosure of the contemplative monasteries and the modified type proper to congregations devoted entirely to active life. The sisters leave the house only in cases of necessity and according to the determination of the superior, always accompanied by another sister and wearing secular apparel. Outsiders are never allowed to enter the part of the house occupied by the religious; separate reception rooms are designated for transacting affairs with outsiders.

VII. The Institute derives its principal means of material support from the interest accruing to dowries which the members provide according to their individual resources. To avoid the possible error of rejecting an applicant with a true vocation, dowry is not required of those who are unable to provide it, whenever ecclesiastical authority and the economic condition of the house permit.

VIII. Aiming solely to promote the greater glory of God and desiring to be free of all temporal involvements, the Institute does not accept compensation for its works of zeal. Persons who wish to make a retreat may reimburse the actual cost of maintenance, if they are able to do so.

IX. Out of consideration for persons who are not endowed with vigorous health, but are called to religious life, the Institute does not prescribe corporal austerities; it requires instead the fostering of spiritual vitality and interior penitence, the practice of detachment and complete self-denial.

By submitting this *Plan* to the Cardinal Vicar of Rome, on April 30, Mother Mary formally presented her Congregation to the Church. In return, as a gesture of favor, the Cardinal visited the convent a week later, on the feast of the Ascension, and celebrated the Sacrifice of the Mass in the sisters' chapel.

Because radical anti-clerical demonstrations were erupting from time to time in Rome, and in Italy generally, all religious were cautioned against appearing in public in their distinctive habits. Similar precautions had to be observed when traveling in and through certain other European countries where religious oppression was rampant.

Whenever the sisters were obliged to go out into the city, they wore the dresses which they had brought with them from their homes. For convent wear they adopted religious apparel which resembled, in a simplified form, the contemporary style in women's fashions. Over the basic habit, designed like a cassock, they wore a wrist-length cape. The accessories were: a silver reliquary cross suspended from the neck, a white upright collar, a black tulle stole draped across the shoulders and clasped in front, a black tulle veil worn with the hair showing above the forehead.[77]

As a natural outgrowth of their inspiration, the sisters tended toward a scriptural and liturgical orientation. In discussing the psalms, Mother Mary assisted them to absorb the sense of eternalism which is above and beyond what is prevalent in any one age or enviroment. This became evident in the evangelical way of their life and in their ecclesial spirit.[78] The incomparable institution which is the Church, thriving in perpetual transformations, emerges always youthful, younger than any of her contemporaries, and those who are carried on her currents of grace experience unfading youthfulness, for she is the hope of the world and of each individual. Thus Nazareth began early to drink at her fountains, identifying the love of the Church with the love for Christ.

When the Foundress was alerted to the first intimations suggesting a Nazareth apostolate in Cracow,[79] she knew she would have to make some important decisions. There was correspondence with Father Leander and Helen Aszperger; there were consultations in Rome with Cardinals La Valetta and Ledóchowski. Then, on the seventh of September, she left Rome to ascertain personally the outlook for the first mission and the type of work open to her sisters.

At the initial interviews, Bishop Albin Dunajewski of Cracow was averse to admitting the Congregation into his diocese; four days later, however, he unexpectedly withdrew his objections and actually encouraged her to settle in Cracow. As her presence became known in the city, persons of influence assailed her with importunities to remove the sisters from Rome entirely and establish the motherhouse in Cracow. This she resisted valiantly, for she was determined to have Nazareth's motherhouse in Rome "even when the Congregation shall have expanded throughout the entire world."[80]

Assured of the Bishop's favorable disposition, Mother Mary left Cracow on October 27, having postponed the opening of a house there to a later date when some of the pressures should relax. During her stay several young women had applied for admission to Nazareth. After serious inquiry into their vocation, two were accepted, Maria Ziętkiewicz[81] and Alodia Malentynowicz,[82] and were sent to Rome for their novitiate.

Mother Mary looked to faith and prudence before finally resolving the question of the location of the motherhouse. She neither relied upon her own preference nor did she incline to the impact of popular sentimentality, but reviewed the matter impartially with the Cardinal Vicar of Rome who, next to the Holy Father, held the highest authority. His unbiased opinion confirmed her very own: to maintain Nazareth's principal house in Rome.

But, just as the Holy Family was obliged to move from place to place, the sisters likewise were not yet established in a permanent dwelling. The owner of the building on the Quirinal served them notice that he wished to occupy all the apartments. The sisters, then, leased a small home in the Esquiline district, at Via Ferruccio, No. 2, into which they moved, December 9, 1880, at a time when the chill of the winter season was acute and the dampness of the new unheated house most distressing.

To add to their trials, Mother Mary developed cardiac neuralgia that incapacitated her for several months. They have also been visited by death for the first time when a promising novice, Sister Antonine,[83] succumbed. To this young sister the Foundress herself devoted countless hours to inspire her with holy dispositions and confidence as she approached the threshold of eternity.

She continued at the same time to instruct the sisters in forming a truly Christlike character through genuine prayer life. Their identification with Christ implied that they should habitually judge and act as he would judge and act under similar circumstances. She would say, "While we are not yet called to an external apostolate, we are doubly obliged to cultivate the spiritual life in an eminent degree; in fact, a person who makes no progress on the spiritual journey is incapable of fruitful external activity for God."[84] Her unique and pervading immersion in the Divine Presence was always an object of awe and edification. With equal fervor she reverted over and over to the work on the constitutions, whether in illness or in health.

At length, on May 30, 1881, Nazareth transferred its location to Via di Santa Susanna, and Mother Mary began planning the trip to Poland and the foundation of the first house in Cracow. She appointed Sister Raphael to be the superior in Rome and Sister Gabriel in Cracow. Before her departure on July 13, she was greatly encouraged by the papal blessing, dated July 9, which endorsed the preliminary *Plan* she had earlier submitted to Cardinal Monaco la Valetta.

On the way to Poland, Mother Mary interrupted her travel to pray at the Holy House of Loreto for guidance and blessing on the future foundation, about which she still had some doubts and fears.

Neither could Bishop Dunajewski indicate specific goals toward which the Congregation might direct its initiatives in his diocese. Mother Mary evaluated the predicament in a manner typical of her. "This is a favorable omen. Christ wants us here and he will himself take care of us without any of the human assistance we may have expected. It is an evident proof that

Nazareth is the work of God and that it remains under his protection."[85]

Although housed in temporary quarters, first at Ulica Karmelicka, No. 143, then at Ulica Kopernika, No. 51, a diversified apostolate sprang up from the beginning. Retreats for women grew in demand; parents requested the religious instruction of their children and their preparation for the Sacraments; study groups in Christian doctrine were organized for older girls; working girls assembled on Sunday afternoons for catechism and recreation under the sisters' guidance. Women of various ages and social conditions, who desired to make the profession of Faith and to be received into the Catholic Church, were directed to Nazareth for instruction and preparation.[86]

Aflame with zeal for the Kingdom of Divine Love in souls, Mother Mary took personal interest in these activities. She was responsive to the particular uniqueness of each person, to the spontaneity of the present moment, and to the vividness of where Christ was for her and for her Congregation. Through association with the sisters in Cracow, many young women recognized the call to religious life and applied for admission to Nazareth in increasing numbers.

In the meantime, in Rome, the sisters were alerted to the opportunity of moving into the building adjoining the church of Aracoeli, where they had originally lived in 1875, at Via Giulio Romano, No. 52. The transfer was accomplished in November and, when Mother Mary returned, December 11, 1881, the apartment was furnished and orderly, in keeping with the familiar convent atmosphere.

Once again the Foundress felt the full burden of a divine imperative demanding of her complete withdrawal from under the influence of Father Semeneńko. Disconcerting though this was to her sensitive nature, she rose to the situation with simple dignity and humility. Father Semeneńko referred to the decisive interview as "spiritual parting," and noted in his diary, "Since she is impressed that it is not the will of God for her to remain under my direction, that is enough for me. I have no personal claims. We parted in peace."[87] Nonetheless the need for an understanding, judicious guide grew the more compelling as some of the prominent spiritual leaders of the day failed to grasp the forward thrust in Mother Mary's ideas differing from the prevalent conventual structures. Though she had the assent of two illustrious popes, the details had to be elaborated with theological competence and unbiased insight.

The sisters in Rome assumed that it devolved upon them to provide spiritual support to that segment of the Community which was emerging into the field of action. They were eager to introduce into their own lives certain austerities and mortifications in behalf of the sisters in the active apostolate. Among other practices, they commenced to rise at midnight to pray the matins and extended the period of daily mental prayer to one hour. Soon, however, Mother Mary concluded against such fragmentation of values, convinced that the total religious life of the Congregation at large must be oriented toward the apostolic spirit, and its apostolate must be given form by the religious spirit of all the sisters.

In this twilight period, veiling the pattern of the Congregation's destined life style, Mother Mary was fortunate to secure for herself and her sisters the bracing guidance of Father Bernardino da Portogruaro, superior general of the Franciscan Friars Minor. He resided at the monastery adjoining the Church of Aracoeli, which was attended by the Franciscans, and willingly consented to assist the Community by spiritual direction, but declined any involvement in the drafting of her constitutions, not wanting to color them with Franciscan elements.

On April 15, 1882, he presided at the religious ceremonies when Sister Raphael had the distinction of being the first to pronounce perpetual vows as a Sister of the Holy Family of Nazareth, while Sisters Josepha, Alcantara and Bernardina were admitted to first vows. At this time, too, Mother Foundress conferred the title of "Mother" upon Sisters Raphael and Alcantara. Somewhat later the names of Sisters Alcantara and Bernardina were changed to Joanne and Bernarda, respectively.[88]

It was May and beautiful springtime in Poland when Mother Mary made her appearance among the sisters she had left six months earlier in the historic city of Cracow. Although frequent correspondence had kept them in close communication, there was much she had to reenforce and revitalize in the newness of pressing demands. It was again her function to emphasize the realities of living the faith, the vows, and the eccesial spirit as essential to any service they might undertake.

That summer she purchased a building with a garden at Ulica Warszawska, No. 13, which after necessary alterations provided suitable accommodations for the multiple services in which the sisters became engaged. Bishop Dunajewski blessed the premises, October 27, 1882, and celebrated the first Mass in their chapel.[89]

Astonishing incidents of the flowering of faith and vocation are recorded in the early chronicles of the Cracow foundation. Perhaps the most extraordinary are those of Rebecca Last and Emma Morgenstern. Rebecca, a young Jewess, exhibited a burning desire for Christianity and, in spite of violent opposition and persecution, received Baptism and later entered the Nazareth Community where she was named Sister Martha. She led an edifying life of humility and piety.[90]

Emma, again, who came from a prosperous Lutheran family, was a well-educated young woman who became attracted to the Catholic Church and secretly succeeded to learn its truths. Her brother, a minister of the small, close-knit Lutheran colony, and her parents, fiercely intolerant of her sympathies for catholicism, made her life miserable. Emma appealed to Mother Mary for protection and decided to accompany her to Rome in disguise, November 8, 1882. Although Emma had executed and filed officially a legal document certifying that she took this action of her own free will, uninfluenced by anyone, the Morgensterns for years attempted to compel her to return. To obviate possible harassment of the Congregation by them and to obliterate the traces leading to her person, Emma changed her surname to Murray.[91]

After her profession of faith she requested admission to Nazareth and received the name of the baptismal patron of the Foundress, St. Frances of Rome. During the formative years in the religious life Emma endured several spiritual crises, which ultimately served to confirm her in the decision once made. Her long life of great dedication and unflinching sacrifice left its mark particularly upon the development of the Congregation's work in England where she was to be known as "good Mother Frances."

In the summer of 1883 Mother Mary retired to Assisi for an extended retreat under the direction of Padre Gregorio, a Franciscan of high regard.[92] She also consulted him about doubtful points in the constitutions, a recurring preoccupation of hers which filled her waking hours. Withdrawn from mounting external claims that encroached upon her time and person, she moved into the very presence of God that encompassed her like consuming fire. The mystical encounter was fraught with the risk of disclosure and discovery which she could not entirely evade. It imposed the price of self-effacing constancy, an unconditional surrender to God at any cost.

Solitude was a grace which ushered in moments of truth and vivid confrontations. Her thoughts again reverted to the person of Brother Stephen whose presence at Nazareth was introducing divisive elements. Capitalizing on the initial role Providence had assigned him, he overreached himself by interfering with the guidance of individual sisters and by insisting on austerities and other practices that were incompatible with the spirit and aims envisioned by the Foundress.[93] Disaster could be avoided only with the aid of clearsighted, wise direction of a priest of God who would be attuned to the promptings of the Holy Spirit and to the new perspectives in the contemporary Church. The crucial question was whether the situation could be eliminated without complication. Doubt stemmed from the fact that the long association with Brother Stephen had become a two-pronged affair: the one, involving him, had to take into account his own self-assertion in the developments of the Congregation; the second concerned the impressionable members who were dazzled by his flights of fatuous piety. She prayed for wisdom and prudence.

While in Assisi, during the month of August, Mother Mary recalled

Mother Gabriel to Rome and appointed Mother Raphael to replace her as the superior in Cracow.[94] In Assisi, too, on August 1, 1883, young Thecla Lubowidzka joined the Foundress with the firm intention of becoming a member of her Congregation.[95] After her father's death and with the consent of her mother she was finally able to realize her vocation. At this point she accompanied Mother Mary to Loreto for the feast of the Assumption which the Foundress observed as her patronal day in the religious life.

It was at Loreto that she learned of Pope Leo's encyclical *Supremi Apostolatus Officio,* in which he exhorted the faithful to sanctify the month of October by the daily recitation of the rosary and the Litany of the Blessed Virgin in all churches. Since the Church was abused and menaced by all sorts of attacks, he proclaimed the rosary, above all practices, as the sword against the evils of the times. In the course of his pontificate, Leo XIII issued eleven encyclicals on the subject of the rosary, all masterpieces of restrained emotion, of faith and fervor, and solid theology. To the litany he added the invocation, "Queen of the Holy Rosary, pray for us."[96]

Mother Mary was quick to recognize the efficacy of the rosary for the Church Militant and in the lives of individuals. To her it was a tender expression of the personal Marian devotion to which she had long been drawn. The pronouncements of the philosopher Pope, the scholar, the statesman, the patron of arts, who put more confidence in praying the rosary than in all other human resources, confirmed her in the desire to adopt it as one of the principal means of honoring the Virgin Mary by the Community and of assisting the Church in its struggles and reverses. Upon her return to Rome she acquainted the sisters with the message of the encyclical, and that October introduced the daily rosary in common.[97] After each decade of the rosary they chose to add the prayer, "Blessed be the Holy and Immaculate Conception of the Blessed Virgin Mary, Mother of God," as a reparatory act, encouraged by the Pope, for blasphemy against the Holy Virgin.[98]

By now the apostolate in Cracow began to attract more vocations to the Nazareth way. They gathered about Mother Mary in the leased apartment near the Aracoeli church, which was becoming too small to house the growing Community. On November 18, 1883, she located and purchased a well-constructed building on the Esquiline, at Via Machiavelli, 18, wherein to accommodate the motherhouse and the novitiate. Under her instructions Brother Stephen was charged with the supervision of the remodeling which had to be carried out before the sisters could move in.[99]

Yet prior to their transfer, the feast of Our Lady of Loreto, December 10, was made memorable for the eager postulant, Thecla Lubowidzka, who was that day admitted to the novitiate in an afternoon ceremony and was named Lauretta.[100] More than any one of her contemporaries, she was to capture the spirit of the Foundress and keep it alive throughout the many arduous years of toil and leadership.

In view of the anticipated change of quarters, a marble altar had been acquired for the new convent and even then replaced the wooden one which was promptly dismantled, awaiting disposal. When word reached Mother Mary that the Resurrectionists had been making inquiries about just that kind of wooden altar, she offered it to them. The procurator general, Father Anthony Lechert, arrived to accept the offer, at which time he made the acquaintance with Mother Mary. By a peculiar faculty of discernment she discovered in him the qualities she had hoped for in a director.[101] At the moment she requested him to visit an ailing novice[102] and to hear her confession from time to time.

On the first Sunday of Advent that year, December 2, Mother Mary for the first time herself approached Father Lechert in the confessional, deriving the long-sought-for light, peace and confidence. This marked an entrance into a new era for her and the Congregation, similarly as the first Sunday of Advent marks the beginning of the liturgical year of the Church. Then on Christmas, at midnight Mass offered by him, Mother Gabriel pronounced her perpetual vows, while Mother Mary made a renewal of hers.[103]

Several penetrating interviews with Father Lechert left her without hesitancy about the advisability of securing his services as the regular confessor of all the sisters. He was agreeable, subject however to the consent of his superior general and the approval of ecclesiastical authorities.[104] When on January 7, 1884 the Cardinal Vicar of Rome imparted the requisite faculties, Mother Mary dispatched a note to Father Lechert, reflecting,

> ... At that time I had no light and probably needed none. When Our Lord inspired faith in me and an inner conviction, which was later confirmed by external circumstances, I implored the Blessed Mother at Loreto to send us a priest of her own choice—one given by her, as it were, not selected by me—a priest who would assist me to find the right road to our destined mission. After all these entreaties you were sent to us. . . . Today I am at peace, knowing that the Lord Jesus has accomplished this. I feel strengthened in faith, and consequently, in hope, believing that what he brings into being, he will likewise bring to fruition. Thus he will not allow human weakness to destroy it, for we are rooted in him and rely upon him for everything: you, Father, for light; I, for the grace of collaboration in alacrity of spirit.[105]

That very day the sisters began transferring their household furnishings to Via Machiavelli, where, on the 18th, Father Lechert celebrated the first Mass in the temporary chapel on the second floor and, after Mass, blessed the entire convent. The permanent chapel was still under construction;[106] four first-floor rooms were being converted to this purpose and a beautifully designed apse was being built to inclose the sanctuary.

With customary tact and gentleness Mother Mary tried to lead Brother Stephen to admit to himself that his function as the instrument of God's will for Nazareth had terminated years ago and that for him at present the will of God was in the monastery of his own order. When to all appearances these efforts were lost on him, she would hasten to the Scala Santa in the Lateran to pour out the anguish of her soul, praying upon the Holy Stairs that Jesus had ascended when he approached the judgment seat of Pontius Pilate. She finally resolved to come to the point and, on February 2, the feast of the Purification of Our Lady, discussed the matter with him decisively.[107] Reluctant to comply with the inevitable, Brother Stephen appealed to Father Semenéñko[108] for support. Since the appeal proved ineffective, he left for Cracow on March 11.[109]

Unwittingly his departure raised seeds of brooding resentment on the part of the first sisters, putting to a severe test Mother Mary's faith in her mission and in the foundation she was heading. She summarized to them the validity of her action in a simple, firm statement, "Believe me, whatever is being done here and now is dictated by the will of God. If I were to die this moment and appear before the living God, I would do nothing to change my decision."[110]

But the Lubowidzki sisters had harbored preconceived ideas of the contemplative life which they expected to be realized in Nazareth and which they fondly aligned with the Brother's desultory notions. To the Foundress the contemplative life was not something to be sought and indulged for itself; it meant, on the contrary, the humble experiencing of the gift of God, freely given, to be utilized for the sake of souls who longed to be inspired, guided, instructed, and served; it was not a flight from the world into the comfortable glow of complacency, but the unremitting building of the Kingdom of God in the world when the presence of God comes closer in the aridity of spirit than in consolation.

By singular coincidence, as if offering endorsement to this principle, a group of children came to the convent unsolicited in this very period, asking to be taught religion. Within the next few days the group numbered eighty boys and girls of varying age levels, so that five classes were formed and five sisters had charge of the instructions.[111]

Learning the language and the culture of the country had been one of the things the Foundress required of every member who arrived in Rome, with view to the future services the sisters may be called upon to render. The same policy was later extended with regard to other countries where their apostolates were initiated in the course of the years. She understood the importance of cultural integration for the effective performance of work in any milieu, and herself set a foremost example of adaptability. For this reason she discouraged nationalistic distinctions among the sisters. The universality of the Church was their standard from the earliest days; they were to stand ready to embrace the whole of the People of God in the charity of Christ.

Early in March, when friendly Cardinal Monaco la Valetta became appointed the Major Penitientiary in the Roman Curia, he was succeeded to the post of the Vicar of Rome by Lucido Cardinal Parocchi. At the first convenient opportunity Cardinal Parocchi received Mother Mary who presented him with a report of the existing status of the Congregation and the general pattern along which it was evolving. Close upon his expressions of interest and forthright good will followed his personal visit to the convent where nothing escaped his appraising eye and nothing incurred his disapproval. Beneath the unhurried, hidden progress, he beheld a forecast of healthy growth in a discipline of expectancy.[112]

4 NEW DIMENSIONS

All the life of Father Anthony Maria Lechert was marked by profound spirituality of purpose. The impact of his presence in any setting was like a stone which has gone down into deep waters but is surrounded by visible concentric circles, the circumference of which expands to an ever greater extent. He had a flair for preaching and spoke out firmly and clearly against the egoism, the mendacity, the godlessness, and the dissipation in the world at large. He had a tremendous feeling for all things Catholic. Given the opportunity, he could have been capable of infusing a dynamic revival within the Church and of reshaping some aspects of its human course, not by a stroke of impetuous action, but in the serene manner of a flowing stream whose steady force carries away everything that is in its path.

This quiet, thoughtful clergyman read the signs of his times and molded the external contours of Mother Mary's inspirations, inserting them into the mainstream of the Church's contemporary life. As a man and as a priest, he enjoyed philosophical discussions and the mathematical precision of logic. In matters theological, St. Augustine came closest to his heart and mind. To those who turned to him he listened with total absorption and complete courtesy, then responded with words of wisdom and flashes of penetration and insight. He was of somewhat less than medium height, but his personality pulsating with the fires of vivid intelligence and inner vision lent him a semblance of physical stature greater than was his in reality.

When Anthony Lechert was born, October 10, 1845, at Witkowo in the Grand Duchy of Posen, the world was tightly wedged about by political contradictions and sociological complexes. His parents, Paul and Frances née Kaczkowska, created a happy, peaceful family life for their children. Besides Anthony, there were two other sons, Francis and Michael, and a daughter, Theophila. The home atmosphere was pervaded by simple Christian virtues and love of God, which contributed to the building of righteous characters, strong in faith.

Having endured the legendary horrors of primary and secondary educational systems under Prussian discipline, Anthony entered the seminary in Posen and received his ordination to the priesthood, August 14, 1870, at the hands of Archbishop Mieczysław Ledóchowski, the future cardinal. He continued advanced studies in Rome where he achieved, with papal honors, the doctorates in both canon and civil laws, and later the doctorate in sacred theology.[118]

Archbishop Ledóchowski, imprisoned under Bismarck's harsh rule, warned Father Anthony against returning to his homeland where persecution of the Catholic Church took on the most severe forms with regard to the clergy. Father Anthony was given leave to go to France, and there he devoted three years to pastoral work in the archdiocese of Paris. Brought into acquaintance with Father Jełowicki and attracted by the spirit of the Resurrectionists, he decided to become a member of this order. With the consent of his ordinary, he entered the novitiate in Rome in 1878 and was admitted to religious profession in 1882.[114]

Father Semeneńko, impressed by the natural abilities and the confirmed virtue of the new confrère, was determined to utilize his qualifications in offices of responsibility within the Congregation of the Resurrection and in the direct services of the Church. His practical sense aptly foresaw the value of allowing Father Anthony to assume the spiritual direction of Mother Mary and of the members of her Congregation.

In this as in all other undertakings Father Lechert was motivated by one dominant idea, the will of God. He aimed to discover it in the mysterious workings of Providence in life's circumstances and in the contemplative encounters with divine light in faith. Once discovered, he pursued its dictates with unflinching fidelity.

He commenced to carry out a methodical program of weekly conferences for the ascetical and theological formation of the sisters. Individually, as they sought his direction and counseling, he helped them to verify the authenticity of their vocation and assisted them to make a genuine, mature response to God.[115]

Concerned about the particular inspiration of Mother Mary, he detected the presence of a paradox in the dual thrust of her spirituality: one, dealing with her own personal journey toward an absorbing union with God; the second, involving her role and responsibility as the foundress. That he succeeded to maintain a delicate balance between these two aspects is a concrete proof of his qualifications for the exacting task he had undertaken.

During the mid-Lenten period of 1884 he conducted an eight-day retreat for the Community. The last day, March 25, was made joyous by the profession ceremonies at which he presided, when Mother Michael pronounced her perpetual vows and the two novices, Sister Columba[116] and Sister Angela,[117] were admitted to first profession.

Since several sisters had already pledged themselves irrevocably by religious vows, Mother Mary wished to ratify formally her own dedication in their presence. For this she selected the anniversary day of her first Holy Communion, May 1.[118] Her own words best describe the occasion about which she wrote to the sisters in Cracow:

My dearly beloved in the Lord,
    I desire to share with you the joy I experienced yesterday by the

grace of God's infinite mercy. Yesterday, on the anniversary of my first Holy Communion, I solemnly renewed my vows in such a manner as if I were making them for the first time, that is, similarly as I made my commitment to Christ eleven years ago. Then I had been almost unaware of his designs; I had surrendered myself voluntarily, but without quite realizing what obligations I was assuming.

Now, after years of trials in which God always manifested his mercy towards me—now, having contended with various adversities and able to discern the path ahead—now, as far as I can judge, having ampler knowledge, understanding and, perhaps, love—now, not alone, but surrounded by the sisters of this house and united in spirit with you—I rededicated myself to Our Lord Jesus Christ unconditionally so that he shall forever be the unique lord, king, father, and spouse of my soul. Prostrate in my nothingness and wretchedness, I prayed in deepest humility, "My God and my all."

O my dearest sisters, at this moment I also offered all of you to Jesus forever, for everything he might wish to do with each of us, for whatever he may have destined for us from all eternity. I am confident that he accepted with favor the offering I made and that he will grant us the grace of fidelity and perseverance. I trust he will give us an increase of ardent love for him, so that we may more effectively die to self and, living solely for him, become identified with him.

Thank God for me, my sisters; praise and adore him for the ineffable mercy he extends to me. Pray for me that I should always remain united with him and that I should not longer live, but that he should live in me.[119]

The formula which she used in the ceremony was inscribed in Mother Mary's own hand; it was signed by her and by Father Lechert, and is preserved in the archives of the Congregation. The act itself meant very much to her, so much so that she henceforth commemorated it annually on the same day, renewing her vows publicly with moving piety wherever she might happen to be.

In July, Mother Mary purchased the adjoining building, at Via Machiavelli, 16, to facilitate the completion of the permanent chapel and to provide needed classroom space and guest accommodations for pilgrims who preferred to reside in a religious house. There were always children for catechetical instruction, as also the poor and the sick of the neighborhood to whom the sisters brought solace and aid. The zealous Foundress participated in these works of Christian concern, setting a glowing example to her companions.[120]

From time to time ecclesiastical dignitaries visited the convent, especially Cardinal Parocchi who was interested in the progress of the chapel, and the newly created Cardinal Ledóchowski, whom the Pope had summoned to make his residence in Rome.

After Mother Michael had gone to Cracow, her sister, Mother Raphael, arrived in Rome, in November, for spiritual renovation under Father Lechert's direction, not only for her benefit alone, but, as one of the elders, for the benefit of those who would come within the orbit of her influence.

Mother Mary was becoming progressively entrenched in the consciousness of Nazareth's corporate entity. Proceeding from this premise, she conceded, all the members should be expected to share the responsibilities of the Community, each one should be allowed to contribute to the extent of her ability, and no one should be made to feel outside the group, least of all the superior. Alert to the potential danger lurking in insidious attitudes that can psychologically separate the superior from the sisters, she deemed it incumbent upon her to strengthen the bond of internal unity within the Congregation definitively. Along with that, for the future, the authority of the highest superior had to be given unequivocal stability, safeguarded against the slightest shadow of a doubt and empowered to sustain the spirit of unity among all members.

On December 5, 1884, in the presence of Father Lechert, she addressed the sisters, informing them that her position among them, as a superior, had no ecclesiastical sanction. She had exercised this function as the foundress until the Congregation would be assured of a sound foothold; now she was convinced that her mission as a foundress was finished and no longer entitled her to continue in the position of authority. With sentiments of gratitude and humility she relinquished it into the hands of Father Lechert.[121]

Promptly he restored the astonished sisters' equanimity with a precise analytical review of the situation. The need for superiors, he explained, arises from the nature of the Church in which everything is lived out in fraternal communion. Since life in communion requires a visible link, it is the vocation of the superior to render to the community this sisterly service. Being in position of authority, the superior has need of the confidence of the members who are bound by obedience. This confidence is to be expressed by their right to elect their highest superior.

Inasmuch as Mother Mary acted within her right when she followed her conscience in submitting her resignation, the Community was instructed to hold an election by secret ballot according to the usual practice approved by the Church under such circumstances. Since but one perpetually professed sister was away at Cracow, the votes of the sisters in Rome would validly determine the choice of the Congregation's superior. He read aloud the names written down by the sisters present, the result being the unanimous election of Mother Mary, with the exception of her own vote which she had cast in favor of Mother Raphael.[122]

Accepting the election as an indication of divine will for her, Mother Mary directed to her sisters a request that was eminently characteristic of her, exhorting them not to be swayed by sentiment or yield to human respect in their relations with her, but to consider her as an instrument of God for the carrying out of his plans. It was always her belief that legitimate human superiors share in God's authority. She looked upon authority, received and exercised in the name of Christ, as the power to serve, to love, to govern, to guide, and to stimulate the growth of persons in the Congregation. The principle that authority is an apostolate of love, she communicated to the sisters who in the course of time were entrusted with authority at various levels.

The next morning, December 6, the Foundress assembled the sisters to discuss with them the feasibility of having Father Lechert as the director of the Congregation in addition to his services in individual spiritual direction of the members. Opinions were freely expressed in spontaneous agreement. The sisters reflected with satisfaction upon the strides they had made in religious formation over the past several months and recalled the priest's competence exhibited in dealing with the situation of the preceding day; they all supported the proposal.

Later in the day, when Father Lechert arrived, Mother Mary presented the proposal to him in their presence. Visibly affected by this manifestation of trust, Father Lechert gave expression of feelings of cordial enthusiasm for Nazareth and its ideals. He acknowledged the apparent will of God in the sisters' full accord and guaranteed his readiness to serve the Congregation's needs and objectives "even unto laying his life for it".[123]

A petition was drawn up in writing, asking him "in the name of Christ to be the spiritual father, guide and director of all the sisters called to the Congregation and of the works of the Congregation." The sisters pledged obedience to him in all things as to the representative of Christ and signed the document in the presence of one another.[124] Father Lechert acceded to their request pending the approval of his superiors, and thereupon he endorsed it with his own signature.

Without delay Mother Mary notified the sisters in Cracow of the events that had taken place in the last two days.[125] She was intent upon giving them an accurate perspective, lest information from biased sources undermine their morale. Until the closing of her life, alike in health and in illness, in travel and well into the late hours of the night, she was tireless in reaching out to her sisters with warmly penned letters of shared information, of encouragement or instruction; letters which, though addressed to individuals or particular Community groups, were at the same time self-revealing.

No cause was too insignificant to command her attention if it pertained to her sisters; in any need, when she could not be there in person, a letter from her would arrive without fail, spanning the distance, overcoming the separation, updating, reconciling, coordinating. Thousands of her extant letters give evidence of her effective use of correspondence to knit a oneness of mind, heart, and purpose, notwithstanding the diversity of age, character, personality, and natural gifts.

At Christmas midnight Mass that year, Mother Joanne was admitted to perpetual profession, Sister Lauretta pronounced her first vows, and postulant Anna Parzyk was accepted into the novitiate and was named Sister Philomena.[126] On this occasion, too, all perpetually professed sisters received selected mysteries from the life of Christ or the Blessed Virgin Mary to complement their religious names. For herself Mother Mary chose Jesus the Good Shepherd.[127] Heretofore she had been in the habit of signing her name simply "Mary of Jesus," but the image of Christ as the Good Shepherd appealed strongly to her with its message of compassion, tenderness and forgiveness. The motherhouse was likewise placed under the patronage of Jesus the Good Shepherd. The practice was thus initiated to adopt at the time of final profession a mystery of the faith which best suited the personal spirituality of a given sister or her devotional bent.

On the verge of the spring of 1885, it was decided to launch a Nazareth foundation in the United States. For weeks Mother Mary had grappled with this proposition in supreme earnestness to establish reasonable certitude for taking the step. She yearned to place the Congregation in the missionary forefront where the inexorable human needs of soul, mind and body beckoned; nonetheless she was troubled by the insufficiency of available personnel and apprehensive of their preparation. The project, however, met with the eloquent support of Cardinal Parocchi and was wholeheartedly welcomed by Cardinal Simeoni, the prefect of the Sacred Congregation for the Propagation of the Faith. The favorable views of other ecclesiatics were also reassuring.

Of the sisters, Mother Joanne instantly volunteered to be sent across the Atlantic, but learned that her mission was elsewhere and, as time went on, her hope of setting foot on the American soil vanished entirely. She was appointed now to be the superior in Cracow, for Mother Michael, who had been temporarily substituting there in that capacity, was returning to Italy for reasons of health.[128]

The arrival of Mother Joanne on Palm Sunday, March 29, was greeted with joy by the sisters in Cracow who had been looking forward to a stimulating leadership. The new superior was radiating precious elements of mystical faith and high principles; she was widely read, charming, intelligent, and had a background of pedagogical experience. Not only was capable management necessary for the volume and variety of services which the sisters were called upon to render, but there were also young women in diverse stages of interest in the religious life to be guided and evaluated. There were the mere applicants, the fascinated aspirants, the eager postulants, and one serious novice.[129]

By May 31, Mother Mary made her appearance at the Cracow convent, bringing with her a small handbook of observances in manuscript, compiled for the harmonious integration of community-living under normal conditions of life and work as religious. In conference and dialogues with the sisters she reviewed the practices described in the handbook[130] and recommended that transcriptions be made for their personal use and reference. The spoken word, being volatile and easily forgotten or misinterpreted, had to be imbedded in tangible form where standard guidelines were concerned. The handbook offered an experimental base from which tried and proven policies would evolve at a future date.

Within a week Father Lechert called at the convent and was introduced to the sisters. Discussions about the forthcoming American foundation culminated in the announcement that Mother Raphael was designated the major superior over the entire new mission and that several sisters selected from the house in Cracow were to join her in Rome at once in preparation for the journey.[131]

On June 8, Mother Mary was already on her return trip to Italy, and on Saturday the 13th, she and the sisters assigned to the United States were received in private audience by Pope Leo XIII who addressed them with appreciative good wishes, then imparted his blessing to each one individually and upon their missionary venture.[132] Father Lechert accompanied the group together with Father Peter Poppe and Brother Ferdinand Idzikowski, Resurrectionists, who were making the voyage. The latter two were assigned to remain in the United States, while Father Lechert was delegated by his superior general to make a visitation tour of the Resurrectionist mission centers in America.

The Foundress believed it her duty to explore the true nature and scope of the overseas field and herself to install the pioneers there. With them she embarked at Naples, June 18, aboard the steamship *Gottardo.* Besides Mother Raphael, the first staff consisted of ten other sisters:[133]

Sister M. Lauretta (Thecla Lubowidzka)
Sister M. Angela (Janine Czoppe)
Sister M. Evangelista (Anna Kijeńska)
Sister M. Frances (Emma Morgenstern)
Sister M. Stanislaus (Josepha Sierpińska)
Sister M. Paula (Maria Czarnowska)
Sister M. Philomena (Anna Parzyk)
Sister M. Cecilia (Elizabeth Sadowska)
Sister M. Agnes (Caroline Łukaszewicz)
Sister M. Theresa (Godwin Czermińska)

5 THE AMERICAN EXPERIENCE

Leo XIII looked with solicitude and admiration to the young American republic making enormous strides in national and economic progress. The tremendous influx of immigrants from Europe had resulted in a rapid expansion of the Catholic Church, under unparalleled conditions of freedom, due largely to the separation of the church and state.[134] Barely had the wounds of the Civil War begun to heal, when a new wave of immigration poured various national groups into the United States in the hope of finding surcease from political and religious persecution that ravaged their homelands. They braved the difficulties of forging a new life, spurred by the anticipation of unfettered pursuit of happiness, of free enterprise and equality of opportunity, and of the inviolability of their conscience.

Inevitably ethnic differences precipitated periodic conflicts among the immigrant groups, and nativists clashed with newcomers in disputes over priorities and civil rights. There was resistance to the infiltration of alien cultures on the one hand, and to the forcible absorption into the mainstream of American life on the other. To safeguard the religious faith of the Catholic community, the Church acknowledged its ecumenical responsibility towards all the faithful.[135]

At the invitation of the Sovereign Pontiff a conference of American archbishops was held in Rome from October, 1883 to March, 1884 to discuss the affairs of the Church in the United States. Meeting at the College of the Propaganda under the presidency of the prefect, Giovanni Cardinal Simeoni, the prelates carefully considered the exigencies of the American pluralistic society in the process of urban and industrial expansion, flanked as it was by phenomenal rural life, and also the urgency to preserve Christian truth and morality among the people.

The result was the convening of the Third Plenary Council in Baltimore, November 9, 1884. The Pope appointed the Archbishop of Baltimore, James Gibbons, to represent him as the Apostolic Delegate and to preside at the Council.[136] Among the far-reaching measures adopted by the Council, parochial schools became mandatory upon the clergy and the faithful for the religious education of both native and immigrant children.[137] Since a large percentage of immigrants came from countries where English was not spoken, the bishops formulated the policy of assigning priests of the same ethnic backgrounds as their congregations, who knew their language and who would be in touch with the spirit and the aspirations of their people.[138] It was understood that actual assimilation would have to be gradual and, hopefully, might be accomplished in a climate of peaceful coexistence without psychological trauma. Just then religion was of prime concern and its ends had to be pursued with judicious propriety.

63

While the agenda for the Third Plenary Council were being readied, there came to Father Lechert an appeal from a Resurrectionist confrère in Chicago, Father Vincent Michael Barzynski, dated October 13, 1884,[139] pressing for European sisters to staff a school and an orphanage. Father Vincent had previously toiled for eight rugged years in Texas, organizing mission stations and ministering to the religious and social needs of the settlers,[140] when in 1874 his assignment brought him to Chicago. The city was throbbing with prodigious vitality in a spectacular rise from the wreckage after the Great Fire of 1871; the demolition had left homeless nearly one third of the inhabitants and destroyed almost the entire commercial area.[141] Chicago emerged briskly, dotted with cultural islands populated by groups of common origin—a veritable cosmorama of languages and customs.

The hub of the Polish community was St. Stanislaus Kostka church where Father Vincent was the pastor. He had an immense energy and a gift for organization, resourcefulness, courage, and determination. As the Polonia branched out towards the outermost precincts of the city, he became known as the superior of the Polish mission in Chicago.[142] In his request to Father Lechert, he minced no words citing the qualifications he expected of the sisters: they had to be "religious according to the Heart of God," "equipped with above-average education," "self-sacrificing," "valiant women, willing to take their stand with Mary beneath the cross of Christ." He added as an afterthought his "fear of costly experiments of worldly-minded religious, who would be incapable of salutary influence upon our families and our women."[143]

Later, in February of 1885, Archbishop Patrick A. Feehan of Chicago addressed himself directly to Mother Mary, urging her to send the sisters by the month of July.[144] He relied heavily on religious orders with a foreign-language manpower pool to help implement the pastoral decrees of the Plenary Council. For weeks, during her hours of solitary prayer, Mother Mary came to grips with God and herself, weighing the probabilities of the American venture. The call of the Church to a participation in the redemptive service of souls induced her to exchange the familiar amenities of European life patterns for the great unknown.

The long transatlantic voyage was wearisome. By the twelfth day the rolling and pitching of the ship broke into a raging bout with battering waves and violent winds. Eventually the sisters reached the shores of New York on the afternoon of July 4 and, the same evening, boarded the train for their destination. Their arrival in Chicago on Monday morning, July 6, was greeted at the railroad station by Father Vincent who provided the transportation to St. Josaphat's. There Father Lechert immediately offered the Holy Sacrifice of the Mass in thanksgiving. The kind women of the parish, rejoicing at the sisters' coming, brought food and household supplies to ease their domestic cares.[145]

Three days later, Mother Mary in the company of Mother Raphael and Sister Lauretta paid respects to Archbishop Feehan and presented letters of introduction to him. The Archbishop, conducting the interview in French, expressed his satisfaction at the sisters' arrival in Chicago, dwelling with fervor upon the extensive apostolate open to them in Christian education, for the preservation of the faith among the immigrants, and for the growth of the Church in America. He repeated with emphasis, "You are needed here".[146]

Amid poverty and privation the sisters were accommodated in the combination building that housed St. Josaphat's church, school and convent. Located on the northeast side of Chicago River, the building was erected in 1884 and remained under the administration of Father Francis Breitkopf, C.R. In August, 1885, however, a new pastor was appointed, Father Candid Kozłowski, who together with Father Vincent and Mother Mary developed plans for the school.

The parish orphanage, initially caring for ten children, increased in occupancy as soon as a sister was placed in charge.[147] In reality it was not an orphanage in the usual sense, but an emergency haven for children who happened to be touched by the misfortunes of life and needed protection and care, either briefly or for extended periods, whether as a result of family stress upon the death or illness of a parent, or when a child's own illness became too great a burden at home, or else in the case of actual orphans, pending the settlement of their custody.

Even before regular classes began in the school, a new spirit commenced to course through the neighborhood tenements and rows of red brick cottages, and through the local shops and marts, for the message of Christ channeled through youth was irresistible to the parents. The sisters formed weekday discussion groups with girls of all age levels, reserving Sunday afternoons for the older ones. Mother Mary would often spend some time with each group to determine the scope of the girls' knowledge of religion and to guide profitably the sisters' planning for subsequent sessions.[148] After each gathering the girls were invited to the church to pray the rosary in unison.

Home visits to the sick of the parish and prayer at their bedside brought considerable solace into the lives of many families for whom Christianity was a practical reality and who in the main aspired to Christian conduct. The purely nominal Catholic was rather an exception to the rule. Long after the good Foundress had died, the memory of her gentle sympathy and sincere warmth thrived among these people in grateful testimony to her desire of helping all in their miseries of soul and body.[149]

Mother Mary's lettter to Mother Joanne revealed some pertinent observations at this stage:

> This is a time of faith in practice, a time of boundless trust in Our
> Lord, a time of love in action. Let not anxiety depress you; for is the
> power, the goodness, and the love of Christ less on sea than on land,
> other in America than in Europe? I do not even advert to the vast
> physical distance which stretches between us; I feel so close to all of
> you, especially at prayer, because we are all united in God and in his
> labors . . . Here our life is quite different, different problems, different
> personalities. The work is unglamorous and simple: the elementary
> teaching of a few hundred children. Materially the situation is very
> delicate, because we do not wish to incur expenses for anyone; we
> accept whatever these good people give us out of their kindness and
> poverty. All this is precious and welcome, coming as it does from
> the Lord's holy dispensation for us.[150]

Even so, her personal attitudes have not made her oblivious to the
sisters' formidable ordeal in the attempts to adjust to the strange environ-
mental conditions and heavy demands. She noticed among them unmistakable signs of dejection that plunged her into a severe spiritual conflict.
Grieved by their distress, she was on the verge of withdrawing from
Father Lechert's direction and of announcing to the Archbishop the
sisters' return to Europe. A heroic act of faith saved her from taking this
fatal step.[151]

Mother Mary's compliance did not stem from a natural predisposition
to submissiveness, for she was naturally possessed of a strong personality,
resolute and decisive. Her diaries reecho the cry to know her true position
with regard to her spiritual director, straining to secure her relationship
above human dross.[152] Trapped in the midst of doubts with which she
wrestled implacably, she cleared away for many the obstacles to achieve
intellectual assent to transcendent values and in so doing enabled them
to face confidently the questions which might haunt them at some other
time.

Father Lechert, on his part, had made no claims. Unperturbed he had
assured her that she was free to act in either instance without affront to
fidelity, if there were supernatural reasons to substantiate such decisions.[153]
It was only normal that in the sisters' work, which was both theirs and
God's, there should occur an admixture of human elements. As Mother
Mary reasonably reminded them that there are other places besides Europe
where God wants to be known and loved, they found it in their hearts to
admit that God in his own way was shaping their lives which they thought
they had chosen for themselves.

The test of their morale came when one of them was called to answer the summons of death. Ever since the stormy episode at sea, Sister Philomena's health had been declining steadily, so that, when on August 2 a torrential rainfall in Chicago virtually deluged the city, she at once fell victim to typhoid fever. With the flooding of the water supply system, water-borne diseases entered the homes of the residents and took toll of hundreds of lives. Sister Philomena gave up her young life on August 11 with sentiments of exemplary piety and resignation to Divine Providence.[154]

Just about then the pastor of the populous southside parish of St. Adalbert, Father John Radziejewski, decided to seek the services of the Sisters of the Holy Family of Nazareth for his parochial school. There were lay teachers of sorts, but to have a staff of religious teachers to direct and coordinate the educational program was the ambition and desire of every parish. Mother Mary consulted the Archbishop about this proposal and received, with his encouragement, the advice to formulate equitable terms of agreement with the pastors that would be acceptable to them and to the Congregation, and would meet the approval of the Archbishop. It pleased him that young women were already indicating an interest in Nazareth as a way of life, and he consented to the admission of suitable applicants. To fortify the spiritual character of the Congregation, he gave permission for the establishment of convent chapels with the Blessed Sacrament reserved and extended this permission to all future convents.[155] He also mentioned discreetly that it was customary for sisters in the United States to cover their hair entirely.

Much was to be accomplished within the rapidly passing days. Relative to the last point, the Foundress enlisted the help of Mother Raphael, who was notably gifted in design and needlecraft. The sisters' headdress was soon transformed[156] to consist of a neat black cap edged with a narrow white band, over which was worn a bonnet-like form with the veil attached to it in smooth folds.

For the use of members and applicants alike, a brochure was prepared in Chicago for publication[157] which embodied fifteen articles of the provisional Constitutions. Although the text was preliminary, it outlined the characteristic elements of the spirit, purpose and principles underlying the total dedication of the Nazareth religious. The timeliness of this action became apparent when the first aspirants were admitted to postulancy: Albertina Szopińska,[158] Balbina Dańczyk[159] and Christina Konior[160], while others were being given an orientation.

An interval in Father Lechert's visitation schedule was utilized for a ten-day retreat at which he presided. The sisters industriously recorded his instructions, which they later transcribed for distribution among the convents as a treasured legacy. They were in the habit of preserving and sharing similarly Mother Mary's conferences in the United States and in

Europe. In view of the scarcity of available ascetical works, these transcriptions, after revision and correction, served to strengthen and mold the spirit of the Congregation in depth and quality.

The best room in the convent section was selected for the chapel and equipped with meticulous care. Father Lechert offered the Eucharistic Sacrifice there for the first time on September the first, and that same afternoon Archbishop Feehan made his first visit to become acquainted with all the sisters.[161] Several days later he arrived to celebate the Mass in their chapel and was also greeted at breakfast by the girls of the sisters' instruction class.[162] The obvious friendliness of the Archbishop generated immense moral support essential to the Congregation in its new setting.

On September 30, the Archbishop of Chicago endorsed the contracts executed by the Foundress and the respective pastors as mutually binding to all intents and purposes.[163]

At St. Josaphat's the regular school program commenced in the early days of September with 200 children attending,[164] while at St. Adalbert's the school opened on September 19 with an enrollment of 500.[165] Responsibilities in local and provincial administration were assigned as follows: Sister Lauretta, superior-principal at St. Josaphat's and provincial assistant to Mother Raphael; Sister Frances, superior-principal at St. Adalbert's, provincial councilor and supervisor of education; Sister Theresa, director of vocations and novices; Sister Stanislaus, director of the orphanage.[166]

Considering the drive that marked the Catholic population to create parochial schools, Mother Mary laid plans for a house of the American province where aspiring candidates would receive religious formation and preparatory education. She discovered what was then estimated a good location along Division street, between Cleaver and Holt streets, where she purchased two existing buildings, one wooden and the other a brick structure, with an adjoining vacant lot to serve as a city garden. Since alterations had to be undertaken in these buildings, Mother Raphael was entrusted the execution of the project after Father Lechert blessed the property and Mother Mary prayed over it.[167]

Departures were already in order; Father Lechert left Chicago on the first of October to travel by way of Canada, where he had to visit a Resurrectionist mission before reaching the port of embarkation. Mother Mary bade farewell to the sisters three days later. They boarded the steamship *Amérique,* which set sail on the sixth and arrived at the Havre on the eighteenth. Father Lechert proceeded at once to Rome, but Mother Mary detoured to Vienna for a meeting on urgent matters with Mother Joanne,[168] after which she stopped at Loreto to pour out all her soul's concerns in the Holy House of Nazareth.[169]

Immediately upon return to Rome she concentrated upon the novitiate, as she was wont to do after any prolonged absence from the motherhouse.

To the novices, who represented to her the future of the Congregation's mission in the Church, she gave of herself unsparingly in guidance and instruction, participating likewise in their activities and chores.[170]

Her correspondence was growing increasingly copious, occupying her mind and time with the affairs in Poland and the United States. It was at this time that she began to suffer with severe eyestrain, which became aggravated through the years and required the aid of eyeglasses for use at close range.[171] But, in spite of personal discomfort in any form, she persisted at the full pace of involvement. The human equation exposed problems that bespoke mysteries to her; to trials and chagrin, mystery added the sweet presence of God who, in the darkness of every problem, brought the manifestation of his inscrutable will. The sisters in America have largely kept the postal communications active and constant, and the interchanging letters between Mother Raphael and the Foundress remain strikingly evocative of the contemporaneous events with which they had to cope.

Many ideas lying restlessly dormant in Father Vincent's subconscious were now thrown into circulation, openly aiming to include the sisters. As a matter of fact, Mother Mary had authorized the provincial superior to purchase the second frame house at the other side of the brick building and also a second vacant lot. In general, the alterations to be accomplished were to be minimal and were to provide only temporary facilities in but one of the buildings, as the Foundress had contemplated the construction, in the near future, of an entirely new convent on that site. Meanwhile Father Vincent convinced Mother Raphael of the expediency of converting the acquired buildings for multipurpose social centers for the women of his parish. He saw fit to assume responsibility for negotiating the additional property and himself took charge of the legal title to it.

The burning needs of the moment drew Mother Mary's willing response to postpone the initial plans in favor of Nazareth's distinct role in the regeneration of the Christian family through the building up of religious, cultural and practical assets in women. St. Stanislaus parish clubs and sodalities of girls and women were to derive these opportunities under the sisters' direction in a family atmosphere of simplicity, informality and refinement. Later similar groups were conducted successfully under parochial auspices at St. Josaphat's and St. Adalbert's with the sisters' cooperation. What became apparent to Mother Mary was the inability on the part of Father Vincent and Mother Raphael to differentiate between the fiscal affairs of the parish and the Congregation. Her precise, practical judgment required clear, factual accounting and recording,[172] but her explanations seemed to baffle the provincial and elude the pastor.

The harsh winter season was causing frequent interruptions in the remodeling of the acquired buildings, so that Mother Raphael and three sisters could finally become established in the provincialate on March 9, 1886.[173] This day of Mother Mary's baptismal patron was marked by a joyous reunion of all the sisters at the Congregation's first American house. Because they wished all the convents in which they would reside to be identified by titles other than those of the parishes, Mother Mary named the house at St. Josaphat's in honor of Child Jesus, St. Adalbert's in honor of the Blessed Virgin Mary (which title was later modified to Our Lady of the Snows), while the provincialate and novitiate in honor of St. Joseph.[174] On St. Joseph's day, the Archbishop celebrated the first Mass in the newly furnished chapel and contributed to the festivity of the occasion by presenting his silver chalice in token of his good wishes.[175]

Satisfying results at school and rapport in parish contacts brought about a proliferation of new proposals, too many and too taxing for the sisters' limited numbers. To undertake additional activities at a sacrifice to their essential aims would be to destroy their effectiveness, and to neglect their primary duty to education would invite disaster upon the fundamental work for which they were asked to come to the United States. Because the deceptive prospect of a harvest for the Lord was apt to rouse their extravagant zeal, Mother Mary admonished them to prudent and balanced judgment after the example of the Divine Master, who chose to be constrained by the limitations of human nature as well as by time and space. Though his apostolate was laborious and supremely beneficent, he neither cured all the sick nor fed all the hungry, nor did he in person announce his teaching to all peoples, but he would ingeniously retire into contemplative prayer to sustain his spiritual integrity in communion with the heavenly Father. To disprove specious arguments that were flaunted before the sisters, she noted:

> . . . True, God does bestow graces more abundantly through some than through others, but that is accomplished when he himself so ordains, not by human choice alone. Hold fast against dispersion of forces; while adhering to principles and rejecting rash opinions, you will build up the potential to bear ample fruit, perhaps not brilliantly astounding, but definitely enduring, because rooted in faith. Humility allows us to view our temporal condition realistically as the will of God for us.[176]

Aside from parish societies, the convent of St. Joseph developed flourishing evening classes for the continuing education of working girls in the subjects of religion, literature, composition, practical mathematics, and useful arts. Interested young women who resided at greater distances formed a Sunday afternoon group which was well attended. The Archbishop, impressed by the cultural scope of the classes, recommended that the program be called an academy.[177] This led to popular requests from the public to establish a formal school for girls with a full-time academic course of instruction, which in fact came into being on October 1, 1887, under the official name of Holy Family Academy. Mother Raphael, who was the local superior and principal in that institution, conducted certain classes, as did Sister Theresa, while few sisters from the parochial schools were assigned to part-time teaching. Qualified lay instructors were engaged to complement the staff.[178]

Among parochial schools of recent date in Chicago, St. Adalbert's achieved early a remarkable status as a result of the acknowledged ability of Sister Frances with the concerted efforts of her associates. They have also been active in the usual collateral services of Nazareth by stimulating leadership in church societies and offering acts of charity to the sick and the needy.

From Rome the news broke across the Atlantic about the Pope's appointment of Father Lechert as rector of St. Athanasius Pontifical College of Greek Rite.[179] His rise in the esteem of ecclesiastical authorities had been rapid, and though doubtless it had been helped by Father Semeneńko, his rise was due chiefly to his own merit. He knew how to be determined when determination was warranted and conciliatory when conciliation was advisable. Unaware of the impression he created, he could with singular charm meet critical situations, unafraid moreover to think out his thoughts to the end. He spoke a half dozen languages and had already occupied the professorship in German at the Gregorian University.[180]

It was then with a sense of personal loss that he learned of Father Semeneńko's death which occurred in Paris.[181] If he had experienced previously to any degree how heavy a burden was the combined gift of intelligence and virtue, he would henceforth suffer more acutely the alienation of his peers who were less endowed.

The new and exacting responsibilities in no way diminished his concern for Nazareth with its new and more remote outposts. In the matter of policy regarding the course upon which the Congregation was entering, he probed the depths of evangelical truth, the better to help solidify its foundations.

The same year the small community was saddened by the announcement of Mother Michael's death in Rome, September 30. In her dying words she freely declared to the Foundress that she had at last regained peace. For long she had been reluctant to concede Nazareth's obvious vocation as it was unfolding in the contemporary Church, but with Mother Mary's inexhaustible patience assisting her through a lingering illness, light made its way through the mental barrier, and with light tranquility.

6 LIGHTS AND SHADOWS

By the end of 1886, two parallel occasions were observed on both continents: in Chicago, at St. Adalbert's, the sisters moved from their provisional accommodations to a newly erected parish convent;[182] in Rome, the slow, faltering progress in the construction of the chapel at the motherhouse was climaxed in a memorable ceremony, when Cardinal Parocchi blessed the chapel on January 3, 1887. The earlier, temporary chapel, which served the motherhouse since its establishment, now became an oratory to provide auxiliary facilities in time of necessity, especially during the influx of pilgrimages in the Eternal City.

Scarcely a month had elapsed since the new chapel was opened and made accessible to externs, when an assortment of provocative disturbances was organized against the convent by the hostile elements of the neighborhood. At first the disturbances consisted of furious ringing of the doorbell, usually when the community was assembled at prayer and, frequently, in the evening hours. Oftentimes, upon answering the doorbell, no one was found present; at other times, ruffians endeavored to force their entry into the convent under absurd pretexts or, remaining behind the door, they would loudly abuse the residents with vulgar invectives. Gradually their vicious activities shifted to an open attack, prowling in the convent garden, peering in the windows, attempting to break down the doors, and, on several occasions, individual sisters were assaulted in the street. The police, however, failed to respond to repeated appeals for protection. With the arrival of Holy Week in April, the momentum of these disturbances increased in intensity, destruction and intimidation; shotguns were discharged at the windows in the convent and the chapel, causing extensive damage and untold fear.[183]

Sectarian groups and isolated revolutionaries, responsible for conspirational raids and acts of violence,[184] disseminated false accusations about the convent, stating that the disturbances proceeded from within. This prevented people of good faith from offering the sisters any form of assistance. When after three months a police inspector appeared at the convent on Easter Sunday, he made a superficial investigation and reiterated the banal rumor of the communist agitators. The attitudes of the police reflected the leanings of the leftists who wielded parliamentary majority in Italy at this time.

With quiet dignity Mother Mary defended the honor of the convent and the innocence of her sisters. Convinced of the futility of police action, she thereupon applied to one of the embassies in Rome for diplomatic intervention to secure the protection of the convent. Continuous surveillance over the entire district was then accorded for a prolonged period until peace and safety were relatively assured.[185] The abuses were also reported to the Cardinal Vicar of Rome.[186] The Holy Father, in a consistorial allocution of May 23, addressed a pressing message to the Italians, denouncing the dark schemes of the sects as a threat to the nation's welfare and its highest interests.[187] On July 27, the sisters for the first time were able to appear in the street in full religious apparel.[188]

The rude encroachments upon privacy did not hinder the Foundress in her work, especially in formulating the Constitutions which were now approaching the final stages. Father Lechert collaborated with her closely, making daily visits in spite of the disagreeable annoyances that could have been hazardous. He was attentive to the details she communicated to him, reading in her fresh ideas a truly charismatic inspiration. Her *Dialogues with Jesus* recorded at that time the outpourings of one moving in the aura of a great call yet striving to find light in faith. Just as the navigator measures the angle from which he sees several constellations to bring his site into accurate focus, so eager was she to verify her course in relation to the truth of God. In the first historical draft of the Constitutions, as in numerous other instances, she documented her belief that Christ was the sole founder of the Congregation;[189] to herself she ascribed the role of his instrument, which role she acknowledged uniformly with total honesty.

Understandably enough, the hour of joy dawned for her when the canonical format of the first part of the Constitutions was completed by Father Lechert, in which the commitment of the Nazareth religious was defined in terms of the Gospel and aligned with practical insights reflecting the life of the Holy Family. The second part, which encompassed the norms of Nazareth's internal government on all levels, was still in the process of refinement.

To provide copies of the document for the existing houses, transcriptions by hand were immediately being prepared. Alive to the scriptural context of the Constitutions, Mother Mary jubilantly referred to them by spoken word and letter as the "Covenant of Love." She wrote to Mother Raphael in Chicago:

> . . . After all these years of longing and waiting, Our Lord in his mercy gave us his Covenant of Love, his holy law, which should direct our life and conduct. You are well aware how our Congregation—not knowing clearly as yet what God's designs were for us—sought among the older orders a rule which could be adapted to our life, to our purpose, but there was nothing that satisfied our spiritual needs . . .
>
> What Our Lord had long ago implanted in our souls, he has now given us in fact. Accept then this holy Covenant of Love, as an expressed will of Christ. Everything that is stated therein is our Divine

Saviour's own wish and is aimed at our sanctification and salvation. It is all taken from the depths of my soul; it had been rooted there; I have yearned for it and desired it ardently.

Receive this grace of Christ with joy and gratitude, and help the sisters who are entrusted to you to live according to this Covenant of the Lord.[190]

Throughout the summer of 1887, while Father Lechert held discourses with the sisters on the Constitutions, Mother Joanne was also there. Meanwhile Mother Mary wrote to Cracow:

. . . Your superior will return on September 8 and will bring with her the Constitutions drafted by our spiritual father, by whom Christ reveals to us his holy will and by whom he chooses to direct us. May these precepts be received by all the sisters with genuine esteem and affection as proceeding from our Divine Lord, and may they be carried out effectively in practice and spirit.[191]

That year a special holiday was established for the novices to be observed annually on November 21, when the Presentation of the Blessed Virgin Mary in the Temple is commemorated by the Church.[192] Also, the first Sunday of Advent was designated to mark permanently the foundation date of the Congregation.

With the increase of membership in the Roman novitiate and the growth of tourism in the city, the purchase of another building, adjoining the one at 18 Via Machiavelli, was highly indicated. This was accomplished on December 19,[193] and the place became available to visitors and pilgrims by February 3, 1888.

The universal popularity and veneration of Leo XIII brought immense pilgrimages from all quarters of the globe to pay him homage on the occasion of his golden jubilee of ordination to the priesthood. Beginning January 1, when he offered the pontifical jubilee Mass of thanksgiving, pilgrims streamed into Rome the year round, presenting testimonials of honor, sympathy, and love, attending audiences, participating in canonizations and beatifications, uniting with him in the magnificent memorial service of expiation and intercession for the souls in purgatory, and visiting the Vatican Exposition where a vast collection of priceless gifts displayed the generosity of the rich and the poor the world over.[194]

Through the arriving pilgrims, lay and clerical, miscellaneous contacts were channeled to the Nazareth Congregation with requests to undertake educational and charitable works in Prussia and France. From Eastern Europe there were invitations, predominantly missionary in character, to work among the Eastern Rite Catholics in Rumania[195] and Bulgaria,[196] and to conduct in St. Petersburg the Institute of St. Catherine, a finishing school for Catholic girls, daughters of high ranking officials who were residing in Russia's sophisticated capital.[197] The latter proposal was first brought to the attention of Mother Mary on August 17, 1887, when she was visited by Reverend John Cieplak, professor of Catholic Ecclesiastical Academy in St. Petersburg.[198] Each time that he renewed the petition either in person or in writing, the vision of this work captivated her with its enormous significance for the faith and the possibility of attracting converts among the schismatics.[199] The same Father Cieplak also pleaded with her the cause of the Siberian exiles in Kamchatka who urgently needed a school for their children.[200]

Regrettably, these invitations had to be declined for lack of personnel, but their recurrence fired the sisters' apostolic zeal in the knowledge of the fields that were open and waiting to be cultivated in the way of salvation. In the meantime, charity, prayer, fidelity to current commitments, and penance, were the means by which they endeavored to exercise a true concern for all peoples who were to be led to Christ.

By literally earning its living, the community aimed to realize evangelical poverty as practiced by the Holy Family, who followed the common law of labor and in their remote corner of the earth worked for their livelihood in the manner of the poor.[201] In this light the Foundress began considering the establishment in Cracow of a residence hall for young women from out of town who were attending studies in the city.[202] Until then, the varied opportunities offered at that convent for personal guidance and religious instruction were gratuitous and had to be subsidized by the Foundress.[203] The residence hall, as conceived by her, was to provide students with appropriate conditions for study, a family atmosphere and intelligent assistance in their religious, personal and social development, and simultaneously would help to uphold the non-revenue-producing programs for other deserving groups. This plan, however, was not entered upon by the incumbent superior, Mother Joanne, as her term of office was coming to a close; she was recalled to Rome, and Mother Gabriel suceeded her in May of 1888.

From the United States there were reports, since the spring of that year, of Mother Raphael's serious illness which, according to medical advice, required several months' rest cure in Italy. Sister Lauretta, as the provincial assistant, shouldered much of the provincial's responsibility throughout this time,[204] and upon the latter's departure in August had to assume its full measure temporarily.[205] Some of the major changes in the American assignments included Sister Lauretta's transfer to St. Joseph convent where she also became the local superior; Sister Theresa then became the superior at St. Josapaht's, while her position as the director of the novitiate was filled by Sister Frances, whom Sister Paula succeeded at St. Adalbert's.[206]

Consistent evidence of Sister Lauretta's loyalty and cooperation gained for her Mother Mary's confidence in her ability to discharge the mounting duties.[207] The Foundress came to recognize that the pure love and the will to sacrifice in the younger nun equalled her own dynamic dedication.[208] Where the Foundress was perceptive, Sister Lauretta demonstrated extraordinary integrity; where the Foundress could rise to inspired words, Sister Lauretta formed practical conclusions. Both by different personality patterns reached the same plane of truth and understanding.[209]

Although Mother Raphael's health was improving in Italy as her nervous exhaustion receded,[210] medical advice was opposed to her return to the United States. With the decision to remain in Europe, she was appointed, October 24, to be the superior at the motherhouse. A week later, Sisters Columba and Alberta departed for Chicago to supplement the sisters' ranks, because another parochial school was entrusted to Nazareth in the new parish of St. Hedwig. Archbishop Feehan formally inaugurated the parish on December 4 with the blessing of the newly completed church, school and convent in a combination building.[211] The first pastor was Reverend Joseph Barzyński, brother of Father Vincent; the initial enrollment in the school numbered 200 children.[212] The convent was placed under the patronage of the Holy Guardian Angels,[213] with Sister Theresa in charge; in her stead, Sister Columba was assigned to St. Josaphat's.[214] To keep abreast of the developments in advancing scholastic standards at the Holy Family Academy, Sister Alberta was appointed the principal of that institution.

This year likewise introduced a change in Father Lechert's position, when, December 13, he was installed by Raffaele Cardinal Monaco la Valetta as rector of the Polish Pontifical College in Rome,[215] where his competence would experience crucial demands. Inescapably he felt himself responsible for his stewardship before his own conscience, before the Church, and before God, mindful that every one of his actions was fraught with eternal consequences for himself and for the clerical students at the College.

Early in 1889 Mother Mary ascertained the need for her presence in the United States. Issues of intricate magnitude called for action and direction with a concern for the present as well as a view to the future. Requests to staff additional parochial schools cast an irresistible appeal, but prompted restraint. A grandiose project of Father Vincent Barzyński glowed with promise, yet savored of dubious outcome. It implied a tacit, unofficial merger for the construction of a pretentious building to house the sisters' novitiate and academy, which would occupy jointly the parish property and the sisters' property on Division streeet. Temporarily the new building was expected to accommodate also the orphanage until a separate home for orphans would be erected in another section of the city on an inter-parochial plan.[216]

Father Vincent originally intended to plunge into large scale operations solely for the building of the orphanage in another location and had enlisted the sisters in fund-raising efforts during the school vacation of 1888.[217] Later he revised his plan in preference to a pseudo merger in connection with a new Holy Family Academy and novitiate. The later project attracted favorable public interest and the sisters found concrete support in the flow of generous donations, which they deposited with the parish savings and loan association. In theory, the Foundress approved the suggested proposal, but with usual foresight and caution advised that legal safeguards be taken.[218] Too well did she know that the world was a world of fact and that a great number of people had to find daily practical solutions to practical problems. In her patient winnowing and probing, she acted with both her heart and mind, unaware of no shortcomings, unappreciative of no merits.

Prior to undertaking the second journey to the United States, Mother Mary was intent on delivering the full text of the Constitutions to the Holy See for a critical scrutiny. To lend support to its factual validity, the document had to be accompanied by episcopal references from the dioceses in which the Congregation existed.[219] She then set aside some time in May to visit the house in Poland to evaluate and strengthen the sisters' efforts,[220] and on June 15 she was at the Havre, boarding the steamship *La Bourgogne*[221] with Sisters Bronislaus,[222] Sophia[223] and Leontine.[224] When the ship came to anchor on June 23, the arriving group detected Sisters Lauretta and Frances at the pier, happily waiting to greet and welcome them.

Together with Sister Lauretta the Foundress first proceeded to Scranton,[225] where Reverend Adolphe Śnigurski for four years thrived on the anticipation of a school conducted in his parish by the sisters. He had personally referred himself to Mother Mary in this matter during her previous visit[226] and now awaited her categorical reply.

The hard-working citizens of the one-hundred-years-old Scranton settlement were performing latterday miracles, converting the undulating low mountains of northeastern Pennsylvania into a commercial and industrial town, prominent for anthracite coal mining. On November 14, 1885, the cornerstone of the church for the newly organized parish of the Sacred Hearts of Jesus and Mary had been laid. To provide for the re-

ligious education of children and to instruct them in other subjects, the
pastor opened two provisional classrooms and engaged lay teachers as an
emergency measure.[227] The city already boasted of St. Thomas Catholic
College which was established in 1888.

On her way then to Chicago, Mother Mary visited the site of the proposed apostolate in Scranton and arrived at an agreeable understanding
with the pastor, who readily consented to provide, before the next school
term, accommodations for the sisters and more adequate schoolroom
facilities. She also suggested that he inform the local Ordinary, Bishop
William O'Hara, of his desire to have the Nazareth sisters in the parish.
Having settled the preliminaries, she hastened to Chicago to meet a full
summertime schedule.

With amazing freshness and directness she matched the lyrical moments
of greetings, bearing the same cordial manners for the new as for the
earlier sisters, which at once established a strong unifying bond among
them. To acquaint the sisters with the nature of her visit, Father Lechert
penned to the community in the United States an open letter, paternal in
tone, articulate and psychologically introspective, outlining the purpose of
religious visitation. Following a cursory review of the graces, trials and
experiences which fell to their lot in the past four years, he continued:

. . . At last your Mother is now with you! I can well imagine the joy
with which you welcome this Mother whom God has given to you.
No doubt, those of you, who had known her earlier, recalled upon her
arrival all the divine favors they received through her in this Congregation of the Holy Family of Nazareth. I visualize, too, how those who
had not known her before are approaching her for the first time as
her beloved, youngest daughters. All of you, the older and the younger,
certainly regard her with love and true reverence, as an angel of peace
sent into your midst by Christ, as the Mother who in his Sacred Heart
loves each of you, who directs you in the name of his holy authority,
who represents his person to you.

This picture of all of you, gathered in the company of your dear
Mother, fills my heart with happiness and immense gratitude to God.
I expect that the love you now entertain for her will not be limited to
this moment of joy, but will become evident in actual situations. Please
remember that God does not send his emissaries in vain. He sends
through them his special graces and expects of us to receive them well
and to employ them profitably . . .

Therefore, I request you, my dear daughters, to utilize to the best
advantage the grace which comes to you with your Mother's presence,
to accept willingly and sincerely what she has to offer, recognizing in

her not only a tender Mother, but a messenger of Christ, invested with his authority to which you are committed by virtue of the holy vows you made to God.

She may find it necessary to renew or improve some aspect relative to your interior or exterior life when it will be conducive to the glory of God and the general good. Respect, then, her decisions, for this is her mission and her prerogative as your superior general . . .

When you will be given the opportunity for an interview with her, be free to discuss frankly and honestly your observations, difficulties and doubts, and be open to accept her response with humility, willingness and love, even when this may not be gratifying to nature. May you be thoroughly convinced of her profound love in God for each one of you. It is for this reason that she can approve and recommend only what redounds to real welfare and happiness, and must condemn or disapprove whatever is detrimental or opposed to sanctity and salvation. So then, if to counteract some weakness, she metes out to one or another a remedy that is not particularly palatable, receive it gratefully as the means for the restoration of full vigor through her kind ministrations.[228]

Naturally the sisters were interested in the place they held in the scheme of things. Their numbers had increased threefold over the pioneer group, and they looked hopefully to the Foundress to uncover for them the realities of Nazareth vocation beneath the ideals and the laws. Imparting her inspiration to them, Mother Mary understood perfectly where to begin, when to stop, and how to explain what happened in the interim. She was fervent in the use of scriptural allusions as guides to captivate them by the eternal timeliness of Christ's Gospel teaching. To avoid the purely human formulation, they would have to enslave themselves to the Gospel, for it characterized the life of Christ as one of mystery and heroism, not as a life of convenience.[229] In guidance interviews she was concerned that they should not be missing the supernatural ingredient[230] in their life of dedication, if they aspired to a life rich in fulfillment; she urged them to perform their services to others when they have first sought a loving union with God.[231] Beneath a manner that was extraordinarily gracious and self-disciplined, her words were refining, elevating, sanctifying.

In reviewing the subject of community life, she touched upon the inmost core essential to mature, formed spirituality, which best portrays the life of the Holy Family of Nazareth in the amiable relationships of family living. Both have the same concept, the same goals, the same virtues, the same bond of charity, the same devotion to the will of God.[232] The Nazareth community is a family in the Lord; it is a holy assembly

that gathers around Christ and remains basically holy because of the love
and fidelity that the members have in common. When they have strong
ties in the human sense, they can present a more striking, a more creditable witness to the cause of Christ. Supported by community atmosphere,
the sisters engage actively among the People of God with benefit to themselves and to others. Without such support, she warned, apostolic work is
apt to consume their individual meager resources, and they may quickly
become vessels without water, incapable of irrigating the vineyard of the
Lord.[233]

It has soon become evident to Mother Mary that she would have to
remain several months, perhaps a year, to unravel the tapestry of the
sisters' life and work on this continent, to project herself fully into the
general tenor of their environment, to try to analyze what was conformable
to the conglomerate culture in which they were moving and what was out
of character.[234] It was sufficiently clear that this was a place of action,
but not yet of answers; that this was the time to synthesize law with love
and to revise some of the more obscure regulations. Nonetheless, the time
was opportune to spark a few clinching answers by introducing precedents,
policies and directives to corroborate sound internal administration and
for the maintenance of the Congregation's juridical integrity.[235] To render
its services effectual and enduring in the universal Church, a religious
community must retain its intrinsic identity; otherwise, to allow to degene-
rate into a mere local agency or an accessory function is to deteriorate
out of existence.

In July, the pastor from Scranton, prodded by impatience for the
arrival of the sisters, appealed to Father Lechert to accelerate action,[236]
but Mother Mary had reasons to withhold deployment of personnel until
all major decisions for the province will have been implemented. Instead,
Father Snigurski was invited to attend in Chicago the laying of the cornerstone of the academy and orphanage building on August 4, when he
delivered an eloquent address on the subject of education of children.[237]

The ceremony attracted city-wide interest and the participation of
Chicago's numerous parish societies with their colorful pageantry of banners and emblems. The Archbishop was represented by Very Reverend
D. M. I. Dowling, vicar general, who officiated, and by Reverend P. O.
Muldoon, chancellor of the archdiocese. Both affixed their signatures to
the parchment document, certifying to the act of the blessing of the cornerstone, along with the signatures of the representative clergy of Chicago
and all the professed Nazareth sisters, headed by the Foundress herself.
Enclosed in the cornerstone cassette, together with this certificate, were
such other documents as the papal blessing of Leo XIII,[238] a congratulatory
message from Father Lechert,[239] and an invocation of blessing written and

signed by Mother Mary. There were also photographs of the Sisters of the Holy Family of Nazareth, of Father Vincent Barzyński and of Father Anthony Lechert.[240]

Despite the tumultuous public ovation, the new project engendered serious apprehensions in the mind of Mother Mary, who wrote, "I hardly know why this building neither pleases nor attracts me . . . Why need we incur the cost of six thousand dollars for stone ornamentations? I knew nothing about this . . . The people will soon tire of these endless collections, but Father Vincent sees everything in bright colors. I fear he will drive us into crushing debts."[241]

Notwithstanding these qualms, she assisted the sisters with dexterity and admirable sensitivity at the annual retreat held in the convent of St. Joseph. Her unforgettable soft voice, wistfully persuasive, encouraged them to unflagging progress, piloted them toward the readiness to give themselves wholly to God and in this giving to belong to all mankind, and led them to build a spirituality of action in harmony with their religious consecration.[242] Continuing ever onward from great moment to great moment, she set the date for the first ceremony of perpetual profession in the United States. It was Thursday, August 22, when the Nazareth community assembled at St. Josaphat's, for there the sanctuary was better suited to accommodate a ritual involving a greater number of persons. During the liturgy of the Mass, Archbishop Feehan received the final vows[243] of Sisters Lauretta, Columba, Paula,[244] Frances,[245] Angela and Stanislaus.[246]

Soon enough another papal encyclical resounded through the world and its message warmed the hearts of the sisters with joy. The gloriously reigning Pontiff, celebrated for his pronouncements on Christian social principles, was no less intent upon the revival of piety, the very soul of Christianity. On August 15, 1889, he issued the encyclical on St. Joseph, *Quamquam Pluries*, in which he extolled the manly virtues and unique qualities of the foster-father of Christ, recommending to his patronage every condition of mankind and holding him up as a model of all laboring classes and of the poor. Implicitly the encyclical endorsed the spirit of the Congregation which embraced as its own the secret of St. Joseph's sanctity and glory. Touching hands with the life of the universal Church, Mother Mary properly followed the Holy Father's wish in adopting for Nazareth the practice of devoting the month of March to the honor of St. Joseph.

Sunday, September 1, saw all the sisters at the convent of St. Joseph, where Mother Mary announced with fitting solemnity the appointment of Sister Lauretta as the provincial superior and instructed the sisters to address her using the title "Mother" in token of respect.[247] Sister Lauretta then pledged her fidelity to the Constitutions and added to her previously professed three religious vows a fourth one: of total commitment to God for the guidance of others and for the performance of any office entrusted to her.[248] Earlier Mother Mary entertained the intention of extending the fourth vow to all members at the time of their perpetual profession, but for the present she decided against making this a general practice and reserved the obligation of the fourth vow to herself and to Mother Lauretta.[249]

Other new appointments in administrative positions introduced the following changes: Sister Theresa, assistant to Mother Lauretta in the management of St. Joseph convent; Sister Frances, principal, Holy Family Academy; Sister Sophia, director of the novitiate and of vocations; Sister Alberta, superior-principal at St. Josaphat's; Sister Leontine, superior-principal at St. Hedwig's; Sister Columba, superior-principal in Scranton. On September 10, Sister Columba with the three sisters assigned to Scranton left Chicago in the company of Mother Lauretta, who remained with them until the early days of October to help with the organization of their activities. Our Lady of Sorrows became the convent patron in honor of the Blessed Virgin's incomparable sorrows. Under this title Mother Foundress venerated Mary with singular devotion and invoked her aid in times of severe trial.

The very day when the sisters arrived in Scranton, they were visited by the pastor from Nanticoke, who wanted a group of sisters to take charge of his parochial school at once.[250] Nanticoke, situated on the Susquehanna river, thirty miles southeast of Scranton, occupied an upland, rugged terrain, rich in anthracite deposits that forecast years of uninterrupted prosperity. The lay teachers, who had been engaged for the school, failed to meet the townspeople's expectations, and the pastor hoped to resolve the thorny problem by bringing in teaching sisters. For practical reasons alone, his request could not be granted that year.

While Mother Lauretta was absorbed with the details of Scranton's convent and school, in Chicago a mood of militancy erupted with startling suddenness, threatening the position of the sisters. The transfer of St. Josaphat's pastor was slanderously imputed to them and incited passionate indignation among the parishioners, who forcibly attempted to enter the convent and wreak their vengeance on the sisters. The violent protest broke on September 14 when Mother Mary happened to be at St. Josaphat's. She summoned the terrified sisters to the chapel, calmly and confidently praying with them to the Sorrowful Mother for deliverance. Four hours later the police somewhat mitigated the uproar, but it was the noble stance and reasonable words of the new pastor, Father Francis Xavier Lange, that succeeded to pacify and soothe the unruly crowd. Splintered groups that continued to bristle intermittently insinuated the real cause of the unrest as resentment of Father Vincent. Believing in their simple-mindedness that the sisters belonged to him, they made them the target of deep-seated rancor.[251]

When the Foundress recounted the episode to the Archbishop, he commended her and the sisters on the manner in which they withstood the insulting abuses.[252] When the parish delegation appeared before him, he declared that the sisters are under his protection and directed a grieved rebuke for the un-Christian riotous behavior and the public disgrace which the parishioners had rashly incurred.[253]

The controversy that swirled about Father Lange's head when he took possession of his parish garlanded him, over the years, with the respect and affection of the faithful. Warm-hearted and sincere, he could be utterly unyielding and direct. Everything he did, he did with all his soul. His life was a tribute to the human spirit and to the individual who, by his vision and decisiveness, was able to translate the ancient virtues of his people into brilliant action that found expression in the magnificent new church (1902) and an excellent new school (1913), memorials to his zeal for divine worship and Christian education.[254] During his long tenure as pastor, 1889-1914, the Congregation has grown in esteem among the people, school enrollment increased consistently, and the parish yielded many vocations to Nazareth.

At St. Adalbert's the sisters were troubled by excessive demands made upon their time and energies above and beyond the terms of the agreement originally ratified by the pastor. With the expansion of the parish, the school enlarged and claimed more concentrated attention and more pains-taking preparation, which they acknowledged as their prime duty in conscience. Agitated by self-appointed advisers, the pastor was irked by the sisters' reluctance to assume additional tasks, and at the height of his displeasure deprived them of the Blessed Sacrament in the chapel. At Mother Mary's intervention, the pastor withdrew his demands but made his dissatisfaction felt long thereafter.[255] He adhered to the notion that the sisters who were assigned to the school remained under his full and exclusive orders.

In her contacts with parochial clergy the Foundress saw the necessity of explaining the relationship of the sisters to the parish in those matters for which their services were enlisted and substantiating the sisters' right to the time and the means for their performance of the religious obliga-tions to which they were committed as members of the Congregation. On the other hand, she instructed the sisters to cultivate towards the clergy in general and demonstrate externally the reverence and the respect to which they as priests of God were entitled.[256]

In the memorandum of this visitation she recorded, "Considering that we have not come to Chicago by our own choice, but that we have been sent by the will of God at the direction of legitimate authority and upon the request of the pastors, only at the indication of the will of God may we leave the city and relinquish our post to others. In the meantime we will work with undiminished dedication, as heretofore, for the glory of God and for the good of his people. I implore Christ to support our sisters in Chicago to persevere to the very end; I beg him also for a change of heart in those persons who are opposed to us, so that they would not prevent us in doing good, but would cooperate in spreading the Kingdom of God."[257]

It was at this time that in Cracow the idea of a residence hall began to germinate. It started as a seedling with five students from outlying areas who were attending teacher training colleges in the city and who desired respectable accommodations in deference to their religious beliefs. With the widespread impact of social consciousness, capable young women, who were eager to contribute to the intellectual advancement of the under-privileged, expected to find in the teaching profession a rare opportunity for leadership, for initiating social concepts and facilitating social projects. The residence hall, serving as their base, could exert a decidedly formative influence.[258]

On November 13, the Catholic Church in the United States marked two historic celebrations, the centennial of the establishment of the American hierarchy and the formal opening of the Catholic University in the national capital. The university was granted the status of a pontifical institution by the brief of Leo XIII, *Magni Nobis Gaudii,* addressed to Cardinal Gibbons earlier that year. The inauguration of the university's academic work was heightened by the presence of the Apostolic Delegate, Archbishop Francesco Satolli, and the President of the United States, Benjamin Harrison.[259] For the sisters, the cause of Catholic education kindled bright moments of optimism despite their own unremitting struggles.

By Christmastime, Father Vincent's audacious undertaking approached completion to the extent that it permitted the placement of the orphans and several sisters in the new building. The legal title to the sisters' entire Division street property, so easily acquired by him, still reposed in his name. All attempts to recover it proved unsuccessful, similarly as were the repeated requests for financial statements of the deposits received from the sisters and of the obligations that were incurred in their name for the construction. Another matter of serious concern was the stipulation of equitable terms for the administration of the Holy Family Orphanage, as it was already called, to avoid the possible difficulties which might arise from conflicting interests. After long and tedious discussions, the principles of operation were mutually agreed upon, and Mother Mary submitted them to the Archbishop for review. He found them satisfactory and endorsed them.[260]

The superior general of the Resurrectionists, Reverend Valerian Przewłocki, who was then visiting in Chicago, expressed full approval of the terms as they were drawn up. However, but three hours after the interview with the superior general, Father Vincent announced that the agreement was rejected and that the School Sisters of Notre Dame were already under contract to conduct the orphanage. It also became apparent that on March 18, 1890 he had conveyed to the diocese the title to the sisters' property and to the new building.

Archbishop Feehan studied the complexity of the situation without prejudice and without passion. Altogether sympathetic toward the sisters' predicament, he concluded that the tangled negotiations nearly destroyed the prospects for their survival in Chicago. His advice was absolute withdrawal from the orphanage and a compromise settlement, whereby the legal ownership of the buildings and land they had originally purchased was restored to them. Furthermore, a nominal reimbursement was made for their section of the land occupied by the new building, and a token refund of their unrecorded deposits in the parish loan and savings account cancelled the affiliation.[261] In the haze of affliction and hope, the Congregation passed through a crisis.

Following the end-of-the-year retreat, Sisters Columba and Paula were admitted to the fourth vow and were given the permanent title "Mother." Few adjustments then became necessary in the appointment of superiors, since Sisters Frances, Cecilia, Theresa and Alberta were returning to Europe with Mother Foundress: Sister Leontine was assigned to the new location in Nanticoke, M. Paula to St. Hedwig's, S. Angela to St. Adalbert's, M. Columba to St. Josaphat's, S. Stanislaus to Scranton, while S. Bronislaus became the principal at Holy Family Academy. Mother Mary and her companions boarded SS. *La Bourgogne,* August 2, and landed in the Havre on the 10th.

Soon after reaching Rome she learned of the saintly death of Father Leander, August 20, 1890, in Cracow. Since her childhood, for twenty-five years he had guided her toward the recognition of her vocation in the Providence of God. Out of deep gratitude and esteem for the spiritual benefits derived through him, she offered tributes of prayer for the repose of his soul.[262]

In the middle of August, when the sisters in Chicago began removing themselves from the orphanage, they were bluntly told that their evening classes and sodality activities were no longer required.[263] The orphanage was relinquished on September 1 to Sister Rogeria of the School Sisters of

Notre Dame.[264] Neither regret nor grievance was voiced by the Foundress upon the dissolution of the tortuous state of affairs; in fact, she welcomed the climax as heaven's release from unsavory developments in the future.[265] She tasted the wondrous coolness of detachment without coldness, a charitable silence that was made of stillness, the silence which was peace. She knew her authority and exercised it with the ineffable combination of strength, intelligence and obliging humor.

But now, with the advent of a new school term, oblique comments strongly discouraged the reopening of the academy program. The Archbishop, on the contrary, favored its continuance, recommended its expansion, and assured Mother Lauretta of his personal support and cooperation in furthering this endeavor.[266] The sisters lived down the strange rumors and absurd reports that had been set afloat against them undercover. The first days' matriculations numbered fifty-eight registrants and more students were applying.[267] In a period of critical employment and low wages, when higher education of girls in a private academy bordered on luxury, admissible to the affluent, the registrations at Holy Family Academy were a gesture of confidence and foresight on the part of the public. Then, too, members of the Young Women's Rosary Society formed the practice of coming to the Academy on Sundays, not anymore as a parish group but informally, to pass the afternoon as an open forum in purposeful discussions with the sisters, concluded with a devotional service.

On September 24, a cablegram from Mother Mary directed the provincial superior to purchase a scenic tract of land in the forested mountains in Scranton, adjoining Connell Park. Negotiations had been opened by the Foundress during her stay in the United States and have now approached a satisfactory point. The site was intended for the Congregation's American novitiate[268] and possibly a home for dependent children.

The ecumenical ideals and principles woven into the texture of the spirit of Nazareth were gently welded into a daily living experience when a three-year-old negro orphan girl was adopted by the sisters.[269] She was brought up at Holy Family Academy and there received her initial education; she pursued further studies in Europe and was later admitted to the sisters' secondary school faculty in Poland.

Two months of that year, until December 9, Mother Mary devoted to the convent in Cracow where, based upon sufficient evidence of need and demand, the future of the residence hall for students appeared settled. Since suitable quarters for this purpose had to be provided, she decided on the construction of a housing unit which would extend into the garden as an annex to the main building.[270]

Quite unexpectedly there came to light the active infiltration of alien ideas disseminated by Brother Stephen's communications to susceptible individuals in Cracow, calling in question the very foundation of the Congregation and militating against the position of the Foundress.[271] The sheaf of her correspondence from this period abounds in the circumstantial information of a valiant woman, carrying the burden of a divinely-imposed mission, whose road was pitted with solitary suffering. In her quest for selflessness the void was filled with an overwhelming awareness of God, for nothing produces a more powerful sense of fulfillment than the conviction that one is the executor of God's will. She remained unshaken even by the puzzling discovery of the epitaph—dictated by someone's misplaced sentiment and inscribed on Father Leander's tomb, "Founder of the Sisters of Nazareth"—knowing that the deceased never considered himself the founder.[272]

Though her times of happiness were few and her disappointments many, she wore lightly the searing experiences that in the final analysis validated her position beyond doubt. She returned to Rome with three candidates and a Carmelite prioress, Mother Joseph-Teresa.[273] The latter had the consent of her superior general to accept the hospitality of Mother Mary when the monastery's physician in Cracow advised her to seek as a therapeutic measure the exemption from the mode of life prescribed by the Carmelite rule.[274]

7 IN THE CRUCIBLE

The question of the viability of the Congregation, from the human standpoint, ceased to preoccupy the minds in the manner it had done during the years of Nazareth's modest emergence upon uncharted waters. There was a quality of enigma in the attitude of the Foundress toward the very substance of time; for the duration of the future hinted at an unbroken continuity in the present, as expressed in the categories of the eternal. In Europe and in America alike she would adapt to nature's own tempo, observing the work of grace within generous souls who embraced the Nazareth way to cooperate in the salvific mission of Christ.

She was in the habit of instructing the superiors to be patient, understanding, and helpful in the face of human frailty, but when overt incompatibilities persisted with no sustained effort on the part of a member to overcome them, Mother Mary advised dismissal. She made it very clear that vocation to Nazareth was not for the fickle or the timid, those who take to half-measures, who yield to compromise or are carried away by superficialities.[275]

The question of the moment was then one of concentration, the constant renewal of the apostolic potential through mystical contact with divine power and goodness in the sanctifying Spirit, the learning of detachment and compassion through industry and adversity. As apostles, the sisters were to realize that their souls were to be at one with the soul of Christ; for as his instruments, of themselves they were capable of nothing, and only united with him were they capable of marvels.

Fresh areas of activity beckoned from the Atlantic seaboard when Reverend Vincent Bronikowski, pastor of St. Casimir's parish in Brooklyn, New York, called on Mother Mary in Rome, requesting a staff of sisters for his school.[276] As soon as necessary arrangements were completed through Mother Lauretta, the sisters commenced work there, March 8, 1891; their convent was named after St. Frances of Rome, and Sister Alberta who had just returned from Europe became the first superior. She brought with her, upon arrival, a pattern for the pleated white collar that was being introduced throughout the Congregation as a final accessory to the sisters' apparel.

Time and again, encouraging invitations were forthcoming from the populous city of Paris, principally from Father Ladislaus Witkowski, C.R., of the Resurrectionist mission, and from Minister Fahrenbach and his wife. To explore the possibilities, Mother Mary went to the French capital, July 22, 1891, accompanied by Mother Theresa Czermińska, who was designated the first superior for the prospective institute, presumably a resident school for girls. The move, however, proved unseasonable and the Mothers experienced disappointing lack of interest and tedious delays due to the absence from the city of persons competent to finalize the required formalities.[277]

In the interim temporary quarters were leased at 32 Rue de Bellefond, and initial preparations were at once begun under the patronage of Our Lady of Loreto to whom the convent was dedicated. The Archbishop of Paris, François-Marie Cardinal Richard, accepted the Congregation into the archdiocese on September 25,[278] and the following January the sisters were authorized to open a school, which they called L'Institut de Demoiselles.[279] By March an unexpected number of applications for admission made it necessary to transfer the school to larger facilities, at 41 Rue Labat, with an additional personnel of qualified lay teachers.

That winter a virulent epidemic of influenza raged in Paris, taking toll of many lives. Although none of the sisters succumbed to it, Mother Mary suffered an acute and protracted siege of the disease. During its severe stage she received news of the frightening tremor that shook Rome in the night of January 22-23. Fortunately, vibrations caused no major injuries or loss of lives.[280]

In Poland, Bishop Dunajewski, recently elevated to the cardinalitial dignity, solemnized the dedication of the newly erected students' residence in Cracow, December 16, 1891.[281] Only six days earlier Mother Gabriel departed from Cracow, succeeded by Mother Raphael as the local superior. For efficiency of operation, Sister Irene[282] was appointed director of the residence hall, and in 1892 Sister Josepha Rembiszewska became the director of novices who were undergoing their religious formation in the Cracow convent. In May, 1892, a municipal committee representing women's colleges for teacher education visited the residence hall and with a vote of approval recommended it to receive a subsidy from public funds.

Impressed by Nazareth's sense of Christian social responsibility for student welfare, Cardinal Dunajewski advocated another timely project, the administration of St. Hedwig Institute in Cracow, whose industrialization, among other large cities of Europe, attracted a significant work force from remote places. Young women, desirous of improving their families' quality of living, found there ample employment opportunities, particularly in textile processing and as seamstresses. To introduce a wholesome influence into their social sector, the Institute of St. Hedwig was founded and endowed by two noblewomen, Princess Marcelline Czartoryska and the widow of Count Andrew Potocki. Collaborating with an interested committee, they aimed to inculcate in the young women the concepts of self-respect, personal dignity, and positive human relations by means of a homelike environment in the Institute. They hoped to achieve these aims by placing the Institute under the sisters' management.

The world was just reacting to Pope Leo's epochal encyclical, *Rerum Novarum*,[283] and Mother Mary, always alert to the pronouncements of the Pontiff, studied his definitions of the basic Christian principles and his concern for the conditions of the working classes. In keeping with the spirit of his message, she acceded to the Cardinal's recommendation and assigned Sister Amantia Gralewska to the position of the superior, who took charge of the Institute with several sisters,[284] March 1, 1892.

In July of that year, at the suggestion of Archbishop Severin Morawski of Lemberg, Mother Joanne and Sister Laurence[285] were delegated from Rome to investigate the likelihood of an apostolate in this thriving grand city at Poland's southeastern frontier. As of September 1, an apartment was leased in a residential district of Lemberg, at No. 5 Ulica Padlewski, and was named in honor of the Holy Family. Favorable contacts in the city insured the success of the small-scale boarding school to which the sisters gave their full enthusiasm and ability.[286] Besides attracting students to a program that promised to be comprehensive and formative, Mother Joanne had the joy of admitting the first aspirant who in time became Sister Faustina.[287]

In the United States the developments were many, rapid, and far-flung. Of the opportunities which presented themselves the Foundress preferred to avoid fashionable locations and inclined to the evangelical counsel in favor of the humbler, the less elegant regions, inhabited preferably by a preponderence of those given to daily toil and scanty gains, who were reticent about their wants and recoiled from being noticed. Such was God's work for the sisters when they came to Philadelphia, January 10, 1892, at the request of Reverend Michael Baranski to conduct the school in St. Stanislaus parish, situated in the industrial section of the city. St. Anthony became the convent patron, and Sister Leontine was appointed the first superior.[288]

In Nanticoke, on the other hand, insurmountable difficulties provoked by the rectory housekeeper rendered the local relationships intolerable, the only alternative being a peaceful withdrawal of the sisters at the close of the school in July, 1892.[289]

With the opening of the next school term, September 1, Sister Leontine, as superior, pioneered with a group of sisters in the new parochial school of St. Michael on the shores of Lake Michigan of Chicago's far south side. The burgeoning of steel mills and iron works offered remunerative employment and drew a marked influx of inhabitants into this area. To distribute the teaching load equitably, in view of the large initial enrollment, Reverend Adolphe Nowicki, the pastor, readily consented to retain the services of lay teachers under the direction of the sisters. At the

insistence of local families, a kindergarten program was likewise organized and made available to pre-school children of the parish. The growth
of the school was astounding, and the convent under the patronage of the
Holy Spirit saw the sister staff increase from year to year.[290]

At Holy Family Academy in Chicago the education of girls was
progressively meeting with greater esteem of those who desired above-
average cultural standards and a creditable moral environment for their
daughters. They supplied the incentives and the stimulus to start work on
the construction of a new academy building which would also provide a
suitable novitiate enclosure for the young sisters, who were in the process
of religious formation.[291] The first step in the long awaited evolution was
to secure the State of Illinois Charter of Incorporation, under which the
Congregation could function as a legal entity, encompassing both present
and future apostolates in educational, health and charitable services.[292]
The charter was issued December 26, 1891. This was followed by the
relocation of the sisters to temporary quarters, few blocks west on
Division Street,[293] and the setting up of provisional classrooms in nearby
apartments to carry on the regular teaching program without interruption.

Demolition of the two wooden dwellings was begun at once, and the
brick building, which housed the chapel, the choir and the room that
Mother Mary had occupied, was moved towards the rear.[294] The new
four-story building was made possible, in part, by voluntary gifts of citizens who understood the challenges and the opportunities dawning for
women at the turn of the century. Archbishop Feehan officiated at the
laying of the cornerstone, July 31, 1892.[295] On December 23, the sisters
have had their housewarming in the new St. Joseph convent and expedited
the furnishing of the academic department for early occupancy by day and
resident students. The successful organization of the plan of instruction
led to the development of a standard four-year high school by 1902, in
addition to elementary school curriculum.

The fourth centenary of the discovery of America, falling due that
year, was noted by the Supreme Pontiff who called it "an immortal event"
which Catholics ought to commemorate in a grateful spirit.[296] Cognizant
of his exalted office in the Universal Church, he sent to the World's
Columbian Exposition in Chicago two rare fifteenth-century geographical
charts from the Vatican collection and a phonograph recording of his
address for the opening of the Exposition.[297]

For the Congregation the voice of the Holy Father rang with a message
of special significance when, on June 14, 1892, the liturgical feast of the
Holy Family was proclaimed as an annual observance within the Christmas cycle.[298] In this connection Pope Leo declared Nazareth "the abso-

lute example for the Church and the individual." Three hymns of his composition honoring the Holy Family have been inserted into the Divine Office as proper for the solemnity.

The ideal of the Holy Family in Christian living commenced to captivate nobler minds as a potent antidote for the ills of society contaminated with the errors of communism. It took root across central Italy, championed in Florence by Cardinal Archbishop Bausa and in Naples by Father Luigi Biaschelli of the Society of Precious Blood. Father Lechert's association with the Sisters of the Holy Family of Nazareth pointed him out to Father Biaschelli as the logical person to approach for the purpose of considering the establishment of pastoral ministry, dedicated to promoting the spirit of the Holy Family, particularly among the working-men's families who were most vulnerable to insidious doctrines. Thus it was that in 1891 few young men were referred to him as aspirants to the proposed Society of Brothers of the Holy Family, and were tentatively lodged in the Nazareth guest quarters for pilgrims.[299]

On presenting this idea in its rudimentary outline to Cardinal Parocchi, the Vicar of Rome, Father Lechert found him favorably disposed; similarly encouraging was the reaction of the Prefect of the Sacred Congregation of Bishops and Regulars, Cardinal Verga.[300]

Meanwhile, a network of episodes disclosed the fact that certain elements, moved by personal animosity, embarked on a denigrating campaign which aimed at the curtailment of his activities. They appeared more eager to block Father Lechert than they were to serve the Church. It seemed not enough that he had accepted without demur the refusal of permission to visit again the sisters in the American convents; he also acquiesced without rebuttal to the plan for his removal from rectorship at the Polish Pontifical College, although the action was contrived unbeknown to the Cardinal Protector of the College, who was ultimately responsible for its administration. He underplayed his interests and avoided flamboyance in conduct, as if to indicate that such display was unnecessary since he was not motivated by personal ambition.[301]

But those who have stressed arguments in opposition to Father Lechert had the fulcrum for which they were looking. In the absence of Cardinals Parocchi and Verga, and based on a collage of skewed information, a decree was issued, October 15, 1892, over the signature of one secretary alone, ordering Father Lechert to relinquish the idea of organizing the Society of the Brothers of the Holy Family, to dismiss the aspirants, and to discontinue all relations, temporal and spiritual, with the Sisters of the Holy Family of Nazareth. In response to all this, Father Lechert said with great calm, "Let us thank God for this cross and humiliation; they are the unmistakable stamp of divine favor."[302] Naturally objective, he was not outraged by human waywardness; he accepted human faults as the residue of original sin which tends to weaken the will and dim the intellect. Father Lechert stood revealed before all men, friendly and hostile, in the full stature of his noble character as he informed his superior general of his readiness to comply with the terms of the decree. He merely requested a leave of one month for prayer and recollection which he susbsequently passed in seclusion at the Resurrectionist motherhouse.

The decree was followed by days of apprehension for Mother Mary who in her profound humility saw herself bereft of the guidance, upon which she knew she ought to rely in faith for the accomplishment of her mission. Yet her distress was not sterile. She understood that these things had to be endured, so that the work of God would be glorified.

As soon as the Cardinals, who should have been the determining factors in these matters, returned to Rome, they received Mother Mary with frank sympathy, openly deploring the course the events had taken.[303] Since the decree contained implications that were damaging to Nazareth's reputation, the fair-minded and perceptive Cardinal Parocchi advised that immediate steps be undertaken to represent the true state of affairs. Accordingly, she prepared two documented statements, vindicating the position of Father Lechert with reference to the Sisters of the Holy Family of Nazareth and elucidating the presence in the guesthouse of the aspirants who desired to become the new male community.[304] To the sisters outside of Rome she communicated the essential details about all these developments to avert a possible threat to the life, unity, and spread of the Congregation.

Without sentimentality Father Lechert pondered the outcome of the crisis during his retirement "in the belly of the whale," as he called the interminable days of his isolation. He had the benefit of surveying the tendency of his congregation's policy-making exponents, who came sporadically to expostulate with him in a rush of self-righteousness and, in consequence, he faced the stark realization that his membership was undesirable. Upon consulting church authorities and foremost spiritual directors, he became convinced of this fact, as well as of his calling to establish the Brothers of the Holy Family.[305] He had identified himself with this cause so completely that he found it impossible to deny it for his own convenience. For this reason he sought release from his religious vows as a Resurrectionist to be free to profess them in his new congregation.

It was in the best tradition of ecclesiastical impartiality to give equal consideration to all sides of the controversy and to act expeditiously once the facts were ascertained. On December 3, Cardinal Parocchi secured from the Holy Father the singular favor by which, as a member of the secular clergy, Father Lechert was permitted to remain in Rome under the Pope's direct jurisdiction.[306] Along with this action the decree of October 15 was annulled and, on December 9, the Cardinal Vicar reinstated Father Lechert as the confessor and director of the Sisters of the Holy Family of Nazareth. The event was celebrated the following day with Holy Mass of thanksgiving in honor of Our Lady of Loreto, which he offered in the sisters' chapel.[307]

The official removal of undeserved censures did not appease the roiled mood of the malcontents, and their aspersions billowed about Nazareth like a sinister cloud.[308] Taking the hopeless vagaries into account, Father Lechert decided upon a period of withdrawal from Italy and left for France early in January, 1893.[309] When two of the initial aspirants followed him there, he at once revived the plans for the male foundation and settled in Sèvres, at 155 Rue Grand, in the diocese of Versailles. Cardinal Richard of Paris and the bishop of Versailles, both in possession of commendatory testimonials from Cardinal Parocchi, granted him the necessary faculties and willingly consented to the new foundation, which he now named the Missionaries of Divine Love.[310]

On January 18, 1893, the Nazareth novitiate in Rome was entrusted to the guidance of the Carmelite Mother Joseph-Teresa, who as a senior nun of a venerable order, distinguished in the Church by many saints, could impart sound precepts to the novices. Having experienced cordial acceptance within this community, she estimated at close range its underlying spirit and was powerfully affected by its evangelical image. This appointment enabled the Foundress to turn with greater ease to the manifold affairs that concerned the widely scattered convents. To safeguard her Congregation against untoward contingencies in the future, she petitioned the Supreme Pontiff to designate Cardinal Dunajewski to be Nazareth's Cardinal Protector. The letter of appointment from the Papal Secretariate of State[311] was delivered on April 21, and two days later the Cardinal, being just then in Rome, was given due honors at the motherhouse in a solemn ceremony when he formally assumed the protectorate over the Congregation.[312] Attempting to restore the climate of peace, Mother Mary took upon herself the burden to open the avenue of reconciliation with the superior general of the Resurrectionists, but was given a cold reception.[313]

That year the faithful of the world have again been flocking to Rome in a magnificent spectacle of homage to Leo XIII on the fiftieth anniversary of his episcopal consecration. Noteworthy among the pilgrimages was the one from England, inspired by Herbert Cardinal Vaughan of Westminster. By one of those unpredictable coincidences which marked Nazareth's unfolding, it was then that he made Mother Mary's acquaintance with the explicit purpose of securing her compassion and cooperation for the spiritual needs of the poorest of the poor in the neglected districts of London.[314] Her compassion was aroused instantly, and she promised to visit London as soon as she will have attended to other pressing matters.

Several messages about her brother's critical condition alerted her to the impending personal grief, which struck when his death occurred on March 19, 1893. He was survived by his amiable, devoted wife Natalie, née Trubert, and two young children, Cecily Frances and Adolphe Joseph. The widow had the comfort of visiting with Mother Mary when she came to Poland on a tour of duty later in the spring, offsetting the disappointment caused by Mother Mary's absence at Adam's deathbed.

In Lemberg the small beginnings already showed optimistic signs of an assured future;[315] in Cracow, the Institute of St. Hedwig exhibited gratifying Christian vitality, and the residence hall for students flourished remarkably well.[316] These developments entailed numerous cares which, even from the material and professional standpoints, the Foundress alone could settle positively. For Mother Raphael harbored fixed reservations, adverse to the Congregation's active involvement in external works, disregarding the summons to the apostolic needs of the Church, heedless of the opportunities to cut a pathway of grace through the world's dreary wilderness.

Aside from the admiration and reverence she professed for the person of Mother Mary, she gave rise to the volatile legend that the key to the interpretation of Nazareth's real purpose and predestined character lay in a strictly contemplative and penitential life, according to Brother Stephen's ideas to which she and her sisters subscribed. The slow, constant seepage of these ideas into the immediate environment was bound to trace a delicate cleavage of the spirit that could end in disaster. Mother Raphael, a romantic idealist, theorized often in a gentle flow of high-sounding contradictory generalities, dwelt on obscure memories in a faintly resentful, unhurried way, and gathered the credulous into her companionate circuit. The Foundress simply bypassed the dissident idiosyncrasies, allowing no diminution of confidence or charity to disturb community relations, in the hope of rehabilitating general good faith eventually. Nevertheless, as late as 1898, she had to admit with sorrow that the Sacred Heart convent in Cracow was still "an impregnable fortress."[317]

Whatever the progress in apostolic ventures, the price paid by Mother Foundress was high in terms of mental stress and in the drain upon her physical health. Already then medical consultation exposed the presence of ascites,[318] attended with liver function failure, difficulty in respiration, recurrent heart ailments, and general malaise.[319] But her singular humility of self-effacement immersed her wholly in the mission she recognized as hers, so that she declined to utilize for definitive therapy the time needed to accomplish the work of God. Satisfied with measures that produced symptomatic relief, she made one reluctant concession: to postpone the plans for another trip to the United States despite the entreaties of the sisters from the American convents.

Enabled thus to prolong her stay in Poland, she divided her time among the three houses, counseling the sisters in personal and professional matters. For the advancement of the respective institutions, Sister Irene was sent as director to Lemberg and Mother Theresa from Paris became the residence hall director in Cracow. In Paris, Sister Tarcisia was placed in charge temporarily.[320]

Finally, by the end of November, Mother Mary arrived in Paris and remained there until March, coordinating the daily activities, establishing proper attitudes, improving the standards of the school. On January 21, 1894, in a private ceremony in the convent chapel at Rue Labat, Sister Bernarda was admitted to the special fourth vow, when the permanent title of Mother was conferred upon her. The following week, January 27, the office of the local superior was filled by Mother Gabriel who moved in lightly with patronizing warmth and charm, an affable dynamo.[321]

In the spring of 1894, every sister in the Congregation received an appropriately revised, printed copy of the directory, a handbook of community observances which had been experimentally put to use in 1885.[322]

When on Easter Sunday Mother Mary arrived at the motherhouse, she found that Cardinal Dunajewski was again in Rome. Through his mediation she was determined to effect a stable reconciliation with the Resurrectionists, to wipe out all differences, and to achieve concord in the forgiveness which she was ready to offer and wished only that it be accepted in its totality. When the superior general of the Resurrectionists relented and made his appearance at the Nazareth convent, a modicum of mutual good will was regained in the long interview that ensued.[323]

Father Lechert, on his part, wished to establish congenial working relations with Nazareth's Cardinal Protector and arranged to see him in Rome, where both occupied rooms in the guesthouse at Via Machiavelli for the duration of their stay. Having bound himself by perpetual vows as a Missionary of Divine Love, in Sèvres, on the feast of Our Lady of Loreto, December 10, 1893,[324] he would have no shadows encroach upon his charity and made the approach to Father Przewłocki, desiring to eradicate whatever antipathy may have arisen as a result of the earlier misunderstandings. These overtures were a moral relief to both congregations in view of the fact that but a year later death claimed the superior general of the Resurrectionists.[325]

Recurring pleas and intentions to visit the American houses were agreeably resolved by Cardinal Dunajewski who, as the Cardinal Protector of the Congregation, delegated Father Lechert to conduct a canonical visitation as his representative,[326] empowered with broad faculties and supported by a formal letter of delegation, dated June 10, 1894.[327] This apparently was the Cardinal's last official act, for upon his return to Cracow he was overcome by a fatal onset of massive pneumonia and died on June 18.

Directly the Foundress applied to the Holy See, requesting that Cardinal Parocchi be designated as his successor in the capacity of the Congregation's Protector. The petition was granted, July 6, 1894, by a document from the Vatican Secretariate of State. Meanwhile, Father Lechert, back in France, prepared for his voyage and sailed from the Havre, July 7, on S.S. *La Touraine.*

8   AHEAD OF THEIR JOYS

Nine years after his first visit to the United States, Father Lechert entered that country the second time in a period of grave economic crisis that held the entire nation in the grips of panic, strikes, poverty and unemployment. In these troubled days the country was saved by the high quality of President Cleveland's statesmanship, while the faith and endurance of the people saved the parochial school system, which had become their valiant manifestation of loyalty to the Church. It is an item of historical record that only religious communities possessed the stamina to cope with the difficult requirement of supplying teaching personnel for a pittance as their voluntary contribution to education at the inestimable cost of personal privations.

In July of 1894 there were nine Nazareth convents existing on the American soil under dissimilar conditions and in varied locations. The Holy Family Academy, called upon to participate in the educational guidance of girls, was in the forefront of cultural activity, proving that the support it received shall have a calculated positive impact upon future family life through the persons of its alumnae. The novitiate, structurally housed with the Academy, was a distinct unit where aspiring young religious were able to capitalize on their opportunities for in-depth personality development.

St. Joseph convent as such, combining both units, was the center of Nazareth vitality in the American province, building up the human fiber of family spirit among the sisters with frequent reunions for days of recollection, retreat sessions, and special observances—festive and recreational. It became axiomatic that the renewing of Christian family life would be unthinkable, unless the sisters' community life were permeated with genuine family spirit. The enlarged scope of the central convent necessitated the appointment of a local superior to direct its countless management details. With Mother Paula in this duty, the provincial superior was in a far better position to analyze, harmonize and guide with creative thinking the assorted endeavors germinating in the province and to promote the welfare of each sister.

Thus far the sisters' efforts were generally concentrated upon the teaching profession, although they extended themselves also in other services and acts of mercy at the expenditure of heavy sacrifices. The sick had an irresistible claim on their sympathy, and those who came to their convents in bewilderment and helplessness were given simple home remedies freely when afflicted with minor ailments. Home visits to the sick were practiced diligently after the example of Mother Mary.

One other medium for the spreading of the Kingdom of God occurred to Mother Lauretta in the form of visits to Catholic patients with language

Mother Mary in the 1870's.

Mother Mary in the first habit of the Congregation.

Mother Mary with the revised headdress, Chicago, 1885.

Mother Mary, in 1891, after the pleated collar was introduced.

difficulties at non-Catholic hospitals.[328] Originally the visits were directed to Cook County Hospital of Chicago, but presently other hospitals were included in turn. A number of languages commanded by the sisters reached patients of several nationalities with the hope and charity of human kindness and brought the consolations of religion to their bedside.

Recent immigrants from Poland were among those who felt keenly the inability to communicate with hospital attendants and the lack of the ministrations of their faith; they were among the first to propose to Mother Lauretta the idea of establishing a hospital in Chicago.[329] By the end of 1893, projects and schema for the sisters' hospital were the subject of spirited discussions in ever-widening circles within the city. In a surge of enthusiasm Mother Lauretta seriously considered retiring from her office in order to devote her energies entirely to the care of the sick. Notwithstanding the crucial economic circumstances of the time, voluntary civic and parochial committees set about the procurement of funds by means of attractive social functions, benefit concerts, regional fairs, and the like.[330]

For the immediate realization of the hospital it was decided to convert the three-story brick residence that had been temporarily occupied by the sisters during the construction of the Academy. It had subsequently been leased to tenants for one year, and upon the termination of the lease animated preparations were begun with the advice of disinterested physicians who formed the hospital's first medical staff: Doctors Charles G. Davis, Frank J. Laibe, George Mueller, W. A. Kuflewski and Albert J. Ochsner, men of unselfish idealism and humanitarian virtues. A round of visits to recommended institutions was made by Mother Lauretta and the concerned sisters for the purpose of orientation with usual hospital routines and policies.[331] On May 6, 1894, Archbishop Feehan dedicated the 24-bed Holy Family Hospital with the participation of jubilant multitudes.[332] The next day, May 7, the first patient was admitted, a six-year old boy suffering from a fractured arm and head injuries.

In the early days the sisters assumed full responsibility for the care of the sick. Under the personal direction of the doctors who admired their spirit of charity and sacrifice, the sisters were instructed in the practical essentials of such functions as nursing procedures, dosage and solutions in medications, special skills in the operating room and laboratory. The hospital became a haven of hope and comfort to the surrounding neighborhoods. To insure for the sisters the continuous support of the Mother of God, the hospital chapel and convent were given the venerated title of the Mother of Perpetual Help.

Understandably the arrival of Father Lechert was looked upon as only second in importance to the arrival of Mother Foundress, and was greeted with sincere joy by the sisters assembled at the convent of St. Joseph. After prayerful moments in the chapel and the beautiful choir rendition of the hymn of thanksgiving *Te Deum Laudamus,* formal salutations followed, one by Sister Bronislaus in the name of the entire province, another by Sister Euphemia,[333] a novice, representing the novitiate. The sisters who were meeting him the first time did not take to him at once and remained aloof; but as he endeavored to know each one individually, they discerned in him the pleasing modesty of manner and the uncommon sweetness of disposition that brought to life the many transcribed conferences of his which they had read and contemplated. Directly the benign warmth of his personality charged the atmosphere with confidence and rapport.[334]

He inspected with absorbing interest the entire academy building and the hospital, called on the Archbishop to present his credentials, and visited the sisters in their respective parochial convents. The month of August was given to two annual retreat sequences at which he presided, available to all in discourses, interviews, liturgical services, and religious ceremonies. At Mother Mary's wish, he conferred the permanent title of Mother on Sisters Stanislaus and Angela, as they pronounced the required fourth vow. He also confirmed and announced the assignments for the year, designating—among others—Mother Paula the hospital superior and administrator, and Mother Columba to succeed her as the superior at St. Joseph's convent. The full complement of the provincial council was established to include: M. Lauretta, provincial superior and treasurer; M. Columba, provincial assistant; M. Paula, provincial secretary; M. Angela and M. Stanislaus, provincial councilors.[335]

Long drawn out controversial problems surrounding the Holy Trinity parish in Chicago[336] required careful study before any responsibility could be undertaken by the sisters for the parochial school. Already in January of 1889, Archbishop Feehan had proposed to the Nazareth Congregation the staffing of Holy Trinity school[337] when the church was about to be reopened for the third time, but disputes over the administrative policies of the parish have within few months necessitated official intervention with the imposition of an interdict. The church was finally reopened in June, 1893 by the Apostolic Delegate, Archbishop Satolli, who also obtained from the Holy Cross Order the appointment of Father Casimir S. Sztuczko, C.S.C., as the pastor. At the outset the school was in a fluid state due to the absence of classroom space on the parochial premises. Teaching was conducted in the rectory with Brother Peter, C.S.C., the principal, two sisters who were coming in daily from the Holy Family Academy, and several lay teachers. Under the prudent direction of the pastor, the parish prospered in peaceable relations, and a school building was erected in

1894. Father Lechert favored the assignment of more sisters, although for lack of a convent they continued to reside at the Academy until 1908. By 1895, the administration of the school was committed to the sisters, with Sister Victoria[338] as the first principal, the arrangement being, however, that the Brothers of the Holy Cross would teach the boys.[339]

On the witness of the religious in the role of school teachers, Mother Mary held explicit convictions, "The teaching of children in school is a work after the very heart of Christ and abounds in great merit for individual sisters. The religious enters the classroom in the name of Christ, and whatever she teaches, she teaches it in his name."[340]

On September 5, 1894, Father Lechert left Chicago for Brooklyn, accompanied by Mother Lauretta and Sister Gertrude.[341] The latter was to be installed as the superior in Brooklyn in replacement of Sister Alberta, who was returning to Europe to take up assigned duties in the house in Paris.[342]

In mid-August, while Father Lechert was going about the spiritual harvest in the United States, Mother Mary, urged by forthright persuasions, proceeded to London with Mother Cecilia.[343] Having accepted the invitation to be the house guests of Lady Herbert, an admirable Catholic who shared Cardinal Vaughan's interest in bringing the sisters to London, Mother Mary found the mansion of their hostess too lavish to be in accord with the Nazareth concept of poverty and, instead, sought to be accommodated at the convent of the Reparatrices.[344] For six weeks she investigated the ambient circumstances of the mission center that was recommended to her, consulted and interviewed informed persons, and contemplated in prayer the indications of divine will. The needs were unquestionably great, but the presence of forceful left-wing activists was known to instigate discord and intrigue that spelled interference and frustrations.[345] She was eager to be of service to these people and expected in a year's time to find there some level of harmony and group solidarity, as a mission prerequisite, to commence the groundwork without squandering the precious but limited potential that was at her disposal.[346]

Back in Paris, she communicated her findings to Father Lechert, and received from him the account of his visit in the United States. To both it became evident that the time was ripe to convoke the first general chapter of the Congregation. With this in view, Mother Mary departed for Poland where, of the three houses, the one in Lemberg claimed most of her attention. The school was transferred to more spacious quarters at 10 Kościuszko Street; members of the faculty, religious and lay, met in conferences with the Foundress for guidelines on Nazareth educational philosophy; the appointment of Sister Laurence as the superior was determined by the recall of Mother Joanne to Rome to assist in the compilation of preliminary materials for the chapter.[347]

Across the Atlantic, Mother Lauretta, before setting out for the chapter, scrutinized the priority components for the health care of increasing numbers of patients who applied to the hospital. As a result of the lingering depression, the majority of those who came for treatment were indigent and unemployed, or so poorly compensated that they were incapable of defraying the cost of the care given them.[348] There were numerous instances of actual deprivation of nourishment on the part of the sisters who chose to do without for the sake of their patients. Replacing the matrons on weekends, school sisters volunteered to do night duty.

The pangs of poverty were prolonged and debts increased, but in many instances suppliers were disposed to extend their credit to the hospital, banking on the immaterial guarantees secured by charity, whereas some market places regularly allocated a quota of farm products gratuitously in behalf of the sick. Benefit entertainments, staged by amateur groups and artists alike, constituted a voluntary financing mechanism which the sisters supplemented by door-to-door collections.[349] The gap between services needed and services provided, along with the pressures to furnish more hospital space, raised specific target areas of concern for optimum development of the hospital care apostolate.[350]

Another urgent matter requiring implementation was the advance planning for a school in Pittsburgh, affiliated with St. Stanislaus Kostka parish, where the convent was given the title of the Most Precious Blood. Mother Stanislaus, the first superior-principal, with a staff of eight sisters arrived there on August 24, 1895, and immediately began to organize the year's program.[351]

In the hope of obtaining a searching appraisal of the Constitutions prior to the chapter, Mother Mary submitted seven copies of the updated, revised text to the special review commission of the Sacred Congregation of Bishops and Regulars.[352] Round about August 12, members of the general chapter assembled in Paris to attend first the twenty-fifth anniversary of Father Lechert's ordination to the priesthood, which was observed on the 14th, and thereupon they proceeded to the peaceful suburb of Chaville, where they had the temporary use of a vacated residence for the duration of the chapter. Following an eight-day retreat, the chapter was opened under the direction of Father Lechert; Mother Mary, the superior general, presided at the sessions.

The authorized capitulants were: Mothers Gabriel, Joanne, Lauretta and Bernarda; Sisters Frances, Laurence and Gertrude; and Mother Theresa, an approved alternate in the place of Mother Raphael who was ill.

The deliberations of the chapter extended until September 5, terminating with the election of the General Council and the ratification of the decrees, which were enacted for the redirection and reinforcement of the Congregation's identity and goals. Members of the general council, elected by secret ballot, were: M. Lauretta, assistant general; M. Raphael, secretary general; S. Frances, treasurer general, and M. Joanne, visitor general.[353] The closing of the chapter was followed by the ceremony of conferring the title of Mother upon Sisters Frances, Laurence and Gertrude.[354]

The next day, at the meeting of the general council, several appointments were made, including the appointment of Mother Lauretta to be the provincial superior for the houses in Poland and the local superior of the Sacred Heart convent in Cracow; Mother Raphael, the elected secretary general, was expected to reside at the motherhouse in Rome. Mother Columba became the provincial superior for the United States,[355] her newly appointed councilors being: S. Bronislaus, provincial assistant; S. Sophia, provincial treasurer; S. Rose, provincial secretary, and M. Angela, supervisor of schools.[356] Mother Frances was named the superior at the motherhouse in Rome, and Mother Gertrude the first superior of the London mission.

Over the intervening months the existing obstacles to the establishment of the mission in London had been successfully removed through the good offices of Cardinal Vaughan. A cottage was leased for the sisters in the East End district, at 313 Mile End Road. On September 16, the Foundress accompanied by Mother Theresa and Father Lechert left for England. Two days later they were joined by Mother Gertrude and three sisters who were summoned from Rome. The opening of the mission convent, under the patronage of the Mother of Divine Love, took place on September 17 with the celebration of Holy Mass in the chapel.

Father Lechert announced to the people an eight-day series of services, morning and evening, at which he preached sermons from the heart, exhorting the listeners to a life consistent with the precepts of faith and nourished at the channels of grace.[357] For the time being he could promise to return each month for a week to serve them until more satisfactory arrangements would be made. During his absences the entire responsibility devolved upon Mother Mary to locate an available priest to offer Holy Mass on Sundays.

By team programming of home and hospital visits, she participated for six months with the sisters in identifying the cultural, social and economic factors that had to be met with understanding and sympathy. Prayerful vigils at the bedside of the sick and the dying, comforting the bereaved, assisting the needy, informal dialogues on Christian doctrine, counseling, practical instructions, preparing the children for the reception of the Sacraments—all efforts, in fact, were employed to elevate the morale of the people who have long hungered for spiritual fare and the touch of Christ's goodness. An interval of two months, March and April, allotted to the affairs that called the Foundress away to Paris and to Rome, was bridged by her return to share again the mission toils, trials and privations in the joy of witnessing Christ come alive in London homes and in daily human occurrences.

Her insatiable zeal and charity lent itself strikingly to Sister Thecla[358] in unsparing devotion and abnegation that endeared her to the poor, the neglected, the underprivileged, and even those who were antagonistic to a religiously oriented way of life. Sister Thecla's contribution lay predominantly in the Lithuanian settlement, known as Silvertown, to which she gave whole weekends.[359] But in London as elsewhere, the good accomplished was similarly attended with an outbreak of active hostility; a mob of bigots stirred up the residual difficulties and for days hurled mud, stones and refuse at the convent windows until late into the night. Police action finally restored order.[360]

On January 31, 1896, Father Joseph Schroeter, the first ordained Missionary of Divine Love, was assigned pastoral duties at the mission. He had completed his studies in Rome, was admitted to the sacred ministry there, and on Christmas Eve celebrated his first Mass in Sèvres in the presence of his superior and confrères. Fired by apostolic fervor, he entered the rhythm of divine operations with consuming selflessness. By mid-April his youthful energies were spent like burnt out incense. Smitten by tuberculosis of the lungs and larynx, he had to leave the mission he loved, compelled to absolute inactivity, with no hope of recovery though under treatment and care.[361] He died in Sèvres, October 19, 1896.[362]

At the friendly recommendation of the Sisters of the Holy Child Jesus, Mother Gertrude and Sister Alphonsus[363] were enrolled at the institute for teacher certification. Successful results after first year's examinations would enable them to establish a school in London, but further attendance at lectures and practice teaching warranted progressively higher qualifications.[364]

The limitations which time and place imposed upon Mother Mary did not prevent her from embracing all of Nazareth's endeavors throughout the world in purposeful vigilance. Unfolding new directions in the United States brought forth the reversal of certain appointments in the interest of the general good. Mother Paula, who had come to Paris prior to the chapter, was asked at the end of February, 1896, to replace Mother Gertrude in England. Early in May the latter left with two sisters on a return assignment to the United States.[365]

In Poland a frustrating situation confronted Mother Lauretta when she arrived, September 11, 1895, at the convent of the Sacred Heart in Cracow. Encounters with subtle opposition and resistance put to test her virtue and the nobility of her character when with tact, humility and gentleness she greeted Mother Raphael, holding in abeyance the just claim to her proper appointment.[366] Two months later Mother Raphael wrote to her sister in Paris, "It is difficult to describe how much the sisters suffer since I announced my withdrawal from office. They are numb with grief . . . they cannot accept the idea of my leaving. They feel they have a superior and delude themselves with the thought that M. Lauretta shall have to leave soon."[367]

That the withdrawal from office was purely verbal was in effect corroborated by her unalterable clinging to the vesture of authority in daily events at the convent.[368] At a later date, still from Cracow, she elaborated on the disappointment she experienced after the chapter in the failure of the anticipated assignment of Mother Gabriel to Lemberg, whose proximity she had greatly desired.[369]

In spite of psychological drawbacks there was much that could be accomplished by the provincial, when the responsibilities of office were conceived as a sacred trust, a sweet yoke to be placed ahead of one's joy. To remedy the overcrowding of the residence hall[370] in Cracow, Mother Lauretta secured the cooperation of a specially constituted commission on development and of the city's school council to expand the students' facilities and the chapel. Public-spirited individuals not only pledged to finance the undertaking but also established grants-in-aid available to deserving needy students to defray their maintenance costs.[371]

In Lemberg again, since the school had already been approved by the department of public instruction, Mother Lauretta pointed out the obligation to strengthen and enrich the curriculum and the necessity of providing a building better adapted for a progressive teaching establishment.[372]

In the rising town of Wadowice, within the diocese of Cracow, new opportunities were brought to the attention of Mother Lauretta by Bishop John Puzyna and others, who were concerned about raising certain local standards through cooperative efforts within the context of Christian consciousness. In the total absence of religious communities of women in the town, the projections for immediate realization by the Sisters of Nazareth encompassed a school, a nursery, an orphanage, and a hospital.[373]

The city council favored the sisters' arrival and encouraged the purchase of suitable property for the care and education of dependent children to insure for the future the sisters' free exercise of their apostolic philosophy. As usual, the work was commenced in small, temporary quarters with Mother Lauretta herself guiding the initial developments, when a day-care center for pre-school children was opened, in February of 1896, under the patronage of Divine Providence. A month later fifty children were enrolled. By the end of March a building was acquired with an ample garden, and provisions were made for the housing of orphans, their education and the teaching of useful crafts. In April, Mother Theresa Czermińska arrived to assume the duties of the superior and director.[374]

The ambitions of the city council of Wadowice were next aroused to improve the patient-care services at the municipal hospital, which were flagrantly unsatisfactory because of the lack of adequate facilities, essential equipment and competent personnel. The sisters were asked to accept the administration of the hospital and, as a result of consultations with Mother Lauretta, the city fathers undertook the construction of a new, well appointed 41-bed general hospital.[375] Sister Irene Marianowska, who had demonstrated outstanding ability for administration in previous assignments, was prepared by a concentrated course of orientation to take charge of the hospital as superior and administrator, when it was dedicated, December 7, 1896.[376]

It was not given to Mother Lauretta, however, to witness the establishment of the apostolate of the sick by Nazareth in Poland. A penetrating observer, she surveyed dispassionately the situation in which she found herself. Her mind was not as unbruised as in the earlier years, but laying hold of knowledge that was fortified with the understanding of the heart led her to sources of timely wisdom. She recommended to the Foundress the reinstatement of Mother Raphael in Cracow and her own withdrawal.[377] Thus she joined Mother Mary in Paris, May 1, and accompanied her to London.

Engulfed in a maze of unfamiliar experiences and besieged with endless demands, the sisters in their mission endeavors in London knew a great practical need of the stabilizing presence of their Foundress, who combined with habitual grace the charity and the simple dignity of the vowed religious. Her guidance tended always toward cultivating in them that personal maturity which is commensurate with one's commitment to God and to man and the deepening to the very core of one's human potential. In confidence she would leave them with the living memory of her words and examples, as she did at this time when she departed with Mother Lauretta for the United States on the *Gascogne,* which sailed from the Havre on August 8, 1896.[378]

9 THE MUSTARD SEED

Upon the termination of the first general chapter, Mother Columba moved into the office of the American provincial superior almost imperceptibly. To begin with, the duties of this office had fallen to her as to the provincial assistant, while substituting Mother Lauretta when the latter was obliged to attend the chapter. She exhibited consummate graciousness and a capacity to serve and plan throughout the heavy summertime period of the year's accumulated problems.[379] Unsuspected dimensions of her spirit came to light in the manner in which she assisted at the annual retreat.[380]

She accompanied the first contingent of sisters selected to initiate the Nazareth teaching apostolate in Pittsburgh, where they were met in welcome, August 24, 1895, by the Fathers of the Holy Ghost who led the local population and throngs of school children in an open demonstration of joy. The earliest fruit reaped of the new terrain was the vocation of four resolute young women who sought the fulfillment of their aspirations in religious life and in fact became: Sisters Joachim,[381] Gregoria,[382] Leocadia,[383] and Margaret.[384]

In Chicago, St. Hyacinth's parish was just being organized in the sparsely inhabited northwest locality of Avondale, when the pastor, Father Joseph Gieburowski, C.R., applied for teaching sisters. On September 3, 1895, Mother Columba introduced Sister Valentine[385] to the new field of work as superior-principal, who with two associates constituted the original faculty. The convent was named in honor of the Immaculate Conception of the Blessed Virgin Mary.

Even before Mother Columba became aware of her appointment to the office of the provincial superior, she was confronted with questions arising from the complexities of the Brooklyn situation. When in 1891 the sisters first came to Brooklyn, the one parish at Williamsburg extended over several city districts. For the convenience of the children who lived at greater distances a subsidiary school was established one year later at South Brooklyn, and soon thereafter at Greenpoint, to both of which the sisters from St. Frances of Rome convent in Williamsburg commuted daily. In proportion as the conditions in Williamsburg were declining, by 1896 the South Brooklyn community developed into a distinct parish, dedicated to Our Lady of Częstochowa, and the sisters' convent was transferred to better serve the growing school at South Brooklyn. The relationship then reversed: the school in Williamsburg became the subsidiary, depending on the sisters who now resided in South Brooklyn.

That same year, likewise, the diocesan authorities decided to organize Greenpoint into a self-contained entity as St. Stanislaus Kostka parish. The school, an integral unit of the parish, began to function on September 8, 1895, with Sister Bridget[386] as the superior-principal. The convent was given the title of the Patronage of Our Lady.

Superficially, the pastor of Williamsburg had reasons to be exasperated. Individual new parishes were arising, while his was dwindling. Sister Bridget, whom he had hoped to retain for the school in Williamsburg, became immersed in duties that totally separated her from Williamsburg. Besides, he was alerted to the fact that the continuance of the sisters' services in his parish would depend upon his correcting the deplorable schoolroom conditions. Furthermore, the teachers' daily commuting across the city depleted the time reserve which they needed for the preparation of their instructional materials and their own professional self-advancement.

As the pressures of conflicting interests increased, the drain upon the fragility of Mother Columba's constitution left her severely indisposed. She also suffered at the hands of the unscrupulous who for their own ends exploited her guileless candor, whereby she trusted too much but not prudently enough. It was at this juncture that Mother Mary made the third visit to the United States, arriving in New York on August 16, 1896. She remained in Brooklyn to determine the exact circumstances under which the sisters' life and work were carried on in the two houses and investigated the conditions at Newtown, later renamed Elmhurst, on Long Island. There, in response to a standing invitation, the proposed school in St. Adalbert's parish was being staffed that summer. Favoring the Elmhurst proposal, she deemed it advantageous to replace Sister Theodora, who had been tentatively assigned in charge, by appointing Sister Vincent[387] the superior-principal. The convent was named after the holy Apostles Peter and Paul.

Mother Columba accepted as a release[388] the decision to return to Europe, hoping to recover her well-being in her native climate. She arrived in France, accompanied by Sister Amata[389] who was destined for the mission in London, and herself proceeded to Poland. On November 4, she assumed the office of the superior in the house of Providence in Wadowice, from where Mother Theresa had been moved to England to fill the vacancy left a month earlier by Mother Paula. The latter, afflicted with acute sciatica and rheumatoid complications induced by insular humidity, required a change of place and intensive, prolonged treatment.

Having gained a true perspective of the eastern seaboard, Mother Mary reached Chicago before the end of August,[390] greeted by all the sisters assembled at the convent of St. Joseph. She announced Mother Lauretta's reappointment as the provincial superior and the appointment of Sister Sophia as the superior at Holy Family Academy. In planning the visitation routine, her heart went out to the sisters in Pittsburgh, Scranton and Philadelphia who were then engaged in preparations for the approaching school term. At once she concentrated upon the houses in the State of Pennsylvania, culminating with the placement of Mother Gertrude in Everson, September 14, to organize the school in St. Joseph's parish[391] and open the convent of the Holy Cross.

During these travels the Foundress received the highly desirable good news announcing the Decree of Praise for the Congregation, issued by the Holy See, September 1, 1896.[392]

While visiting the convent of St. Anthony in Philadelphia, Mother Mary took the opportunity to pay her respects to Mother Katherine Drexel (1858-1955), who founded the Sisters of the Blessed Sacrament for Indians and Negroes in 1891. Observing the countryside on the return trip, Mother Mary indicated a certain place to Mother Lauretta, saying, "Here I should like to see a house of Nazareth established for the perpetual adoration of the Blessed Sacrament." At that moment they read the placard at the trainstop which identified the site as Torresdale, a northeastern suburb of Philadelphia.[393]

To have a chapel of perpetual adoration, a house of prayer, was Mother Mary's recurring desire which she entertained to the end of her life. She saw it as a superb restorative of the sisters' inner rhythm in prayerful confrontation with eternal realities, and it occurred to her that it may serve as a radiation center of grace to the world-weary who could find respite before the face of the Lord in a fellowship of prayer.[394]

Archbishop Patrick John Ryan of Philadelphia was agreeable to the idea of a chapel for perpetual adoration as such, but on investigating the matter with his consultors he decided against it for the simple reason that perpetual adoration was already in existence in the archdiocese and that numerous churches and Catholic institutions regularly conducted Eucharistic devotions with exposition and benediction of the Blessed Sacrament.[395] Although the Foundress did not live to see a house of prayer realized as a distinct apostolate, the emphasis on sisters' prayer life and the availability to externs—individuals and groups—of opportunities for a prayer experience were always present in Nazareth since the days of its foundation. With the flowering in the Church of Eucharistic worship in paraliturgical services, the veneration of Christ's most sacred mystery pervaded the very lifestream of the Congregation. It constituted the source and summit of internal unity through shared communal prayer and the power of return to the fold of the estranged through expiation and reparation.

Instead of a chapel of perpetual adoration, the site indicated by

Mother Mary became, twenty-five years later, the location of the Immaculate Conception Province headquarters at Grant and Frankford Avenues.

When the Foundress resumed her work of visitation in Chicago, Mother Lauretta allocated her time to the more recently opened houses in New York and Pennsylvania. Inasmuch as the situation in Williamsburgh gave neither evidence nor hope of improvement, it was judged advisable to withdraw entirely from the area and to channel the sisters' efforts in the direction of optimum utilization. As a measure of expediency in so vulnerable a situation, proper adjustments in personnel had to be implemented promptly and deliberately to circumvent a whole array of misunderstandings.

Some four years earlier Mother Lauretta had intimated the practicality of forming two provinces in the United States to facilitate intra-provincial communication and administration.[396] This subject, now posing even greater urgency, was revived in the light of the diffusion of apostolic works,[397] but definitive action was postponed.

The immediate objective of Mother Foundress was to focus her attention upon the role of local superiors who in their leadership position were responsible for knitting together the local community. It was incumbent upon them to fashion each house as a representative unit by which the Congregation realized its purpose and justified its charismatic existence in the Church through the integrated efforts of individuals. She outlined strong, sober directives for guiding the sisters by charity and prudence and by the power of exemplary virtue, especially the little virtues of the hidden life and the family spirit. The Nazareth religious had to strive for excellence in a duty well done without seeking renown or acclaim, the total abandonment to the will of God and detachment from self-interest, and an all-embracing, generous love. To foster the bond of unity at the leadership level, she slated blocks of time for meetings with the superiors to inveigle them in an intelligent exploration of the decrees of the first general chapter, to research with them the rationale behind the recommendations, and to encompass the directions Nazareth must take, as a viable organism, in preparing for the dawn of the twentieth century.[398]

After careful study and observation of trends, needs, and reasonably predictable possibilities, she endorsed the undertaking of several fresh enterprises in the immediate future. The acute shortage of space in the hospital was remedied provisionally by the purchase of four neighboring vacant lots and of a two-story building which was converted into a 20-bed women's pavillion.[399] First attempts were initiated to bring to life the Ladies' Auxiliary, a society of women willing to further the charitable endeavors of the hospital.[400] While many prominent women of good will and social standing proved the sincerity of their interest, the society actually evolved as a formal organization after a lapse of years, November 27, 1904.

The hospital's new superior-administrator became the capable Sister Sophia who, after seven years as director of novices and the one year as superior at the convent of St. Joseph, was given the title of Mother. The novitiate then passed under the direction of Sister Lucille,[401] a person of uncommon insight into the psychology of youth and of inspired skill in the techniques of guidance and formation. She died nineteen years later among her beloved novices, having served them to the end and mourned by all who knew her.

Likewise in Chicago, negotiations with the pastor of St. George's parish, Reverend Michael L. Krusas, have reached the point of agreement that sisters would be provided for the school he strived to open. The parish consisted predominantly of Lithuanian element, both immigrant and derivative, and the Lithuanian clergy here as elsewhere displayed eagerness to preserve the faith by means of parochial schools. In the absence of an ethnically Lithuanian sisterhood in the United States, the Lithuanian clergy decided at a national meeting, two years earlier, to aim to organize a Lithuanian teaching sisterhood and, in the meantime, to establish parochial schools on the best compatible terms.[402]

Nazareth's ecumenical resilience was not a secret, alike with regard to the admission of members of all nationalities as to the recipients of its services. Historically since the fourteenth century, the Lithuanian people in Europe were united with Poland into one political entity by which they enjoyed the extrinsic advantages of the union and were assured their intrinsic liberties. The prime condition for the union was Lithuania's rejection of pagan beliefs and acceptance of the Catholic faith. The protagonists in the event were the youthful Queen Hedwig of Poland and Grand Duke Jagiello of Lithuania, whose marriage won a whole nation of souls for the Church of Christ.

The motive to be all things to all people brought the Sisters of the Holy Family of Nazareth into association with the friendly community at St. George's. They opened the school, October 7, 1897, with Sister Ladislaus, the first superior-principal.[403] The convent assumed the title of Our Lady of Ostra Brama to honor the famed Lithuanian shrine of the Blessed Virgin Mary.

In the extraordinary growth of Pittsburgh's St. Stanislaus parish, the population swelled to such overwhelming proportions that the Fathers of the Holy Ghost were commissioned to organize the parish of the Immaculate Heart of Mary on Herron Hill nearby. An overflow of four hundred children transferred from the first school when, September 8,

1897, Sister Leontine, superior-principal, and her staff of eight sisters took charge at Herron Hill.[404]

Pittsburgh appeared to the Foundress as a promising fertile field in the cause of God and man. Contemplating the welfare of the sisters in this teeming, smoky city, she inspected a small, hilltop villa in out-of-town Emsworth, with the intention of testing its merit as a resort for vacations and retreats, rest periods and outings, to preserve the sisters' health for apostolic service.[405] The villa was leased on trial basis to allow sufficient opportunity for appraisal and was designated as an affiliate of the Precious Blood convent.

Following repeated invitations from the bishop of Trenton in New Jersey, Mother Mary consented to blaze the trail yet in this one other diocese, in the city of Camden. Sister Theodora, as superior-principal, was assigned with an associate group to St. Joseph's school in September, 1897.[406] Unfortunately, the original congenial outlook of this locality deteriorated sharply, and the sisters were withdrawn in the spring of 1900.

This third and last visit to the United States, to which Mother Mary gave a full laborious year of pilgrim service, she summarized in retrospect in her report to the second general chapter:

> . . . In all the houses the sisters exhibited genuine good will, docility and obedience, and caused no difficulties. Their attitude was one of respect for the authority of Our Lord represented by their superiors with whom they cooperated wholeheartedly . . . There were inescapable situational problems, but with divine help and episcopal support these were resolved amicably.

Her belief in the future of Nazareth in the United States became stronger and brighter as time for her return to Europe drew closer. She signified this by accepting American citizenship in the formal act of naturalization, July 26 1897.[407] The sympathy she felt for the United States, because of its freedom of worship and equality of opportunity, convinced her that by acquiring American citizenship she and other sisters likewise may be more effective in the American apostolate.

On August 1, she embarked on the steamship *La Touraine,* landed at the Havre on the 9th, and proceeded through Southampton to London. The London convent of the Mother of Divine Love had been relocated[408] to Mayfield House at Old Ford Road in Bethnal Green, in the vicinity of St. Joseph and St. Casimir church on Cambridge Road East, which Father Lechert had acquired in August of 1896.[409] It was in this church that Mother Mary was present at the first Mass celebrated, August 14, by Father Joseph Bakanowski, a newly ordained Missionary of Divine

Love, who was assigned to the pastoral work here.

The dire poverty which the sisters shared with the poor of the district troubled Cardinal Vaughan lest they should be compelled to depart from London for lack of reasonable subsistence. Immensely gratified by their influence for the good, he visited Mother Foundress at the convent to convey to her not only his appreciation but also the recommendation to establish a private finishing school for girls of the middle class.[410] The plan was practical and immediately acceptable, for Mother Theresa's professional competence qualified her as the director, and her proficiency in French and the fine arts equipped her for instruction. Other subjects were assigned to Sisters Alphonsus and Amata.

10 A BURNING TORCH

Early in October of 1897, Mother Mary was again in Rome. She had been traveling with Sisters Rose and Antonia[411] from the United States, and now appointed Sister Rose the assistant to the local superior in the motherhouse, and Sister Antonia the director of postulants. The one novice and three candidates, who had departed from the United States at that same time, came to Rome in August immediately after their landing in France.[412]

There was an element of urgency in the little time the Foundress saw ahead, as she glimpsed her future closing in. Neither the tedium or inconvenience of third-class travel, nor the adjustments to the fatigue of changing environments, nor even the exhaustion from multitudinous demands that were made upon her could eclipse her inner vision. Like a burning torch, her unwavering sense of mission led her onward, regardless of the cost in personal sacrifice or hazard to her health and life. The voice of obedience alone had the power to mitigate the intensity of her zeal, for she acknowledged in faith the delegated authority of Christ in the person of Father Lechert, who was her director and superior.[413]

The Decree of Praise accorded the Congregation by the Holy See had been accompanied by a list of emendations to the Constitutions. It was necessary to revise the text of the Constitutions, as recommended, and to submit it to another scrutiny. Substantially, the changes indicated were minimal, largely stylistic,[414] requiring the substitution of formal terminology that was then in customary usage for the informality of expression in the original text.

Of the recommendations given, three were of major importance. One referred to the fact that the vows professed by the Sisters of the Holy Family of Nazareth were simple, not solemn, and since the outstanding distinction was within the context of the vow of poverty, it was mandatory to state in the Constitutions the canonical attributes of the simple vow of poverty which differentiate it from the solemn vow.[415] Another point was concerned with the Apostolic decree *Quemadmodum*, issued December 17, 1890, for all women religious as well as men who were not priests; this had to be included in the Constitutons, since all religious congregations were required to insert it in their respective constitutions and were obliged to have it read aloud to the community at least once a year.[416]

The third noteworthy observation was directed against the practice of permitting certain members to pronounce a fourth vow. Where all members made three vows at religious profession, there may not be a provision for a fourth vow to be taken separately by some, who then formed a distinct group within the Congregation.[417]

The work of rewriting the Constitutions was undertaken with the advice and assistance of Father Lechert. He was in Rome that autumn, establishing a house of studies, at 10 Via Alfieri, for the clerics of his congregation who matriculated in Roman universities to pursue the courses in theology and philosophy.[418]

When the recast format of the Constitutions appeared relatively satisfactory, Mother Mary went to Poland in July of 1898, after a four-year interval since her last visit. Confronted with the apostolic responsibility that challenged her constantly to go where she had to be for others, she concentrated on the needs of every house and of each person. Thinking of those who were receiving her message, she reviewed with them in detail the decrees enacted by the first general chapter and implemented their adaptation. She also sought expert consultation for the progressive and efficient stewardship of the institutions that were conducted by the sisters[419] to ensure their evangelical witness.

In Wadowice, in the house of Divine Providence, Mother Columba had been relieved of her duties the previous year, due to advancing degenerative arthritis aggravated by chronic enteritis which incapacitated her permanently. Mother Paula, who replaced her then, was now appointed superior at Lemberg, and Sister Rose took charge of the house of Providence. At the Institute of St. Hedwig in Cracow, the Foundress accepted Mother Joanne's request to withdraw from the office of superior-director and assigned in her stead Sister Jerome.[420]

This last visit of Mother Mary to Poland was made memorable by Pope Leo's felicitations on October first, noting the twenty-fifth anniversary of the papal blessing imparted by his predecessor for the foundation of the Congregation.[421] But she was not wont to dwell on comforting memories. Heeding the signals of distress from England,[422] she departed, October 4, for heavy clouds gloomed over the London mission with a dramatic resurgence of upheaval.

The attempt to establish a private school resulted in but a brief career of unfulfilled hopes for lack of students. In consequence, Mother Theresa Czermińska diverted her creative energies to the relief of the disadvantaged who were committed to the district workhouse. Her earlier experience in the house of Providence in Poland impelled her to accept dependent and neglected children into private custody under the care of the sisters. The work was being accomplished at the price of untold personal sacrifices and privations. By far the most cruel suffering was inflicted by a core of restive individuals who set about maligning the sisters publicly and discrediting them by slanderous reports to Cardinal Vaughan.

Although the Cardinal had not given credence to the reports, he welcomed Mother Mary's objective exposition of the events that had conspired to disgrace the sisters. With Mother Joanne as her visitation companion, she sorted out the values of what was right, in the functional sense, to salvage the mission enterprise. In her accustomed gentle manner, she went about modulating attitudes and relationships outside the Congregation, and adjusting duties and personnel within the mission group. Mother Theresa, who suffered most severely the brunt of the critical months, was granted a respite in the motherhouse when Mother Gertrude arrived in November to succeed her.[423]

As soon as the severity of the situation in London abated, the second general chapter was convoked to assemble again in Chaville[424] to consider the collective problems associated with the evolution of the Congregation in the contemporary world. At this time, similarly as at the first chapter, Mother Raphael sought exemption from attendance and asked to be relieved of the office of the secretary general to which she had been previously elected.[425]

Father Lechert, delegated to the chapter by the Cardinal Protector as his representative, read the Decree of Praise to the capitulants at the opening session, February 20, 1899. One of the major points on the agenda was the review of the Constitutions, modified according to the emendations propounded for inclusion in revising the original text which had been submitted to the Holy See in 1895. The revised text had to be implemented experimentally within the entire Congregation over a minimum of three years before resubmitting it to the Holy See, at which time a commentary appended to the text should denote the methods employed in the actual application of specific provisions, or, if experience proved a certain provision impractical, the reasons for an alternative were to be stated.[426] The era of theory was over.

Unanticipated by the capitulants was Mother Mary's resignation from the position of the superior general and her impassioned exhortation urging them to elect one better qualified, more competent. She had long been aware of the dispositions of some members who, regarding themselves as co-foundresses, entertained notions contrary to the patterns of service emerging in the Congregation in response to the palpable needs of society. Now she signalled the opportunity for the Congregation to determine, in the light of the Holy Spirit, the course it envisioned as its proper contribution to the life of the Church.

Therefore, when the votes of the capitulants clinched her unanimous election, she requested a second voting; when these results were identical, she pleaded for a third ballot. Father Lechert decided against repeating the procedure, declared the elections closed, and advised her to yield to the united will of the chapter. With touching humility the Foundress expressed her consent in the words of the Holy Virgin, "Ecce ancilla Domini, fiat mihi secundum verbum tuum." The chapter was concluded on March 9, the day of Mother Mary's baptismal patron, St. Frances of Rome.

On behalf of the American province, Mother Lauretta gained the understanding and the endorsement she desired for the development of the hospital in Chicago. There, popular interest and enthusiasm had pledged full support to the construction of a professionally planned hospital building to accommodate the growing health care demands of the locality. Despite the existing technical shortcomings in structural design and equipment with which the physicians had to contend currently, they continued their noble cooperation, perceiving themselves hopefully as a force at the foundation of true Christian involvement in a professional setting. Even under the restrictive conditions of the original hospital, a school of nursing was contemplated. Early in 1900, Miss Theresa Smith, R.N., director of the school, organized a standard program of nursing education for the first historic class of six students, among whom Sister Alexis[427] was the first Nazareth sister to achieve state certification. In a word, the upswing of American economy during the presidency of William McKinley (1897-1901) justified undertaking the proposed expansion.

Again the exalted spirit of Leo XIII inundated the universe when, at the approach of the new century, the Pontiff proclaimed a Holy Year of grace and benediction. By way of preparation for the solemnities, the Holy Father announced in the encyclical *Annum Sacrum*, dated May 25, 1899, the consecration of mankind to the Sacred Heart of Jesus as a tribute of the whole human race to Christ. The date set for the universal act of consecration was June 11, 1899. One month later the Sacred Congregation of Rites invited the extension of the practices of devotion to the Sacred Heart, especially the consecration of the month of June to the Heart of Christ by various homages of piety and by the special observance of the First Friday of each month.[428] These practices found a warm response in Nazareth spirituality and have been incorporated into its devotional calendar for the regeneration of the spirit.

Within the immediate months following the second chapter, the Foundress noted that she had not been spared the ordeals experienced by other founders and foundresses before her time and those to be relived in times to come—the grief caused by defections of members who have already traversed a long distance in the religious life.[429] Nevertheless, she invariably referred to those persons with moving compassion and charity. A sorrow of a different nature was caused by the step taken by Mother Theresa Czermińska which separated her from Nazareth when she made the authorized transfer to the Congregation of the Assumption to devote the remainder of her life in greater abnegation and contemplation.[430]

In London the outlook for Nazareth commenced to change in July,

1899, with the acceptance of the suggestion of the Reverend G. Thompson, the sisters' confessor, to take charge of the school in Bow Common, at 187 Devon Road, attended by Catholic and Protestant children alike. The Franciscan sisters who heretofore conducted the school were being withdrawn by their superiors, but two of them, Sisters Josephine and Raphaela, expressed a desire to remain in this particular apostolate and wished to become members of the Sisters of the Holy Family of Nazareth. To this Cardinal Vaughan gave approval on condition that they be required to make their novitiate in Rome. Upon their admission to the novitiate they received new religious names: Reginald[431] and Scholastica,[432] respectively.

To give fresh orientation and steady direction to the work in London, Mother Mary remained there with the sisters from July until January.[433] She entrusted the school in Bow Common to Mother Gertrude's responsibility, and appointed Mother Laurence superior at Mayfield House.[434] Father Lechert, in turn, commissioned another of his Missionaries of Divine Love, Father Ladislaus Bajerowicz, to the pastoral ministry in this area.[435]

In the midst of the affairs that absorbed her wholly in London, Mother Mary received the notice of her mother's death which occurred in the nursing home at Kowanówko in Poland, September 5, 1899, at the age of 79.[436] All through the long period of disability during which she suffered several paralytic strokes, she was well attended spiritually and physically, and was fortified by the Sacrament of the Sick while still relatively lucid. In her demise the Foundress mourned a beloved parent and a very dear religious whom she admired for the fervor of her total self-giving, although this act of hers was abruptly intercepted as a result of the illness from which she never recovered. Interment took place at the local cemetery in the vicinity of the nursing home without the participation of Mother Mary. She recommended the soul of her mother to the prayers of the community, pointing to the fact that her mother made the profession of religious vows as a Nazareth sister and that her religious name was Mary Rosalie.[437]

In France, threatening clouds were accumulating at the instigation of a government that was inimical to religion. The trial of Alfred Dreyfus unleashed violent emotions which were on the verge of erupting by either of the contending parties, anti-Semitic or anti-Catholic, regardless of outcome. Particularly relentless and subtle was the growing persecution of the Catholic Church and, at the turn of the century, religious orders were menaced by the introduction of legislation that aimed to wield them a deathblow. Apprehensive for the survival of L'Institut de Demoiselles at Rue Labat, Mother Gabriel maintained close vigilance over the fluctuations in the political climate and alerted Mother Mary of any signs of imminent crisis which should necessitate deliberate, organized action.[438]

At this time two eminent ecclesiastics demonstrated a benevolent interest in the Sisters of the Holy Family of Nazareth in Rome, Father Hyacinth M. Cormier, O.P. and Father Wilhelm M. Van Rossum, C.Ss.R., both consultors of the Holy Office, who in a staggering era of tumultuous complexity offered the expertise of their knowledge, wisdom and virtue to Mother Foundress and her sisters.[439] As the pressures of diversified activity within the Congregation gathered force, Mother Mary's attention was redirected to the idea of a house of prayer with a chapel of perpetual adoration.[440] She was enamoured of the hidden God who so utterly concealed his greatness and grandeur solely to draw mankind into the one unique relationship of love with him. Her letter to Father Lechert on this subject, penned at the advice of Father Van Rossum, is a flaming revelation of the intimate concerns, ingrained in the very fiber of her soul, for divine glory through atonement and for the infusion of the sacred into the secular.[441] Ultimately these concerns brought her face to face with the insight that each Nazareth convent should be a house of prayer in a real, pervading sense, and each convent chapel a chapel of adoration given to the veneration of the Sacramental Presence throughout the hours of the day[442] and accessible to the laity.

11 INTO THE HOUSE OF THE LORD

The assassination of Italy's King Humbert during the opening year of the twentieth century shocked the world with its inane pointlessness, but did not prevent the flow of pilgrimages from converging upon the Eternal City for the Holy Year observance. At Via Machiavelli the Nazareth guest house provided its share of hospitality to the incoming visitors. Mother Mary, having remained in Rome over the larger portion of that year, dispensed endless gracious acts of kindness in her concern for the welfare of the guests.[443]

Some of the visiting clergy and hierarchy were instrumental in crystallizing the idea that led to the establishment of a house of the Congregation in Częstochowa. A pilgrimage city in its own name, Częstochowa for centuries was the spiritual capital of Poland, drawing the hearts of the faithful to the shrine on the Bright Mountain. It was the hope and the aspiration of every Pole in the land, peasant and noble alike, to visit there —at least once in the lifetime—the basilica of Our Lady with the miraculous picture of celebrated antiquity.

Although Częstochowa was situated in Russian-dominated sector of Poland, well-intentioned friends of Nazareth periodically alerted the sisters in Paris, Cracow and Rome to the unexplored fields of service in Mary's holy city. The Fathers of St. Paul the Hermit, who staffed the monastery on the Bright Mountain, saw in the underlying spirituality of Nazareth the qualities particularly conducive to an effective apostolate, if the sisters but braved the repressive Russian edicts. Furthermore, Mother Mary received for the Congregation an estate in Częstochowa which was inherited jointly by Sisters Kunegunda[444] and Maria-Josepha,[445] and their brother, Msgr. Peter Waskiewicz, for the explicit purpose of opening a boarding school. The estate included a handsome residence with a spacious garden, located at the proverbial stone's throw from the shrine. The income accruing from the Waśkiewicz family investments was destined to provide for the school's support and maintenance. One precautionary measure was requisite, namely, secular apparel would have to be worn by the sisters until such time as a change in the political situation should render this practice unnecessary.

There were likewise other encouraging voices that could not be ignored. Consequently, Mother Joanne was delegated by the Foundress to proceed to Częstochowa and evaluate at close range the immediate possibilities.[446] For three months she took up residence with the Waśkiewicz sisters in their family homestead where she sought to determine a feasible mode of operation that would carry appreciable advantages.[447] At length, in 1902, the convent under the title of the Patronage of St. Joseph came into being and Sister Kunegunda became its first superior.

Its object could initially be realized as a workshop of handicrafts in embroidery and liturgical vestments, opening to needy young women an opportunity to engage in remunerative employment. Simultaneously they were able to pursue basic courses in religion, church history, mathematics, and other practical subjects taught by the sisters.

In the American province the inscrutable ways of Divine Providence signalled to a new undertaking. The sisters' rest home in Emsworth, Pennsylvania, was suddenly transformed into an orphanage when, September 1, 1900, Father Caesar Tomaszewski, C.S.Sp. brought to them three small children who had lost both parents in a fire; few days later two little orphan sisters were accepted. As the number of children needing shelter and care increased unpredictably, a nearby building was acquired to meet the growing demands. The influx in this highly industrialized area was occasioned largely by occupational hazards to which the fathers of families were exposed. In general, many lives of young parents were lost due to the lack of protective safety regulations and to inadequate enforcement of public health ordinances. The eighth of September went on record as the date of inception of the Holy Family Orphan Asylum, as it was originally called; later the name was changed to Holy Family Orphanage, and in more recent times, in line with other developments, it became known as Holy Family Institute. Sister M. Leontine was appointed the first superior.[448]

In Chicago, the hospital project was gaining momentum. Once the uncertainties and delays over title and credit were removed, a vacant square block near the western city limits was selected as the building site in view of a promising locality shift.[449] Cost estimates were carefully prepared and architectural plans were designed under competent advice with the open approval of Archbishop Feehan and upheld by Mother Mary's confident hope.[450] Accompanied by the architect, Mother Lauretta visited several prominent hospitals in New York and, later, St. Mary's Hospital in Rochester, Minnesota. Before the onset of winter, excavations were completed, tying in with the construction plans which were to be set in motion early in the spring of 1901.[451]

Meanwhile the sisters in London struggled against the problems of bias and distrust peculiar to the milieu within which they labored. Moved by the difficulties of their predicament, Mother Mary went to them in October, 1900, to build up their morale in the interest of general good. She decided to transfer Mother Gertrude to the motherhouse in Rome and placed the energetic and astute Mother Frances in charge at Bow Common.[452] The exchange took place in the first days of 1901, although the Foundress had gone to France before then, in November, to make timely dispositions in the face of rising intransigence against religious orders.[453] The French government did not favor the religious, looked askance at them, and sought to annihilate them.

After almost ten years of service to a discriminating segment of the population in Paris, the school and student residence attained an honorable reputation which spread even beyond the boundaries of France. It is noteworthy that during the crucial period when the fate of religious orders was in the balance, the Institute at Rue Labat had among its residents a gifted young pianist, Bella Marcinkowska, a protégé of Ignace J. Paderewski, whose studies in the French language he financed.[454]

The decree of July 1, 1901, abolishing the orders which were not authorized by civil law, has not found Mother Mary unprepared.[455] To avoid possible expulsion and the confiscation of property, the ownership of the Institute was transferred to the name of one of the teachers who was willing to conduct it for the Congregation until the political atmosphere should become more favorable. The sisters who were not of French origin were withdrawn and replaced by those of French nationality. Thus it was that Mother Gabriel returned to Rome, January 23, 1901, and Sister M. Redempta replaced her as the superior;[456] the sisters who remained in France adopted secular dress for the duration of the emergency.[457]

With the controversy about religion at its peak, simple survival dictated that Father Lechert relocate his Missionaries of Divine Love in a circumspect move. Fifteen members were accommodated in Rome, leaving the house in Sèvres in the custody of two brothers.[458]

While the clouds of skepticism and unrest were gathering over France, the announcement of Queen Victoria's death, January 22, 1901, was broadcast across the English Channel. Historically, it terminated that eventful era associated with her long and prosperous reign which produced a nation infinitely certain of itself and of its purpose in the world.

Mother Mary's return to Rome in March that year marked the close of her travels. She concentrated intensively on the evolving aspects of the Congregation in the world, analyzing the adaptability of the Nazareth way of life in the emerging phases of apostolic activity.[459] Besides the intimate, direct, and time-consuming attention with which she treated individual matters that claimed her interest, once again she plunged into a meticulous review of the Constitutions.

The Apostolic Letter of Pope Leo, *Conditae a Christo*, promulgated December 8, 1900, was a call to religious communities to promote by their rules the harmony and order which must prevail in every respectable society. The rise of many new communities with specific new objectives made it mandatory to establish and define the basic common principles requisite for the canonical status of religious life. A set of precise norms supplemented the Apostolic Letter to guide the communities in revising their existing constitutions or framing new ones.

Reports from the United States exposed a ruck of vexing events that surrounded the hospital building project, but there were also brisk over-tones of progress and popular enthusiasm quite evidently generated by Mother Lauretta's studied determination and tact. Actual construction was begun, March 9, 1901,[460] and the ceremonial laying of the cornerstone was scheduled for June 16.[461] For this occasion Mother Mary secured the papal blessing in writing, which she forwarded with her own ex-pressions of heartwarming wishes for the sisters, patients and benefactors of all times.[462] In genuine accord with the undertaking, Father Lechert extended his message likewise.

A month later, he set forth on the *Gascogne* for the American shores[463] to devote three indefatigable months to the visitation of all Nazareth con-vents, incorporating in his program the direction of annual retreat sessions wherever they were planned and making himself available in special situa-tions where his intervention was desirable or necessary.[464] He had ob-tained the willing consent of Father Van Rossum to attend to the spiritual needs of his own community in the interim.[465]

Effective at this time in the United States were several transfers and appointments oriented to the human reality of Nazareth's state of affairs. Of these, three concerned the institutions of the Congregation, namely, Holy Family Academy received Mother Stanislaus for its superior-prin-cipal; the orphanage at Emsworth, open to the rapidly unfolding needs of society, was committed to Mother Sophia's prudent management as supe-rior-director; and the challenges of the hospital in Chicago fell to the enterprising spirit of Sister M. Donata,[466] who for nine years directed its course as the superior-administrator.

Before sailing back to Europe, October 10, 1901,[467] Father Lechert experienced the American national tragedy of President William McKin-ley's assassination by an anarchist and witnessed the nation's days of prayer and mourning proclaimed by Vice President Theodore Roosevelt. Upon his arrival in Rome, pressing matters awaited him. For as early as April of that year, Bishop Domenico Ambrosi of Terracina, through his secre-tary, Canon Guiseppe di Girolamo, had been in the process of negotiating an arrangement whereby the Missionaries of Divine Love would take charge of one of the churches in his ancient seaport diocese.

When Count Alessandro Antonelli intervened with an offer of a resi-dence in Terracina, as his gift to the Missionaries, the community's groping for a foothold ceased in the bright hope of stability. Situated fifty-six miles southeast of Rome along the Tyrrhenean coast, the exuberant district held abundant opportunities for zeal and good works.[468] As soon as it became practicable to liquidate the household at Via Alfieri, a small inexpensive apartment was acquired at 219 Via Merulana for the convenience of the members of Father Lechert's community when they were in Rome.

By January of 1902, Mayfield House in London reached the point of diminishing returns. Near-heroic efforts to house and care for forty-eight waifs, although subsidized by Mother Mary and Cardinal Vaughan, failed to arouse comparable support from the public, and the undertaking had to be discontinued.[469] In Bow Common again, under woeful conditions of neglect and indifference, the sisters contended in vain against progressive hostility to elevate the standards of the school. But Mother Frances, the superior at Bow Common, unwilling to see the collapse of Nazareth mission work in England, was receptive to the proposal of Reverend A. O'Gorman to come to Enfield, a suburb of London. Within the confines of his parish, a city school was being established which could be conducted by the sisters who possessed the required qualifications.

Furthermore, a private finishing school for Catholic girls was in the offing. As a unit distinct from the city school, it was to occupy a section of the convent building, where instructions would be offered in fine arts, languages, and religion. Upon thorough investigation, the plan was approved by the Cardinal and accepted by Mother Foundress together with the withdrawal of the sisters from Bow Common.

At the trimester beginning May 1, 1902, the sisters commenced teaching in Enfield, but temporarily resided at Mayfield House and commuted daily. In September their Enfield convent, The Holmwood at Bycullah Road, under the patronage of the Holy Family, was ready for occupancy.[470] After Mother Mary, who planted the Nazareth ideal of life and service upon British soil, the one person who for years nurtured it with persevering faith and courage was Mother Frances Morgenstern. The teaching apostolate in England waxed strong and continued to flourish unimpeded despite subsequent wartime difficulties and under stringent regulatory measures in peacetime.

In Chicago, the building operations of the hospital, which was now renamed St. Mary of Nazareth,[471] approached successful completion. Although the plans had been carefully scrutinized and approved, Mother Lauretta occasionally registered qualms which, in turn, Mother Mary pacified in her unique understanding manner, "Why do you fear that I should find the hospital too imposing, too large? I know well enough that it would have been impractical to construct a smaller building at this time. I trust you have a sufficient number of sisters to staff it, and may their work in the spirit of sacrifice and dedication glorify God."[472]

The patients were moved to the new hospital, March 18, 1902,[473] and the following day, the feast of St. Joseph, Holy Sacrifice of the Mass was celebrated there for the first time. Instantly the number of patients increased from day to day; the free dispensary, too, was actively patronized by ambulatory patients in need of advice, medication or dressings.[474] The solemn public dedication of the hospital, May 25, 1902, was performed by Archbishop Feehan with the participation of the clergy and the leading civic groups.[475] Into the vacated premises of the original hospital, refurbished and rearranged, the novitiate was transferred from the academy building, thereby gaining space, privacy and a hedged in garden plot.[476]

Absorbed in matters essential to the holiness of the vowed life and to the Congregation's mission of word and charity, the perceptive Foundress secured from Cardinal Protector Parocchi his approval of Father Cormier, as his delegate, to oversee the aligning of the Constitutions with the recently issued precepts.[477] For not only was Father Lechert engaged in Terracina and could scarcely afford frequent visits to Rome, but his relationship to the Sisters of the Holy Family of Nazareth had undergone a change under the new norms, since the norms prohibited founders of newly established male congregations from serving in the capacity of directors to newly founded congregations of women.

Mother Mary and Father Lechert, in the nobility of their souls, bowed in compliance to the requirement as behooved those who exist under the aspect of eternity. Father Lechert, in fact, viewed with satisfaction the saintly Dominican's unquestionable influence for good in Nazareth's forward course.[478] Nonetheless Mother Mary's esteem for Father Lechert has never waned, as she expressed it simply in one of her latest letters to him:

> I am confident that this little Nazareth shall never depart from the path you had outlined, that it shall always hold in grateful memory what you imparted to it, and shall cherish what our Divine Lord accomplished for it through you and what he will continue to do because of you.[479]

On occasion Mother Mary intimated that she was called to implant the spirit proper to the Congregation and to communicate to its members a corresponding interior life, whereas Divine Providence would summon others after her to the task of perfecting the externals of community life and polity.[480] She had parceled out her message in untechnical terms, allowing the seed to germinate and mature in time, confirmed in the faith that through stages of inner growth it will reach the full stature of spiritual development in the souls.

Father Cormier lent his excellent gifts of learning and experience to advance the work of which he was thoroughly convinced as having intrinsic value.[481] Approaching it with his customary method of respect for freedom and discretion, he recommended the collaboration of several sisters who, by virtue of personal contact with the problems of life and service over the years, had acquired direct knowledge of the varied structures of society to which they had to relate responsibly as religious.[482] When in June the advisory core group at Rome was joined by Mothers Lauretta, Laurence and Paula with several representatives, they entered upon the epic study and appraisal of the constitutional revisions proposed by Father Cormier. In thirteen lengthy sessions the groundwork was laid for the special general chapter which convened promptly on July 16 and at which Father Cormier presided. Heedless of the midsummer climate, the chapter extended into sixteen plenary sessions and closed on August 26, 1902.

Along with the adaptations introduced in deference to the promulgated norms, the position of the Carmelite, Mother Joseph-Teresa, had to be subjected to practical scrutiny. For nearly twelve years she had annually conveyed in writing her pledge of loyalty to the Carmelite superior general, but upon consultation he gave his considered opinion indicating that her return to the Carmelite rule of life was a foregone issue and advised her to apply for formal admission to Nazareth. Mother Joseph-Teresa accepted the counsel with good grace and, on August 28, filed a petition to the Holy See for an indult of adjustment in her canonical status.

With the election of new members to the general administration, the policy was charted obliging them to reside at the motherhouse for reasons of availability to the superior general in sharing the service of authority through assistance and advice. The new constituents were Mother Raphael, assistant general; Mothers Joanne, Joseph-Teresa and Gertrude, Councilors; Mother Bernarda, secretary; Sister Antonia, treasurer. Mother Raphael's position in Cracow was to be filled by Mother Gabriel.

In the midst of its deliberations the assembly was astounded by the circulating news of the martyrdom, on July 6, of teenage Marietta Goretti who gave her life in defense of purity at the seaside village near Nettuno. Later in the month, transatlantic communications reported the lamented death of Archbishop Feehan of Chicago, a beloved and revered shepherd, a leader of great ability, and a man of prayer and of peace.[483]

On another note, Mother Lauretta was informed of the urgent request, directed to Mother Sophia by Father A. Zubowicz, C.S.C., to take charge of St. Casimir's parochial school in South Bend, Indiana, in replacement of a mixed group of lay teachers who had conducted the school for three previous years. Responsive to the mission goals in American Catholicism to be attained through education, Mother Lauretta was returning to the United States early in September gratified in the knowledge that the preliminaries had been bridged; the first superior-principal appointed for South Bend was Sister M. Celestine, and the school convent was to bear the title of Our Lady of the Rosary.

On the other hand, Paris that summer witnessed harrowing scenes of forcible dissolution and dispossession of religious establishments under the violent application of the Law of Associations. With the closing of the school term in June, 1902, the sisters withdrew from Rue Labat for fear of possible recognition and repressions, their disguise notwithstanding. They moved into a remote part of the city, where their identity as religious was entirely unknown and, in October, opened a private day school at Rue St. Dominique.[484]

As soon as Mother Mary was assured of the safe return of all the chapter participants to their respective destinations, she retired to the Benedictine monastery in Subiaco for a retreat of three weeks, September 24 to October 15, 1902. By special exemption she was admitted into the pontifical enclosure of the nuns, joining them in choir and community,[485] and returned thereafter to Via Machiavelli with refreshed spiritual vigor and renewed vitality of interest. The prepartion of manuscripts of the revised Constitutions, however, was as yet temporarily held in abeyance. Father Cormier desired to examine again the amended provisions and to verify their validity and practicality before presenting the document to the Holy See.[486] He warned against hasty action, lest changes should be found necessary after the revised text had been submitted for approval.[487]

November 12 marked the sixtieth birthday for Mother Mary, a day which she passed without drawing particular attention, except for the time she gave to more contemplation and prayer. She surprised the novices by advancing their annual festival to the following day, when the Church honors St. Stanislaus Kostka, a Jesuit novice of extraordinary fervor— instead of observing the holiday on November 21 as in former years. Her presence in the novitiate brought to the young religious hours of unforgettable charm and joy, touched by flashes of spontaneous humor that usually enlivened the periods of recreation whenever she attended them.

In the evening Mother Mary experienced a feeling of general malaise with a slight elevation in temperature. The day after, on the fourteenth, when the sisters gathered in her room, she addressed her last conference to them on the theme that always lay at the root of her concerns, charity. "Nazareth," she emphasized, "and lack of charity can have nothing in common." As symptoms of her illness grew more pronounced, the gravity of her condition became apparent, but medical treatment proved ineffective. Quite unexpectedly, on the nineteenth, the hopes of the community were buoyed by a semblance of an improvement, when her mounting fever and intermittent chills subsided abruptly.

But the consulting physicians were agreed upon the diagnosis of acute general peritonitis and recommended an immediate surgical procedure,[488] "similar to the one performed upon the King of England."[489] When

Edward VII, at the age of sixty, was to succeed his mother, Queen Victoria, to the throne, his coronation had to be delayed due to a sudden attack of appendicitis;[490] whereupon an emergency operation was successfully performed,[491] followed by his complete recovery. In her case, though, Mother Mary believed that surgery would be futile, and she was reconciled to inevitable death.[492]

The visits of Fathers Lechert, Cormier and Van Rossum, who spent lingering hours in the convent chapel, brought her moral support and the sustenance of sacramental grace. She took an affectionate leave of the sisters as they approached her bedside individually. On the morning of November 21, the Holy Father sent his special blessing to her for the hour of death, and later in the day Cardinal Parocchi arrived to bestow his blessing. On noticing the sisters' grief, the Cardinal suggested to Mother Mary to ask God for the recovery of her health. With a clear recognition of the divine will for her now as ever, she replied, "Your Eminence, God is already calling me." Other dignitaries also came to convey their devout commendations.

Willingly and knowingly she was leaving to the Providence of God two hundred and ninety-one professed sisters on both sides of the Atlantic, and a total of seventy-two youthful novices and postulants who would find in Nazareth their incentives to scale the heights she had envisioned; she was relinquishing without misgivings twenty-nine houses of Nazareth, centers of apostolic services in Europe and the United States. Death occurred peacefully at three o'clock in the afteroon in the presence of her praying sisters and the three spiritual directors. Her last audible words were an affirmation of implicit confidence and faith, "In domum Domini ibimus,"[493] for in the house of the Lord she would be reunited with the nineteen sisters who had embraced the Nazareth way and preceded her into eternity.

The news of Mother Mary's death spread quickly through Rome, attracting many persons, otherwise unknown at the convent, who arrived to pray at her bier and to recommend their needs to her intercession. The liturgical burial services were conducted on Monday, November 24, and the remains of the saintly Foundress were laid to rest in the tomb at the Roman cemetery of Campo Verano.

Telegraphic dispatches immediately announced to the Congregation everywhere the crushing loss it suffered in the death of its Foundress. The mourning was shared in poignant sincerity by vast numbers of the clergy and laity who deemed it a privilege to have known Mother Mary in life. The most significant tributes were the countless memorial Masses offered for the repose of her soul.

By protocol, Mother Raphael, as the assistant general, should have assumed the functions of the vicar general, but having failed since her election to arrive at the motherhouse to date, the choice of the vicar general remained to be resolved among the other members of the general council who were then present. There was a kind of reverent reluctance on their part, constraining them from taking upon themselves a responsibility that was in a way reminiscent of Mother Mary. Because over the years only Mother Gertrude has had minimal personal association with Mother Foundress, and was perhaps better equipped psychologically to meet the demands of the moment, she was asked to discharge the duties of the vicar general until the election of the superior general. Father Lechert and Father Cormier alike concurred in this move, and the special electoral chapter was convoked to assemble on February 3, 1903.

III

Age of Growth
1902-1942

1 TO BEAR FRUIT IN PATIENCE

The death of Mother Mary laid a pall of sadness upon Nazareth's motherhouse, the convent of the Good Shepherd, while an undercurrent of apprehension and anxiety for the future spread through the Congregation. The sense of loss increased vastly when on January 15, 1903 Cardinal Protector Parocchi also died. Meanwhile Fathers Cormier and Van Rossum visited the Roman convent frequently to offer to the sisters their counsel and encouragement out of the regard in which they held the deceased Foundress and whose unique charisma they openly acknowledged.

Nonetheless, when the capitulants began to assemble for the electoral chapter, there was a lack of the usual easy spontaneity in their approach, which was characteristic of former arrivals at the motherhouse. Drawn by filial piety, they lingered in the third-floor room, formerly used by Mother Mary and in which she died, yet the onus of their present responsibility weighed heavily upon them.

The fifteen sisters who were authorized to participate in the elections included the general administration and the representatives from the United States, Poland, France and England; of these Mother Raphael did not find it possible to attend. Three days of recollection and prayer preceded the opening date of the chapter, February 3. The recently appointed Cardinal Vicar of Rome, Pietro Cardinal Respighi, presided at the elections and was assisted by Father Van Rossum.

According to the Constitutions then effective, two-thirds majority was required for the election of the superior general. After the votes were cast three times and have not yielded the required majority, the Cardinal decided to present the record of the elections to the Sovereign Pontiff. Ten days later Father Cormier, delegated by Cardinal Respighi, informed the capitulants of the Holy Father's decision to postpone the selection of the superior general to a later date and recommended that all who had arrived from out of Italy should return to their respective countries, except Mother Lauretta who was to remain until further notice.

About this time the Eternal City was again to witness Christendom's manifestation of honor and esteem for Leo XIII in the solemn observance of his twenty-fifth anniversary of election to the Chair of Peter on February 20. Finally, on March 28, 1903, Father Cormier was the bearer of the decree of the Holy See,[1] processed by the Sacred Congregation of Bishops and Regulars, by virtue of which Mother Lauretta was granted all the rights and powers of the superior general. The decree, signed by Dominic Cardinal Ferrata, prefect, and Philip Giustini, secretary, carried the official text:

Following the death of Mother Mary Frances, foundress and superior general of the Institute known as the Sisters of the Holy Family of

Nazareth, the Sacred Congregation of Bishops and Regulars, concerned lest this Institute suffer any impairment in its vigor, has taken under consideration the particular circumstances of the present moment. To provide continuing adequate administration of this religious family, Mother Mary Lauretta is by the terms of the present decree delegated and appointed by the Holy See as the Vicar General of said Institute and is entitled to all the faculties, privileges and rights to which superiors general of said Institute are eligible. Moreover, the above mentioned Sacred Congregation directs all the sisters of this Institute, regardless of rank, position or seniority, to recognize Mother Mary Lauretta as the Vicar General and to render her the reverence and obedience due her office.[2]

When a copy of the decree, accompanied by Father Cormier's letter explaining the juridical prescriptions, reached the houses of the Congregation, the decision was received with an optimistic outlook. The intervention of the Holy See was welcomed with enthusiasm, for it terminated what appeared a virtually insoluble situation. Mother Raphael was among the first to respond in a cordial letter written to Mother Lauretta, pledging fidelity and cooperation.[3]

At the time when the responsibility for the direction of the Congregation devolved upon Mother Lauretta, she was 41 years of age. She came to the task with a background of authentic experience acquired during her remarkably successful fourteen years' tenure as provincial superior in the United States. On her previous visits to Rome, Fathers Cormier and Van Rossum noted that she was naturally endowed with executive ability and with the gifts of heart and mind necessary for leadership and guidance. Above all, she assimilated the inspiration of Mother Mary and made it her rule of life. With convincing singlemindedness she henceforth dedicated her efforts to cultivating the spiritual legacy of the Foundress as a thriving reality in the sisters' personal encounters with God and in their communal relationships, as well as in the quality of their apostolic services.[4]

Soon after the acceptance of her appointment, Mother Lauretta withdrew for several days to the Benedictine monastery in Subiaco to clarify her perspectives in reflection and prayer. One of her first acts afterward was to secure for Nazareth, early in May that year, the official protectorate of Cardinal Respighi, who succeeded Cardinal Parocchi in this capacity. The new Cardinal Protector was quick to discover the assets inherent in the Congregation whose Foundress had so aptly read the signs of the times and translated them into a dynamic life style of ecclesial dimensions.

The second major step undertaken was to complete the editing of the Constitutions as they were drawn up after the revisions adopted by the chapter of 1902. Sister M. Norbert Sliwińska, who operated the small printing press at Holy Family Academy in Chicago, processed the copies of this edition for distribution to the sisters for their individual use. The experimental period allowed for adaptation and appraisal was expected to give palpable indications for future adjustments in the articles of the Constitutions.

By June 27 Mother Lauretta was ready to begin her first canonical visitation, when she left Rome for England in the company of Mother Gertrude. Immediately she gave her full attention to the promising work of the sisters in Enfield. Subsequently she found that the services of the Mayfield House convent have become superfluous in view of London's changing social scene. The convent was closed, the sisters were reassigned to other posts, and the superior, Sister Rose, returned to the United States during the month of July, having accompanied the Vicar General on the transatlantic voyage.

The news of Leo XIII's death reached them belatedly, for on July 20 he had departed this life. It is noteworthy that his public genius, as an advocate of Christian principles to all mankind, was followed by the holiness of Pius X, the Pope of religious living in the purest sense. In his first encyclical, *E Supremi,* Pius set forth the one purpose of his pontificate: "to restore all things in Christ."

Mother Lauretta's five-month sojourn in the American province was occupied in dealing with unfinished matters during the period of transition.

When she paid her respects to Archbishop James E. Quigley, recently installed to the see of Chicago, he recalled the hospitality he had enjoyed at the motherhouse in Rome in 1900, where, as Bishop of Buffalo, he celebrated Mass in the sisters' chapel.[5] As a gesture of magnanimity he now donated to the Congregation 56 acres of land in the suburb of Des Plaines[6] for the building of an adequate central house of the province and for the accommodation of the novitiate. Although it was not possible to carry out his intention at once, the Archbishop's provident gift, in fact, soon became the site upon which the necessary convent was erected.

The office of the provincial superior, vacated by Mother Lauretta, was entrusted to Mother Sophia, who until then was the superior-director at Holy Family Institute, Emsworth, Pennsylvania. To strengthen and safeguard the new provincial's position in the face of civil law, Mother Lauretta conveyed to her the power of attorney couched in a formal document.[7] Then, at the opening of the school term, she saw Nazareth branch out into two additional parochial locations: in Chicago, the school and convent under the patronage of St. Ann, and in Pittsburgh, the school and convent under the patronage of the Holy Family.

Once the needs arising from these situations were regulated and the annual review of personnel assignments accomplished, Mother Lauretta concentrated on a searching exploration of the total American mission. At this juncture the fate of Holy Family Institute in Emsworth had to be ascertained. It had been accorded legal standing under a charter of incorporation issued to the Sisters of the Holy Family of Nazareth, May 29, 1903. But, with the growing volume of petitions for the placement of children, the public urged an expansion program in land and buildings which, she found, exceeded the financial possibilities of the Congregation. To remove this obstacle, the Vicar General consented to a daringly uncommon reorganization of the corporation, whereby interested laity of the surrounding community might be admitted to its membership and vote.[8] Father Caesar Tomaszewski, C.S.Sp., was thereupon elected to the position of superintendent of the Institute, while the sisters retained direct management functions and the care of the children.

In December, 1903, she sailed for Europe, conscious that the world atmosphere was charged with excitement and expectancy for the outcome of the flying experiment, staged in North Carolina by the Wright brothers, Wilbur and Orville. Wrestling with a stiff wind that whipped flurries of sand across the field, they succeeded to raise their airplane in full flight. The epochal achievement was received with mixed reaction. The Cincinnati *Enquirer* gave it a front-page coverage with flaming headlines; other publications mitigated their fervor; some bypassed the enterprise with awkward silence.[9] Whatever the reaction, the twentieth century was heralding an age of change and of striking technological innovations.

The accelerated tempo of the new age imposed unavoidable demands. Like Paul of Tarsus in his evangelizing journeyings, the Vicar General became a veritable pilgrim for the cause she represented. Twice in 1904, in January and September, she went to Poland, and each stay involved her in helping to overcome the economic and political problems peculiar to the settings in which particular houses existed. In fact, she made it a practice to visit regularly, in alternate years, the sisters in the United States and in Europe until the outbreak of the First World War restricted her movements.

To her satisfaction the municipal hospital in Wadowice prospered and gained in reputation and prestige under Sister Irene's capable management. Frequent, unannounced inspections by board of health commissioners repeatedly confirmed its high rating.[10]

In the same city, the House of Providence showed the need for more extensive accommodations, were it to properly care for the orphaned children whose number was constantly increasing. There were no public funds available for their maintenance and education, so, for the support of this work, the sisters relied upon private charity and other sources, such as Bishop Anatole Nowak's pledged monthly subsidy, periodic appeals to society at large, the sale of handicrafts and needlework, and occasional benefit performances. When in 1907 a commodious building was erected to house the children,[11] the Austrian Emperor Francis Joseph I established an endowment fund, the income from which supplemented the institution's resources.

Knowledge of the sisters' hidden undertaking in Częstochowa was spreading discreetly among sympathetic individuals. It led them to present to the sisters yet another part of the spectrum of life. In the shadows of the miraculous shrine of Our Lady, a shelter had been contrived for the aged and homeless who hovered about the hill. Some had traveled from distant places with group pilgrimages and chose to remain; others, miserably solitary, simply lingered on the fringe of existence. A local benevolent society supervised the shelter and supplied the material necessities, but wished the sisters to provide a draught of fresh hope to the derelicts. In the course of daily visits and encouraging friendly conversation, the sisters first buoyed their awareness of the brotherhood of man and of their own human dignity, then steered them to the paths of interior peace and ultimately assisted them in crossing the threshold of eternity.[12]

The early years of Mother Lauretta's tenure marked the entry of the Congregation into other regions in Poland which were under Russian domination. In spite of recurring political complications, the sisters accepted the challenges of the remote northeastern frontier when, at the invitation of the prominent citizens of Vilna, they planted there the kernel of their zeal in 1906. Inconspicuously housed in the mansion of Madame Maria Jeleńska, they organized a thorough program for teacher education under the cover of a manual training school. Catholic young women who aspired to elevate the cultural standards of rural schools in the country were eager for opportunities where they could acquire sound pedagogical preparation with a strong foundation in religion and patriotic indoctrination.[13]

In this sector of occupied Poland strict Russian policies controlled all institutes of learning; schools of trades and crafts alone were allowed to be conducted by the Poles. It was of the essence of Nazareth's apostolate just then to be both visible and invisibly committed, to engage externally in utilitarian endeavors and to remain devoted to the sacred ideologies of faith and patriotism. Apart from the inconvenience of its catacomb-like existence, the school afforded decided advantages to the students. When they passed the rigid qualifying examinations, they were able not only to contribute invaluable service as rural teachers, but also taught household skills to women and girls, especially the weaving of cloth, knitwear and rug-making which they themselves had learned.

In Częstochowa again, through the generosity of Monsignor Peter Waśkiewicz, an attractive corner property was purchased in 1907, in the residential part of the city at 19 Ulica Dąbrowskiego, and given to the sisters for a school. The population here enjoyed a temporary reprieve from the prohibitions affecting the conduct of schools and the freedom of worship. Religious orders, however, still suffered under the stigma of suspicion ascribing to them anti-Russian conspiracy and could not appear openly under any circumstances. Being in possession of recognized professional certificates, the sisters soon gained a large enrollment of students, but they did not escape the furtive curiosity of informers. When the occupation forces revoked all permits for private chapels, a wave of raids and persecutions was at once set in motion. The sisters submitted with quiet grief to the unreasonable ruling, dismantled the chapel furnishings and the altar, but stood firm in the performance of their duty as they saw it, even at the risk of being denounced.[14]

Archbishop Edward Ropp, whose episcopal jurisdiction encompassed the eastern outposts of Poland, offered to the Sisters of the Holy Family of Nazareth, in 1908, the vacated Bridgettine monastery in Grodno. But one of the Bridgettine professed nuns, Sister Scholastica, was still there and remained with the Nazareth group of sisters until her death in 1919. There were also two Bridgettine postulants; one of them transferred to Nazareth and took the name of Sister Cornelia, while the other, a proficient music teacher, stayed on as a convent affiliate.

The nature of the sisters' involvement in this as in other territories under Russian rule called for the sacrifice that obliged them to conceal their identity. They had to devise ways by which they might reach the youth of this area without incurring political censures, since the severity of regional authorities precluded all plans for formal education. Although the inhabitants here were of divers persuasions: Roman Catholic, Eastern-rite Catholic, and Eastern Orthodox or schismatic, there was no delay in discovering cooperative and willing persons through whom safe contacts could be made. Too many of them had already been exposed to the pressures and threats in schismatic proselytizing as a tactic of forcible russification.

Now the peaceable, unassuming presence of the sisters generated a sobering influence. Daughters of the gentry from outlying districts were recommended to them for residence while attending Russian schools away from home. Other avenues of association opened to them through membership in the sodality of Our Lady, the young people's choir, and the incidental tutorships.

In France, the difficulties of the sisters have not at all been alleviated during the first decade of the century. As a matter of fact, the conditions became aggravated when diplomatic relations between the French government and the Vatican were severed. For security purposes, Sister Redempta and her staff of sisters transferred as lay teachers, in 1906, to a diocesan school in the district of Gentilly, at 58 Avenue Raspail.

In England, on the other hand, the attempt at starting a private boarding school in Enfield was amply justified by the steady increase of students. In the progress report of 1907, Mother Frances gave pressing reasons for moving to larger, better suited quarters in a contemporary homestead, the Juglans Lodge, situated at 52 London Road. The purchase price of the Lodge was absorbed by the liberal bequest which at this time fell to Mother Frances upon her father's death.

With the shifting character of London's East End, Father Lechert's mission activities were discontinued by the sheer force of circumstances. He relinquished the administration of the church to the Assumptionist Fathers and concentrated on the religious formation of the priests, brothers, clerics and novices of his congregation. Not unlike all beginners, ordained priests, who were attracted by the missionary spiritually he propagated, also underwent a period of novitiate at Terracina. In the year 1904, the Missionaries of Divine Love came to the United States and were accepted by Bishop Michael J. Hoban to the diocese of Scranton.

Following a meeting with Francesco Cardinal Satolli, former Apostolic Delegate to the United States, together with James Cardinal Gibbons, Archbishop of Baltimore, and Bishop Denis J. O'Connell, Rector of the Catholic University of America, Father Lechert took to the idea of founding a scholasticate for his members and other likely applicants in affiliation with the Catholic University. A temporarily acquired building for the scholasticate in Washington was to have been superseded in the near future by a nobly conceived St. John Cantius College.[15] Over the years this plan failed to rise above initial steps, not because it lacked in perspective but dimension—the material dimension of capital.[16]

Uncomplainingly Father Lechert shared his time and energy between his duties in Europe and the obligations assumed in the United States.[17] On both hemispheres his relations with the sisters remained cordial as ever, and his visits, though infrequent, were regarded by them no less than a marvelous favor.[18] The memory of Mother Mary's exceptional personality knit an imperishable bond among them, which Father Lechert extended likewise to Fathers Cormier and Van Rossum in the fraternal courtesies of men of God.[19]

In 1908 word came to Nazareth's general council in Rome about an emerging social situation in Vienna for which a core group of sisters was urgently requested. In a colony of migrant workers, consolidating into a more or less permanent settlement, there was a distinct need for a school, a home for orphaned and dependent children, and a student residence for adolescent girls. Princess Maria Lubomirska, chairman of St. Vincent de Paul Society, and her two daughters, on fire for the welfare of the disadvantaged, appealed to the Christian sensibilities of Viennese friends to finance the project through a joint voluntary endeavor. The settlement, moderated by the Resurrectionist Fathers, who provided the spiritual care and liturgical services, unfolded into an active mission center.[20]

Present in Mother Lauretta's memory was the wish of the Foundress which was now revived by the gift of land that the Congregation had received from the Archbishop of Chicago in 1903. More than once Mother Mary had said, "I should like to see the novitiate moved away from the disturbances and hubbub of the city to enable the novices to acquire the spirit of the Holy Family of Nazareth in the reflective atmosphere of peace, prayer and work."[21] Although, in truth, the introductory period of the aspiring religious is brief, it does allow the individual sufficient amount of time to experience uncertainty, to strain through some soul-searching and to mature her character while evaluating life's priorities and her own potentials. It facilitates a view of life not centered on, or restricted by, the time-consuming task of striving after formal education or other temporal ends.

Simultaneously Mother Lauretta's thoughts ran along parallel lines relative to the Roman novitiate, housed at the convent of the Good Shepherd. This Mother Mary had desired to be the central novitiate for the formation of young members selected from the entire Congregation. Since multiple activities at the motherhouse began to impinge upon one another in the course of their operation, the manifest purpose of the novitiate had to be safeguarded by providing separate premises. In the Apennine foothills of Albano there was a wooded suburban villa with an existing building that answered the purpose admirably.[22] On May 26, 1906, twenty novices with Mother Joseph-Teresa and the assistant director, Sister M. Victorine Podgórska, departed from Via Machiavelli to be installed at Villa San Giuseppe, as the property was then named.

For the building in Des Plaines Mother Lauretta discussed the architectural designs with competent advisers before executing a contract. The construction of the American novitiate, in combination with the seat of the province, was completed in 1908. Anticipating the relocation of the novices, the general plans first called for their return, as early as December, 1904, to the convent of St. Joseph from the original hospital quarters at Division and Paulina Streets. By May of 1905, these quarters became converted into Holy Family Working Girls' Home, where unattached young women found friendliness and warmth, reminiscent of the candor of family environment.

On March 8, 1908, a group of twenty-two novices, accompanied by Sister M. Lucille Bielecka, their director, and Sister M. Domicille Wiśniewska, assistant director, were led by Mother Lauretta into the long-awaited new convent, filling it with an air of happiness and ease as they disappeared into its welcoming halls and dormitories. The ceremonial dedication was set for the following day, March 9, in deference to Mother Mary's baptismal patron, St. Frances of Rome, whom she venerated all her life. Archbishop Quigley reserved for himself the liturgical functions of the day and the formal opening of the novitiate.[23]

After the novices moved to Des Plaines, the working girls were transferred to the former novitiate area of St. Joseph's convent and the property at Division and Paulina was sold. Gradually, as life situations changed, the number of residents decreased and the project in behalf of the working girls was allowed to phase out.

In June of 1908, the Chicago sisters at the Holy Spirit convent in St. Michael's parish experienced the joy and honor which fell to the lot of the parish upon the elevation of its pastor, the Reverend Paul P. Rhode, to the episcopal dignity as Auxiliary Bishop of Chicago. Invariably the life of a particular parish drew upon the capacity and sacrifices of local sisters and in a sense enveloped them in the grandeur of great issues and in the tedium of petty ones. Remaining true to their code, they preferred to accentuate intentionally their role behind the scenes, for it was of not so much importance to them to have their deeds proclaimed to the world as to know that they have served its human needs wherever they happened to be.

In general, the following year, 1909, may not have been extraordinary in certain aspects of human endeavor. Child labor was still practiced here and there. Diseases were not under control. Anarchists threw bombs. Labor unions were looked upon as necessary evil. Women were not allowed to vote. But 1909 represented the coming of age of the Nazareth Congregation. Under the date of the New Year the Holy See conferred upon Mother Lauretta the title of superior general, as evidenced by the document which bears testimony to that fact:

> His Holiness Pope Pius X, at the recommendation of the Cardinal Protector, decided to grant to Mother M. Lauretta a proof of his benevolence and an encouragement in her unceasing efforts for the progress of the good work of the Congregation of the Sisters of the Holy Family of Nazareth,
>
> THAT henceforth she shall not be addressed Vicar General, but Mother General or Superior General, for as long as the Holy See shall deem it expedient to leave her in charge.[24]

Pope Pius, like his great predecessor, was in the habit of proving his benevolence in various delicate ways. One of these was the assignment of an invocation to the Holy Family explicitly for the Sisters of the Holy Family of Nazareth, personally written and signed by him and blessed with an indulgence.[25]

But no greater encouragement could have come to Mother Lauretta and to all the sisters than the approval of the Constitutions, issued on August 2, followed by the definitive approval of the Congregation on August 5.[26] Consequently, the fifth general chapter which convened to consider current affairs was of short duration and jubilant. Assembled in Albano, it remained in session from August 11 to 15, presided over by Father Cormier, superior general of the Dominican Fathers, who was assisted by Father Van Rossum, consultor of the Holy Office.

Members of the general administration, confirmed or elected by this chapter, were: Mother M. Gabriel, assistant general; Mothers Gertrude, Joanne and Joseph-Teresa, councilors general, and Mother M. Paula, treasurer general.

The chapter's deliberations were concerned predominantly with the list of emendations which applied to a number of articles in the Constitutions. These were reviewed, probed, and discussed broadly. One of the measures inserted into the Constitutions and immediately implemented was the change from gold profession rings to silver in keeping with evangelical poverty. Gold rings had long been used by nuns of various congregations and were adopted by Mother Mary for Nazareth. Father Van Rossum revealed to the sisters the extent of her love of poverty, when on one occasion she was determined to surrender her gold ring had he not dissuaded her from this action as inopportune at the time.[27]

Another provision of the Constitutions standardized the use of the title "Mother," limiting its application to the sisters who were superiors, local or major, and members of the general administration, but only while they were in office. The superiors general alone would retain the titles even after the expiration of their term.

The usual policy governing the composition of religious constitutions recommended brevity and terseness. Father Cormier explained that the Vatican approving commission, motivated by respect for the fruit of the work of the Foundress, had chosen to deflect the force of this policy with regard to the text of Nazareth Constitutions. Aiming to preserve intact the original spirit embodied in them, deletions had not been required merely for the purpose of bringing about a condensation in structure. The chapter was adjourned on the prophetic note of faith and courage.[28]

Houses of the Congregation
opened since the death of Mother Mary of Jesus the Good Shepherd,
1903 through 1909:

Year	*Location*	*Convent-Apostolate-First Superior*
1903	UNITED STATES Pittsburgh, Pennsylvania	Holy Family convent; Holy Family parish school; Sister M. Aloysius Żmich

Year	Location	Convent-Apostolate-First Superior
1903	UNITED STATES Chicago	St. Ann convent; St. Ann parish school; Sister M. Victoria Fatz.
1904	UNITED STATES Chicago	Presentation of Our Lord convent; Holy Cross parish school; Sister M. Justine Kozłowska.
1904	UNITED STATES Dillonvale, Ohio	St. Hyacinth convent: St. Adalbert parish school; Sister M. Josaphat Gaffke.
1904	UNITED STATES South Bend, Indiana	St. Dominic convent; St. Stanislaus parish school; Sister M. Bonaventure Kołowska.
1905	UNITED STATES Philadelphia	Convent of the Agony in the Garden; St. Adalbert parish school; Sister M. Bonaventure Kołowska
1905	UNITED STATES Chicago	St. Gerard convent; Providence of God parish school; Sister M. Bridget Bartkowska.
1906	POLAND Vilna	Eucharistic Heart of Jesus convent; teacher education; manual arts and crafts for girls; Sister M. Valeria Czarnowska.
1906	ITALY Albano-Ariccia	Patronage of St. Joseph; novitiate; Mother M. Gabriel Lubowidzka.
1906	UNITED STATES Calumet City, Illinois	Our Lady of Loreto convent; St. Andrew parish school; Sister M. Bronislaus Grudzińska.
1907	POLAND Częstochowa	Patronage of Our Lady convent; boarding school for girls; Sister Maria-Josepha Waśkiewicz.
1907	UNITED STATES Pittsburgh, Pennsylvania	Patronage of St. Joseph convent; St. Casimir parish school; Sister M. Josaphat Gaffke.
1907	UNITED STATES Chicago	Assumption B.V.M. convent: Assumption B.V.M. parish school; Sister M. Ildephonse Gums.
1907	UNITED STATES Brooklyn, New York	Presentation B.V.M. convent; St. John Cantius parish school; Sister M. Salomea Kalwa.

Year	*Location*	*Convent-Apostolate-First Superior*
1907	UNITED STATES Cleveland, Ohio	Convent of the Sacred Hearts of Jesus, Mary and Joseph; St. Stanislaus parish school; Mother M. Stanislaus Sierpińska
1908	UNITED STATES Des Plaines, Illinois	Holy Family convent; provincialate and novitiate; Mother M. Sophia Kulawik, provincial and local superior.
1908	POLAND Grodno	Annunciation B.V.M. convent; student residence; cultural and religious youth activities; Sister M. Paul Gażycz.
1908	AUSTRIA Vienna	Mary, Help of Christians convent; elementary school; orphanage; student residence; Sister M. Adolorata Pągowska.
1909	UNITED STATES Derby, Conn.	Mother of Good Counsel convent; St. Michael parish school; Sister M. Philomena Górska.

House closed:

| 1903 | ENGLAND London | Mother of Divine Love convent (1895-1903); home and hospital visits; catechetical work. |

2   AS A ROSE OF JERICHO

In England, Florence Nightingale was approaching her ninetieth birth-day in 1909 and saw nursing, her life's ruling passion, securely taking its place among the world's honorable professions. Society was withdrawing its queasy objections to nursing that had branded it with a gamut of dis-paraging epithets—from unsuitable to disreputable—as a career for any young woman. Not only have glowing reports of her ministrations to the sick and the wounded, alike on battlefield and in civilian life, circled the globe, but by dint of relentless effort and research she became the founder of modern nursing. Mounting admiration for her humanitarian zeal, coupled with the Christian ideal personified by the sisters in the service of the sick, attracted each year some of the finest applicants to St. Mary of Nazareth School of Nursing from Chicago and out of State.

St. Mary's personnel found the height of a glorious experience in their self-giving when, heeding Archbishop Quigley's emergency call, they volunteered for rescue work in the mine disaster at Cherry, Illinois, November 13, 1909.[29] A corps of nurses, headed by Sisters Callista, Cyrilla, Genevieve and Febronia, met the Red Cross team and other volunteers at the mining village to learn that an explosion of a miner's lamp started the fire that trapped 565 miners. By the time 185 had been brought out to the surface, eleven rescue workers lost their lives in the blazing pit, and the mine was sealed in a final effort to extinguish the flames.

The men, suffering acutely from severe bodily burns, exerted every vestige of fortitude to bear the pain manfully. They bravely attempted to smile a little when spoken to by a sister, and some even reached out for a sister's hand to kiss it in gratitude. Grieving women, defenseless against the misfortune that befell them and their bewildered children, needed material and moral comforting to help them reknit the tenuous fabric of their life struggle.[30] The presence of the sisters among them sustained them through the uneasy days that still lay ahead, leading them gently to faith in God by that divine charity which is a transposition of love.

On the sixth day after the outbreak of the disaster, 80 of the entombed men were discovered alive, in a state of collapse, with seared flesh and festering wounds.[31] Sister M. Cyprian with another group of volunteer nurses from St. Mary of Nazareth Hospital joined additional workers who were arriving not only to take care of the survivors but also to attend to the dead and to aid the families of the victims. When the endless hours of arduous days and sleepless nights finally closed, there remained the after-taste of subdued compassion that lingered on in the memory of those who witnessed the holocaust.

For Nazareth sisters, who cared for the sick and the injured, to live well meant to serve, and to serve genuinely it was impossible to live comfortably. Their future years were interspersed with occasional major emergencies involving mass casualties, caused by such acts of God as tornadoes, cloudbursts, river flood and epidemics, and by accidents of catastrophic magnitude as train derailments and fires in densely populated buildings. Ranking next in gravity to the Cherry mine tragedy was the explosion which occurred twenty-six years later in the public school of New London, Texas.

But the undramatic daily heroism of quiet service at the hospital bedside or in public health activities was no less demanding. Specialized responsibilities which became increasingly essential to the field were undertaken by the sisters, including hospital pharmacy by Sister Wilhelmina Konopinska, x-ray technology by Sister Febronia Netzel, and laboratory analysis by Sister Fidelia Creed. The widening role of the emerging professional nurse implied that nursing measures, under all circumstances, had to be administered with skill, dispatch and discriminative judgment.

To this end, between the years 1910 and 1920, notable revisions were introduced in the whole sphere of nursing, and were expertly incorporated in the program of instruction implemented at St. Mary of Nazareth School of Nursing by the school's two outstanding directors, Sister M. Ambrose Krueger (1908-1913) and Sister M. Dolores Mahoney (1913-1918). When the state legislature ratified the official organization of a State Society for Nurses, St. Mary's graduates of 1911 were the first to take State Board Examinations, and in 1912 the school became accredited by the Department of Registration and Education. On the basis of this accreditation, earlier graduates of the school were granted certificates of registration by waiver, without examination.

Having overcome the sense of unfamiliarity that colored the many new developments, Nazareth looked back in 1910 upon its first quarter of a century on the American continent as on a period of both fulfillment and promise. Rooted in the inspiration of Mother Mary of Jesus the Good Shepherd, who in 1885 launched her mission in Chicago, divers aspects of service blossomed into flourishing works of the Church. Even when these did not conspicuously deal with the spiritual dimension of man, the sisters were wont to give evidence that for them this element was always in the foreground.

The silver anniversary was fittingly observed with the participation of Archbishop Quigley, Bishop Rhode and Father Lechert in solemn religious functions. Prominent on the social calendar was a benefit concert presented by the Ladies' Auxiliary of the Holy Family Academy as a jubilee tribute to the Congregation.[32] The general public, both native and immigrant, were accorded grateful recognition for their cooperative good will and confidence in supporting the charitable and educational efforts of the sisters.

Education in the parochial school system of the United States realized broadly one of the leading ideas entertained by Mother Mary, namely, the development of Christian character founded on belief in God and made manifest by sincere practice of religion and the example of virtuous living. In the parochial school, through an expanded curriculum the sisters were further able to guide the children's intellectual development and form in them a well-rounded personality. The schools exerted a considerable impact on homelife, and the three—home, school and church—were unified in the exercise of their duty: to engage in the issues of life, to interpret them in the light of human experience and divine law, and to act and teach as honestly as limited human knowledge made it possible.

Catholic schools, organized on a diocesan plan, constituted in each diocese a separate unit with an autonomous school administration that complied in principle with the State Department of Public Instruction. Under frontier conditions, before the standards and programs became stabilized, the innovative thrust and initiative of the sisters were reflected in the courses of studies they implemented. The first Nazareth school supervisor, Mother M. Frances Morgenstern, was appointed by the Foundress in 1885.

At a time when education, even elementary education, was far from universal, the early sisters, who were educated women with a European background, contributed significantly to the effectiveness of the schools where they were placed. To acquire the language of the land and the knowledge of its history, they engaged reputable instructors who tutored them in their respective convents. They, in turn, prepared the Congregation's young American members, indoctrinating them in elements of pedagogy[33] and imparting advanced content courses in basic elementary school subjects.

When the school boards around the country were still advocating high school education, or its equivalent, as a requirement for elementary school teachers, the Sisters of the Holy Family of Nazareth reacted with alacrity to the progressive policy of De Paul University in Chicago which opened its doors to women in 1911, established summer sessions, and offered throughout the school term late afternoon and Saturday classes. The first registrants to avail themselves of these opportunities were the backbone of the Holy Family Academy, and over the years ardent promoters of higher education: Sisters Euphemia Dahlke, Basilla Frelich, Severine Wysocka, Virginia Grzędzicka, Loyola Jastroch, Liliosa Melerska, Theophane Machan and Amabilis Kudialis.

In regions where the Nazareth membership was more widely dispersed, the cause of teacher education was steadily propagated by Sisters Pancratius Ławecka, Chester Polentz, Ildephonse Gums, Agnes Kosiba, Liguori Pakowska and Electa Glowienke under academic sponsorship of the universities of Villanowa in Philadelphia, St. John's in Brooklyn and Duquesne in Pittsburgh.

At the cost of additional sacrifice and effort, full-time teaching sisters pursued higher studies to better equip themselves for the task they held sacred. College degrees were not always aimed at, and ordinarily they were not then essential. But the twofold responsibility, classroom teaching and their personal advancement, had to be shouldered concurrently.

Unmitigated population growth in the country gave rise to continuing proliferation of parishes in unexpected places, each of which aspired to have a school for the children of its parishioners, though the rising new communities had not yet developed sufficient group identity and cohesiveness to risk the funding of joint projects. More often than not, the parish complex—church, school and convent—started out with tentative lodgings that were meager and inadequately equipped. The people's struggle with poverty and want was shared by the sisters. Dutiful and cheerful in their dedication to Christ's poor, they cherished their own evangelical poverty in the reality of daily living. The reality was necessarily carved out of the hard granite of forbearance and self-denial.

A formal contract, approved by the bishop and executed by the pastor and the provincial superior, stipulated the conditions for staffing a school and the incidental parish relationships. The indicated rate of salary was subjected to unpredictable undercutting when unemployment or inflation depleted the regular sources of income, and when accidents, illness or untimely death deprived families of their breadwinners, but the pupils whose families happened to be touched by misfortune that resulted in economic disability were not rejected. Even at the Holy Family Academy, where the student population was reputed to represent economically well-situated strata of society, poverty was not a deterrent to admitting girls who had the requisite scholastic and moral qualifications. The sisters' acceptance of nominal compensation pointed up the priorities they upheld in their service of love and availability, not estimated in terms of a hireling. Their adherence to a pattern of Eucharistic community life, combined with the sisterly sharing of possessions in actual poverty, enabled them to reproduce the message of the Gospel in spirit and in truth.

Flowing out of its initial corporate commitment to the Church, the Congregation repeatedly affirmed its position of fidelity upon every admission to another diocese and in the contractual arrangements with every pastor. Through the mediation of major superiors, Nazareth maintained the undertaken apostolates in continuity and stability; in this way the sisters, too, were assured of realizing their primary vocation and of its temporal validity.

In England, their educational work has been consistently rising in acceptability and, by 1911, enjoyed a measure of prosperity. Capitalizing on favorable indications, Mother Frances gained substantial private support to be able to remodel Juglans Lodge and to acquire an attractive neighboring property, Roseneath, for the housing of foreign students.

While the external works grew and waxed strong, the internal forum of the Congregation was building up its staying power by an incisive study of the Constitutions. In reviewing the recently promulgated enactments there arose a question of seemingly minimal consequence concerning the use of the title "Mother" to which, unaccountably, considerable interest became attached and brought it to the attention of the Sacred Congregation of Religious. The issue was resolved by the decree of March 12, 1913, which declared that the title shall be borne by the superior general while in office and thereafter for life, by the general councilors during their terms of office, and by those sisters who were given the title by Mother Foundress.[34] Of the original seventeen upon whom Mother Mary of Jesus the Good Shepherd conferred the permanent title "Mother," eleven were living when this decree was formulated.[35]

Ten years after the death of Mother Mary, at the request of the sisters, a burial chapel was erected over a spacious crypt at the Roman cemetery of St. Laurence in Campo Verano. The chancel above-ground was furnished with an altar for the celebration of memorial services. On May 3, 1913, the remains of Mother Mary were translated to a niche in the chancel and placed behind glass through which the casket was visible. The same day, the remains of ten sisters who had died in Rome were likewise disinterred and entombed in the chapel[36] to await there the dawn of resurrection, as in time would all others who ended their earthly pilgrimage in the Eternal City.

Several days later, May 11 witnessed the inauguration of Wilhelm Cardinal Van Rossum as Nazareth's Cardinal Protector, filling the vacancy created by the death of Cardinal Respighi,[37] which occurred March 21, 1913. Two years earlier Father Van Rossum was elevated to the cardinalate in recognition of his service to the Church; in his new and eminent dignity his consent to exercise a protectorate over the Congregation which he had known long and thoroughly was indeed a gain of no slight value for Nazareth.

Death had also caused a breach in the membership of the general administration with the passing of Mother Joseph-Teresa (March 29, 1911), general councilor and, for eighteen years, director of novices, and of Mother Paula (February 4, 1913), treasurer general. Appointments to the positions held by them were made in accordance with the provisions of the Constitutions and were to be effective until the next general chapter. Mother M. Clare,[38] who had arrived from the United States to be present at the translation of the remains of the Foundress, was called upon to be a member of the general council, while Sister Mary Magdalene[39] was entrusted the duties of the treasurer.[40] The responsibility for the formation of novices fell to Sister M. Bożena Staczyńska who, as director, shared it with Sister M. Alma Sebowicz, assistant director.

The summer of 1913 brought Mother Lauretta to the United States where the rapid increase of new locations placed in charge of the sisters claimed her attention. Furthermore, with the changing social and economic character of the population, new types of work were arising. In Conshohocken, Pennsylvania, Father Benedict Tomiak invited the collaboration of the sisters in caring for and teaching of orphan boys at St. Mary's Home which he founded in 1911. In Chicago, St. Adalbert's parish, in addition to its well-established parochial school, saw the development of a day-care center, opened in 1913, for pre-school children of working mothers.

Archbishop Quigley, like his predecessor, took occasion to visit the sisters informally at intervals, while in conjunction with formal functions he would prolong his stay to inquire leisurely into their problems and hopes, as well as successes and hardships. That year a fair opportunity for such an exchange of insights came about after the ceremony of perpetual profession in the provincialate at Des Plaines. Accompanied by Mother Lauretta, he made an impromptu tour of the novitiate section, which he concluded with the observation, "You need a larger house and a permanent chapel to replace the present makeshift arrangement."[41] He went so far as to describe how the proposal might be realized. His practical and timely suggestion took into account the high-spirited group of novices, ninety-six in number, who had come from far removed points in the United States.

Without delay Mother Lauretta laid comprehensive plans for the enlargement of the building in Des Plaines to be completed with architectural harmony, as she had done the year before for the Roman novitiate. Considering the immediate needs and looking into the future, she also promoted the addition of two parallel wings to St. Mary of Nazareth Hospital: the south wing to provide more facilities for patients; the north wing to meet the exclusive purpose of the school of nursing, including both the living quarters for student nurses and the educational areas with lecture rooms, laboratories and library. The American building projects were finished in 1914, months after her return to Europe.

Meanwhile dark shadows were lengthening across the convulsive, fragile continent of Europe. Along with industrial leviathans and high society's elegant charm came socialism and militant suffragettes. The seven-month Balkan conflict (1912-1913) generated new provocative tensions; all over Europe governments were shaken by strikes, sabotage and assassinations. When on June 28, 1914 Archduke Franz Ferdinand, heir apparent to the Austrian throne, was assassinated by Serbian conspirators, Europe, like a massive locomotive, lurched recklessly toward the abyss.

Enmeshed in a network of interlacing alliances, some diplomats exerted frantic efforts to keep the peace and fumbled. The network ruptured in a series of declarations of war that became known as the Great War, and was later named World War I. Peace was beyond recall.

Pope Pius X, in sympathy with all the calamities that befell mankind in his time—volcanic eruptions, earthquakes, floods, massacres, revolutions, injustices—was overwhelmed with horror and pain at the impending tragedy of the Great War which his diplomatic intervention could not avert. His public exhortation to peace was recorded in *L'Osservatore Romano* of August 2, 1914; he died eighteen days later.

His successor, Benedict XV, in his entire pontificate concentrated upon the problems of the war, which involved millions of Catholics on both sides of the conflict, and on exploring all possibilities that might lead to peace. He added the invocation, "Queen of Peace," to the litany of the Blessed Virgin Mary and urged the leaders of belligerent nations to embrace the spirit of Christian brotherhood.

On the brink of the international crisis the Sacred Congregation of Religious granted to the Sisters of the Holy Family of Nazareth a rescript, August 3, 1914, authorizing the establishment of a novitiate in Grodno. The visitation of the houses in Poland, concluded by Mother Lauretta that summer, had apprised her in the nick of time of the political dilemma that confronted the czarist government, which indirectly brought a degree of relief in matters of religion to the territories under its control. It was opportune to move the novices from Cracow to this remote location, away from the line of expected military activity. The artist, Sister Paul Gażycz, conversant with the unsettled regional complications of the moment, was charged with the dual position of local superior and director of novices.

On the dismal probability that an interruption in communication might occur in the event of war, Mother Lauretta delegated emergency powers over the houses in Poland to Mother Raphael, the superior in Cracow.[42] Another decision dictated by prudence was to determine points of contact for dispatching correspondence to and from Rome in order to preserve the inner bond of unity in spite of continental hostilities.

It was impossible to steer Europe's nations away from a collision course. The embattled countries turned on each other in a succession of furious assaults. The neutrality of non-belligerents was violated. The three enemy powers, occupying Poland since the close of the eighteenth century, made of it the stamping ground for their military operations and dragged its people into fratricidal struggle by exacting compulsory service in opposing armed forces. But Russia, notwithstanding its immense army, was unready for tactical warfare. Its regiments disintegrated before the advancing German columns and retreated from Polish provinces, leaving arson and devastation in their wake.

Częstochowa, situated in the Russian sector, lay in the path of traversing German divisions which, in the absence of Russian troops in the city, sought to intimidate the civilian population by opening fire against the townspeople in the vicinity of the monastery and basilica. The sisters from the nearby convent of the Patronage of St. Joseph, together with their students and a group of civilians, fled to safety in the farther removed convent of the Patronage of Our Lady. Later, upon returning, they found utter destruction and pillage on the premises they had left. The second convent was obliged to relinquish a part of its building to the German army to be utilized as a military hospital for eleven months. Regular classes, however, were allowed to continue normally in the reduced facilities without interference.[43]

After the first year of war, the convents in Austrian-occupied Poland were required to release accommodations for the care of combat casualties. With the exception of the city hospital in Wadowice, which was permitted to retain its civilian status, the sisters converted large sections of their houses into provisional military hospitals and themselves rendered Samaritan services in varying capacities alongside the military medical and nursing personnel. A similar situation prevailed in the mission center in Vienna. In each case, to the extent that it was possible, a segment of the initial apostolate was maintained active. Only the Institute of St. Hedwig discontinued its original function completely, because the out-of-town working girls, who had been housed there, left Cracow in panic to rejoin their families, and the entire building became a military hospital for the duration.

The sisters' dominant role in this period was notably in restoring and fortifying the human morale of the soldiers through meaningful religious influence and familial atmosphere. Participation in chapel devotions was a spiritually satisfying experience to the men who were not totally confined to bed. Threaded through the sequences of hospital routine were planned holiday observances and sporadic on-the-ward entertainments, replete with moments of gallant comradeship to season the time of enforced inactivity. The men whose health could not be restored and life sustained were assisted to accept their condition with Christian dignity and faith. Those, who were dismissed on recovery or transferred to other installations on medical advice, sent testimonials of gratitude and moving sentiments in the letters they mailed to the sisters from their stations.[44]

Impressed by the beneficent undercurrent of Christian compassion, neither intrusive nor conventional, to which the disabled soldiers were exposed, the military authorities applied to Mother Raphael to assign groups of three or four sisters to other temporary installations. The conditions of these assignments respected the religious character of the sisters, assured them of private living quarters on location, and approved the establishment of chapels and programs of worship for the battle-scarred invalids.

Grave concern for the destitute, helpless children stricken by the ravages of war prompted Mother Lauretta to propose to the American sisters a campaign of mercy among the parochial school children in the United States in honor of the Divine Child Jesus. Their voluntary offerings were presented to Pope Benedict XV who allocated the funds to the needy through his private channels. To the children whose names were submitted to him on the list of donors he imparted a special blessing as a token of heavenly graces.[45]

By 1917, a children's relief committee of the Red Cross planned to evacuate a transport of war orphans and homeless children into Switzerland and appealed to Mother Lauretta for a staff of sisters to conduct there a child-caring home. She responded without hesitation, and Sister M. Alma Sebowicz, as superior, arrived with a group of sisters from Rome on August 1. As soon as the children began adjusting to normal living in the peaceful protected environment at Villars sur Glâne, in the canton of Fribourg, the committee assumed the responsibility for tracing the whereabouts of the children's relatives. As a result, some families were brought to Switzerland for a happy reunion, while others, prevented from traveling by wartime obstacles, remained in contact with the committee until the dissolution of the home when, May 22, 1919, the children accompanied by two sisters returned to their native land.[46]

In the midst of the world's turmoil, Nazareth convents everywhere eventually learned of the death of Father Hyacinth M. Cormier, O.P. Commenting on his demise, Father Lechert expressed a succinct tribute, "I have always regarded him as an extraordinarily holy religious; I bear in my heart a great, undying gratitude for him."[47] News of other deaths which touched the Congregation deeply were those of the early members: Mothers Columba, Gertrude and Joanne, and of Sister Lucille, director of the American novitiate for nineteen years. Sincerely regretted in Nazareth was also the death of Archbishop Quigley,[48] whose evident interest in the welfare of the sisters and in the progress of their apostolate left a lasting memory in the Congregation. He was succeeded by Archbishop George Mundelein from the diocese of Brooklyn, where in the founding years he had on numerous occasions advised and supported Mother Lauretta during her tenure as provincial superior.

As the politics of war underwent strategic changes, the United States was drawn into the allied effort against the aggressive maneuvers of a common enemy. One month later, the first of a series of apparitions of the Holy Virgin occurred in Fatima, summoning the faithful to penance and devotion to her Immaculate Heart in the cause of world peace.[49]

The hope of the resurgence of a free and united Poland was revived in the minds of its people and spurred them steadily towards that one supremely sensitive goal which now appeared attainable. Reading into the premonitory signs, the sisters in Poland looked expectantly to the speedy return of religious and civic freedom. It has already become possible for them to wear the religious habit openly wherever that practice had been prohibited formerly.[50] Their undercover educational activities also surfaced without impediment where previously they had been severely forbidden.

But ruthless miltary operations left city residents bereft of money, food and work, while rural regions were brought to the verge of starvation by the destruction of crops and animals. The sisters conducted free soup kitchens for the impoverished, while they themselves suffered distress in their congested convents, gave long and exhausting hours of service, and in many instances paid irreparably with their health. In the United States the burdens of the war were carried in untold sacrifices, privations and the soaring cost of commodities caused by the outlay in equipping and supplying American troops on foreign fronts and by the outpouring of relief to check the wave of misery in invaded areas. In England, France and Italy, each wrestling with the conditions imposed by war, the sisters were oppressed by the same strain of uncertainties, terrors and food shortages that beset the civilians at large, yet by the charity of their hearts they aimed to temper the misfortune and sufferings of those about them.

When the armistice of November 11, 1918, was finally declared, the bloodiest war ever fought until then came to an end. Methodically the works of the Congregation resumed their proper direction, unfolding like a rose of Jericho planted near running waters, where it opens up its petals.

Mother Raphael brought full-scale consideration to bear upon the probing of opportunities for future development in Kalisz and Warsaw. Sisters Maria-Josepha and Victorine, in an interview with Msgr. Achille Ratti, Apostolic Visitor to Poland, were impressed by him with the importance of taking up the work of Catholic education at this point, especially in cities ruined by war. He encouraged and blessed the plan to establish a school and an orphanage in Kalisz as a vital contribution to the reconstruction of the city that had been razed by bombardment during enemy siege. To realize this purpose, the industrious Sister Maria-Josepha set about restoring and remodeling an abandoned monastery building which was eventually dedicated, in 1919, by the same Msgr. Ratti, who later became Pope Pius XI. The occasion marked one of the first joyous manifestations in the postwar period for the townspeople and the crowds from outlying countryside.[51]

In this climactic period Warsaw was obviously a key city. The Papal Nuncio advised moving into it to form as soon as possible a nucleus of an apostolate that should be most needful and particularly desirable to society. The beginnings were slow and faltering, not for lack of public interest—that was enthusiastic enough, but for lack of a suitable locale and sufficient funds. Nevertheless, classes for girls on the secondary level, arranged at first in a rented apartment on Ulica Wilcza, later in a leased building on Ulica Litewska, began to forecast a hopeful prospect.[52]

Even before the termination of the war, a disaster of a different kind gripped the world in the form of epidemic influenza which took toll of thousands of victims. Schools in the United States were closed and all public assemblages discontinued as a preventive measure against the spread of infection. The sisters joined forces with Red Cross personnel in caring for the stricken, who were accommodated in emergency centers that were set up to alleviate undue crowding of hospitals. Having taken courses in home nursing at the outbreak of the war, the sisters attended the sick in their homes with skill and devotion and, where whole families were prostrated, they performed the daily details for human survival, prepared the food, heated the homes, managed the domestic chores of hygiene and sanitation.

In an era prior to the introduction of antibiotic therapy, St. Mary of Nazareth Hospital, along with all other hospitals in the nation, served to the limits of its capacity, redoubling its efforts in treating influenza patients whose condition, aggravated by critical complications, required strict isolation and around-the-clock medical and nursing teams. In agonizing instances, when all human means failed to save the lives of loved ones, the sisters revealed colossal resources of Christian faith and selfless love in the support and solace they gave to the bereaved.

At this stage, the small Providence Hospital in Argo, in the southwestern suburb of Chicago, dispensed like services to the local community. Organized under the auspices of Corn Products Refining Company, it had been placed under the direction of the sisters, March 19, 1917, to be available primarily to the company's employees in case of accident or sudden illness. When unexpected needs arose as a result of the raging epidemic, it responded to all with an open heart and ready arms,[53] and when some fifty casualties were brought in from a train wreck, which occurred at the nearby railroad crossing, the spirit of Nazareth united all personnel through the stressful hours of the night, carrying out triage, treatment and identification.

Still, the ordeals of war and epidemic have in no way interfered with the growing number of parochial schools in the United States. This factor, together with the diffussion of locations where the schools were situated, rendered the administration of the province progressively more unwieldy. With these problems in view and relying upon the alleged estimates of a swift conclusion of the war, Mother Lauretta and her council had planned to convoke the regular chapter of the Congregation in August of 1915.[54]

When it became apparent that the predictions were abortive and the outlook for peace elusive, the notion of holding the chapter was abandoned. As an alternative, a program of official visitations was designed to be accomplished by delegated visitors-general during the winter-spring term of 1917-1918. The superior of the provincialate in Des Plaines, Sister M. Valeria Kapcia, was assigned to visit the houses within the State of Illinois, except the provincial house; Sister M. Bronislaus Grudzińska, superior at the convent of Our Lady of Loreto in Calumet City, was entrusted the visitations in Western Pennsylvania and in Ohio and Indiana; while Sister M. Antonia Danisch, superior at the convent of the Sacred Hearts of Jesus, Mary and Joseph in Cleveland was delegated to conduct the visitations in Eastern Pennsylvania, New York, Connecticut, Massachusetts and in the provincialate. In Poland, the visitations were carried out by Sister M. Antonina Kalicka, superior-administrator of the city hospital in Wadowice.[55]

Disrupting external conditions and gnawing cares have not prevented the superior general from enlarging upon a broad scope of concerns essential to the vitality of the Congregation. Among these was the publication of the Nazareth prayer manual, *Jesus, Mary, Joseph,* which she forwarded to the sisters for the Christmas of 1917. Steps were undertaken for the preparation of the biography of Mother Mary of Jesus the Good Shepherd, to be written by Archbishop Vincent Sardi, who had known the Foundress personally. In this connection, the sisters were asked to submit facts and incidents known to them individually to contribute to the presentation of the life and work of Mother Mary in full light.[56]

Mother Lauretta's loyalty to the heritage of the ecclesial spirit, transmitted to the Congregation by Mother Mary, was emphasized by her attitude of uncompromising faith and compliance when the new *Code of Canon Law* was promulgated. The project of the codification was initiated by St. Pope Pius X and was completed during the pontificate of Benedict XV.[57] Part two of the Second Book, containing 195 canons (Nos. 487 to 681, inclusive), was devoted to the religious of the Catholic Church. The constitutions of all approved congregations had to be adapted to the new *Code* and its prescriptions to be embodied in the pertinent chapters of the constitutions for the immediate and general instruction of all the sisters in each congregation. Although fundamentally no contradiction existed between Nazareth Constitutions and the *Code*, the adaptation of the text required another revision.[58]

The reports of the delegated visitors-general supplied the general council in Rome with indispensable information for considering the state of the American province; the surveys were then studied factually in consultation with ecclesiastical authorities. With the approval of the Holy

See the houses in the United States were formed into three provinces to facilitate intra-community solidarity and the efficacy of operation under the leadership of three provincial superiors, each being responsible for an administrative unit limited to a definite geographic area.[59]

The Sacred Heart province, having its provincialate in Des Plaines, consisted of the houses in Illinois and Indiana, with Sister M. Antonia as the provincial superior; Sister M. Celestine, provincial assistant; Sister M. Donata, councilor; Sister M. Ignatius, treasurer; and Sister M. Euphemia, secretary.

The Immaculate Conception province, encompassing Eastern Pennsylvania, the State of New York and the New England States, with Sister M. Valentine as the provincial superior, established its principal office temporarily at St. Mary's Home in Conshohocken. The members of the provincial council were Sister M. Lucy, provincial assistant; Sister M. Aloysius, treasurer; Sister M. Rosalia, secretary; and Sister M. DeSales, councilor.

St. Joseph province, with Sister M. Bronislaus as provincial superior, extended over Western Pennsylvania and Ohio, and its administrative building was provisionally the convent of the Hidden Life of the Holy Family at Wesleyville, a suburb of Erie. The provincial council consisted of: Sister M. Ildephonse, provincial assistant; Sister M. Amata, treasurer; Sister M. Redempta, secretary; and Sister M. Renata, councilor.

The center for the formation of novices of the three provinces continued to be the novitiate at Des Plaines.

Houses of the Congregation
opened in the years 1910 through 1918:

Year	*Location*	*Convent-Apostolate-First Superior*
1910	UNITED STATES Chicago	St. Mary of the Angels convent; St. Francis of Assisi parish school; Sister M. Hilary Okon.
1910	UNITED STATES Kankakee, Illinois	Our Lady the Good Shepherdess convent; St. Stanislaus parish school; Sister M. Denis Kanarowska.
1910	UNITED STATES Philadelphia	Convent of the Holy Wounds; St. Hedwig parish school; Mother M. Cecilia Sadowska.
1910	UNITED STATES Utica, New York	Convent of the Hidden Christ; Holy Trinity parish school; Sister M. Patricia Krusse.

Year	*Location*	*Convent-Apostolate-First Superior*
1910	UNITED STATES New Haven, Connecticut	Our Lady of Grace convent; St. Stanislaus parish school; Sister M. Leonia Deja.
1911	UNITED STATES Manayunk, Pennsylvania	Queen of Virgins convent;* St. Josaphat parish school; Sister M. Florence Gawrych.
1911	UNITED STATES Chester, Pennsylvania	Virgo Fidelis convent;*** St. Hedwig parish school; Sister M. Pancratius Ławecka.
1911	UNITED STATES Philadelphia	Holy Face convent; St. John Cantius parish school; Sister M. Ignatius Romanowska.
1911	UNITED STATES Conshohocken, Pa.	Our Lady of Częstochowa convent; St. Mary's Home for Boys; Mother M. Cecilia Sadowska.
1911	UNITED STATES Jamaica, New York	St. Clement convent; St. Joseph parish school; Mother M. Laurence Królikowska.
1911	UNITED STATES Westville, Illinois	St. Casimir convent;** Sts. Peter and Paul parish school; Sister M. Tharsilla Bogdziunaite.
1912	UNITED STATES Cicero, Illinois	Queen of Virgins convent; St. Anthony parish school; Sister M. Irmina Skorupa.
1912	UNITED STATES Cicero, Illinois	Our Lady of Lourdes convent; St. Valentine parish school; Sister M. Fidelia Ciszewska.
1912	UNITED STATES McKees Rocks, Pa.	St. Thecla convent; Sts. Cyril and Methodius parish school; Sister M. Josephine Retman
1912	UNITED STATES Chicago	St. Stanislaus Kostka convent; Immaculate Heart of Mary parish school; Sister M. Regina Wentowska.
1913	UNITED STATES Argo, Illinois	St. Raphael Archangel convent; St. Blase parish school; Sister M. Julia Kitowska.
1913	UNITED STATES Whiting, Indiana	St. Joachim convent; St. Adalbert parish school; Sister M. Hippolyte Kruczkowska.

Year	*Location*	*Convent-Apostolate-First Superior*
1913	UNITED STATES Gallitzin, Pennsylvania	Queen of the Sacred Heart convent; Our Lady of Częstochowa parish school; Sister M. Desideria Suchomska.
1913	UNITED STATES Maspeth, New York	St. Gabriel Archangel convent; Holy Cross parish school; Sister M. DeSales Przybylska.
1913	POLAND Stryj	St. Joseph convent; elementary boarding school; Sister M. Irene Marianowska.
1914	UNITED STATES Norwich, Connecticut	St. Michael Archangel convent; St. Joseph parish school; Sister M. Pancratius Ławecka.
1914	UNITED STATES Harvey, Illinois	St. Gerard convent; St. John the Baptist parish school; Sister M. Vladimir Jóźwiak.
1915	UNITED STATES Erie, Pennsylvania	Most Holy Redeemer convent; St. Stanislaus parish school; Sister M. Ildephonse Gums.
1915	UNITED STATES Worcester, Massachusetts	Our Lady of Victory convent; Our Lady of Częstochowa parish school; Sister M. Valentine Kapcia.
1915	UNITED STATES Chicago	St. Tarcisius convent; St. Ladislaus parish school; Sister M. Fidelia Ciszewska.
1916	UNITED STATES Cambridge, Massachusetts	Queen of Peace convent; St. Hedwig parish school; Sister M. Euphemia Dahlke.
1917	SWITZERLAND Villars sur Glâne, Fribourg	Patronage of the Holy Family convent; home for war orphans; Sister M. Alma Sebowicz.
1917	UNITED STATES Argo, Illinois	Divine Providence convent; Providence Hospital; Sister M. Florentine Bieschke.
1918	POLAND Warsaw	Holy Name of Jesus convent; secondary school for resident students; Sister M. Antonia Iwanowska.

Year	Location	Convent-Apostolate-First Superior
1918	POLAND Kalisz	Patronage of the Holy Family convent; secondary school for resident students; orphanage; Sister Maria-Josepha Waśkiewicz.
1918	UNITED STATES Erie, Pennsylvania	St. Casimir convent; St. Casimir parish school; Sister M. Anatolia Dylnicka.
1918	UNITED STATES Detroit, Michigan	St. Aloysius convent; St. George parish school; Sister M. Justine Kozłowska.
1918	UNITED STATES Wesleyville, Pennsylvania	Convent of the Hidden Life of the Holy Family; temporary provincialate of St. Joseph province; Sister M. Bronislaus Grudzińska, provincial and local superior.

Houses closed:

*1912	UNITED STATES Manayunk, Pennsylvania	Queen of Virgins convent; St. Josaphat parish school;
1914	UNITED STATES Chicago	St. Gerard convent (1905-1914); Providence of God parish school.
**1916	UNITED STATES Westville, Illinois	St. Casimir convent; Sts. Peter and Paul parish school.
***1917	UNITED STATES Chester, Pennsylvania	Virgo Fidelis convent; St. Hedwig parish school.
1918	POLAND Cracow	Institute of St. Hedwig (1892-1918); working girls' home; provisional military hospital during World War I.

3   LIKE A BUDDING OLIVE TREE

The creation of three Nazareth provinces in the United States, from the original one, was linked to a moment in the stream of time that bespoke the splendid economy of God and a challenge to human intelligence. Resilience was a necessary ingredient in the branching out into distinct, though essentially not different, units. It tested and proved the values that undergirt the life of the Congregation for the fulfillment of what is best in life. The ingenuity, vision and resourcefulness of the provincial superiors, their councils and the sisters at large resolved many of the new situations and discovered, at the threshold of new possibilities, true unity underlying a functional diversity.

The Sacred Heart province had an obvious headstart in the new design; the roots of the American foundation were there with an established provincial seat and novitiate. In the east, the Immaculate Conception province continued to be administered for a few years from Conshohocken, Pennsylvania, from St. Mary's Home for Boys, which was given in full possession to the sisters by Father Tomiak, the unacclaimed apostle of youth. The centrally located St. Joseph province experienced several changes in the placement of its principal house before a final settlement was determined.

For months before the matter of the three provinces had become a reality, Mother Lauretta was offered by Reverend Andrew Ignasiak thirteen acres of land, at Mill and Shannon Roads in Wesleyville, Pennsylvania, whereon he was erecting a small residence. He proposed that the building be used as a vacation and rest home for the sisters engaged in the two Erie parishes.[60] It seemed opportune to assign there the provincial superior and her staff tentatively, at least for the period of their orientation. In the course of reviewing all facts pertinent to the affairs of the province, Sister Bronislaus was advised of legal flaws in the title to the Wesleyville property. Since these would unwittingly impose heavy burdens on the Congregation, it was impractical to become fettered with the undesirable ownership. A formal investigation and report,[61] directed to Mother Lauretta, resulted in withdrawal from the property.

St. Joseph provincialate then moved onto the grounds of the Holy Family Institute and temporarily occupied the bungalow at 11 Maple Avenue, where the work of the orphanage had initially begun. At this point in time, infants and toddlers were housed there. Through the courtesy of Father Francis Retka, C.S.Sp., the Institute's superintendent since 1915, the children were accommodated in a section of the main building until more feasible arrangements would be completed.[62]

When civil tranquility returned to the world and the allied leaders deliberated at Versailles after the end of the war, Poland arose from the

161

dèbris of enslavement, an independent, sovereign republic. The sisters eagerly turned to the huge task of reconstruction and stabilization of their peacetime endeavors within the context of native culture and faith. They developed the power of living and working with greater intensity, free of pressure, for through deepening reflectiveness they were capable of listening to life and to the many ways by which the Lord communicated his message.

The Nunciature Apostolic in Warsaw took cognizance of their total contribution to the preservation of the faith through education. Sister M. Valeria Czarnowska[63] was singled out to receive, May 27, 1920, the papal medal "Benemerenti" and a citation signed by Pope Benedict XV. For thirteen critical years Sister Valeria had guarded and guided the witnessing to Catholic principles in the programs of instruction conducted in Vilna. Her moral strength and compelling personality withstood the threats and anti-religious demands of changing occupation forces until the day of liberation from foreign control arrived. To her faculty and students she represented a symbol of courage for justice sake, a living exponent of fidelity.

Typical of the wider view now coming into focus were two postwar foundations in 1919. Though seemingly new in character, in reality they complemented the Nazareth vocation and conveyed the best of it where the need was greatest. The first of these, a home for children in the health resort of Rabka, passed a long phase of preparation. As early as 1913, it had been recommended to Sister M. Tarsicia Bzowska and had been tenderly promoted by her through experimental stages and difficulties.[64]

Endowed with thermo-mineral springs, Rabka was a mecca for health seekers of all ages. Its pine-saturated mountain air was particularly conducive to the successful treatment of pulmonary ailments. The sisters were called upon to consider assuming responsibility for the welfare of children whose parents were unable to remain with them for a season of weeks, sometimes extending to several months. This entailed providing a controlled homelike environment, looking after the regular carrying out of the treatments as prescribed by physicians, the planning and supervision of recreational activities, and cultivating religious, social and intellectual attitudes in keeping with the children's age levels and health.

To give the project a fair trial, Sister Tarsicia leased a villa for the children of interested parents for the season commencing late in the spring and closing on the brink of autumn, just before the first anticipated snowfall. The resort village of Rabka, set against a gorgeous background of rolling landscape in southern Poland, was an island of peace in a strife-torn world. The sisters' villa was a perfect answer to the parental concern for the care and safety of many a frail child. From year to year increasingly larger facilities were reserved in answer to the growing influx of advance applications. In 1919 the general council welcomed the new direction the apostolic efforts of the sisters were taking. Until a permanently workable scheme should evolve, a lease was negotiated for year-round occupancy of an existing villa. Girls of school age who, under medical advice, required prolonged, uninterrupted climatic therapy were offered a modified program of instruction that enabled them to take state examinations for credit. This was the beginning of what later developed into a recognized open-air sanitarium and school for girls.[65]

That same year, a nucleus for a Nazareth house of studies was formed. When the Apostolic Nuncio gave the incentive for the erection of the Catholic University of Lublin with pontifical status, its rector aimed to incorporate such programs of enrichment that would popularize the widespread higher education of women. He suggested to Mother Lauretta to undertake the establishment of a residence for female university students which could also serve as a center for the sisters who would study at the university. Unfortunately, it was not possible to struggle long against the economic slump which was then crippling Europe's initiative, and the project soon had to be abandoned.

In Rome, however, at the behest of the Holy See, a guest house for pilgrims was opened adjoining the church at St. Stanislaus, at 15 Via delle Botteghe Oscure. The church, sacristy and guest quarters were actually committed to the Congregation on January 21, 1918, but unforseen complications delayed the necessary renovation of the premises, so that they at length became available to the public in May of 1920.[66]

After a lapse of eleven years, the sixth general chapter of the Congregation assembled in the novitiate house at Albano, and was opened on June 5, 1920 by Wilhelm Cardinal Van Rossum, C. Ss. R. The fourteen-member body consisted of the five officers of the general administration, the three provincial superiors from the United States—each with one elected delegate from her province, Mother M. Frances from England, Sister M. Redempta from France and Sister M. Bożena from Poland.

This being an electoral chapter, the protocol then in effect ordained the election of the general administration as the first item on the chapter agenda. By unanimous vote Mother Lauretta was reelected for a second twelve-year term. Other members elected to comprise the general administration were: Mother M. Clare Netkowska, assistant general; Sisters Adolorata Pągowska, Redempta Seifert and Virginia Grzędzicka, councilors general, from among whom Sister Adolorata was chosen to the office of secretary general; and Sister Mary Magdalene Szeligowska, treasurer general.[67]

Adaptations of the Constitutions to the new Code of Canon Law were carefully studied and voted upon, preliminary to applying for full ecclesiastical approval. A proposed Book of Customs was discussed for the purpose of amplifying the original Directory and aligning it with contemporary usage.[68]

Impartial and reasoned consideration was given to the request of Lithuanian clergy in the United States who sought to form a separate province of Nazareth sisters who were of Lithuanian ancestry.[69] A practical reason which militated against acceding to the request was the inadequate number of these sisters in order to maintain a functioning administration of the province. Of the thirty-two professed, one-fourth did not qualify as teachers, whereas five parochial schools were currently staffed in the so-called Lithuanian parishes. It was important, furthermore, not to lose sight of the fact that, for approximately twelve years, there was already in existence a new diocesan congregation of sisters, founded and flourishing in Chicago, with the explicit aim to serve the Lithuanian Catholics.[70] In general, the consensus of the chapter declared nationality distinctions among members untenable, being contrary to the spirit and the letter of Nazareth Constitutions,[71] while the provinces were to represent broadly integrated geographic components regardless of their ethnic elements.

The question of establishing a formal province to encompass the houses in Poland in a canonical unit was referred to the Holy See and, in the meantime, Sister M. Valeria was designated the visitor-general for that area with unspecified tenure. The chapter also reviewed the factors leading to the withdrawal of the sisters from several recently opened houses and agreed to hold in abeyance the trend of too rapid expansion. It endorsed, instead, the decision to concentrate upon the strengthening of professional standards in the interest of existing apostolates if they were to be served well.[72]

To solve some of the recurring problems of local superiors, a series of consistent policies was formulated for their guidance. At the closing session, June 18, the Cardinal Protector in his address to the capitulants accentuated the exercise of great care in the formation of novices and, for the entire Congregation, the revival of fidelity to the teachings of Mother Mary of Jesus the Good Shepherd.[73]

Scarcely had the chapter adjourned and the delegates departed when the news of a formidable Bolshevik invasion, pressing westward, alarmed Europe. For months vagrant skirmishes had been exploding all along the eastern districts of Poland, inundating the borderlands by armies on the march. On July 17, the novitiate was suddenly evacuated from Grodno in the hope of finding refuge at the Sacred Heart convent in Cracow. The unexpected arrival of 41 sisters—professed, novices and postulants— distressed the convent, for it already housed other arrivals from the frontier houses of Lemberg, Stryj and Lublin, while the restored regular activities in the Cracow convent left it with no space to spare. Like the Holy Family in its flight to Egypt, the novices and postulants with their director, Sister Alma, proceeded to the House of Providence in Wadowice for lodging.[74]

There was excitement in the western capitals when the movements of the invaders indicated that capture of Warsaw was their objective. The Polish people went from church to church in penitential processions chanting prayers for the safety of the city. On August 15, the avalanche was stemmed at the very walls of the city in a decisive battle, known as the miracle of the Vistula, which routed the foe and ultimately cleared the way for peace negotiations. Italy, at this time, heaved with Benito Mussolini's rise to power as the leader of fascism, an original contribution to modern political experience.

By April 1, 1921, the novitiate returned from Wadowice to Grodno, finding Sister Thecla Targońska engaged in endless tasks which had developed in the interim. In the drear, uncertain days of the past summer, when the novitiate was evacuated, she had volunteered to guard the convent and the church. With unshaken confidence in divine protection, she applied sober judgment and a rare sense of humor against the importunities of the besiegers, preventing the profanation of the sacred precincts.[75]

The aging and the sick, fearful of remaining in the city but unable to flee, had come to the Grodno convent for security. A group of local girls banded together about Sister Thecla as relief service aides in the work which now became her inescapable occupation. Besides the newly acquired household of assorted residents, she received with cordial hospitality many a forlorn wanderer in need of food, rest and moral uplift. She performed these duties and all that came to hand, quietly, unobtrusively, not even conscious of the humility she had assumed. She spent a great deal of the night on her knees in prayer, and knew a great peace.

After the cessation of hostilities, countless road-weary returning soldiers, on the way to join their military units, were common visitors at the convent at all hours of the day. She welcomed and honored them as the defenders of faith and country, and replenished their knapsacks to capacity for the remainder of their journey.[76]

When life regained its normal pace, Sister Thecla directed her zeal to the rugged inhabitants at the fringe of the city. With the help of her Ladies of Charity, she plunged into the religious and social rehabilitation of children, youth and adults, mindful of the vivid experiences she shared with Mother Foundress in the early days of the London mission. She now descended along the slope of mercy until she reached the very abyss of ignorance and superstition where the Shepherd of souls himself was found leading the way to gather up what may have been lost.

It came as a tremendous surprise to her that her accomplishments were noted by the highest officials of state, when, at the age of 72, she was presented in public ceremony the Gold Cross of Merit. The award, accompanied by a citation signed by the President of the Republic of Poland, was conferred in recognition of the distinguished services she performed over and above ordinary civic duties.[77]

The general council was meanwhile giving serious attention to the constant flow of testimonies bearing evidence of unusual favors obtained through the intercession of Mother Mary of Jesus the Good Shepherd. Mother Lauretta and the councilors addressed a petition to the Sacred Congregation of Religious, December 2, 1920, requesting the examination of available facts and statements in the light of possible beatification of the Foundress. The request was well received and, on December 10, Monsignor Giovanni Bressan, former private secretary to Pope St. Pius X, was appointed the postulator. When the preliminary details were organized and approved, the Vicar of Rome Basilio Cardinal Pompili, instituted the canonical tribunal, January 8, 1922, to initiate the Ordinary Informative Process.

Interest in the person of Mother Mary was further heightened in ecclesiastical circles and elsewhere with the appearance of her biography, at first in Italian in 1921,[78] followed by a translation in Polish in 1924,[79] and an adaptation in French in 1926.[80] The work undertaken by Archbishop Vincenzo Sardi, who had known Mother Mary personally, was interrupted by his death, but was subsequently finished according to his original plan by Archbishop Carlo Sica. Since then, numerous minor biographical works and articles were published in several languages.

The first issues of Mother Mary's biography were off press too late to be received by Father Lechert. This was the final disappointment of his life; he died on January 15, 1921 at St. Mary of Nazareth Hospital, after a brief illness. Only the preceding summer, Benedict XV remembered him with a telegraphed message[81] on the occasion of his fiftieth anniversary of ordination to the priesthood. This was one of the high points of his career, similarly as at an earlier date when he had been drawn into a confidential interview with the previous Pontiff, Pius X.[82]

Conscious to the end, he radiated the serenity and charm of spiritual faith that had always marked his manner. He voiced the keynote of his life in a memorable statement he made during the closing days, "May one refrain ever resound in my soul, 'His will be done.' "[83] To Sister Antonia, the provincial in Des Plaines, he entrusted the disposition of his house in Washington, D. C., and its contents. Reverently preserved there was the vast correspondence of Mother Mary, which Sister Antonia dutifully forwarded to the archives of the generalate in Rome.[84] The house, situated at 922 Girard Street, became incorporated in the Immaculate Conception province, but was to be available to all the provinces as a house of studies for the sisters who would attend the Catholic University of America. The site, however, had definite drawbacks, and an even exchange was legally transacted for a comparable building at 1243 Monroe Street N. E.[85]

Before the small company of Father Lechert's Missionaries of Divine Love a yawning vacuum opened wide; no one seemed capable of taking up the torch of leadership. His priests admired him and remained devoted to the principles of his spirituality, but in the absence of an inspired leader they chose to join the ranks of diocesan clergy; the brothers, in turn, offered their services in parish rectories; thus the congregation as such gradually passed out of existence.

One other person who had looked forward to the publication of the biography and did not live to see it was Mother Raphael in Cracow. She died on March 20, 1921. Throughout the last years of her life, during the period of stress and peril beginning in 1914, she gave invaluable service and support to the convents in Poland in the role of coordinator. The sisters within the country and the general council in Rome were amazed at her ability and tact to function under pressure when it was necessary to make instant decisions effectively.

In collaboration with her sister, Mother Gabriel, she prepared a manuscript containing their reminiscences of Mother Mary of Jesus the Good Shepherd. She also produced four reflective works, bringing to the personal awareness of the sisters, for whom they were intended, that which stands at the very heart of the Nazareth ideal, as the titles clearly indicate: *Marya Niepokalana Naszym Wzorem* (Mary Immaculate Our Model),[86] *Jezus Chrystus Naszym Życiem* (Jesus Christ Our Life),[87] *Cnoty Droga Uświęcenia* (Virtues, the Road to Holiness),[88] and *U Stóp Najświętszej Eucharystii* (The Eucharistic Presence).[89]

In the United States, two of the new provinces, having solved the immediate technicalities of organization and management, established their central houses. The Immaculate Conception province acquired for that purpose the Middleton Estate in Torresdale, a suburb of Philadelphia, and occupied the premises in February, 1921. St. Joseph province again, moved in September, 1920, into its third place, a small residence in the subdivision of Avalon, near Pittsburgh.

About this time, a thorny problem was coming to the fore in Pittsburgh. The sisters in St. Casimir's convent were at the focal point, processing with the Lithuanian group in Chicago the arrangements to form a separate religious congregation with ethnic objectives in view. Bishop Hugh Boyle of Pittsburgh agreed to accept them as a diocesan community, and Mother Clare, assistant general, was delegated in January, 1922, to wind up the affairs with a delicate touch.

Canonical prescriptions had been carried out under instructions from the Sacred Congregation of Religious. What remained to be done was the personal approach to particulars through interviews held with the Ordinaries of Pittsburgh and Chicago, with the pastors of involved parishes, and regretfully with the sisters concerned. From the inception of the Lithuanian sisters' movement to withdraw, eight of the group were determined to remain with Nazareth. Mother Clare advised the others about the points of canonical procedure obliging them under the circumstances. Severance took place in the summer of 1922, and the Franciscan Sisters of the Providence of God came into being.[90]

Apart from settling the Lithuanian question, Mother Clare toured the convents in the United States, contributing broad insights to help the sisters bridge the transitional age. Since the Roaring Twenties have been revolutionizing the mores of the world, she pointed to genuine Christ-centered performance of the religious as a natural balance for the feverish activity and the new-found sense of adventure. In her travels she observed the incredible growth of schools which spurred the spontaneous construction of buildings, replacing those outworn, providing more and better equipped classrooms, erecting respectable convents for the staffs of teaching sisters. The people who supported the private educational system were gratified by the results it yielded over the years and inaugurated fund-raising campaigns to assure its progressive development.

The professional education of sisters was generally becoming oriented toward academic degrees in specific fields. In each of the American provinces the course schedules were individually adapted and guided by the deans of studies: Sister M. Agnes Kosiba, Chicago; Sister M. Neomisia Rutkowska, Philadelphia and the east, and Sister M. Chester Polentz, Pittsburgh. Artistic interests, especially instrumental and vocal music as well as painting and drawing, were earnestly cultivated, allowing latent potentials to emerge. The incubation time for new advances was long, and sustained faith and vision continued to be needed.

The year 1923 signified a milestone toward still newer dimensions in the life of Nazareth—in the world, though not of the world. On June 4, the Constitutions were accorded the definitive decree of approval by the Holy See,[91] confirming the Congregation in its character and purpose.

Incidentally, the reports of Sister Valeria's frequent and extended visits to the individual convents in Poland, followed by a personal visit of Mother Lauretta in the tidal era of national reconstruction, justified the recommendation to form yet another province. The number of houses and variety of services, the promising number of vocations and the densely occupied novitiate were statistics indicating healthy vitality. The only thing lacking was capital, and for that all eyes were turned hopefully to the sisters in the United States for assistance. On March 18, 1925, the province of the Holy Name of Jesus became canonically erected; Warsaw was its designated administrative seat, and Sister M. Bożena Staczyńska was named the provincial superior. The first provincial council consisted of Sister M. Anna, assistant; Mother M. Sophia, councilor; Sister M. Ancilla, treasurer, and Sister M. Emmanuel, secretary.

Bishop Achille Ratti, Nuncio to Poland, became Cardinal in Milan in 1921, and a year later, upon the death of Benedict XV, was elected to the papacy as Pius XI. He chose as his motto, "The peace of Christ in the reign of Christ" and, as a means of universally realizing it, he proclaimed 1925 a Holy Year, inviting all as one great human family, united in peace, to partake of the spiritual treasures of the Church, to enliven the faith at the ancient shrines of Christendom, and to venerate in fraternal harmony the relics of saints and martyrs for Christ.

Plans for the Holy Year introduced the possibility of accelerating the intermediate general chapter which normally should have been meeting in 1926. An earlier convocation enabled the chapter delegates to take part in the observances of the year of grace in Rome. Known as the chapter of affairs, the intermediate chapter assembled in Albano from July 17 to 27, 1925, to coordinate the common endeavors of religious life and apostolic work of the entire Congregation. Community practices, consistent with the provisions of the Constitutions, were discussed and agreed upon to enhance certain outward characteristic features of Nazareth mode of life.[92]

A review of the Congregation's withdrawals from particular locations since the chapter of 1920 led to an analysis of the criteria to be weighed seriously before moving into a new location or engaging in a new type of work. In retrospect, except in cases of emergency, three points were found essential to corporate continuity and productivity when considering new work, that is, the actual presence of a local need, a favorable response to the services proffered by the sisters, and an appreciable degree of local cooperation.

The chapter was briefed about the major undertakings current in the provinces, namely:

In the Sacred Heart province, Sister M. Antonia Danisch demonstrated the need for two building projects: one, a convent adjoining St. Mary of Nazareth Hospital in order to release the hospital rooms occupied by the sisters (completed in 1925); and the second, Holy Family Academy expansion of high school facilities (completed in 1927);

Sister M. Regina Wentowska, St. Joseph's provincial superior, presented the indications for erecting a composite structure including the provincialate, the novitate, and high school department named Mount Nazareth Academy (completed in 1927);

The provincial superior of the Immaculate Conception province, Sister M. Celestine Piekarska, outlined similar construction plans for the provincialate, the novitiate, and Nazareth Academy (completed in 1928);

Sister M. Bożena Staczyńska of the Holy Name of Jesus province reported the hope of completing the boarding school and provincialate in Warsaw with subsidies forthcoming from the American provinces (completed in 1926).

For the Sisters of the Holy Family of Nazareth everywhere, the Holy Year of 1925 closed with a special commemoration of the Congregation's fifty years of existence. Hosts of friends, clergy and lay, filled their chapels to join them in the liturgical services of gratitude to God, celebrated with appropriate solemnity on the first Sunday of Advent, the official foundation date. At its midcentury, the Congregation numbered 1,180 professed sisters and 79 houses.[93]

Houses of the Congregation
opened in the years 1919 through 1925:

Year	Location	Convent-Apostolate-First Superior
1919	POLAND Rabka	Our Lady the Good Shepherdess convent; open-air sanitarium and school for girls; Sister M. Tarsicia Bzowska.
1919	UNITED STATES Emsworth	St. Joseph convent;* temporary provincialate of St. Joseph province, transferred from Wesleyville, Pa.; Sister M. Agnes Kosiba.
1919	UNITED STATES Monessen, Pennsylvania	Virgo Fidelis convent: St. Hyacinth parish school; Sister M. Desideria Suchomska.
1919	UNITED STATES Ambridge, Pennsylvania	Our Lady Help of Christians convent;*** St. Stanislaus parish school; Sister M. Margaret Ruszkowska.
1919	UNITED STATES Cleveland, Ohio	Bl. Bronislava convent; Our Lady of Częstochowa parish school; Sister M. Gracianne Gadacz.
1919	UNITED STATES Springfield, Mass.	Our Lady of Consolation convent; Our Lady of the Rosary parish school; Sister M. Methodia Grubczak.

Year	Location	Convent-Apostolate-First Superior
1919	POLAND Lublin	Presentation of Our Lady convent** Nazareth house of studies; residence for female students attending Catholic University of Lublin; Sister M. Paul Gażycz.
1920	ITALY Rome	St. Stanislaus convent; guest house for pilgrims; Sister Maria-Josepha Waśkiewicz.
1920	UNITED STATES Brooklyn, New York	St. Francis Xavier convent; Sts. Cyril and Methodius parish school; Sister M. Charitas Nikielska.
1920	UNITED STATES Avalon, Pennsylvania	St. Joseph convent; temporary provincialate of St. Joseph province, transferred from Emsworth, Pennsylvania; Sister M. Agnes Kosiba.
1920	UNITED STATES Farrell, Pennsylvania	Holy Cross convent; St. Adalbert parish school; Sister M. Catherine Bombich.
1920	UNITED STATES Chicago	St. Francis of Assisi convent;**** Immaculate Conception parish school; Sister M. Baptista Laurinaite.
1921	UNITED STATES Philadelphia	Immaculate Conception B.V.M. convent; provincialate of the Immaculate Conception province; Sister M. Valentine Kapcia, provincial and local superior.
1921	UNITED STATES Washington, D.C.	Mother of Divine Love convent; Nazareth house of studies; Sister M. Sylvia Danisch.
1921	UNITED STATES Clayton, New Mexico	Patronage of St. Joseph convent; St. Joseph Hospital; Sister M. Amata Menge.
1923	UNITED STATES Chicago	St. Catherine of Siena convent; St. Camillus parish school; Sister M. Ladislaus Dahlke.

Year	Location	Convent-Apostolate-First Superior
1924	UNITED STATES Portage, Pennsylvania	St. Therese of the Child Jesus convent; Sacred Heart parish school; Sister M. Yvonne Poklenkowska.
1925	UNITED STATES Ozone Park, New York	St. Andrew Bobola convent; St. Stanislaus parish school; Sister M. Clarisse Siudowska.

Houses closed:

Year	Location	
1919	UNITED STATES Wesleyville, Pennsylvania	Convent of the Hidden Life of the Holy Family (1918-1919); temporary provincialate of St. Joseph province.
1919	SWITZERLAND Villars sur Glane, Fribourg	Patronage of the Holy Family convent (1917-1919); home for war orphans.
*1920	UNITED STATES Emsworth	St. Joseph convent; temporary provincialate of St. Joseph province; property absorbed by Holy Family Institute.
1920	AUSTRIA Vienna	Our Lady Help of Christians convent (1908-1920); elementary school; orphanage; student residence; provisional military hospital during World War I.
1920	UNITED STATES Cicero, Illinois	Queen of Virgins convent (1912-1920); St. Anthony parish school.
1920	UNITED STATES Everson, Pennsylvania	Holy Cross convent (1896-1920); St. Joseph parish school.
1920	UNITED STATES Argo, Illinois	Divine Providence convent (1917-1920); Providence Hospital
**1921	POLAND Lublin	Presentation of Our Lady convent; house of studies; residence for university students.

Year	Location	Convent-Apostolate-First Superior
***1922	UNITED STATES Ambridge, Pennsylvania	Our Lady Help of Christians convent; St. Stanislaus parish school.
****1922	UNITED STATES Chicago	St. Francis of Assisi convent; Immaculate Conception parish school.
1922	UNITED STATES Pittsburgh	Patronage of St. Joseph convent (1907-1922); St. Casimir parish school.
1922	UNITED STATES Detroit, Michigan	St. Aloysius convent (1918-1922); St. George parish school.
1923	UNITED STATES Chicago	Our Lady of Ostra Brama convent (1897-1923); St. George parish school.
1924	UNITED STATES Chicago	Presentation of Our Lord convent (1904-1924); Holy Cross parish school.

4 IN VERDANT PASTURES

The year 1926 recorded the twenty-eighth International Eucharistic Congress, held for the first time outside of Europe and detailed with matchless grandeur in Chicago under the auspices of George Cardinal Mundelein, the first cardinal of the West. For months the nationwide preparations for this event focused the attention of the Catholics in the United States upon the ineffable mystery of Christ's Sacramental Presence. The doctrine of the Eucharist and the practice of eucharistic faith were the high points of homilies and sermons for adults and of religious instructions in parochial schools. At the opening of the five-day ceremonies, a chorus of 62,000 school children sang the exquisite *Missa De Angelis* in Soldier Field, which in itself was a rewarding experience for the sisters who had invested generous hours of drill and practice to achieve its success.

That same year, by virtue of the solemn proclamation made by Pope Pius XI,[94] the Kingship of Christ was observed for the first time in the universal Church. By instituting an annual feast, the Supreme Pontiff desired to affirm Christ's social dominion over the world as King of souls and consciences as well as of peoples and nations. The liturgical triumph of Christ's eternal royalty sounded a familiar note in all the convents of Nazareth, for time and again Mother Mary of Jesus the Good Shepherd had referred to Christ as the Founder, Master and King of the Congregation, and unfolded in impassioned terms the role of the sisters in spreading the Kingdom of his love.[95] On this occasion Mother Lauretta, the superior general, relayed a formulation of insights based on the acknowledged reality of Christ's supreme reign having a direct bearing upon the attitudes of every Nazareth religious.[96]

The world in general was settling into an era of normalcy with comfortable optimism. Wherever the war wounds had not yet been stanched, the adjustments came about somewhat groaningly. It was a vigorous and enterprising time with a pronounced impact upon the social, economic and cultural structures transforming society on both sides of the Atlantic. Technology and industry celebrated the boom of profuse inventions and growth. Production of consumer goods spiraled upward in volume and variety. A widespread, intensified drive towards quality education swelled parochial and private school enrollments to unprecedented numbers.

The process of merging the reunited regions of Poland to function as an organic entity in various aspects of national life placed heavy demands upon the population of that country. Differing political views in government required the precious element of resilience, tested in patience, to arrive at a cooperative level of understanding among the leaders. An uncertain economy, incapable of providing security with progress, struggled for international credit and confidence, while life at home attempted to reshape the vestiges of dignity.

174

To meet the costs and consequences of rational human progress, Nazareth in Poland was caught between its moral commitments and the material limitations of its milieu. Although the repressive legislation formerly affecting schools that were conducted by religious groups was promptly repudiated, universal trends in education imposed soaring professional requirements including school buildings and equipment.

It was from the original inspiration of the Foundress that the institute, which grew out of it, derived the vital principle of continuing development. Not restricted to the place and period in which Nazareth became established, the principle ingrained in the concept of community extended to the evolving needs of all the apostolic works which the Congregation embraced throughout subsequent ages. From the earliest days of its existence the practice of sharing material assets through central channels of administration had been enjoined upon the sisters by Mother Mary of Jesus the Good Shepherd. The houses with inadequate resources and those being in more prosperous circumstances shared, as in the breaking of the bread of personal life, the enrichment they jointly offered others in the discovery of new vision and broader knowledge.

This practice, incorporated into the Constitutions to give witness to sisterly unity and Christian charity, was now more urgently invoked by Mother Lauretta.[97] The houses in the United States rallied to support the common cause which they recognized in the larger objectives of the Congregation's total mission. Out of the vowed evangelical poverty of their lives, individual and corporate, they assumed the responsibility for loans contracted to finance the necessary construction of Nazareth convent schools in Warsaw, Vilna, Kalisz, Częstochowa and Lemberg, and the combined school and sanitarium facilities in Rabka.

Since the loan funds were insufficient for building a school in Stryj, the flourishing program conducted there in a converted private residence was denied official approval by the Department of Public Instruction. Much to the regret of local citizens the sisters discontinued their work and withdrew in 1927. Eight years later they returned to Stryj with plans to resume their activities in a new context.[98]

Socially, the convent schools were not exclusive. Student admission policies, however, were selective to the extent that each school should fulfill its intellectual, social and religious aims. Mixed faculties, religious and lay, male and female, were appointed for their distinction in wide-ranging achievements and for their ability to advance the horizons of learning. The sisters were at last unhampered in their own pursuit of higher studies in the nation's leading universities in Cracow, Warsaw and Lublin and in other centers.

By 1929, the Grodno convent established as its affiliate a regular mission center in the rural community of Kochanów, inhabited by few

Byzantine-rite Catholics, fewer Roman Catholics, and predominantly by schismatics who had been forcibly separated from Catholic unity by intimidation and ruthless persecution. The change in political conditions awakened in the hearts of this frontier population the desire to return to Catholic orthodoxy. With the encouragement of the local deanery and the aid of the sisters, the ancient, deserted, rustic church of St. Michael the Archangel was reconditioned and restored to the worship of God. In a pervading religious awareness the people found the true and satisfying meaning of their existence through the sisters' catechetical instructions at all levels and the practical guidance for living the faith in actual daily situations.[99]

About this time, Bishop Zygmunt Łoziński requested the sisters to venture farther east—to Nowogródek situated on the banks of the Niemen river—where the need for cultural and religious rehabilitation was perhaps even greater. Their convent was arranged in the meager quarters of a poor rented dwelling. Despite the favorable reaction of the common people, the outlook for the sisters' future was at first severely shaken by antagonistic officialdom still wielding power in some positions of authority. Gradually the prejudices melted and vanished, and Nazareth pastoral ministry saw fruition in a warm acceptance and successful organization of an elementary school with the material support of local contributions.[100]

A proposition for a health resort in the enchanting foothills of the Tatra Mountains brought the sisters to Komańcza, the farthest southeasternly point overlooking the Czechoslovakian border. Among the towering pine forests covering the gentle slopes, the mountain air dissipated a magically clear and sparkling quality, wholesome and invigorating. Even before the amenities of the health resort were made available, the mountain folk of the region claimed the sisters' ministrations in the form of assistance for the sick at home, religion instruction of children, and the care of the small neglected church.[101]

In view of the widely scattered places where the sisters in Poland were engaged, their houses became grouped administratively to comprise two provinces with relation to 51° north latitude: in the north, Holy Name of Jesus province with the provincialate in Warsaw, and in the south, Holy Name of Mary province with the provincialate in Cracow.[102] The first provincial superior appointed to the latter province was Sister Anna Łyszczyńska.

In England, likewise, private schools were not exempted from state regulations and had to move in the general direction of progressive education to maintain an acceptable status. On the recommendation of Sister Virginia, secretary general, who visited Enfield, the sisters who staffed Holy Family convent school updated their qualifications[103] by complying with the latest requirements in teaching skills and content. This strengthened the prestige which the school already enjoyed and elevated its goals to a plane equivalent to that of junior high school.

They were asked forthwith to take full charge of St. Mary's parochial school in Ponder's End, a subdivision of Enfield, where until then a loose arrangement existed with the first Enfield convent for sister-instructors who commuted daily. That same convent was also approached to assign at least two competent sisters to help organize the faculty and construct the curriculum for the new neighboring school in St. George's parish. The association with St. George's was not permanent, but Sister Ancilla Dritz and Sister Berchmans Hickey were instrumental in opening up its paths to a sound and stable future.

While Sister Antonia Danisch managed these school and convent affairs[104] in Enfield, Mother Frances Morgenstern found that the mood in France towards the clergy and the religious orders was changing. In those years of the twenties sisters were still disqualified to teach, but were left undisturbed in other external activities and in their religious life. The small valiant group, teaching incognito in Gentilly, saw this as an opportunity to reestablish the apostolate Mother Mary of Jesus the Good Shepherd had originally envisioned for Nazareth in France. Equipped with a long and adventurous experience under one political crisis after another earlier in the century, Sister Redempta, now councilor general, arrived to survey the likely prospect at the moment.

Truly, a climate of tolerance prevailed by tacit agreement with public authorities and the allegiance of the faithful. The separation of Church and State was complete, but no longer inimical. Against the uneasy vacillations of French law and philosophy, it was a carefully contemplated choice just then to avoid the capital and remain in Gentilly. There a student residence was opened, at 63 Rue Montrouge, under the name of "Association Familiale pour la Protection des Etudiantes Etrangères." The purchase transaction was formally concluded, March 19, 1927, in the name of Sister Blanche Girardin, superior at St. Saturninus school in Gentilly.[105]

According to the laws regulating the ownership of property intended for public or social service, legal title was granted to chartered agencies with a governing board of at least seven members and a minimum membership-at-large of 100. In the light of past experience and fluctuating political trends, it was a delicate process to secure endorsements of French citizens which in a sudden change of fate could incriminate those who wished to be helpful. Fortunately, in this time of need, the good will and courageous support of numerous acquaintances were not lacking.

Sister Blanche piloted safely the student residence in its initial stage until Mother Frances came from England to take charge as the superior. Within a few months of operation so many students sought to obtain rooms there that a larger building became an evident necessity. To concentrate on the expanding project, withdrawal from the parochial school was smoothly carried out as soon as the transfer of the *foyer*[106] from Gentilly to Paris had been determined.

If any apprehensions overshadowed the idea of again going to Paris, they were replaced by the sense of preparedness coupled with knowing expectancy. On June 19, 1928, the sisters took possession of the building at 49 Rue de Vaugirard which, prior to the dispersion of religious orders in France, served as a house of studies for the Society of Priests of St. Sulpice. It was a joyous relief for the sisters to be able to wear the religious habit once more without fear of reprisal or reproof.

To record the steady wave of events and share the experiences of the Congregation with all the houses, the novitiate printshop in Albano began publishing a Nazareth news digest in 1927.[107] The first major work published there was the *Book of Customs* which had been under preparation since 1920.[108] Its first part, printed and distributed in 1928, drew upon the instructions communicated by the Foundress in her letters and conferences and aimed at cultivating within the Congregation a conscious Nazareth identity. The second part, which appeared in 1929, contained the analyses of the Congregation's administrative positions and their interrelating aspects.[109]

That the life of the mind and the life of the spirit need not be things apart was realized more and more in the sisters' work in the United States. The growth and vitality of Catholic parishes was matched by the striking growth of parochial schools, many of which numbered just under one thousand children, and some reached or exceeded two thousand. For tuition-supported schools these were amazing statistics. Rightly were they attributed to those who, prompted by demanding educational priorities, did not hesitate to move onward, to create and innovate. They understood that schools exist for the children who are contemporaries of their age, where the best of both worlds must be imparted to them: the wisdom of the past and the vision of the future, and where at the same time the accent must be on the present. People wanted education on this scale not because they desired ornamental knowledge of social graces, though these would be acceptable as by-products, but because it was needed.

The list of deans of studies and regional school supervisors, who set the creditable pace in that period, represented a cross-country team of far-sighted educators, namely, Sisters Euphemia Dahlke, Charitina Renklewska, Ildephonse Gums, Chester Polentz, Neomisia Rutkowska, Antonilla Zielińska and Laura Ławecka. Similarly, through the efforts of Sister Agnes Kosiba and Sister Loyola Jastroch, a preparatory program for prospective teachers was instituted in Des Plaines. Under the State of Illinois charter it was registered in 1927 as De Lourdes College.

In Pittsburgh, after the impressive dedication of the provincialate headquarters by Bishop Hugh C. Boyle, May 30, 1927, eighteen novices of St. Joseph province were brought from Des Plaines, August 8, to complete their religious formation in their own province.[110] They were accompanied on the train journey by Sister Renata Gapczyńska, newly appointed director of novices for the Pittsburgh novitiate, and Sister Anania Schmidt, assistant director. The arriving group joined nineteen younger novices who had only recently been admitted to the novitiate in Pittsburgh.

Simultaneously, in another wing of the provincialate building where Mount Nazareth Academy was to commence high school classes, Sister Chester was investing her energies as the principal. By 1930, the high school merited State approval by the Department of Education of Pennsylvania.

In Philadelphia, when in 1928 Sister Celestine was ending her term of office as provincial superior, the provincial house under construction, though habitable, was not yet finished. Her successor, Sister Idalia Górka, who had served as director of novices in Des Plaines over the preceding five years, arrived on August 21 with 35 novices who were to pursue the second-year novitiate program in Philadelphia. After their departure from Des Plaines, there remained in the novitiate of the Sacred Heart province 33 second-year novices and a group of 35 beginning the first year.

The first director of novices in the Immaculate Conception province, Sister Hyacinth Górecka, together with Sister Noela Linkowska, assistant director, installed the newly arrived novices and the following day all witnessed the reception ceremony of 52 postulants as first-year novices.[111] Formal dedication of the provincialate building by the Archbishop of Philadelphia, Dennis Cardinal Dougherty, took place on October 7, 1928.

The organization of Nazareth Academy as a high school unit in the new building was entrusted to Sister Neomisia, now appointed the principal. Advance announcements of the school's opening as of September, 1929, exerted immense pressures not only from a purely academic standpoint, but to a large degree because the availability of the school premises was uncertain due to the contractors' falling behind their work schedules.[112] Nevertheless, the school term opened, as announced, with a two-year academic program which was expanded the next year to a full four-year curriculum, accommodating those students who had already taken some courses elsewhere. In 1931, the academy was accredited by Pennsylvania State Department of Education.

The dual goals of the schools, to inculcate intellectual knowledge and to lead the young to Christianity, were promoted by two outstanding organizations, the National Educational Association and the National Catholic Educational Association. Both aimed at improving educational programs by improving the corps of teachers responsible for these programs in order to benefit the nation and the Church. Nazareth teachers actively subscribed to the pronouncements voiced by national leaders in fundamental and in higher education, and themselves participated productively at seminars, lectures and national meetings.

In nursing education important strides were taken in St. Mary of Nazareth School of Nursing when, in 1926, the regular nursing curriculum was coordinated by De Paul University with a sequence of college courses leading to the Bachelor of Science degree. By 1931, Sister Therese Netzel, director of nursing education, completed the satisfactory groundwork upon which formal affiliation of the school with the university was founded. In 1935, St. Mary's was "the only Catholic nursing school and hospital in the country wherein every sister in charge of any department has at least a Bachelor of Science degree in addition to her qualifications as a registered nurse."[113]

Religious, being ascetics by profession, are given to the austerity of self-discipline and the pursuit of excellence in their personal lives and in external commitments. The Nazareth religious, never actually intending to be looked upon as a group apart, considered seriously the responsibility for their social impact under the accelerated conditions of modern existence. For them, therefore, the reports of the steps undertaken towards the beatification of Mother Mary of Jesus the Good Shepherd revived the memory of the Foundress in the moral strength and beauty of an admirable life which they hoped to reflect.

In the five years devoted to the Informative Process, sworn testimonies were obtained from surviving witnesses wherever Mother Mary had spent a significant length of time and from others who had known her. The purpose of the inquiries was to accumulate opinions regarding Mother Mary's holiness as supported by factual accounts and to ascertain that neither her person or her relics were accorded the cult that is reserved to the saints who are recognized as such by the Church. For the completeness of this Process all the writings of Mother Mary were also collected.

On June 8, 1927, records of the testimonies were collated and presented to the Sacred Congregation of Rites in an official act known as Introduction of the Cause of Beatification. This Process was in turn concerned with the translation of all depositions into Latin, as well as the preparation of a text containing biographical data, an authentic summary of the testimonies thus far received, and the examination of Mother Mary's writings.

Suddenly, into the buoyant mood of the new era, when the world was rushing out of the twenties into the thirties, the panic of general economic collapse exploded in the United States with dismal repercussions around the globe. Beginning on the tragic Tuesday of October 29, 1929, bank failures at an alarming rate were precipitated by massive withdrawals of savings by the public. Merchants and manufacturers went out of business. Mine and metal industry ceased to function. The sharp drop in prices for farm products became a threat to the integrity of rural life. Average workingmen, dependent upon regular wages, were gripped by the terror of unemployment, the fear of a hard winter and the specter of starvation.[114] Employment at any type of occupation was a privilege, and education in private schools a commodity which few could afford.

One-half to two-thirds of the parochial school children transferred to public schools, and for those who remained tuition rates were flexible, frequently charged to the future. Teaching assignments, in consequence, were revised, and sisters possessing an aptitude for health care services were released to undertake specialized studies in paramedical fields.

People in the parishes remembered the sisters with gifts in kind during the grim, lean years of the depression, for adversities and frustrations did not harden many, but bred compassion for their variously beset fellowbeings. When mothers of families looked for jobs and took them on hard terms in the quest for normal and stable existence, parish kindergartens and nursery centers were established for pre-school children under the care of the sisters. Free lunches to undernourished children of regular school age became the usual order of the day in addition to those served to pre-schoolers. For similar reasons, this type of service developed also in Poland in connection with Nazareth-owned schools.

The European nations had been struggling to recover from the crippling aftermath of the first world war, tasting the bitter fruit of unemployment, inflation and government relief. The entire structure of postwar reconstruction in Europe had been built upon war loans advanced by America. In reflex action, the crisis of 1929 unleashed disruptive social havoc in the relatively homegeneous world and aggravated international tensions.

If breadlines were the barometer of unemployment, St. Mary of Nazareth Hospital in Chicago reviewed the readings in the steady flow of two hundred hungry men who patiently came with humble dignity three times daily for the substantial lunch they knew they would receive. But neither was the hospital spared the distress of these unhappy times. In the absence of health care insurance, the number of patients declined and uncollectible accounts surpassed the revenues. Were it not for the unlimited credit granted by suppliers, the hospital would not have been able to continue in the midst of the vast economic upheaval. Were it not for the dedication and essential charity of those persons who—in exchange for sheer daily maintenance—gave their services in professional and household areas, the effectiveness of the hospital would have been paralyzed.

The force of the depression wrought drastic changes in culture and mores with no discernible sign of recovery. This, and the fact that the term of office of Mother Lauretta as the superior general was ending, were weighty grounds in support of holding the Eighth General Chapter in 1932, as forecast. The capitulants assembled in Albano were addressed by Cardinal Protector Van Rossum on the opening day of the chapter, June 2. He laid emphasis upon their obligation in conscience to elect to the general administration the best qualified members, known to be intent upon preserving the purpose for which the Congregation was founded and fully cognizant of the primacy of supernatural goals to which it was pledged.[115]

Referring to the questions which had been privately directed to him concerning the election of the superior general, the Cardinal explained openly the canonical legislation governing this matter. Nazareth Constitutions, definitively approved, prescribed a twelve-year term for the superior general with the possibility of reelection for another twelve years, but not beyond. Mother Lauretta, having been elected to two successive terms, could not validly qualify for election at this time. However, Cardinal Van Rossum brought to the attention of the chapter the exception permitted under extraordinary circumstances,[116] whereby what could not be accomplished by standard electoral norms might be achieved by postulation, that is, by requesting the Holy See to approve a desired choice. To gain such consideration, at least two-thirds of the votes would necessarily have to show *postulo* written in with the name of the nominee.[117]

Elections were held the next day under the presidency of the Cardinal Protector. Impressed by the unanimous postulation in behalf of Mother Lauretta, he declared in the Gospel words of the Nativity, "I announce to you the good news of great joy: Mother Lauretta is your superior general." He stated that he had been empowered by the Holy See to lift the statutory ban and grant the chapter's request.[118]

Reelected to the general council were Mother Clare Netkowska, as assistant general, and Sister Redempta Siefert; newly elected councilors were Sister Agnes Kosiba, chosen also to be the secretary general, and Sister Jerome Gostomska. Sister Mary Magdalene was retained in the office of treasurer general.

In the first part of the discussions the chapter concentrated on the quality of religious life in the Congregation. The delegates reviewed specifics for building the self-concept of the sisters in dignity and confidence through a deeper appreciation and deliberate practice of the vows in the context of daily living. Much importance was attached to related aspects contained in the trenchant encyclicals of Pope Pius XI in which he clearly demonstrated the primacy of spiritual values.

His call instructing the faithful in their duty of reparation towards Christ[119] revived the selfsame message, often addressed to the sisters by Mother Mary of Jesus the Good Shepherd. His recommendation to begin a reform from within, by means of prayer and soul-searching reflection in retreats,[120] introduced the movement to enrich the usual monthly retreat days in each Nazareth convent with the aid of zealous directors. Appropriate opportunities were provided for the superiors to assist them in their personal growth and at the same time to open avenues to enlightened consultations. Outstanding in the wise and helpful guidance given the sisters over the years were Fathers Richard Bakalarczyk, M.I.C., and Bruno Hagspiel, S.V.D.

The Supreme Pontiff further appealed for prayer of expiation to the Sacred Heart of Jesus[121] to instill among the faithful a powerful current of gratitude for the Savior's redemptive love and invoke his saving mercy upon the world in distress. His summons shed a renewed eminence upon the sisters' own practice of reparation and confirmed their offering of the midnight hour before the first Friday of each month as a prayer vigil of atonement. Once again strengthened in the mystery of God, they were reminded that as members of the human race their prayers like their apostolic works were meant to be a service for all mankind.

Amid the drastic dislocations of society, the Popes' timely statements on Christian education of youth[122] enlisted the noblest incentives of religious teachers to broaden and intensify their teaching apostolate in the crucial moments when all indeed might have been lost.

The encyclical on Catholic Action,[123] originally addressed to the bishops of Italy, gave impetus to a tremendous movement that encircled the world. Because of their contact with youth, the sisters as moderators conveyed the underlying ideas to their students, defining the proper and indispensable role of Catholic laity in the mission of the Church. As a preparation for future leadership in the lay apostolate, they were instructed in the various opportunities open to them by giving an example of credible Christian living, by the exercise of good works in the supernatural spirit, and by cooperating to restore the temporal order in society.

A Catholic Action branch, associated with the motherhouse in Rome, was the Holy Family Circle begun by Sister Benilda Józefowicz It consisted of several age groups and perdured to our times. Over and above other diocesan and national youth organizations, the Catholic Action groups flowered into many-sided interests on both hemispheres. Flowing out of the Nazareth inspiration, there were those dedicated predominantly to religious activity, as the Eucharistic Crusade, the Living Rosary, and the catechetical aides; of charitable and social nature were student mutual assistance clubs, Junior Red Cross, child welfare groups concerned with the needs of pre-school children of indigent families; of patriotic and humane interest were the Youth League for Air Defense and the Friends of Animals. Alumnae associations also gained new vitality and fresh motivation.

Gradually parents of students mobilized their initiatives in mothers' and fathers' clubs, joining forces to help establish school libraries, plan hot lunches for the children, organize vacation camps and educational and recreational outings. Periodically, programs for adults were offered to expand their cultural knowledge and religious values.

As in the founding days of Nazareth, lay retreats were again sponsored to lead souls of good will to the greater love of those truths which should enable them to live as children of God. Outstanding in this endeavor was Sister Charitina Renklewska. A dynamic educator, always completely aware, sensitive, affable in her many contacts, she kindled the mystic spark of enthusiasm among lay associates and friends in Philadelphia who became eager for the outpourings of grace in the intimacy of a retreat. The first such retreat was given in the Advent season of 1934 as a day of recollection and was repeated the next spring during Lent, after which three-day retreats were introduced at the wish of the retreatants. Planned by the sisters and presided over by retreatmasters, these encounters with God became regular happenings acclaimed by the participants for the benefits they derived.

Barely had the decisions and directives of the Eighth General Chapter been dispatched when the unanticipated death of Cardinal Van Rossum, August 30, 1932, deprived the Congregation of its ecclesial protector and advisor. He was esteemed by popes and dignitaries of the Roman Curia for his wise, indefatigable service to the Church.[124] His work as the Prefect of the Propagation of the Faith was marked by sincere cosmopolitan approaches, pointing out the complementarity of diverse traditions to achieve the spirit of Christian brotherhood. His life as a Redemptorist was a model of unshakeable loyalty that lay deep at the very heart of his strength.

Of foremost importance to Nazareth was his personal acquaintance with Mother Mary of Jesus the Good Shepherd for whom he had high reverence and referred to her even at the recent chapter as "your holy Mother Foundress."[125] The vacant position of Cardinal Protector was filled on June 10, 1933 by Eugenio Cardinal Pacelli, the Secretary of State of Pope Pius XI.

Houses of the Congregation
opened in the years 1926 through 1932:

Year	Location	Convent-Apostolate-First Superior
1926	UNITED STATES Gary, Indiana	Patronage of the Holy Family convent;** Holy Family parish school; Sister M. Vladimir Jóźwiak.
1926	UNITED STATES Latrobe, Pennsylvania	St. John the Evangelist convent;* St. John the Evangelist parish school; Sister M. Ludvina Strzelecka.
1926	UNITED STATES Dearborn, Michigan	Sacred Heart convent; St. Barbara parish school; Sister M. Nazarene Niewiadoma.
1926	UNITED STATES Detroit, Michigan	St. Aloysius convent; Transfiguration parish school; Sister M. Gracianne Gadacz.
1926	UNITED STATES Ansonia, Connecticut	St. Agnes convent; St. Joseph parish school; Sister M. Noela Linkowska.
1927	UNITED STATES Pittsburgh	Patronage of St. Joseph convent; provincialate and novitiate of St. Joseph province, also Mount Nazareth Academy; Sister M. Lucy Madaj.
1927	UNITED STATES Paterson, New Jersey	Holy Name of Jesus convent; St. Stephen parish school; Sister M. Charitina Renklewska.
1927	UNITED STATES Baltimore, Maryland	Nativity of Our Lord convent; Sacred Heart of Mary parish school; Sister M. Camilla Lange.
1927	FRANCE Gentilly and Paris	Mother of Divine Providence convent; residence for female university students; Mother M. Frances Morgenstern.

Year	*Location*	*Convent-Apostolate-First Superior*
1928	UNITED STATES Philadelphia	Immaculate Conception B.V.M. convent; provincialate and novitiate of Immaculate Conception province, also Nazareth Academy; Sister M. Idalia, provincial and local superior.
1928	UNITED STATES Philadelphia	St. Clare convent; St. Mary of Częstochowa parish school; Sister M. Domina Krzewińska
1928	UNITED STATES McAdoo, Pennsylvania	St. Martina convent; St. Kunegunda parish school; Sister M. Rosalia Łagodna.
1928	UNITED STATES Lansing, Michigan	Christ the King convent; St. Casimir parish school; Sister M. Regina Wentowska.
1928	UNITED STATES Harvey, Illinois	St. Francis of Assisi convent; St. Susanna parish school; Sister M. Tatiana Zalewska.
1928	POLAND Komańcza	St. Therese of the Infant Jesus convent; health resort; pastoral ministry; catechetical instructions; Sister M. Clemens Korkuć.
1929	POLAND Nowogródek	Christ the King convent; pastoral ministry, elementary school; Sister M. Flora Nagłowska.
1929	ENGLAND Ponders End, Mddx.	Loreto convent; St. Mary's primary school; Sister M. Alphonsus Leggett.
1929	UNITED STATES Dalhart, Texas	Our Lady of Loreto convent; Loretto Hospital; Sister M. Edith Cummins.
1930	UNITED STATES McKees Rocks, Pa.	Our Lady of Perpetual Help convent; Ohio Valley General Hospital and School of Nursing; Sister M. Ambrose Krueger.

Year	Location	Convent-Apostolate-First Superior
1930	UNITED STATES Linden, New Jersey	St. Therese convent; St. Therese of the Child Jesus parish school; Sister M. Lucidia Gajewska.
1931	UNITED STATES Mineral Wells, Texas	Holy Family convent; Nazareth Hospital; Sister Marie de Lourdes Mazalewska.
1931	UNITED STATES Chicago	St. Angustine convent; Holy Rosary parish school; Sister M. Perseverance Szymańska.
1931	UNITED STATES Pittsburgh	Mary Mother of God convent; St. Hyacinth parish school; Sister M. Catherine Bombich.
1932	UNITED STATES Philadelphia	Mother of Divine Love convent; sisters' infirmary and rest home; Sister M. Amata Menge.

Houses closed:

Year	Location	Convent-Apostolate-First Superior
1927	UNITED STATES Avalon, Pennsylvania	St. Joseph convent (1920-1927); temporary provincialate of St. Joseph province; provincialate transferred to new quarters.
1928	FRANCE Gentilly	Our Lady of Loreto convent (1891-1928); St. Saturninus diocesan parish school.
*1929	UNITED STATES Latrobe, Pennsylvania	St. John the Evangelist convent; St. John the Evangelist parish school.
1931	ITALY Rome	St. Stanislaus convent (1918-1931); pilgrim house.
**1932	UNITED STATES Gary, Indiana	Patronage of the Holy Family convent; Holy Family parish school.

5 FRUITFUL AS A VINE

For all believing Christians and for the world at large, the Sovereign Pontiff proclaimed the year 1933 a jubilee of grace. Mankind had arrived at the nineteen-hundredth milestone of Christ's incomparable act of Redemption which endowed it with the hope of future life in glory by the fact of his Resurrection. Generally speaking, jubilees are a pause at a landmark of one's pilgrim road to contemplate the meaning of life in the passage of time through the process of a spiritual audit and adjustment. Although the graces of the jubilee were primarily associated with visits to the Roman basilicas, for those who were unable to travel the Holy Father extended the same benefits on easily substituted conditions.

The emergence of a man called Adolf Hitler appeared as an antithesis to the work of grace. His devious political dealings began to impinge upon world consciousness. Already by 1933 the European pleasure resorts were emptying in consternation and tourists kept a wary eye upon the gathering cloud of distrust that rose from the flurry of shrewdly calculated non-aggression pacts, disarmament agreements and peace treaties.

Meanwhile, for four bleak years since the financial crash of 1929, social patterns sagged in the depths of the depression, afflicting family life with disastrous reverses. It was in a true spirit of the Nazareth vocation that the sisters turned with solicitude to the commonplaces of family existence to help safeguard family living in unity and dignity by investing their own humanity in the current need. Their visits to the homes grew into a large scale design for pastoral and social ministry, couched in the charity of Christ that expected neither recognition nor reward. They met the families on their own ground and shared their human values and cares through the little work of many hands.

With the fundamental changes that occurred in society, special religion classes for non-parochial school children developed quite naturally. These led to more extensive missionary objectives. The sisters accepted summer assignments in remote places where frequently one priest alone served unaided several widely scattered communities the year round. In populous cities, during summer vacations, they found collaborating teams in diocesan and civic programs, conducted in public parks and other centers, not only to bring in the poor from the streets but also to introduce them to books, beauty and culture. Arts and crafts, hobbies and games, story hours and music ensembles were all geared to be experienced together in a Christian atmosphere in order to give the young a natural foundation to discover the meaning of religion in real life.

On another level, there was a trend among teachers to exchange practically rewarding insights in the common search for improvement and relevance. Sisters Infanta Kurcz, Oswaldine Marcinska and Adria Grochowiak conducted periodical demonstrations of successful innovative primary-

188

grade methods which were open to interested religious of all congregations.

Because life had to go on in the present and in the future as well, it was necessary to look beyond the helplessness and desperation that covered the world like a pall. Though recovery from the depression was painfully slow and long, the Congregation steered its members toward continuing preparedness through qualifying teacher education courses. To reach large classes of sisters at any one time, the courses were organized in the respective provincialates as university extensions under the authority of select universities.

No less fertile in the scope and quality of influence for the future have been the fresh approaches to advanced studies outside of one's native country. Annually during this period, the advantages of a sabbatical year, or longer, opened new sources for intellectual exploration. The representative trickle of American sisters to European universities commenced in 1932 with Sisters Bonosa Siedlecka and Veronica O'Donovan who went to England. But destiny trailed Sister Veronica; she consented to teach in Enfield and remained abroad permanently. For Sister Bonosa the foreign experience was colorful and varied; having completed the projected studies in London, she became the principal in Enfield, was then appointed to the high school faculty in Warsaw, and at the outbreak of World War II proceeded to the motherhouse in Rome to work in the archives.

In 1933, the first three who matriculated at the University of Cracow were Sisters Reginia Zielińska, Pulcheria Pol and Liguori Pakowska. Upon their return to the United States, both Sisters Reginia and Pulcheria became high school principals, although Sister Pulcheria had taken an added year of studies at the University of Warsaw before returning. Sister Liguori, moreover, after fulfilling the requirements for a doctorate, administered the high school in Warsaw for one year and later served in a similar capacity in Pittsburgh. Her liberal contributions to the learned journal, *The Polish American Historical Studies*,[126] were the fruit of her unceasing interest in historical research. In richly documented articles she highlighted persons of Polish ancestry whose careers ennobled the American way of life.

For three years, beginning in 1936, several sisters with advanced university standing were recipients of one-year scholarships at the University of Warsaw.[127] The scholarship program, funded by the World Federation of Poles Abroad, encompassed Polish heritage studies—language, history, literature, art forms and folkways—that carried credits recognized by American universities.

The first Nazareth religious from the United States to study in Paris, Sister Theophane Machan, was awarded a diploma by the faculty of French letters at Sorbonne University, designating her as professor of French language and literature. Subsequently, as high school principal for fifteen years and head of the department of modern languages, she continued to teach French classes with brilliant success. To benefit from an extended sojourn in Paris, Sister Laurence Crowe from England and Sister Ezechiela Szupenko from Poland also came to the French capital in this period.

Charting an important course in the Congregation's education mission fell to Sister Neomisia Rutkowska when, in 1934, she began teaching at the Sisters' College of the Catholic University of America. Then, in 1937, she was invited to join the faculty of the Department of Slavonic Languages. Concurrently with this appointment she completed the doctoral dissertation which had been in progress when the latter position was offered to her. She was associated with the Catholic University of America until, in 1943, she was called upon to fill offices of responsibility within the Congregation.

Implicit in the cultural perspectives of individuals and groups, music always held a unique opportunity for the sisters, a common bond linking all artistic forms and responses with warmth and charm. Not only was individual talent encouraged to grow and blossom, but the creative force of music, instrumental and vocal, found its expression in the communal effort of provincial choirs and provincial orchestras of the sisters. Much of the appreciation and understanding of music among the religious at this particular point in time was due to the enthusiasm of Sisters Amabilis Kudialis, Lucille Doyno, Anatolia Dylnicka, Electa Glowienke and Alma Kowalska. Liturgical music as such received proper emphasis and refinement through the specialized attention of Sisters Theobald Jaskulska, Assumpta Strenkowska, Amata Łokuciewska and Charitas Mikosz.

Similarly, interest in music and acceptance of it throughout Nazareth's elementary schools in the United States can be credited to the initial attempts of Sister Joanine Niewiadoma and the persevering guidance for twenty years of Sister Cordia Skonieczna. The observations and personal conclusions accumulated while imparting methods in music education inspired Sister Cordia to enlarge the children's contact with music beyond the basic repertoire traditionally available for school purposes. Together with Sister Amabilis, she compiled two volumes of Polish songs, popular and classical, to give the pupils a new lyric experience tinged with the fascination of old world melodies.[128]

In Poland, the year 1934 saw country-wide implementation of the school reform that fitted the school system to twentieth-century education. It had been long apparent that the residual system from the past, bearing the markings of foreign rule, inhibitive and suppressive, was unsatisfactory and had to be replaced in order to conform to contemporary society. Nazareth schools have at once adopted the new organizational structures of elementary, secondary and junior college levels with respective grade classifications. The transition was costly and complicated and required parallel planning for some years to provide for two categories of students, namely, those who had begun their education under the old system and had to be guided methodically to completion, and the new registrants upon whom the new system was being built.

Under the revised school system the sisters were better able to utilize the psychological equipment of their Nazareth spirituality. Respecting the personality of every student and considering the natural endowment of each, they dealt with a harvest of souls and a potential intellectual force for the future. Developing the whole person by integrated education aimed to increase the value of growing Christians under their direction while they were helped to discover and use the gifts of God that awaited the acceptance of a challenge.

The fiftieth anniversary of Nazareth's foundation in the United States, in 1935, was a spiritual celebration commemorated in solemn liturgies of thanksgiving through the Eucharistic Sacrifice and in the unity of spirit renewed through the personal visit of Mother Lauretta. For her the observance brought distant memories of the first landing in New York and the arrival in Chicago, in 1885, with Mother Foundress and ten other pioneers. As a memorial of the golden jubilee, a wayside shrine of the Holy Family on the provincial grounds in Des Plaines, facing River Road, was dedicated by the Auxiliary Bishop of Chicago, William D. O'Brien, on July 14, 1935. It was financed by Holy Family Ladies Auxiliary, a goodwill society, organized October 29, 1934, for the purpose of raising funds for the education of aspirants to the Sisters of the Holy Family of Nazareth.

In announcing her intention for the jubilee visit, Mother Lauretta made an explicit plea to the superiors and sisters to maintain unaffected simplicity in all preparations. The better to partake of the unencumbered joy of the children of God, she urged them to preserve the outward restraint of religious poverty as being consistent with the overwhelming poverty that stalked the world. For, carrying even into the innermost recesses of private life, the voluntary poverty they embraced for the kingdom of heaven equipped them to proclaim convincingly the beatitude of poverty to the poor and to inject dignity into their frugal living.

Despite the unrelieved tribulations of the times, two fields of fruitful apostolic activity opened separate historic chapters. One was the expansion of hospital care of the sick in new locations; the second, the extension of negro apostolate into unfamiliar environments.

Two small hospitals in southwestern United States heralded in fact the growth of Nazareth hospital services. At the request of Archbishop Albert T. Daeger of Santa Fe, the provincial superior, Sister Antonia Danisch, took charge of a seven-bed sanitarium in Clayton, New Mexico, in 1921, and named it St. Joseph Hospital. Situated on a high plateau, Clayton, a county seat in the northeastern corner of the State, was inhabited mostly by plodding farmers and small ranchers. Because the mild, dry climate was particularly beneficial to persons suffering with respiratory ailments, the next provincial, Sister Ignatius Romanowska, was assured that many patients would be referred to Clayton if sufficient provisions were made to accommodate them. In 1928, St. Joseph's was enlarged to a three-story, 25-bed hospital with standard clinical departments for total health care.

That same year, Sister Ignatius received from the Chamber of Commerce of Dalhart, Texas, a tract of land upon which to build another hospital. Bordering with New Mexico and stretching just across the State line from Clayton, Dalhart was similarly engaged in farming and cattle raising and enjoyed the same bracing climate. It had the additional advantage of an active railroad junction where convenient hospital facilities for trainmen and their resident families had been repeatedly urged by railroad officials. On May 1, 1929, the 40-bed Loretto Hospital was opened to the public after dedication by Bishop Rudolph A. Gerken of Amarillo.

The beautiful vision of a healing apostolate for body and soul was dimmed when the great depression descended upon the whole country. The woes of the times were multiplied in the southwest by harvestless years caused by a long, persistent drought and devastating sandstorms. Staggering losses in agriculture and livestock, as well as curtailed railroad timetables, forced many people to move away. The sisters remained with the impoverished population and the few sturdy characters who with them upheld the sense of mission in these remote and strangely isolated places, scarcely touched by religion.

But hospitals everywhere bowed beneath widespread misfortunes. Many of the proprietary hospitals under secular management were compelled to close, while others applied to Catholic sisterhoods to assume charge. Ohio Valley General Hospital, a 70-bed institution with a school of nursing, owned and conducted by a Board of Incorporators in McKees Rocks, Pennsylvania, was confronted with such predicament. Rather than deprive this industrial suburb of Pittsburgh of medical treatment and care for its residents by withdrawing, the Board invited Sister Hilary Okon, provincial superior of St. Joseph province, to acquire the hospital. In the final agreement the Board of Incorporators retained the ownership and the sisters accepted full responsibility for administration and service, beginning November 1, 1930. Four professionally qualified sisters with a background of experience were the key personnel who came from the Sacred Heart province. Among them were Sister Ambrose Krueger, superior-administrator, and Sister Margaret Mary Wilkowska, director of nursing education and nursing service.

The provincial of the Sacred Heart province, Sister Ignatius, was at this time in the midst of a building project. A six-story north wing to St. Mary of Nazareth Hospital had been proposed, encouraged and planned, and was now under way without interruption, for she was a woman of faith and prayer, and of action likewise. She had came to the office of the provincial with a five-year service record as hospital administrator at St. Mary's —always equal to the present moment, the contemporary moment, and equal to the future as well. When a new 40-bed hospital building in Mineral Wells, Texas, was offered to her, she recommended the purchase to Mother Lauretta and obtained the general council's approval, December 29, 1930.

The town of Mineral Wells in north central Texas grew in attraction and popularity because of its natural mineral wells with curative properties. It was a health and pleasure resort, and the processing of mineral crystals was its principal industry. To house the increasing volume of visitors during the boom years, new hotels were erected and also the hospital which suddenly had to close its doors after a brief one year of operation. When on January 13, 1931 six sisters from Chicago arrived, they organized the hospital anew, naming it Nazareth Hospital. It was dedicated with public ceremony, June 7, by Bishop Joseph P. Lynch of Dallas.

Influenced by this turn of events, Dr. Robert L. Hargrave of the Hargrave-Walker Hospital in Wichita Falls, Texas, lost no time in trying to interest the Sisters of the Holy Family of Nazareth in his 35-bed institution. Located in the eastern part of the State and near the Oklahoma border, Wichita Falls is a residential city of successful oil industrialists and grain and cotton growers whose fields spread out deep into the heart of Texas. The proposition—though tabled by the Congregation's general council on March 25, 1931, for lack of qualified sisters at the moment—was revived three years later and terminated in a satisfactory arrangement on the last day of 1934. On New Year's day the sisters took legal possession of the hospital property which from then on became known to local and neighboring communities as Bethania Hospital. Here, too, Bishop Lynch officiated at the dedication which was performed with civic and religious solemnity on March 19.

Almost simultaneously, in the province of St. Joseph, deliberations were carried on between Mercy Hospital Board of Directors of Altoona, Pennsylvania and the provincial council concerning the terms of an option under which the Congregation might obligate itself to administer Mercy Hospital without acquiring its ownership. The hospital was in existence since 1910 in Altoona, a bituminous coal region with a sprinkling of textile factories. It had grown to 160-bed capacity and was now in administrative difficulties.

When an equitable contract was negotiated, the sisters arrived on May 1, 1935 to take over the essential tasks. The province already had a number of professionally prepared members for hospital duties, and was assisted by the Sacred Heart province with the person of Sister Isabella Jóźwiak to be the superior-administrator, the position she previously held with distinction at St. Mary of Nazareth Hospital. From the Immaculate Conception province came Sister DeChantal Krysińska, a competent registered nurse, to take charge of the nursing department as its director. Five days later, Bishop John McCort of Altoona celebrated the first Holy Mass in the hospital chapel and delivered a memorable homily.

And in Philadelphia, where in 1934 Sister Ignatius followed Sister Idalia as provincial, careful plans were being advanced as early as 1935[129] for the establishment of a hospital in the Immaculate Conception province. Because of the prevailing economic conditions, stringent budget limitations were experienced with unavoidable delays. These were counterbalanced in hope by the continuing interest of Cardinal Dougherty, who was impressed that the sparsely inhabited northeast sector of Philadelphia would develop into a thriving district of the metropolis at which time the realities of hospital services should be recognized.

The Congregation's general administration affirmed the validity of the project and approved it. Eventually the confidence of the local public, expressed by underwriting the costs through voluntary contributions, culminated in three unforgettable events graced by the Cardinal Archbishop of Philadelphia: March 25, 1939, groundbreaking; September 10, 1939, blessing of the cornerstone, and March 9, 1940, ritual dedication of the 150-bed Nazareth Hospital.

During this time, Sister Regina Wentowska, provincial superior in the Sacred Heart province, was unexpectedly informed in 1936 by Archbishop Rudolph A. Gerken, now of Santa Fe, of the gift which Mrs. Mabel Dodge Luhan wished to make for hospital purposes. It was an estate with a newly built mission-style mansion in Taos, New Mexico, a spectacular village resting at the foot of a chain of the Rocky Mountains, known as the Sangre de Cristo Mountains. Aside from the artists' colony, the seasonal skiers and the pueblo Indians which add greatly to the charm of Taos, the population was predominantly Spanish-speaking. Upon legal transfer of the property title to Nazareth and after appropriate alterations in the building, it became Holy Cross Hospital with a 20-bed capacity, dedicated and opened on January 30, 1937.

Another hospital dedication, scheduled for March 19, was to be held at Tyler, Texas, a throbbing commercial and industrial city, the rose kingdom of the south. Designed to serve 60 patients, the hospital was built as a municipal project under the Public Works Administration, which was one of many government agencies organized for unemployment relief. After months of consideration and discussions between Tyler and Nazareth authorities, workable terms for a five-year lease were agreed upon with the option to renew the lease at the end of that period or to purchase the building. To honor the Foundress of the Congregation, it was named Mother Frances Hospital.

Its formal opening was antedated by the sisters' response to the emergency occasioned by the school explosion in nearby New London, March 18, 1937, when the doors of the hospital were thrown open to receive and treat the victims. In a simple dedicatory ceremony the next day, Bishop Lynch fittingly pointed out that the hospital was consecrated by the sufferings of over one hundred persons, children and adults, who were the first patients, and by the compassionate care given to them.

It was through the mediation of Bishop Lynch that Sister Regina's attention was brought to Vernon, Texas, a town of cotton gins and oil refineries. There Dr. Thomas A. King, owner and administrator of a 30-bed hospital, decided to withdraw his proprietary interest in the hospital, offering it to the Sisters of the Holy Family of Nazareth. The legal transfer of title was followed by a formal opening, June 4, 1937, under the new name of Christ the King Hospital.

The last addition to St. Mary of Nazareth Hospital, which was completed in 1931, made possible the admission totaling upward of 300 patients to various clinical services. The effectiveness of these services was attended early by the scientific approach to patients' nutritional needs through the individualized planning and personal instructions of Sister M. Laurettana Bogacz, therapeutic dietician. To facilitate and coordinate the professional administration of the hospital, the practice of dual authority was initiated in 1937. The local superior retained the responsibility for the convent and for the spiritual and temporal welfare of the sisters, while the administrator was charged with the direct responsibility for the operation of the hospital, its professional quality and spiritual vitality. Sister Therese Netzel became the first administrator to receive the separate delegation of authority.

Then, in 1938, Sister Aloysius Żmich was appointed vicar provincial for Texas and New Mexico with delegated powers in the administration of regional affairs affecting the seven hospitals of the Sacred Heart province. The regional office was established at Loretto Hospital, Dalhart, Texas.

The advancing standards in medicine, technology and nursing were paralleled in all the hospitals by the special touch that came at the hands of womanhood consecrated to the things of God. Many persons began to take religion seriously when they became strikingly aware of death and then turned to the sisters for a supportive message and prayer. The cheer and friendly humanity of the sisters, without proselytizing, made Christ present to the patients and medical staffs alike. Their diligence and honest sympathy motivated the hospital personnel and drew the general public into the orbit of hospital-related activities in the form of auxiliaries, guilds and clubs. Wherever Catholic population was in the minority, the hospital sisters gave of their time to conduct classes in Christian doctrine and sacramental preparation for children and, incidentally, for adults.

In Poland, the sisters assumed the responsibility for patient care and the management of a small county hospital just outside the manufacturing town of Równe, northeast of Lemberg. In the course of 1937-1938, Bishop Edward Szelążek, distressed by the deplorable conditions which he discovered there during his pastoral tour, appealed to Mother Lauretta whose boundless concern for the welfare of the sick was widely known. By October, 1938, arrangements with the administration were concluded and eight sisters with many-sided qualifications arrived at the hospital, introducing order, efficiency and Christian atmosphere.

The second significant apostolic field opened to Nazareth the hard problems involved in bringing about humane social change to negroes in their northern isolation and their southern insulation. The charity of Mother Mary of Jesus the Good Shepherd traced a blueprint for the sisters of the future to follow when God should summon them to the task in his own good time.

The time was ripe in 1933, prior to the days of effective racial integration. Father Arnold Garvey, S.J., was faced with teacher recruitment for St. Joseph mission school in Chicago, an offshoot of a parochial school where segregationist pressures had prevailed against a uniform admission policy. It was then that Sister Regina Wentowska accepted the staffing challenge for the Sacred Heart province. All her life she held dear the memory of Mother Foundress with whom, as a young religious, she had occasion to become personally acquainted during her last twelve-month visit to the United States; now she recognized in the mission call the charisma of the Foundress for the Congregation.

A private home, converted for the mission's purpose, became the center of activity. The sisters lived in improvised convent quarters; the chapel as also the improvised schoolroom facilities were all housed under the same roof. Without some measure of austerity, they realized, they had no right to teach democracy or Christianity. They were almost the only white people on this inner city island, but their nearness and understanding established through the children a kind of kinship with the adults that tended to eradicate the hot resentment engendered by what they had felt was unfair treatment.

Fortunately, interest in intergroup relations ran high among unbiased, generous individuals from other parts of the city who voluntarily promoted the work of the sisters. The local inhabitants, taking their cues on the rebound, banded into mutual aid groups to help themselves over the hurdle of marginal poverty, caused by the helplessness of their limitations and the appalling unemployment that plagued the country. Reassured in their self-esteem, they were strengthened in their natural sense of religion, whatever their creeds, so much so that within several months after the sisters' arrival the law enforcement officers reported the disappearance of disturbances and misdemeanors known to be a common occurrence in this locality.

On the eastern seaboard, in 1937, Sister Ignatius responded readily to Msgr. Bernard J. Quinn's invitation to staff the Little Flower House of Providence, a child-caring institution from which another sisterhood had withdrawn. It was one of the works of St. Peter Claver Apostolate in the diocese of Brooklyn, founded in 1920 by Monsignor Quinn in Wading River on a high bluff overlooking Long Island Sound. The 123 acres of rolling land included a beach that excelled in wild beauty, with sand cliffs towering above the water's edge and luxuriant bayberry filling the clefts between the cliffs.

The twenty Nazareth sisters, who arrived on June 26, found 314 children whose blurred backgrounds and vexing problems had one common denominator: "starved for love." Boys and girls, taken from broken homes and unwholesome environments predominantly from New York City and the counties on Long Island, ranged from six to seventeen years of age. In a majority of instances, they suffered from the effects of privation and social maladjustment. Consequently, their program of guidance, education and living was so correlated as to prepare them for life.

Within a family-type environment and religious atmosphere, they were educated in community standards and given pre-vocational training for useful occupations. In accordance with the policy under which the institution was conducted, the children were returned to their parents or relatives when satisfactory home conditions had been established; others were placed in foster homes when the particular needs of certain children warranted such course.

In August of the same year, the sisters took charge of the school in St. Peter Claver parish in Brooklyn from which a former staff had resigned. Besides the regular teaching schedule, they became immersed in work that was thoroughly missionary in character, for they devoted their efforts to instructing non-Catholic children in addition to those who were of the household of the Faith. The weekly released-time program for religion classes assembled the children who attended public schools; vacation school projects were conducted each summer for boys and girls of the neighborhood to combat juvenile delinquency. Convert classes for adults were in progress for the year round, available to any and all who were ready to heed the voice of God and for their continuing Christian formation. With the cooperation of private societies in the city, clothing was supplied to the poor children of the school who were the hapless victims of desperate circumstances.

The next year a call came to Nazareth from the Cotton State of Alabama, a land of mesquites and cottonwoods where St. Jude Negro Apostolate, inaugurated with the blessing of Bishop Thomas J. Toolen, had been founded in Montgomery, in 1934, by Father Harold Purcell for the spiritual and material betterment of the negroes. Friends of the Apostolate throughout the country have been its constant source of support, realizing that the greatest gift of all, the gift of Faith, was given them not solely for their own benefit but also for the benefit of others. Only about two percent of the negro population were Catholics, and many of the others professed no religious belief.

Obviously, the first appeal to the poverty-stricken, sick and dejected had to be directed along the lines marked by Christ himself. He who was chiefly concerned about souls, was also very much concerned about people's temporal necessities and his most numerous miracles were exquisite manifestations of his love and concern.

By 1938, the headquarters of the Apostolate at Montgomery, called the City of St. Jude, embraced the beautiful church, a functional school, a dispensary and a convent. Having deliberately volunteered to this distant and unfamiliar region in the deep south, the sisters—ten teachers and two nurses—offered their services within the context of a religious dimension, in living faith. They had an opportunity to identify the broad areas of suffering, death, loneliness, hope and joy. In their visits to the ramshackle plank-board shacks that were home to thousands of negroes and in the people's visits to the dispensary they had opportunity to share some of life's serious moments with other human beings.

There were abundant compensations in the school, as young minds tasted the fascination of new-found knowledge and the diocesan school supervisors evaluated St. Jude's to be at high level of educational performance. The joy of new, clean school uniforms and the relish of nourishment in growing bodies seeped into the children's young life with a warming thrill. Their souls, too, opened eagerly to the revealed truths of divine love for man, and the religious instructions they absorbed went far to correct many of the depraved primitive habits which had been ingrained through social indifference and disdain.

All the services which had taken the sisters to racially disadvantaged points developed further, in time, not in segregated areas alone, but radiating towards integrated groups to help heal their alienation and to strive for a new mode of life which would rectify the imbalance of society.

Among other charitable pastoral works the sisters' ministry began to function, in 1936, in Du Bois, a depressed mining region near Altoona.

In a small bungalow, which served as a convent, the basement was transformed into a youth center with classroom space for scheduled religion and music lessons for grade school and high school students, and also recreation and hobby rooms. Why so many parents wanted their children to participate in these programs, when they could have taken on petty jobs to add their trifle earnings to the family income, was their driving concern for the children's moral and religious training.

The sisters' visits to the homes in the district uncovered human needs which were alleviated, sometimes totally, sometimes in part, but always with the compassion and dignity that inspired the people with courage to shoulder the burdens of life. For the sick and the aging the visits were channels of cheer through which life could be accepted in terms of "the possible" and with reverence.

In Conshohocken, when after 25 years, St. Mary's Home for Boys was no longer suited to be all things to the ever increasing numbers sheltered within, Cardinal Dougherty of Philadelphia advised the acquisition of more spacious accommodations, even in the face of the prolonged economic crisis. The auction of a beautiful estate in Ambler proved to be auspicious to the purpose though funds were scarce, for reliable credit was acceptable in preference to any nominal security. On June 28, 1936, Sister Modesta Sowinska, superior-director of the Home, was welcomed at the new St. Mary's with the transferring staff of teachers and housemothers with their charges.

The grounds had been named Lindenwold after the thousand linden trees within the cultivated park. Visible from afar were the mansion's turrets and battlemented parapet reminiscent of the Windsor Castle. The large array of rooms supplied the needs of home and school for the boys and set apart in convenient privacy the convent quarters for the sisters; chapel specifications were met in the large, elegant ballroom.

Beyond the regular course of studies obliging in the archdiocesan school system, the boys were at liberty to engage in a variety of outdoor and indoor sports and to pursue extracurricular activities under competent direction. Eventually, with the addition of adequate facilities, the admission policy included girls, and later a limited number of neighborhood children were allowed to register at St. Mary's as day students. The change of policy was aimed at the normal sociological development of the children.

The original St. Mary's Home in Conshohocken, after complete renovation, was renamed St. Joseph's Home for the Aged and in November, 1936, began accepting elderly retired residents. There had been many voices urging the sisters to undertake this type of housing arrangement for senior citizens, whether couples or individuals. They adapted easily to the new family they created, contributing to one another's interests in their relaxed associations. Abruptly their peace and security were shattered by the night fire of January 30, 1938, which arose from unidentified causes. With the assistance of neighbors and local agencies the people were safely removed, without any loss of life, to the Middleton residence on the provincialate grounds in Philadelphia, which until then was used as the convent infirmary. To cope with the emergency, the sisters from the infirmary were taken into the main building. By 1942, the project for the care of the aged gradually went out of existence.

After the fire the building in Conshohocken was beyond restoration; only charred walls and a sagging roof remained. To make an ambitious start anew in the light of an unprepossessing future was contraindicated when other tangible ventures were already under consideration. Moreover, the site in Conshohocken attracted willing buyers and was ultimately surrendered on agreeable terms.

In Poland, the counterpart of the House of Providence at Wadowice was the Home for Boys in Łuków, an industrial town known for leather works and petroleum products. At the recommendation of Bishop Henry Przeździecki, Mother Lauretta consented, in 1935, to add this Home to the Congregation's roster in order to give the youths the cultural advantages which had been lacking under previous management. Before long, the Home proved that it was capable of maintaining a program that embodied collaborative relationships, civil and diocesan. Agencies representing both domains sought placement there for their wards.

In northern France, in the Department of Calvados, two centers were opened, in 1938, for sisters' pastoral ministry in the mining towns of Potigny and St. Sylvain. Sisters qualified by prescribed certification dispensed clinic services to ambulatory patients and attended to the sick who were unable to leave their homes. Accidents in the mines, when life was at stake, were not uncommon, requiring instant availability on emergency summons at any time. Among the regular functions at both centers were religion instructions and sacramental preparation of the children, as also a responsibility for the sanctuary and sacristy of the church in the mining community.

In the United States, year after year the genius of President Franklin D. Roosevelt masterminded bold measures and upheld those proposed by others for economic rehabilitation and for the recovery of individual and family respectability through gainful employment at a living wage. Close upon the enactment of the new policies, new movements began stirring with an edge of militancy working out of the inner dynamics of modern society. The Social Justice groups, the National Negro Congress, the Farmers Union, and the National Youth Congress were representative of the spreading special awareness. But hardly had the acute signs of distress begun to taper off when a recession came in, another downhill slide, a depression within the depression. Only about the middle of 1938 a steady surge of confidence was marked.

Nevertheless, the events of the present moment were productive of new formulations for the future. The clergy of leading parishes in larger cities laid plans for stable educational mooring for the American youth at greatly reduced tuition. With the full approval of diocesan school boards and the cooperation of the sisters, parochial high schools evolved within the standard framework that insured state accreditation. Although each of these high schools was an undertaking of a particular parish, it was intended to serve students coming from a wide radius outside the parish boundary.

In Worcester, Massachusetts, St. Mary's High School[130] was organized in 1936 with Sister Hyacinth Górecka as the principal. The next year, two parochial high schools came into being in Chicago: St. Michael's,[131] under the direction of Sister Vitalia Grubinska, and St. Ann's[132] through the efforts of the first principal, Sister Secundilla Kniszek. Paradoxically, St. Stanislaus parochial high school, which existed in Erie since 1920, closed in 1935 as a result of unfavorable conditions.

As a part of the total educational mission of the Church, new approaches in the parochial school system included the addition of ninth and tenth grades, or of one or two years' curriculum in office procedure and commercial courses. For the students who learned the basic clerical skills or acquired some advanced academic knowledge, the short programs had immediate value in negotiating employment. They also afforded a headstart for the students who at a later date decided to resume their higher education. In time these programs were modified, absorbed or discontinued, depending upon the specific factors in every situation.

Similarly in Poland, practical reasons induced the sisters to develop trade schools for girls and young women during the latter years of the thirties. Classes in dress design and sewing gained popularity in Rabka and at the House of Providence in Wadowice. The remarkable output of a variety of knitwear at Wadowice grew into a succesful private enterprise that helped to maintain that institution and assured the apprentices of their means of support. In Grodno, knitwear was likewise the outstanding craft, with second-ranking interest in rug-making, basket-weaving and embroidery.

The general administration of the Sisters of the Holy Family of Nazareth rightly anticipated the Ninth General Chapter to be fraught with thought-provoking appraisals and resolutions in the process of examining the Congregation's position in the Church and the world. Though the far-reaching changes, woven into the fabric of its apostolate, could not be surveyed in full detail, they had to be put into a realistic focus. The great depression, perhaps more than any other single force thus far, tested the compatibility of Nazareth's heritage and charism with the temporal reality of the world in progress.

When Cardinal Granito di Belmonte, Bishop of Albano, formally opened the chapter, May 28, 1938, he read to the nineteen assembled capitulants the letter of Cardinal Protector Eugenio Pacelli. It contained a message from the Supreme Pontiff, Pope Pius XI, exhorting the chapter to evaluate the role of the Congregation in a perpetually changing world and to determine it in the light of its capacity for adaptation and the vigor of its spiritual principles.[133] Following this guideline, the chapter reaffirmed its belief in the validity of the Nazareth way of religion dedication and in its ability to respond to the need of mankind in whichever age it may be called upon to share in the plans of God.

This attitude of the capitulants was heightened by Mother Lauretta's report that, November 27, 1937, the Holy See issued the decree of approval for all the writings of Mother Mary of Jesus the Good Shepherd. Thus, progressively, the mystery of sanctity was being probed, for saints typically remain hidden by their works, but are not buried in them. If only few are perceived and fewer still understood, it is because the saints transcend the natural plane while the average person regards transitory aspects alone.

The truth of this was seen in areas where the Congregation broke new ground without contradiction to principle or precept of the Constitutions and in the expansion of the works already in existence. The chapter debated whatever controversial questions arose from the completely new situations and analyzed the points which required revision or strengthening. The decree of the chapter reflected the orientation to new relationships in the world with the awareness that unchanging principles must always be applied in a changing world.

The reports to the chapter accounted for a total of 116 houses, some of which engaged in multiple endeavors attached to an initial chief purpose. In the personnel statistics the membership tabulated 2,007 professed sisters and 195 novices and postulants.[134]

Two replacements were in order to fill the vacancies in the general administration following the appointment of Sister Agnes Kosiba to the position of superior in Ponders End, England.[135] Effective until now was the optional arrangement of allocating to one of the councilors general the office of the secretary general, which practice no longer proved feasible. Consequently, the separate appointees were Sister Theobald Jaskulska, councilor general, and Sister Antonina Kalicka, secretary general.

Houses of the Congregation
opened in the years 1933 through 1938:

Year	Location	Convent-Apostolate-First Superior
1933	UNITED STATES Chicago	St. Frances of Rome convent; St. Joseph mission school; Sister M. Milton Mach.
1933	POLAND Ostrzeszów	Immaculate Heart of Mary convent; junior high school for girls; Sister M. Euthalia Wismont.
1935	UNITED STATES Wichita Falls, Texas	Jesus Infinite Goodness convent; Bethania Hospital; Sister Marie de Lourdes Mazalewska.
1935	UNITED STATES Altoona, Pennsylvania	Infant of Prague convent; Mercy Hospital; Sister M. Isabella Jóźwiak.
1935	POLAND Łuków	St. Stanislaus Kostka convent; diocesan home for boys; Sister M. Charitas Mikosz.
1936	POLAND Ostrzeszów	St. Michael convent; St. Anthony parish kindergarten; Sister M. Anece Uss.
1936	POLAND Olsztyn	St. Anthony convent; catechetical center; affiliate of Patronage of Our Lady convent in Częstochowa.
1936	UNITED STATES Du Bois, Pennsylvania	St. Augustine convent; St. Michael mission center; Sister M. Berchmans Hejnowska.
1936	UNITED STATES Conshohocken, Pa.	Patronage of St. Joseph convent; St. Joseph Home for the Aged; Sister M. Virgil Mackowiak.
1937	UNITED STATES Taos, New Mexico	Holy Cross convent; Holy Cross Hospital; Sister M. Grace Young.
1937	UNITED STATES Tyler, Texas	St. Frances of Rome convent; Mother Frances Hospital; Sister M. Ambrose Krueger.
1937	UNITED STATES Vernon, Texas	Christ the King convent; Christ the King Hospital; Sister M. Emmanuel Mazurowska.

Year	*Location*	*Convent-Apostolate-First Superior*
1937	UNITED STATES Wading River, New York	St. Therese of the Child Jesus convent; Little Flower House of Providence; Sister M. Pancratius Ławecka.
1937	UNITED STATES Brooklyn, New York	Christ the King convent; St. Peter Claver parish school; Sister M. Josephine (Alphonsilla) Zane.
1937	UNITED STATES Throop, Pennsylvania	Our Lady of Perpetual Help convent; St. Anthony parish school; Sister M. Caledonia Słomska.
1937	POLAND Posen	St. Anne convent; residence for university students; Sister M. Ambrose Groblewska.
1937	POLAND Wilczkowice	affiliate of the Sacred Heart convent, Cracow; day-care center for peasant children; Sister M. Virginia Komar.
1938	POLAND Równe	St. Andrew Bobola convent; county general hospital; Sister M. Regina Budzyńska.
1938	FRANCE St. Sylvain, Calvados	Holy Face convent; pastoral ministry, catechetics; Sister M. Eugenie Roy.
1938	FRANCE Potigny, Calvados	St. Michael Archangel convent; clinic, pastoral ministry, catechetics; Sister M. Michaela Kosińska.
1938	UNITED STATES Montgomery, Alabama	St. Jude convent; City of St. Jude: school, dispensary, pastoral ministry; Sister M. Anthony Kajzer.

House closed:

1938	UNITED STATES Philadelphia	Mother of Divine Love convent (1932-1938); sisters' infirmary and rest home, incorporated in the provincial house.

6 HOUR OF ADVERSITY

The death of the great peacemaker, Pope Pius XI, on February 10, 1939, caused universal mourning. Providentially, the election of Cardinal Pacelli as Pius XII[136] did much to assert the influence of the papacy in one of the gravest hours through which the Church and the world had to pass. With personal majesty of bearing he combined an engaging simplicity of approach, and with just such simplicity he acceded to Mother Lauretta's petition to remain Nazareth's Protector even as the Supreme Pontiff.[137]

If the spirit of the age was preoccupied with technology, intellectual processes and aesthetic qualities, the schools—from the lowest levels upward—were representative of these trends with an intensified emphasis upon a culture that should be central to the good of society. In the United States fresh incentives were imparted by educators who were in the front lines on the path of progress, among them being Sisters Clarissa Siudowska, Liliosa Melerska, Dulciosa Rejrat, Emnilda Opps, Laurenta Okray and Slava Rostkowska.

Enrichment through ethnic cultural studies was made available in the schools where a concentration of a particular national ancestry existed. In St. Joseph province, Sister Hilary Okon, provincial superior, placed these efforts high in the scale of values and furthered them by her overflowing zeal. For her contribution to the advancement of Polish studies, the Government of Poland awarded her the Gold Cross of Merit which was presented in public ceremony, June 18, 1939, by the Polish Consul General, Dr. Heliodore Sztark.[138]

Special recognitions were also conferred upon Sister Ignatius Romanowska and Sister Regina Wentowska who received the Distinguished Service Cross from the Catholic Hospital Association for outstanding achievements in the hospital field.[139]

Renewed widespread enthusiasm in scholarship prompted Mother Lauretta to recommend the organization of inter-provincial educational conferences in the United States. Without slighting the requirements and directives of local and national authorities in education, the conferences were to provide a Nazareth forum for the sisters' exchange of ideas and experiences in teaching, for mutual assistance and consultation, and for the purpose of mastering the relative educational perspectives in the light of Nazareth ideals and the evolving contemporary patterns.[140] The conference task force consisted of three provincial working committees which coordinated their plans through the conference committee under the general chairmanship of Sister Liliosa Melerska.

In a cross-country representation over three hundred sisters attended the first conference which was held at the Holy Family Academy in Chicago, from June 25 through 29, 1941. The committee on proposals and recommendations, headed by Sister Neomisia Rutkowska, summed up in a comprehensive report the expectations, needs and projections of the Nazareth teaching apostolate in the changing world. This report, together with the addresses and papers presented at the conference, was published in the Proceedings of the First Educational Conference.[141]

In Poland the sisters likewise pursued long-range plans with determination. Convent school buildings were going up in Kalisz and Lemberg, and hopeful efforts were mustered to bring about improvements in Ostrzeszów. Suddenly, their exquisite plans were shattered. Europe blazed in a conflagration of bombing raids after the Nazi forces launched a fierce assault on Poland in an undeclared, provocative war. In the dawn hours of September 1, 1939, the massive invasion poured in by land, air and sea, from the north and northwest, south and southwest, and along the Baltic seacoast, converging upon Warsaw and converting the entire country into one ravaged battlefield.

Volumes of documentary accounts and personal memoirs have pieced together the scattered aspects of the Second World War. But each of the Nazareth convents in Europe suffered in a distinct manner the tragedies of war inflicted by rocket and mortar barrage and by enemy occupation. The sisters lived through terrors of bombardment and ruthless pillage of towns; they were caught in torrents of gunfire, faced personal indignities, eviction and dispersion, and agonized over the persecution of religion. The provincial houses in Warsaw and Cracow were woefully damaged and all communication was impeded.

After the cessation of bombing, under Hitler's decree of October 8, 1939, the western provinces of Poland became arbitrarily incorporated into the Reich and the population was dispossessed. Affected by this order were the convents situated in Posen, Ostrzeszów and Wadowice. From Posen the sisters were evicted with a minimum of their belongings and, after confinement in a detention camp, they were released and found their weary way to Komańcza. When it became apparent that the two establishments in Ostrzeszów shall have to be abandoned, Sister Anna, the provincial superior, recalled the sisters to Warsaw before any action had been taken by the invaders.

In Wadowice the state of affairs was somewhat different, although the city was under constant enemy surveillance and a squad of military police occupied a section of the House of Providence. The courses of sewing for older girls which were offered with some cultural subjects had to be discontinued; a program in textile crafts and embroidery was merely permitted. By 1941, when the threat of eviction hung heavily over the sisters and their wards, Sister Noela Linkowska, the local superior, obtained from Mother Lauretta a document issued by the Italian government which testified to the Congregation's ownership of the property. The alliance then binding Germany and Italy exerted the desired effect and the sisters were not compelled to depart.

In the hospital at Wadowice, when the lay personnel were seized by the general panic that descended upon all citizens, they scurried to safety in flight, leaving the sisters to long hours of duty. As soon as a German medical officer arrived to take charge of the hospital, he ordered the instant removal of the patients who were then under treatment and brought in others of his own selection. The sisters' services, however, were retained.

Since Italy did not enter the war in its early stages, it was possible for news to seep into the motherhouse in Rome by way of refugees, diplomats, members of the Allied forces and occasional correspondence.[142]

The large central part of Poland, devastated by heavy air strikes and ground fire, though not outright incorporated into the Reich, was abruptly occupied and oppressed. Nazareth schools saw the urgency of reopening their classrooms without delay, but were limited to elementary education only; high schools and junior colleges were prohibited. There were, moreover, other activities occasioned by time and circumstance which engaged the sisters completely. They distributed food to the continuous flow of homeless multitudes of refugees and displaced persons from the incorporated regions; many were given long-term hospitality and, if necessary, asylum was provided. Starving, mistreated prisoners of war in transit were fed secretely, under the penalty of death, when they halted in a convent courtyard.

For the children of resident families, Nazareth convents dispensed supplementary meals because the supply of food was generally restricted in quantity and quality and the prices were exorbitant. Those sisters who possessed a fluent command of the German language succeeded to establish satisfactory communication with the officials of the occupying forces and secured food products for their unending relief work.

Under the auspices of the Citizens' Protective Committee, day-care centers were developed for the poorest children of pre-school age who could remain from eight to fifteen hours in the sisters' charge and receive ample feedings, while their mothers struggled to earn a living. In Częstochowa, a child-caring home was officially opened in August, 1941, for the housing and elementary education of the orphaned daughters of prisoners of war, of soldiers who lost their lives in resistance and defense, and of victims incarcerated in the concentration camps. Alongside the official institution, there was an unofficial one, conducted under cover, where any child who had a desire to study and had no guardian was befriended, given nourishing meals and a bed. Here Jewish girls were also accepted at grave risks to the establishment and to the sisters.

Transports of wounded Polish troops were welcomed at the resorts in Komańcza and Rabka for recuperation and rest. Eventually, the Nazis requisitioned a part of the building in Komańcza for their purposes and evicted the sisters in Rabka from their beautiful open-air school sanitarium.

Throughout the years of Nazi occupation, practically all candidates to Nazareth were directed to the convent in Kielce for the period of their postulancy. They not only shared the uncertain fate of the nation and the Congregation, but also had the advantage of remarkable guidance by Father Charles Schrant, C.SS.R., as a preparation for their religious commitment and participated in the relief work of the convent. In addition to the regular food service organized for the needy of the city, hospitality was extended to evicted clergy and to a group of Passionist nuns.

At the outbreak of the war, the novitiate at Grodno numbered forty novices whose safety was the concern of the local superior, Sister Lucilline Stelmaszuk, and the director of novices, Sister Alphonsa Sawicka. After consultation with the diocesan dean, they advised the first-year novices to return to their families and those in the second-year had the option of remaining. The latter group with Sister Alphonsa was transferred to the convent in Vilna where peace seemed to prevail.

But on September 17, 1939, the pincers closed in on the nation with the entry of Soviet troops into the wide stretch of the eastern frontier. The country has always been a living epic to its people, though an errant illusion to others who despised it according to their bias. Thus in a sudden lurch of neighborly collusion the glorious epic crumbled overnight.

At the county hospital in Równe, the sisters were promptly replaced by other personnel. Assuming civilian attire to deflect attention from their persons, they departed for Vilna. Evictions from the convents and schools in Stryj, Nowogródek and Lemberg forced the sisters to live in dispersion, to abandon wearing of the religious habit, and to take on whatever employment they could find, whether tutoring and private music lessons or textile crafts and domestic household tasks.

Besides the hospital sisters from Równe, two from Nowogródek and the novitiate group from Grodno who were housed at the Vilna convent, numerous refugees from central Poland congregated here. Up to 400 meals were served daily and food rations were dispensed to poverty-stricken families. The local superiors, Sister Fides Tomkowicz, not deceived by the apparent calm in the city, began early to condition the sisters to the imminence of eviction, deportation or possible imprisonment. Not only did she instruct them to have some ordinary personal necessities in readiness for a hasty departure, but helped them to deepen their outlook upon life in faith and in absolute confidence in God.

On June 14, 1941, twenty-nine of those sisters who had taken refuge in the Vilna convent, among them seven novices, Sister Alphonsa and the hospital superior, Sister Regina Budzyńska, were exiled to Siberia. In the course of transportation six were detached and, on reaching Uzbekistan, joined the Polish military hospital. Their services merited lofty approval alike from the patients and the commanding officers, with outstanding recognition for Sister Dobrochna Dobrońska.

The core group of the exiled sisters, with Sister Regina, were jammed in the cattle freight cars and were deported into the northern Ural region. In a taiga of primeval firs and birches that stretched endlessly beyond all horizons, they were charged with felling trees and clearing swaths of forest lanes, had to manage the primitive commune household and care for the sick. Their life was a daily martyrdom imposed by the presence of vulgar and depraved elements and by the unremitting exploitation of arduous toil. They suffered from abject privations, and even more from the absence of spiritual resources.[143]

At the expense of rest and sleep, they assembled early in the morning and after work in the evenings to pray in common and hold the customary religious exercises of the Congregation. The Sacrifice of the Mass was substituted on Sundays by readings from the missal of prayers and scriptural passages proper to the season, rendered by Sister Regina. She was a gentle, serene woman of patient dignity and at the same time a tower of strength to the sisters who drew from her the courage of their noblest ideals. Considering herself as given a special task among them, she approached it heroically, true to her intelligence, making of it a fountain of holiness for herself and for them.

From the utter helplessness of arctic cold and unspeakable hunger, and from the derision and the crowding they had to bear in the crude barracks, these sisters were released in January, 1942, at the intervention of Bishop Joseph Gawlina, Military Vicar of the Polish Armed Forces. They were detailed from the forest labor camp to Nizhny Tangil where they were required to work at digging up peat deposits. With few exceptions, their co-workers were people who looked to them for the inspiration of religion. Oftentimes they joined the sisters at prayer and eagerly participated in the worship meetings sponsored by them. Alert to the opportunities of the moment, the sisters spread the Gospel, performed baptisms and in the midst of their strenuous labors went about doing good.[144] Sharing their doom with the Siberian exiles, "they accomplished a historic mission for Christianity."[145]

In August, another change of place and work took the sisters to a steppe in Kazakstan where they were engaged in harvesting and processing cotton on a collective farm. Here Sister Celine Bednarska gathered about her the children of the exiles and imparted to them the fundamentals of education.[146] Of Sister Fidelis Minte, whom the guards had isolated from all others at the time of deportation, it was learned that after a bout of illness she died, May 12, 1942, and was buried in Turkestan.

France, in the meantime, following the German attack upon Poland in 1939, viewed her own prospects with alarm; men walked between brittle confidence and gnawing fear. Neither have foreign students found it conducive to affiliate with the renowned institutions of Paris. But the Nazareth *Foyer* at Rue de Vaugirard was not wanting in purpose, for Bishop Gawlina took up his residence there, October 14, 1939, and the *Foyer* became a religious base for the units of the Polish Army which were being constituted on French soil. Encounters and conferences with the Bishop and other ranking clergymen have been as essential to their mental, spiritual and moral well-being as tactical maneuvers for their military expertise. They were proud to receive at the hands of the sisters the insignia made by them for their uniforms and to carry the banners they had embroidered for the army.[147]

The *Foyer* was a temporary oasis to the priests who had been released from the concentration camps by some strange logic of the enemy and to the many wanderers who hoped to find in a friendly country an escape from the terrors of war that wracked their homeland. But soon, out of the fateful darkness, long before the daybreak on May 10, 1940, German forces sprang forward towards France in a blasting deluge and pressed on furiously, until a month later Paris fell and the country lay prostrate, in agony, under the aggressors' rule and military occupation. Consigned among thousands of unfortunate victims to concentration camps were Sisters Mary-Ann Charleston and Eugenie Roy.

Without respite, directly on July 10, the Battle of Britain commenced with a violent bombing onslaught that continued for ten months, causing severe stress and aiming at the total destruction of the island from the air. Repeatedly London was the enemy target for heavy concentrated air raids. Months before the invasion the sisters had been instilling in the school children all the precautionary measures under "alert" and "alarm" signals, preparing them for orderly evacuation to shelter areas. Too frequently actual warning signals could not be sounded in time due to the overlapping phases of the raids, so that the escape to safety zones had to be negotiated in extreme danger. The convent buildings in Enfield and Ponders End were extensively damaged under the pressure of bombardments at which time several sisters sustained bodily injuries.

During those bleak and brutal years there was no relaxation of fervor and interest in researching the life of Mother Mary of Jesus the Good Shepherd in Rome. All the work accomplished up until the approval of her writings has once again undergone meticulous scrutiny by canon lawyers to ascertain the validity of the successive steps and to investigate and clarify any points of doubt which may have arisen. The resulting material, thus far accumulated with ample documentation, was published as a voluminous position paper, *Positio,* and was formally discussed,

December 3, 1940, by the working Commission with members of the Sacred Congregation of Rites and members of the hierarchy.

By joint action it was recommended the following day to His Holiness Pope Pius XII for the purpose of initiating the Apostolic Process.[148] Thereupon, the first stage, the long legal procedure was concluded, and the cause of beatification officially entered within the exclusive competence of the Sacred Congregation of Rites.

About this time the reshuffling of German plans for world conquest diverted the air attacks from England. Nazi forces were being deployed across Poland for a vast eastward campaign of betrayal against Russia to open crushing operations in June, 1941. They left a grim trail of new terror, pillage and suffering. Waves of Soviet troops were forced to abandon the eastern outposts they held in order to escape the onrushing Nazis. By 1942 the Gestapo became firmly entrenched in a systematic effort to uproot religion and destroy the Church.

The night of March 25-26, thirty sisters who still resided in the Vilna convent were arrested, were ordered to put on convict uniforms, and were cast into prison. Twenty-three were confined in one cell together with Sister Fides; the remaining six were joined to the Bernardine sisters in another cell. Through the kindness of imprisoned priests, the Blessed Sacrament was reserved among them. Daily Mass prayers and other devotions, conducted in common, compensated for the absence of Eucharistic Liturgy.

Released after two months, they were forbidden to resume community living and the wearing of the religious habit, and were compelled to seek employment. They lived and worked in dispersion in various parts of the city, meeting once a week with Sister Fides in the farmhouse of an eminent surgeon, who, though a Protestant, respected and guarded their secret. These assemblies were occasions for prayer meetings and religious practices; they also facilitated the sharing of food and funds with those among them who suffered want because of meager earnings.

In other cities on the eastern strip the Nazareth sisters were obliged to organize their lives in a similar manner. They were prevented from any significant works of charitable or religious nature, and their attempts at the sacramental preparation of children necessarily had to elude observation. In spite of all opposition, their influence quietly insinuated itself into the minds of men, grew and increased in the strength of the spirit, and without ostentation inaugurated a reformation of morals.

On December 7, 1941, the surprise attack on Pearl Harbor roused the world to an immeasurable chain of calamities that lay ahead. Four days later, Mussolini, who had thrown in his lot with Germany and Japan, declared war on the United States on the rebound. Until then, sympathy and moral support, as well as immense quantities of defense materials and food supplies were the American contribution of humanitarian concern to the victims of war. Now the nation's actual involvement required greater sacrifices and consistent preparedness on the home front. Over and above their personal input of effort, the sisters initiated productive youth and adult civilian defense programs, simulated disaster exercises, processing of first aid supplies with Red Cross volunteer crews, recruitment of volunteer workers to replace the professional hospital personnel who enlisted in the armed forces, nursing classes for emergency treatment of casualties, management of air raid shelters over extended periods. The needs were many and great.

The octopus of war, reaching to the farthest regions of the earth, barred the free communication among the convents and with the motherhouse in Rome. Correspondence through Vatican channels has on occasion been denied the international immunity to which it was entitled and was subject to delays caused by wartime priorities. The blank periods of suspense and silence that separated the sisters at various points weighed with anxious care upon Mother Lauretta and the administration. However, a glimmer of consolation and confidence waxed strong with every wisp of news that penetrated the barriers and revealed to what extent the charity and ecumenism, infused by Mother Foundress, had taken root in the Congregation. For, individually and as a Community, the sisters recognized their mission in the Church and in the world, as religious, placed in the very center of unnatural and perilous circumstances.

The Nazareth motherhouse likewise realized its function of emergency service in the many acts of hospitality to homeless travelers who fled the fury of war, arriving in Rome in quest of peace and safety. But even here peace was already threatened and safety was uncertain. Mother Lauretta was spared the approaching miseries and confusion on the Italian scene. She died piously, June 15, 1942, after an exhausting heart attack during which she preserved her clarity of mind. As a parting gesture she traced the sign of the Cross on the forehead of each sister in blessing. Her last words were, "Pray, sisters, that the divine will may be accomplished." It was a muted end for the superior general whose very name connoted vigor and leadership. For thirty-nine years she wore the mantle of authority with becoming modesty, dignity and grace. Without lapsing into circumlocution, she spoke out firmly and clearly on the issues that were vital to Nazareth as an arm of the Church.

Her remains were laid to rest in the burial chapel at the Roman cemetery of St. Laurence in the niche next to Mother Mary of Jesus the Good Shepherd. *Precious in the sight of the Lord is the death of his faithful ones.*

In accordance with the provisions of the Constitutions, Mother M. Clare Netkowska became the vicar general.

Houses of the Congregation
opened in the years 1939 through 1942:

Year	Location	Convent-Apostolate-First Superior
1939	POLAND Kielce	Holy Spirit convent; pastoral ministry; Sister M. Beatrix Kirkor.
1939	UNITED STATES Roundup, Montana	St. Scholastica convent; St. Benedict parish school; Sister M. Columbine Kowalska.
1940	UNITED STATES Philadelphia	Infant Jesus convent; Nazareth Hospital; Sister M. Camilla Lange.
1940	UNITED STATES Park Ridge, Illinois	Sacred Heart of Jesus convent; house of prayer; retired sisters' residence; Sister M. Crescentia Drzonek.
1941	UNITED STATES South Heart, North Dakota	Queen of Peace convent; South Heart public school; Sister M. Esther Weiss.
1942	FRANCE Chevreuse, Calvados	St. Therese of the Child Jesus convent; pastoral ministry; sacramental preparation of children; Sister M. Eugenie Roy.

Houses closed:

Year	Location	
1939	POLAND Równe	St. Andrew Bobola convent (1938-1939); county general hospital; sisters evicted.
1939	POLAND Posen	St. Anne convent (1937-1939); residence for university students; sisters evicted
1942	UNITED STATES Philadelphia	Patronage of St. Joseph (1936-1942); St. Joseph home for the aged.

IV

Age of New Frontiers
1942-1959

1 SHADOW OF THE CROSS

The complications of global warfare prevented the immediate convocation of the special general chapter for the election of the superior general. It was far from safe for the delegates to attempt to travel, whether by land, sea or air, when all routes were rendered hazardous by strategic operations of the belligerents.

With the rights and authority normally vested in the interim office of the vicar general, Mother Clare was destined to bear for four and a half grim years the afflictions, risks and dire responsibilities in a darkening world. Girded for the test of the spirit by an unalterable devotion to the Cross of Christ, she sought in the contemplation of its mystery and meaning to discover in its shadows the saving will of God for the Congregation and the world, and for herself.[1] Those who came to know her were convinced that they had been in the presence of moral grandeur. Now, from the hidden reservoir of the spirit, she drew stillness in the eye of the storm, herself an image of strength and solace to the sisters.

Ever since Pope Pius XII had been the Cardinal Protector of Nazareth, he knew Mother Clare as a member of the general council who occasionally filled also the office of the local superior at the motherhouse or of the director of novices in Albano. It was this personal acquaintance that lent a note of true cordiality to the letter in which he acknowledged the felicitations and spiritual tributes presented on the twenty-fifth anniversary of his episcopal consecration. These had been accompanied by a gift of liturgical vestments and altar linens for the Pontiff's distribution to needy churches. He wrote, in part,

> . . . It is Our desire to convey Our personal gratitude for this gift and to state how much We value your benevolent activities, and how deeply We sympathize in the present trials with you and with those among you who are suffering for God's holy cause and for their brethren. We are confident that your suffering will bear the seeds of sanctity and will promote the growth of your apostolic works. Praying to God for the intentions of the deceased pious Mother Lauretta and imploring his merciful protection and consolation for the entire Cogregation, We impart Our blessing to every one of the sisters, especially to those who are afflicted by the tribulations of war.[2]

The Pope's insistence in diplomatic circles upon the establishment of an international program for a just and lasting peace was paralleled by his efforts to bring spiritual principles to bear on the solution of contemporary problems. The roar of artillery could not halt the impact produced by his consecration of the world and mankind to the Immaculate Heart of Mary on the twenty-fifth anniversary of the Fatima message. Families and societies, dioceses and parishes reenacted the consecration with revived devotion and hope. The same response occurred at the motherhouse of the Good Shepherd and was followed by Nazareth's provinces, convents and individual institutions.

Wherever the sisters were untouched by active combat, they took cognizance of the one-hundredth birthday anniversary of Mother Foundress in November of 1942, commemorating it in solemn liturgy and community assemblies. Much of the joy of the occasion was eclipsed by the knowledge of what hundreds of their fellow sisters suffered in war-beleaguered target areas.

Within Italy itself the government's collaboration with Nazi Germany plunged the country into acute distress. The lot of the civilians, marked by progressive food shortages and accented in fear by the recurring air raid alarms, befell the motherhouse and the novitiate. Material aid could reach the convents in need only through American voluntary organizations which were internationally acceptable. Throughout the years of war-time emergency the provincials in the United States, Sisters Richard, Electa and Eusebia, were united in providing substantial relief to the sisters in Europe and those exiled to the Middle East and later to Africa. The means of survival and sustenance were assured through the good offices of Bruce Mohler of the National Catholic Welfare Conference, and under the personal supervision of Msgr. Edward C. Swanstrom[3] and Joseph Wnukowski, both of War Relief Services, and of Florian Piskorski, overseas representative of Polish American Relief Council.

Special problems in relief and correspondence arose for a group of twenty-seven sisters who were compelled to abandon their convent in Kalisz, September 12, 1942. Under Nazi patrol they were conducted by van to Bojanów, south of Posen, where they were confined within the precincts of the municipal penitentiary converted into a labor camp for approximately 500 nuns of various orders and detained there until February 15, 1945. Divested of their religious garb and prevented from communicating with anyone outside the compound, they were enslaved in hard, ceaseless toil, always in the presence of scathing ridicule, always under the threat of being denied the only concession to which they could look forward—that of attending Sunday worship.

Officers of the enemy occupation forces would select young persons in good health from among the inmates of the camp in order to take them into servitude as domestics in their private households in Germany. There the sisters were similarly exposed to frustrating, unreasonable treatment by members of the officers' families.[4] The camp also farmed out a quota of its workers to the tuberculosis hospitals in Gostyn and Gostynin to perform heavy housekeeping chores. The sisters' religious character was a common knowledge, yet their unruffled composure and diligence with incredible feats of endurance were baffling to the environment. This induced some of the overseers to seek discreetly the path of faith in the God who exerted so amazing an influence upon the lives of his believers.

Fragments of information, vaguely drifting about Poland, in time penetrated the walls of secrecy. Sister Noela Linkowska and Valeria Czarnowska, from their locations in Wadowice and Stryj respectively, sent food items at intervals out of their frugal convent supplies to supplement the hunger rations doled out to the captive sisters.[5] Thus were shared the food and clothing parcels shipped by the American convents to known points of delivery, assisting others whose fate and whereabouts were generally unknown, though their need was not less.

Distressed by the infamous treatment of the sisters in the labor camp, Sister Bożena Staczyńska, the provincial superior in Cracow drafted an appeal to Pope Pius XII, asking his intervention in their behalf. The letter was dispatched through confidential sources with every assurance of safe passage, but contrary to expectations it was intercepted in Vienna by Nazi officials and its contents branded as an unpardonable offense against the Third Reich. Couriers, sent to the headquarters of the police districts in Poland, carried orders for the instant arrest of Sister Bożena as one condemned to the extermination camp in Oświęcim (German name *Auschwitz*). The first inkling of the pursuit came to light in February of 1943 when three German officers arrived at the convent in Cracow demanding to see her. Her absence at the moment and her frequent changes of place, caused by traveling to alleviate the sisters' needs and difficulties, protected her against a possible encounter and fatal discovery.

When the Gestapo search for Sister Bożena grew in force, the sisters at the Cracow convent were informed that unless the provincial superior gives herself up, two sisters will be taken each week and imprisoned as hostages. The first two, taken January 5, 1944, were Sister Lydia Malinowska, convent superior, and Sister Chrysantha Szypula. Three months later they were released through the mediation of Archbishop Adam S. Sapieha and no other hostages were claimed; the heat of the pursuit was also quashed.

Meanwhile, as the German campaign against Russia pressed onward into its interior, the Gestapo rule of terror flamed out along Poland's eastern territory. In Grodno, following the transfer of the novices, the remaining thirty professed sisters were engaged in numerous charitable services of the moment, aiding the needy transients, housing the destitute aged, and caring for hospitalized prisoners of war. When in 1942 a

German official was killed by an unidentified assassin, one hundred Grodno citizens were arrested as hostages including the sisters who, however, were not mentioned individually by name. Instead, Sister Lucilline Stelmaszuk, superior, was required to appoint one half of their number to join the other hostages in prison. When she refused to comply on the grounds that she exercised no right over the sisters' life, all of the sisters offered to accept the imprisonment. The astonished deputy made a random choice of fourteen sisters, and these Sister Lucilline voluntarily decided to accompany. They were fully aware of the death penalty that awaited them in the event the killer's identity remained undisclosed. Two weeks later, twenty-five hostages were executed; the others and all the sisters were freed. Beyond doubt there was more horror, courage, shock and foreboding stirred up within that short span of time than could have been normally sustained.

Back in 1940 the Germans established the notorious concentration camp in Oświęcim, an ancient fortress town in the province of Cracow, not far off from Wadowice. By 1942, when typhoid fever, dysentery, tuberculosis and other communicable diseases were rife among the internees, the hospital facilities in Wadowice were enlarged by the building of barracks for prisoners who would be selected to receive treatment there. The sisters cared for these patients with special solicitude, pleased to be able to communicate with them in their particular languages according to the countries of their origin. To bring about as complete a return to health as possible, the sisters bent their efforts to prolong the hospital stay of these unfortunate persons. They even grasped opportunities to procure an occasional deliverance from the camp.

Governed by the policy of systematic extermination, genocidal and cultural, of ravaged countries, the invaders prohibited all education on secondary and higher levels, both academic and professional. Elementary schools alone were allowed to exist with a prescribed seven-year program of instruction, stipulating that during the last two years classes be held but once a week. These minimal concessions to education were bound up with contrived obstacles which hampered the free conduct of student activities, since a section of each of Nazareth's school buildings was occupied by enemy troops. Their demands for additional room space obliged the sisters to organize the periods of instruction in double sessions.

Intent upon a plan for the intellectual impoverishment of youth, the Germans stripped the teaching program of social studies, religion and science. At once the Nazareth schools in Poland matched the challenges offered by secret national commissions of public instruction which guided and certified the continuing prewar programs conducted under cover. When in the next stage of repressive tactics private schools were totally banned, this posed not only greater difficulties but also aroused higher incentives to preserve and cultivate the educational priorities at all cost. By skillfully switching to such ventures as an apprentice school of dressmaking or a home for dependent children, the sisters introduced high school classes on the side and, together with lay faculties, followed the standard course schedule to enable their students to earn valid credits issued by the secret boards of examiners.

To further the cause of education, despite cramped quarters and obvious dangers, Nazareth convents in Poland accommodated several university professors who desired to hold classes for advanced students in the subjects of classical philology, educational psychology, history of education, history of philosophy, and theology for seminarians.

It was in the spirit of service to the Church and to society that the sisters took a stand against injustice and denial of fundamental rights by using such natural means as they were best qualified to employ. Wherever they happened to be, regardless how widely the conditions of life differed, they made clear their interest in youth and in the helpless. Although actual war operations had not exploded on the American continent, there was much to be accomplished—for the present and the future—through positive indoctrination of the school children and older students. They had to be made to understand the true value of the tremendous sacrifice of thousands upon thousands of Americans in the armed forces who were defending the heritage of freedom around the globe. In an earlier age, tides of European migrations flowed into the New World now the descendants of immigrants were turning the tide in gallant action in the lands of their forefathers.

With understanding there came the deepening of patriotism which inspired the youth to practical conclusions of service and sacrifice in ways that were open to them. They displayed a generosity in giving up their leisure to part-time occupations, filling the vacancies created by the call to arms and other essential demands which adults had to face. Quickly they discovered the supporting role that could be theirs by contributing of their own savings to the national defense fund. That role was uniquely amplified when they formed the Student Defense Legion to promote Allied victory and just peace. To this end they adopted the practice of frequent participation in the Eucharistic liturgy and Holy Communion, setting aside a definite period daily for mental prayer and for instructive religious reading. Fortified in this manner, members of the Legion pledged themselves to volunteer duties in Civil Defense, Red Cross, or adjunct junior military divisions.

To underscore the influence of aviation upon national security and world progress, aeronautics was incorporated into the high school curriculum. As one source of students' educational enrichment it was an introduction to expanding career opportunities. The course was designed by Sisters Chestine Dziekońska and Canisia Majewska on a broad scientific background involving aeronautics theory and flight technique.[6]

In the spring of 1943, through Allied intervention, the Polish government-in-exile concluded its negotiations concerning the uncared for orphans and children separated from their families in the Siberian plains. They were relocated to a home founded by the Polish Combat Engineers in Teheran and placed under the guardianship of fourteen sisters who, with Sister Regina at the head, were given leave to cross the boundary from Siberia into Iran; somewhat later four other sisters joined them. The children began to live and learn in surroundings resembling a normal pattern as nearly as possible, and their number continued to increase without stopping. Scarcely one year later, complicated international politics forced them to be on the move again, this time to Tanganyika, a British Trust Territory in East Africa, to the district of Morogoro. In the cloying tropical climate of the strange environment they groped for the frayed ends of a life that dragged on wearily.[7] The small native huts, roofless and without flooring, in which they were housed, were no protection against malarial mosquitoes and swarms of pernicious tsetse flies.

By November, when uninterrupted heavy rainfalls commenced the long wet season, the children stood little chance of survival. To salvage them from the effects of prolonged illnesses and to build up their physical resistance, the entire group together with the sisters was transferred to the settlement at Rongai in Kenya, which was then under British protectorate also. The refreshing moderate climate of the highland region proved singularly beneficial to the well-being of the children.[8] Before long, a transport of three hundred children from Uganda was added on to this group, giving rise to a provisional child-caring institute which flourished until 1947, directed by Sister Alma Puchalska.

Since the sisters' departure from Siberia, the American provincial superiors, encouraged by Mother Clare, endeavored to bring the migrant group into the United States. Contending with wartime immigration policies, rigid and exacting, it has taken over four years to complete all security formalities and obtain entry visas to the United States for the sisters and their charges based in Africa.[9]

In spite of the problems precipitated by the world at war, budding vocations to the religious life have not been blighted by apparent obstacles. The exiled sisters in Africa saw the evangelical inspiration sprout and grow among the young women of the settlement, and these were admitted to share the Nazareth way. They probed and tested the stability of their resolution in the long postulancy that of necessity extended until the disbanding of the settlement.

Neither have the hardships occasioned by the Nazi occupation of France prevented eager aspirants from applying to the convent in Paris. Beginning in 1943 and for the duration while the emergency lasted, the local superior, Sister Virginia Grzędzicka, had the approval of the Sacred Congregation of Religious to conduct the novitiate program at Rue de Vaugirard, since travel routes out of the country, including Italy, were bristling with dangers. The novitiate in Paris was discontinued in 1946 when normal transportation to Italy became again available.

Poland likewise saw many candidates who would not be deterred by the Nazi rule and its violent inroads on religion. Of the postulants and novices who had been advised to return to their families at the outbreak of the war, not all accepted the easier course of presumptive safety outside the convent, and others persisted in the determination to strive for their life's fulfillment as Sisters of the Holy Family of Nazareth. In the minds of the major superiors not a shadow of doubt appeared as to what should be done, though the canonically established novitiate in Grodno had been evacuated, and not one of the convents still held by the sisters offered the requisite conditions for a novitiate where the fundamental two-year formation could be undertaken successfully. The ecclesiastical consent to open a provisional house of formation left it to the discretion of the superiors of the Congregation to determine the best suited time and place.

Eventually a spacious villa was leased some eighteen miles southeast of the capital, surrounded by a screen of pines in a dense forest preserve. During the prewar years it had been a favorite site for student outings from the Warsaw school. At a distance there were two small cottages maintained by two different groups of nuns; otherwise the seclusion and peace afforded virtual privacy, for no marauders had been observed in the woodland even at the height of enemy activity. In an interval of comparative calm, on October 2, 1943, eighteen postulants were admitted to the novitiate at a reception ceremony in the Warsaw provincialate chapel. At once they departed with Sister Ezechiela Szupenko, formation director, to become established in the forest novitiate which they named Bethania. Father John Mackowski, Pallotine, provided the regular ascetical instructions and personal spiritual guidance to the novices. Other reception ceremonies followed later and, in 1945, the first novices of Bethania made their profession of the religious vows.[10]

The perils stalking civilian travelers across Europe had cut off the influx of novices to the international novitiate in Albano. The four last novices, who had been admitted to religious profession, September 12, 1941, were joined to those who had been professed since 1939 and comprised an advanced formation unit, the scholasticate, entrusted to the

direction of Sister Frances Sikorska. The young religious devoted themselves, among other pursuits, to regular sessions of teaching children of
school age to counteract the interruption in public education caused by
the war.[11] When the American sisters were given the option of either
returning to the United States or remaining in Italy, the choices went both
ways and were accommodated accordingly. Those who remained had the
rare opportunity of spreading abroad to the full the advantages of American citizenship in the course of wartime developments.

The idea of the scholasticate, originated by Mother Mary of Jesus the
Good Shepherd, aimed to deepen the theological knowledge and the
Nazareth spirituality of the young religious and to make available to them
the means for apostolic preparation. While in the early years of the
foundation Mother Mary had personally assumed the responsibility for
directing the formation of the sisters at all stages, by 1890 she placed the
scholastics in charge of Mother Frances Morgenstern. The first general
chapter of the Congregation affirmed in its decrees the importance of
guiding the sisters to religious maturity in a well-balanced scholasticate
program.[12]

In the years that followed since the turn of the century, the demand
for sisters' services had reached such proportions that for the sake of the
Lord's harvest the scholasticate was being gradually sacrificed until at
length it disappeared as a formation unit. It became necessary, instead,
to harmonize the sisters' extensive apostolic labors with their continuing
efforts at self-improvement. Mother Lauretta's hope for the restoration of
the scholasticate was realized in 1939 in Albano, and her exhortations to
the provincial superiors yielded results in the American provinces thereafter.

Unable to withdraw all at once a significant number of sisters from
their assignments for a full-time scholasticate, Sister Electa began, in
1942, to summon each year the young religious of the Immaculate Conception province to the provincialate in Philadelphia for the entire summer
vacation.[13] The same method was employed by Sister Richard in the
Sacred Heart province beginning in 1943.[14] For each summer sequence,
a comprehensive program, oriented to the perfecting of one's total personality within individual means, was drawn up with a staff of instructors
selected from among the Congregation's members and others from reputable centers around the country.

Philadelphia's proximity to the Catholic University of America and
the deferential attitude of the university's officials to Nazareth's educational endeavors opened the possibility for establishing, in 1942, a model
primary school on the provincialate grounds, approved for teacher education purposes. With Sister Antonilla Zielińska, as dean of the affiliate

college for teacher education, the theoretical and practical aspects of the program achieved academic vitality, geared toward state certification, which commenced to draw students from outside the Congregation additionally.[15]

In the Sacred Heart province somewhat different approaches were traced to realize similar goals. Supplementing the annual coming together of the younger members to the provincialate, Sister Liliosa Melerska had suggested that the administration of De Paul University accept the commitment to a new campus unit, the normal college, to meet responsibly and creatively the educational needs of aspiring teachers who were able to matriculate for full-time study. Concurrently, for the benefit of in-service teachers, she proposed a wide range of desirable courses in content and method, yielding college credits through the university's department of education. Both programs were received with general favor, attracting a steady flow of interested students, religious and lay.

The year-round scholasticate in residence, however, evolved at a later date in all the provinces, in Europe and in the United States, after a period of experimentation, evaluation, and judicious adaptations applied regionally.

While in one part of the world the instruments of peace through faith and education were advanced by persons of good will to weld intelligent associations of mankind in charity and justice, the eastern hemisphere groaned across seas and continents under the acts of rabid inhumanity. In the town of Nowogródek temperamental outbursts of Nazi hostility and violence without cause were witnessed from the moment the German forces had taken over the municipal headquarters in 1941. Twelve sisters under the superiorship of Sister Stella Mardosewicz were evicted from their convent and school and supported themselves by manual labor; one of them, Sister Margaret Banaś, was engaged in the local hospital. Privately they formed religion classes of the children who were being prepared for the reception of the sacraments. Their quiet life, pious and unpretentious, inspired the people with trust in God and the simple courage to carry on.

By 1943, as the German reverses in the Russian campaign increased, the tense atmosphere in occupied areas grew ominous. Nightly arrests and mass executions without trial spread terror among the townspeople. Upon a wave of arrests, that spring, a fearful lament came up from the homes from which the menfolk had been seized and doomed to extermination. Impressed by the immensity of the tragedy racking the people, the sisters agreed among themselves to pledge their lives in exchange for the imprisoned husbands and fathers of families. They confided to the chaplain, Father Alexander Zienkiewicz, that this was what they prayed for. Some days later, quite unexpectedly, the men were released unharmed.[16]

The chaplain, whose zealous ministry about town was well-known, has also become the object of Gestapo's designs. When a rumor of an attempt upon his person threatened to be probable, the sisters assured him of their readiness to offer their lives for his safety, because they believed that in his priestly capacity he was needed more than they.[17] Suddenly afterwards the news filtered through the town that eleven sisters were shot and buried in the nearby woods during the predawn hours of August 1, 1943. Sister Margaret, having been on hospital duty, had not been with them, and it was her lot to discover the common grave into which they had been hurled and hastily covered over with soil.

Exhumation was accomplished after the Nazis had been repulsed from the country. The remains of the sisters were then identified, each was placed into a separate casket, and on March 19, 1945, brought back to the parish church in a triumphal procession for a solemn burial service.[18]

Led by Sister Stella, the victims who joined the radiant army of martyrs were:

Sister M. Imelda Zak
Sister M. Canisia Maćkiewicz
Sister M. Raymunda Kukolowicz
Sister M. Daniel Jóźwik
Sister N. Canuta Chrobót
Sister M. Sergia Rapiej
Sister M. Guidona Cierpka
Sister M. Felicitas Borowik
Sister M. Heliodora Matuszewska
Sister M. Boromea Narmontowicz

There is little to remind the emerging generation of the sacrifice, known to God, which these noble women made of their lives that others might live. There is but the testimonial brochure, *No Greater Love*,[19] in which Father Zienkiewicz reflected the events from the broad perspective of twenty-five years as survivor and witness.

A huge canvas in oil by the celebrated artist, Adam Styka, vividly depicts the moment of the execution of the eleven sisters. Commissioned by Mother Bożena, superior general, the painting was executed under the patronage of Sister Neomisia Rutkowska, provincial superior of the Immaculate Conception province. The painting was unveiled in April of 1948, and in 1965 it was transferred to the generalate in Rome. A copy of the original is displayed at the provincialate in Philadelphia.

2 WITH ANXIOUS CARE

The war rolled on, and in Italy the summer of 1943 brought the fall of Mussolini. Agitated by a strong popular revulsion against his alliance with Hitler, the liberty-loving Italians hailed the arrival of British and American troops as saviors of their national dignity and independence. The professionals and public office-holders, eager to strike up a rapport with the representatives of the Allied Military Government temporarily functioning on the peninsula, at once sought out the American sisters in Albano and Rome to form adult classes in the English language.

In retaliation for the Italian accord with the allies, the Germans were determined to attack strategic points south of Rome from the fortified positions they held in the north, which they continued to strengthen. The novitiate house, Villa San Giuseppe, being in the path of the action, resounded with the thundering of air-borne divisions in their interminable flights over the Alban hills. The drone of motors became a part of the rhythm of life. Convoys of enemy troops and heavy armaments rumbled directly in front of the convent in a constant movement along Via Appia Nuova, the principal road leading to Naples. The sounds of explosives bursting in the street added to the sisters' apprehension that had already been aroused by the fact that neighboring villas were occupied by enemy units.

It was the fearless ingenuity and tact of the superior, Sister Ludvina Lachmayr, that dissuaded the requisitioning officer from appropriating the convent for his men. In reality the soldiers stood in a kind of awe of the sisters and some, stirred by childhood recollections of religion, came secretly to the convent chapel to assuage their inner conflict. There were also Poles, Italians and Frenchmen who had been compelled to don the German uniform, and they, too, would come for a respite of prayer, an occasion for confession, or a nostalgic talk with the chaplain or a sister. The midnight Mass at Christmas assembled a large company of soldiers for the festive observance of the coming of the Prince of Peace and united all voices in the carols of joy as they were brought into marvelous harmony with life's eternal values.

Few days later, a German military physician applied for two sisters to be assigned to the field hospital conducted in one of the villas to help attend the men who had been wounded in action. His reason for the request was that the sisters' presence should contribute to the better management of the hospital and the improved care of the patients. In this request there was no mistaking of Christ's appeal voiced in the Sermon on the Mount. The beatitude of the merciful and the beatitude of those who suffer persecution for the sake of justice were clearly summed up for Sisters Reparata Rulewska and Brunona Blach in the mission to which they were then detailed until the hospital should be moved away, closer to the combat zone.

Such were the gratifying highlights of the sisters' relationships on a Christian level, divorced from political antagonisms. These, however, were mingled with the frightful interludes of heavy aerial bombardment, near and far, the awful trembling of the convent building under the shattering impact of the bombs, and the exhausting rush at all hours to reach the shelters in the garden. Shortages of the most ordinary supplies were severely felt, but in this emergency the friendly American army invariably came to the sisters' aid. Through thick and thin, Mother Clare shared with the sisters in Albano the hard, long months of uncertainty, reviving anew their confidence in St. Joseph to whose honor this convent was specially dedicated.[20]

The massive Allied landing at Anzio opened the raging Battle of Italy centered at Monte Cassino, where the Germans had built and manned formidable defenses. All the hazards of war lying round about were a signal for immediate evacuation. On February 2 and 3, 1944, the sisters proceeded to the papal villa at Castelgandolfo where accommodations were made available to the stricken refugees. After two weeks they were transferred by Vatican vehicles to the motherhouse in Rome.[21] The perilous days snailed along while the enemy hung on desperately until they were thrust back with staggering losses beyond the Alban hills. On Monday evening, June 5, 1944, Rome was liberated from the encircling clutch of the foe as the victorious Allies entered Piazza Venezia in the heart of the city to the sound of pealing church bells.

The next day the long-concealed plans for the liberation of occupied France came to light with the surprise operations from the English Channel breaking in on the shores of Normandy. The liberating forces moved inland arduously, clearing the colossal opposition inch by inch, until on August 25, 1944, the enemy's resistance was broken in Paris. In the last days street fighting had erupted within several yards of the convent at Rue de Vaugirard, but the French troops, having taken possession of St. Sulpice Quarter, were at once in full command. The sisters confidently prayed their thanks to God in the chapel, while the jubilant population filled the Notre Dame Cathedral in solemn dedication.

One week after the Normandy landings had begun, the Germans launched a campaign of retaliation against England in an intensive onslaught upon London. The capital and its boroughs were incessantly plagued by long-range pilotless missiles which exploded in the air, dropping their volcanic flames in a blaze of conflagration. These flying bombs, popularly known as "doodle-bugs" for the strident sound of their motors, gave warning of their approach and enabled the sisters to withdraw the children in sufficient time into deep shelters. Fraught with greater and insidious dangers were the unmanned rockets which superseded the flying bombs, because their approach was silent and therefore more terrifying.

Finally, on September 8, the Battle of London was won and the bombardment ceased. The Enfield convent was reduced to a ghastly skeleton and a part of the school building had been destroyed. Later, in the process of national reconstruction, the British government made adequate provisions for the building of a new convent and the restoration of the school. Before that could be accomplished the sisters moved into Roseneath, the foreign students' residence, where a chapel was temporarily arranged for the community.

In the struggles for the deliverance of Rome, Paris and London two issues hung in the balance: the morale of the people and the subsequent expulsion of the enemy from each of the countries. In Poland, where Nazareth's European apostolate was most extensive and widely diversified, the same objectives were sought. The hour for action struck in January of 1944 when the German forces driven from Russia entered the Polish frontier, harrying and devastating the cities, villages and farms. The network of the Polish Resistance Movement against German occupation started a spirited campaign to break the concentrations of the enemy in transit. But it was not possible to beat down the conflagration set up in the beautiful city of Vilna and to save Nazareth's large new school building and convent from the devouring flames. Here Sister Adela Antczak was found among the city's casualties, mowed down by a machine-gun blast.[22] Neither was it possible to protect from artillery discharges the convent in Grodno where Sister Jucundine Duplaga was killed by an exploding shell.[23]

On August first, the forlorn Battle of Warsaw began. Prevented by Soviet obstinacy, both American and British governments were thwarted in their efforts to assist their Polish Allies to liberate and hold the capital. They were compelled to bear the onslaught alone and unaided to the end while bombs were turning homes into incinerators and countless lives of civilians were sacrificed.

The school and convent in Warsaw had already witnessed scenes of aggravated danger to the lives and safety of many persons when, at the same time, the provincial superior, Sister Ann Łyszczyńska, and the local superior, Sister Euthalia Wismont, have risen to heights of heroism despite the sorrows and privations they had to endure. At this tragic hour they housed the inmates of an institution for the aged who were left homeless when the establishment was ruined. A band of Germans, in a confrontation with a detachment of Polish soldiers within the convent, brutally killed these defenseless old people. Compelled to flee from the site of the encounter, the sisters went forth into the unknown, dependent solely upon Divine Providence. Under the stress of the situation, Sister

Notburga Małochleb died then as a result of an acute heart attack.[24]

By October 2, the reserves of the fighting Poles were depleted. The Red Army openly hailed as accomplished facts the Soviet domination of every province through which it passed across Poland in pursuit of the retreating Germans. It halted inactive at the suburbs of Warsaw, waiting for the anihilation of the city's defenders. When the Red Army finally moved in and the Soviets seized control, the entire city was an enormous sepulcher with burned out buildings and the dead lying in the streets.[25] As soon as cautious investigations proved reassuring, the sisters returned to Warsaw. They found their convent and school building a shambles, but not beyond repair; the interiors were defaced in the process of outright cremations, while all furnishings and school equipment had been deliberately destroyed.

The war on the giant scale dragged on. The enemy was yet to be expelled from sections of the occupied European territories which had not been liberated. But the inhabitants of Rome and its environs were already abounding with mercurial optimism, though a great many problems and hardships oppressed them. Reacting with friendly sympathy towards the Allies, they were eager to come out of their shell and clamored for instructions in foreign languages. Several sisters formed classes in English, Polish and French in continuous sessions for learners of all ages.[26]

The American soldiers who were on active duty within the vicinity of Albano adopted Nazareth's novitiate chapel as their preferred place of worship which they attended in large numbers with or without their military chaplains. Vocal participation in the prayers of the Mass and choral singing were a common practice among them. For the benefit of newcomers they erected a bulletin board off the street announcing the services, and posted a series of arrows along the way leading to the chapel.[27] They deemed it their natural duty to ease the material cares which burdened the sisters on finding the havoc done during the disastrous bombings. Not only did they discover and deliver glass panes to replace the shattered windows and brought other scarce building supplies, but from time to time provided them with food items while the food shortage was critical. The first relief parcels and cases of food and clothing from the United States began arriving in February of 1945 when foreign transports could safely enter the Italian ports.[28]

The sisters, in turn, gave of themselves with ready hand and heart to help where the need was greatest, the people poorest, and the prospects hardest. An industrious cluster subscribed to the reconditioning of clothing that had been received by the Vatican charities administration from various sources for distribution to those in want. Five sisters joined the Information Bureau, organized in the Vatican by the Secretariat of State for the purpose of maintaining informational services concerning lost persons and providing assistance in the search. For the destitute and unemployed, impoverished through the vicissitudes of war, the Holy Father subsidized the free feeding center where the sisters prepared nourishing meals and dispensed them daily.[29]

At Rome and in Albano the sisters conducted free schools for the children of the poor and made rounds caring for the sick and the aged in their homes and hovels. As early as the month of August after the liberation of Rome, twelve sisters have enlisted their services in Red Cross hospitals on the Adriatic coast, at Casamassima and Noci southeast of Rome and at Senigallia in northern Italy, where they remained on duty for two years. Assigned to the convalescent divisions of these hospitals, their presence restored to the soldiers a sense of real achievement and purpose, inspiring them with renewed faith and courage to meet the future.[30]

Although the painful and overwhelming course of the war imposed hampering burdens and limitations upon the sisters in the American provinces, they remained open and attuned to arising human demands where they could effectively heal, help and teach. It was in that spirit that staffs of sisters have made their entry, for the first time just then, into the States of Montana and North Dakota and onto the island of Puerto Rico to conduct schools, and with that aim engaged in new forms of child care activities in Alabama in two additional centers. In Cleveland, Ohio, a parochial high school evolved successfully, in 1942, in conjunction with St. Stanislaus primary school, under the direction of Sister Humiliana Szałkowska. A first attempt to establish a retirement home for sisters was also made in this period by the Sacred Heart province.

These new developments and others of varying dimensions in existing locations prompted Mother Clare to write to the sisters in the United States of her great desire to visit them and their works. However, in the face of the unresolved world conditions which prevented her, she delegated three visitors-general to make the visitations on her authority, namely, Sister Hilary Okon in the Sacred Heart province, Sister Aloysius Zmich in the Immaculate Conception province, and Sister Idalia Gorka in St. Joseph province.[31] The visitations were commenced promptly after the New Year of 1945.

On a wave of inexpressible relief the war in the European theater ceased at midnight on May 8, 1945. The task of reconstruction began at once, and for the sisters life was slowly returning to normal after an invigorating retreat and spiritual renewal in the reconstituted convents. But, in view of the residual obstacles to international travel, the convocation of the general chapter had to be postponed. The Sacred Congregation of Religious decreed that the general administration of the Sisters of the Holy Family of Nazareth remain vested in the same persons as heretofore.[32]

In the recapitulation of the war years, Mother Clare contemplated the gift of suffering which Nazareth offered to God in the name of the Church. If suffering is man's life companion in a greater or smaller degree, it is the uncontested lot of the religious who have accepted the mission of atonement as inseparable from their dedication. The material losses, privations and sacrifices, sustained by the sisters even to the laying down of their lives, were a precious investment of death and glory into the coffers of eternity.

Evacuation from the convents and forcible dispersion had been an acute trial to the sisters. They endeavored to counterbalance it by keeping alive the invisible, powerful bond of unity among themselves and with their superiors. To the extent that external conditions made it feasible, they preserved fidelity to the Nazareth lifestyle and communal prayer, which were to them a source of inner strength and of religious identification. Throughout the anxieties and fears of the troubled times their thoughts turned to the one focal point, the motherhouse in Rome, the anchor of their life's ideals and aspirations. It was then that they understood with sudden clarity the wisdom of the Foundress, expressed in one of her letters, "For us nothing can replace Rome. To part from it would be our undoing."[33] Whether near or far, alike in adversity as in fair circumstances, the Roman motherhouse remained a visible, tangible, vital bond of unity, sealed in an undivided commitment to the Church through the Congregation.

Now there was eager readiness in the Enfield school, in England, when the notice arrived of a general inspection to be held in June, 1945, by the Ministry of Education. Ten inspectors carried out detailed examinations lasting one week which culminated in a full-fledged recognition of the school. In Paris, the *Foyer* became a halfway house for the priests liberated from German concentration camps where they found hospitality for as long as they needed it. It served also as a place of refreshment where released prisoners who were in transit were offered free meals by the sisters.

The eight sisters detained in Uzbekistan in 1943, with Sister Hyacinth Bienkowska at the head, seized upon an opportune moment to set out on the long homeward trek that brought them to Warsaw in the summer of 1945. When the Iron Curtain descended across the European continent, the provincial superiors in Poland recalled from dispersion the sisters whose convents were cut off from the west and confiscated because they could no longer exercise an apostolic mission. But Sister Berchmans Drozdowska with nine companions had won permission to dedicate themselves to the service of the people of Grodno after the frontier would be closed.[34]

In Nowogródek, similarly, Sister Margaret volunteered to remain alone, not only as guardian of the martyred sisters' graves but also of religion. Her death, which occurred on April 26, 1966, was mourned deeply by the townspeople to whom as a valiant and enterprising nun she had brought much comfort.[35] Among the messages of esteem and gratitude, directed to the generalate in Rome in acknowledgement of her contribution to the religious life of the locality, was one from the Apostolic Administrator, Msgr. Michael Krzywicki.[36]

Sister Deodata Markiewicz, having been isolated and removed from the labor camp in Bojanów, was taken to East Prussia as a nurse and governess to five young children in a German officer's family. Freed upon the entry of the Allies, she immediately joined the transit camp for liberated prisoners in the Bavarian town of Coburg to teach the teenage youth who had been cruelly mistreated and utterly neglected during the years of their imprisonment. With unspeakable joy she took out her religious habit which she had kept hidden for nearly three years, grateful to be able to wear it again unreproached and happy to signify her Nazareth membership.[37] By December she found it possible to be reunited with the community in Rome,[38] and the following month proceeded to Trani, in the province of Bari, to teach in a refugee camp until its liquidation in September, 1946.

The former superior from Kalisz, Sister Immolata Krajewska, who together with her sisters had endured the ordeals of the labor camp, was given—after the cessation of the hostilities—the assignment to an entirely new mission opened in Żdżary. The splendid ancestral estate of Mother Mary of Jesus the Good Shepherd had been parcelled out into small land holdings following her brother's death, and the two wars left a corrosive imprint upon the once well-cared-for stretches of forest, park and farms. From year to year Mother Lauretta had hoped to realize the Congregation's desire to establish there a lasting memorial to the saintly Foundress, and the hope began to take form when her personal visit to Żdżary, July 25, 1927,[39] facilitated the purchase of a tract of land around the parish church erected by Mother Mary's grandfather.

At the conclusion of the general chapter of 1932, the American delegates had made a pilgrimage to this cherished place associated with the heavenly favors that Mother Mary experienced in her youth.[40] One of the annual projects developed by the high school students in Warsaw was a Christmas fête for the farmers' children in Żdżary with gifts of handmade practical knitwear, holiday items and a decorated Christmas tree.[41] The sisters from Warsaw, again, would make a summer mission visit there for several weeks,[42] but no stable plan had taken root until 1945, when upon postwar ruins a day nursery, catechetical center and dispensary were begun.

Another new undertaking was the Mater Dolorosa Institute, a nursing home for the chronically ill, which the Apostolic Administrator of the diocese of Wrocław entrusted to the sisters. At this time of adjustment and adaptation the temporary novitiate, ensconced in the forest seclusion in the vicinity of Warsaw, was moved, September 17, 1946, to the Immaculate Heart of Mary convent in Ostrzeszów.

The fulfillment of one other uncompleted project of Mother Lauretta's came to pass in Loreto. She had wanted to honor the memory of the Foundress in some manner near the sanctuary of the Holy House of the Annunciation to which Mother Mary made her way repeatedly to pray for inspiration and grace. Here, too, the sisters participating in the general chapter of 1938 had an opportunity to make a pilgrimage as a group,[43] and two years later, when the war was already in full swing, Mother Lauretta went there with Mother Clare to select a suitable place for a foundation. The place acquired was indeed ideally located, near the Basilica of the Holy House, overlooking the brilliant Adriatic with the shimmering Apennines dipping into its waters, but the building—a kind of warehouse—was not habitable. Eventually war-time refugees occupied it, pleased to have a roof over their heads for the time being.

Situated but a short distance from the sanctuary was the military hospital in Senigallia from where the sister staff made visits of piety to Loreto. When on December 6, 1945 the refugees departed from the sisters' building, it was in turn requisitioned by the Polish Army Corps for its temporary post.[44] By July of 1946 two incidents occurred in favor of the prospective Loreto convent: the sisters' tour of duty in Senigallia was terminated and the troops stationed in Loreto were transferred to England. Sister Ludvina Lachmayr with seven associates converted the building into provisional accommodations to serve their immediate needs. At the outset the sisters' work consisted of pastoral ministry and social service among the families of Polish soldiers married to Italian wives, to whom Polish and Italian speaking sisters brought the means for a happy mutual understanding and harmony.

At the recommendation of the Polish Army authorities, the sisters were commissioned to supervise the Polish Military Cemetery on the slope leading from Loreto's basilica. Besides having the responsibility for the care of the graves, they took charge of the records of the soldiers and officers resting there, who gave their lives in the Allied effort during the Ancona campaign and in defense of Loreto,[45] in order to provide information to visitors and correspondents. Several times each year open-air memorial services at the field altar of the cemetery are also arranged by them.

Though outward recognitions had not been sought by the Congregation nor did they motivate its members, the Polish government-in-exile, at the temporary headquarters in London, took grateful cognizance of the public merit in certain outstanding deeds they had performed. Acting without delay, it conferred the Order of *Polonia Restituta* upon Sister Agnes Kosiba, superior at Ponders End, England, who was instrumental in setting up an Information Bureau for refugees, exiles and displaced persons from Poland. The sisters of the convent extended help and solace to these persons by conducting an interpretation center, search unit, letter-writing station, and travelers' aid.

In the United States, Sisters Electa and Richard, provincial superiors, likewise received the same distinguished Order for promoting extensive social services to incoming displaced persons, so that narrowing down the strangeness of new environments the immigrants should be able to reach a plateau of adjustment from which their children could ascend to higher achievements. The provincials have also given firm support to relief and rescue work for the victims of the war, and generous cooperation to Prince Jan Drucki-Lubecki in organizing the Catholic League for Religious Assistance to Poland.

To Sisters Liguori Pakowska and Liliosa Melerska, the President of the Republic of Poland made the award of the Gold Cross of Merit for their effective widespread support of Polish studies among teachers and students. Furthermore, it was upon Sister Liliosa's initiative that the chair of Polish language and culture had been introduced by De Paul University on both undergraduate and graduate levels and drew endorsement and interest from discriminating quarters.

Despite the turbulent era of war, the Sacred Congregation of Rites proceeded to implement the Apostolic Process concerning Mother Mary of Jesus the Good Shepherd, which now entailed the critical analysis of individual Christian virtues manifested in her life and the favors attributed to her intercession. There was an obvious urgency to accomplish this re-examination while the primary witnesses were still living and capable of bearing credible testimony. Auxiliary tribunals, appointed in each of the countries where Nazareth was represented, interviewed the witnesses under the auspices of the Vatican office and transmitted the text of their findings. This work occupied the years from 1941 to 1946, and was followed by the exacting procedures of translation, verification, transcription and printing, which were completed in 1950.

The grim aspect of open and secret antagonisms that seeped into the liberated countries disturbed the efforts at peaceful national reconstruction. Political unrest unavoidably interfered with private lives. Rather than undertake visits of dubious usefulness in Europe, Mother Clare was advised by the Sacred Congregation of Religious to schedule a personal tour of the convents in the United States,[46] which could be considerably expedited on the basis of the reports submitted to her in the previous year by the three delegated visitors.

In anticipation of the journey, Mother Clare was received in audience by Pope Pius XII on March 27, 1946. She requested that he give her a message for the sisters, coming from him as the Protector of the Congregation. After a moment's profound reflection, he said, "Please tell the sisters that their principal concern should be to cultivate the life of spirituality. The life of the spirit should be at the center of their activity; for all external activism, not permeated with the current of spirituality, is empty. Externals acts to be truly meaningful must be the outgrowth of a flourishing interior life."[47] Three weeks later Mother Clare made a trans-Atlantic flight accompanied by Sister Theobald Jaskulska, secretary general,[48] and Sisters Frances Sikorska[49] and Josephine Wąsikowska,[50] arriving in New York on April 14. She commenced the visitation with the easternmost houses, progressing westward with gentle vigor and remarkable insight.

Meanwhile, Archbishop Sapieha of Cracow was in receipt of the communication from the office of the Sacred Congregation of Religious, summoning to Rome the provincial superior, Sister Bożena. She departed from the airport in Warsaw, November 29, 1946, in the company of Sister Fides Tomkowicz.[51] By the decree issued on November 25, 1946,[52] Mother Bożena was named the superior general[53] for three years experimentally —*ad triennium et experimentum*—and was authorized to select the members of the general administration for the same period. Her ceremonial installation took place at the motherhouse in Rome on December 5.[54]

Mother Clare received the news of the nomination by way of telegram from the Apostolic Delegate in Washington, when she was already in Chicago. She, in turn, notified the sisters throughout the United States and continued her work of visitation until its completion, as was expected of her. Content in the knowledge of God's designs for her, she accepted them unconditionally on his terms, whatever the price, and emerged finer and stronger.

With reference to these developments she wrote to Sister Pia Kasperska, "Divine Wisdom guides the incomprehensible events which nonetheless tend to realize God's unfailing plans that are unknown to us. Let us love the cross of the divine will and allow the daily trials, pains and contradictions to enrich our souls. All these shall pass away like a shadow when life eternal will open to us. In the meantime may our love and union of hearts at Nazareth thrive in sincerity and truth."[55] These sentiments, characteristic of Mother Clare, were a refinement of the rule of life she had professed twenty-five years before, in another letter wherein she commented on the chagrin suffered by someone over a bitter disappointment, ". . . it is always well to be disposed in advance to face disappointments; one becomes less given to feelings of frustration when disclaiming one's supposed merits in the light of stark reality."[56]

The thirty-three years she had spent in Rome at the service of the Congregation were an epiphany of a soul immersed in God, and now she knew she would not return. For she was destined to remain in the land of her youth where she had responded to the mystic call to Nazareth and lived her early years in the joy of its blessings as teacher and religious superior. She accepted now the position of provincial assistant in the Immaculate Conception province and, in addition to the duties of her office, devoted much time to visiting the patients at Nazareth Hospital in Philadelphia with words of human understanding and spiritual uplift.

Houses of the Congregation
opened in the years 1943 through 1946:

Year	Location	Convent-Apostolate-First Superior
1943	UNITED STATES Mobile, Alabama	Infant of Prague convent; Zimmer Memorial Home for children; Sister M. Alexis Wesołek.
1943	POLAND Karczew-Warsaw	Bethania,* temporary novitiate; Sister M. Ezechiela Szupenko, director.
1944	UNITED STATES Hato Rey, Puerto Rico	Jesus, Mary and Joseph in Nazareth convent; Colegio Espiritu Santo; Sister M. Theotime Pokorska.
1944	UNITED STATES Footedale, Pennsylvania	St. Clare convent; St. Thomas parish school; Sister M. Titus Kutka.
1945	POLAND Żdżary	St. Frances of Rome convent; pastoral ministry, catechetical center; Sister M. Immolata Krajewska.
1946	UNITED STATES Montgomery, Alabama	St. Peter Claver convent; care of spastic children, pastoral ministry; Sister M. Infanta Kurcz.
1946	ITALY Loreto	Virgo Lauretana convent; family apostolate, pastoral ministry, supervision of military cemetery; Sister M. Ludvina Lachmayr.

Year	Location	Convent-Apostolate-First Superior
1946	POLAND Wróblowice	Our Lady of Perpetual Help convent; catechetical center; Sister M. Amanda Bostnowska.
1946	POLAND Wrocław	Sorrowful Mother convent; "Mater Dolorosa" Institute, nursing home for the aged and chronically ill; Sister M. Angelica Kułach.

Houses closed:

Year	Location	
1943	FRANCE St. Sylvain, Calvados	Holy Face convent (1938-1943); pastoral ministry, catechetics.
1945	POLAND Wilczkowice	affiliate of the Sacred Heart convent, Cracow (1937-1945); day care center for children.
1945	POLAND Vilna	Eucharistic Heart of Jesus convent (1906-1945); junior college, teacher education; evacuation and dispersion.
1945	POLAND Stryj	St. Joseph convent (1913-1945); elementary boarding school; evacuation and dispersion.
1945	POLAND Lemberg	Holy Family convent (1892-1945); junior college and high school for girls; evacuation and dispersion.
1945	POLAND Nowogródek	Christ the King convent (1929-1945); elementary school, pastoral ministry; sisters executed, convent confiscated.
*1946	POLAND Karczew-Warsaw	Bethania; temporary novitiate; transferred to Immaculate Heart of Mary convent, Ostrzeszów.

3 MINDFUL OF HIS MERCY

The new superior general moved quite smoothly into the concerns of the Congregation. A servant versatile and cautious, sensitive to the signs of the times and to effective ways and means, she ascended from the office of the provincial as easily as from a launching platform. By suffering and introspection she had learned her own strengths and shortcomings, the intrinsic character of Nazareth in its variegated totality, and the character of the circumstances in which the sisters lived, that is, not merely the circumstances of the respective and separate communities, but of the whole world society bearing down upon them. With new-found patience she could then determine the interplay between their character and the circumstances. Through all this she displayed qualities of leadership and the ability to make judgments and decisions for which there had been no precedent.

Among the first acts undertaken by Mother Bożena was to consider the proposal of Reverend Stanley Belch, spiritual director of the Polish colony in England. At the recommendation of the British hierarchy he requested the establishment of a home for the orphaned children of the members of Polish military forces, who had been based in England and who had been engaged with the Allies in combat. To investigate the possibilities and details of the proposal, Sister Bonosa Siedlecka was relieved of her duties as superior at Albano and departed for London, February 5, 1947.[57] During two trying years of postwar want and hunger she had plied the affairs of the Albano convent with great courage and resourcefulness. Equipped with the certifications from American, British and Polish universities, she was singularly qualified to prepare the terrain for a new type of work, custodial, educational and bilingual, to which she was assigned.

In May, the sprawling estate known as Pitsford Hall, situated on the borders of Northampton, was purchased from the British government and was blessed, in August, with the participation of the sisters from Enfield and Ponders End. It was a charming property, though perhaps a triffie bleak in winter, but the views were magnificent, and it afforded a promising outlook for the future. In the meantime, the East African settlement of exiles in Kenya was liquidated, and the sisters departed in groups to Poland, Rome, and England. They had declined the opportunity of going to the United States on the advice of Bishop Gawlina, Vicar for the Polish people who had been uprooted and displaced by the misfortunes of war.

On the eighth of October, Sister Regina, the intrepid superior, arrived in London with seven sisters and five postulants and proceeded the following day to Pitsford Hall. Actual working situations altered the admission policy of the home. It became a resident school for girls, accepting also the orphaned children from the temporary refugee camps in England. As a junior high school, its curriculum complied with that prescribed by the Ministry of Education.

Promptly in 1947, the project in Loreto also began to assume its intended features, when the plans for erecting a pilgrim and retreat house, with accommodations for Catholic Action youth activities, were set in motion. In honor of the Blessed Virgin Mary, whose Holy House is enshrined in the nearby basilica, the American convents defrayed the cost of construction. Sunday, October 31, 1948, marked the solemn dedication of the building, preceded by the ritual consecration of the altar in the chapel.[58]

The march of time pressed for the reactivation of the central novitiate in Albano. A few postulants at the motherhouse were ready for the second stage of their religious formation; in England there were the native recruits as well as those who were arriving from Africa; and there was one who had risked the three-month voyage from New Zealand. To form the core of the revived novitiate, ten novices from Poland were selected to make the transfer together with Sister Ezechiela, as director. Following the delay involved in exit formalities, they reached Italy, September 19, 1947.[59] After years of turmoil, they finally tasted a life of hope and serenity in the intense happiness of dedication to God. When the American novices came, they rounded out the number that made for the international character of the novitiate.

Once Mother Bożena was able to lead off in the right direction the matters of immediate urgency in Europe, she turned towards the United States. She was not a stranger to the American apostolate, for she had made its first acquaintance back in 1935, when it had reached the fifty-year milestone since the first sisters set foot in the New World. Travel meant the gentle confrontation of different cultures, a profound examination of possible barriers to communication, a confirming of basic cordiality and large-mindedness that embraced all the differing backgrounds in order to proclaim validly the Gospel message of unity and love from within a strongly united, loving sisterhood in truth.

She urged the sisters not to be diverted from coming to grips with the spiritual realities that were the foundation of faith and religious life. Despite her undeniable credentials and talents, these concerns led to an anxiety produced partly by the questions that preoccupied them and partly by the questions she herself was asking. In the light of the contending forces of the period she knew that to respond rashly was as fatal as to fall behind.

Historically, the aftermath of wars have been bewildering changes in the mores of the people with an admixture of disorientation and disorganization. To offset the gathering disorientation, the Congregation was assisted by Reverend Francis A. Cegielka, theologian-scholar of the Society of the Catholic Apostolate, permeated with the burning zeal of the founder, St. Vincent Pallotti. Shortly after his release from the Nazi concentration camp, Father Cegielka devoted himself largely to Nazareth in the United States and delved into the study of the life and inspiration of Mother Mary of Jesus the Good Shepherd, which enabled him to probe the underlying spirituality of the Congregation and its mission in the world. Though his association over many long years to come proved genuinely profitable, other perceptive and pious clergymen have also had a part in illuminating the concept of life as seen in the contemporary issues through reflection, prayer and discourse.

In the summer of 1947, after preliminary meetings in the United States, Mother Bożena announced the appointment of the provincial superiors: Sister Hyacinth Gorecka, St. Joseph province, Pittsburgh; Sister Neomisia Rutkowska, Immaculate Conception province, Philadelphia, and Sister Aloysius Kozlowska, Sacred Heart province, Chicago-Des Plaines. The vicar for the southern region of Texas and New Mexico became Sister Richard Rutkowska, who had served since 1938 as the provincial in the Chicago area.[60] To fill the office of the provincial in Cracow, left vacant by the departure of Mother Bożena, Sister Assumpta Hermanska had been named the successor.

Having completed a cursory visit of the provinces, the superior general returned to the motherhouse in November. Among matters of importance that claimed her attention was the general administration which had to be duly constituted and briefed. It consisted of the following officers: Sister Marie de Lourdes Mazalewska, assistant general; Sisters Mary Magdalene Szeligowska, Ezechiela Szupenko and Berchmans Hejnowska, councilors general; Sister Fides Tomkowicz, treasurer general, and Sister Honesta Jastrzembska, secretary general.

In Warsaw, Sister Beatrix Kirkor succeeded Sister Anna as provincial superior in 1948; and in Cracow, in 1950, Sister Deodata Markiewicz replaced the ailing Sister Assumpta.

By the decree of the Sacred Congregation for Religious, dated November 25, 1949, the tenure of Mother Bożena as superior general was approved to extend until the expiration of the twelve-year term in 1958.[61] The duration of the offices of the general administration was to coincide accordingly.

Whatever wartime lag had hung over the essential pursuits of the sisters, the sweep and surge of peacetime advances rushed to overcome it. Graduate studies in theology were gaining significant emphasis among them in quality, scope and method. Opportunities in specialized fields of interest became increasingly available to them in outstanding foreign universities, and doctorates have come to be attained more frequently as the means to greater achievement.

In a period of swift change and vigorous competition, the will to live — not merely to survive — had to be fired once more, and the key could be found within a revitalized system of artistic flowerings and exciting talents of students. The convent academies and parish schools have been building up a well-earned art reputation under the tutelage of scores of creative artists. Notable for originality of design and variety of media in their own works as well as in formal art instruction were Sisters Silveria Labacz, Plautilda Pachucka and Alberta Zenderska. Traditionally it has been a labor of tears to care for the arts, but cultivating art appreciation through practice led not infrequently to the discovery of a genuine gift that determined some students' entire future.

Literary skills, fostered and encouraged in creative writing by enthusiastic teachers, found their exponents in Sisters Florence Tumasz and Edith Wierzbowska. Both prolific and graceful writers, they merited unstinted acclaim by contemporary poets for their poetical compositions, lyrical in concept and beauty. All things considered, it turned out to be a long-lasting banner season of scholastic accomplishments, high in awards and honors earned by individual students and entire divisions, in regional as well as national performances within the broad spectrum of their studies.

The magnitude of surfacing social problems gave rise to a wide new field of social services and opened noble options to the sisters to help rehabilitate those who were unable to help themselves. Sisters Clemens Pionke, Angela Kuzia and Medarda Synakowska received graduate degrees in social work and placed the social service departments of their respective institutions on a professional footing.

As caseworker, and later as superintendent of Little Flower Institute in Wading River on Long Island, Sister Medarda brought expertise and dignity to its services which necessarily had to be correlated with the diocesan office of Catholic Charities and the State Department of Public Welfare. Already in 1945 the policy of racial desegregation became effective at the Institute, and the negro children saw other races admitted and learned to live with them as one human family. Another social service development on Long Island met with considerable success when the sisters staffed St. Christopher Home in 1947. Conducted under the auspices of the Children's Division of Catholic Charities, it cared for infants and pre-school children awaiting placement in foster homes.

In Chicago, at the explicit wish of the Archbishop, Samuel Cardinal Stritch, Sister Clemens initiated at St. Mary of Nazareth Hospital a temporary placement service for infants born of Catholic mothers at Cook County Hospital, who were surrendered for adoption. In cooperation with

Catholic Charities, before these infants were released to their adoptive parents, they were given a thorough pediatric examination and were placed under observation for several days. During their stay, they were baptized by the hospital chaplain. The baptismal and health records were given to the adoptive parents, with the infant, by the caseworker of the Catholic Charities Bureau, who had attended to the adoption proceedings. Gradually, other services were offered by the hospital's social service office for the benefit of the needy, the stranger, the perplexed. Gradually, too, social service offices and departments were established elsewhere and staffed by qualified sisters to maintain institutional liaisons with related public and charitable agencies for available assistance.

In the tidal wave of scientific knowledge and health care systems the hospitals have not delayed rising to the expectations of an informed society and a progressive medical profession. The intelligent concern for the preservation of health and the early treatment of disease had to be equalled with expanding facilities, a demand which involved each of the American provinces in major building programs in this period:

Bethania Hospital, Wichita Falls, Texas: hospital additions, 1942 and 1948;

Mercy Hospital, Altoona, Pennsylvania: hospital sisters' convent, 1951;

Mother Frances Hospital, Tyler, Texas: purchase of the hospital building upon the expiration of the ten-year lease, 1947; hospital addition, 1948;

Nazareth Hospital, Philadelphia, Pennsylvania: hospital sisters' convent, 1952; departmental expansions, 1952, 1953, and 1954;

Ohio Valley General Hospital, McKees Rocks, Pennsylvania: new hospital building to replace the obsolete structure, 1949; nursing education building and student residence, 1956;

St. Mary of Nazareth Hospital, Chicago, Illinois: nursing education building and student residence, 1955.

To provide educational opportunities to health workers interested in paramedical services, certified curricula were organized within the hospitals in radiologic technique, medical technology, anesthesiology, and nuclear medicine. The schools of nursing at St. Mary's, Ohio Valley and Mercy hospitals, which for years held reputable standards, have been expanding their regular programs of instruction and opening to professional nurses post-graduate courses in nursing specialties, such as pediatric nursing, obstetrical nursing, newborn nursery care, and operating room supervision. Besides meeting the accreditation requirements of the respective State Boards of Nurse Examiners, the schools voluntarily adopted the more exacting educational policies enunciated by the American League for Nursing.

In Texas, both Bethania and Mother Frances Hospitals introduced broad programs for practical nurses who, upon the completion of prescribed theory and practice, could be accorded state registration as vocational nurses. Each term fresh corps of skilled women and men went out into the community at large to function responsibly as auxiliary personnel in hospitals and other health organizations.

Under a scholarship from the Catholic University of America, Sister Janine Polinska had prepared for psychiatric nursing care and, in 1955, organized the psychiatric unit at Mother Frances Hospital. She subsequently merited the public service award from the city of Tyler for a community-wide mental health program which was acclaimed for its constructive educational value.

But in a technological era there is the inclination to acquire a limited view of man, to recognize man only for what he does or produces and to lose sight of the source of his innate dignity. Against the lurking dangers of a purely utilitarian ethic, the newly formulated graduate-level studies in hospital administration came as a counterpoise in the development of prospective administrators and in-service administrators.

Deriving from sound scientific and philosophical principles, they were qualified to affirm in practical situations that the patient is a person, a member of society, a personality in a culture, made in the image of God, and that from the moment of conception to the moment of death he is worthy of the full support of the human family. This became a rallying point in time of testing. Thus, a new line of hospital administrators, confirmed in their creed and equipped for the ways of modern leadership and management, was begun in 1953 by Sisters Edith Szczepanska and DeChantal Dylewska when they earned the Master of Science in Hospital Administration degree and later became Fellows of the American College of Hospital Administrators.

Concern for perpetuating the durable qualities of life through education and good citizenship placed a unique demand upon the sisters who taught in the primary and secondary divisions of the public school at South Heart, North Dakota. For seven years North Dakota's Department of Public Instruction had been pleased to have the Nazareth group on its force when teacher shortages were experienced in its rural and small town public schools. Besides meeting the strict requirements uniformly insisted upon of all teachers, irrespective of the locality to which they were assigned, the sisters accepted the peculiar conditions of the straggling farm region.

The widely scattered population pooled their arrangements for bringing the children to school, yet the enrollment was small enough to warrant combining the elementary grades under three teachers and dovetailing the high school courses over a four-year period under two teachers, one of whom was the principal. As in all public schools in the nation, instructions in religion may not be offered on the premises of the school. Instead, the sisters complied with the popular desires of the district, dominantly Catholic, by holding classes in religion in the church after Sunday services and during summer vacations.

It came as a shock to the people of South Heart and thereabout, when in the spring of 1948 the state legislature, influenced by the strong anti-Catholic sentiment of its members, enacted the Anti-Garb Bill. The contention was that the religious habit worn by a sister teaching in a public school was a sign of religious witnessing, consequently, incompatible with the non-sectarian education required of public schools by law.

At the request of Bishop Vincent J. Ryan, who voiced the wishes of the faithful of the diocese, the general council of the Congregation consented to the continued staffing of the school and to the sisters' changing into secular apparel for classes. Reliving the experiences of Mother Mary of Jesus the Good Shepherd, who fifty years earlier had not withdrawn the sisters from France under similar difficulties, Sister Flavilla Fiederowicz, superior-principal, instilled in her four associates the sense of mission for the cause of faith. In the diocesan publication, *Dakota Catholic Action*,[62] they were named "God's Heroine's."

The news media of the world gave notice to the fact that Pope Pius XII will have reached his fiftieth year of priestly ordination, April 2, 1949. The Pontiff, however, declined the proposed plans for a public observance of that event, desiring preferably to concentrate on the Holy Year of 1950, when pilgrims from all parts of the world would come to Rome to gain universal pardon for sin and international reconciliation through prayer and penance. As teachers of youth, the sisters were engaged in the spiritual and intellectual preparation of their students for the Holy Year objectives of world peace and brotherhood. The patients in hospitals, on the other hand, were encouraged to join in a crusade of prayer and suffering as their contribution for the peace intentions of the Holy Year.

For Nazareth, a singular jubilee of grace dawned that year, the seventy-fifth anniversary of its foundation. The years had been productive, teeming with unsung deeds and hidden joys, rich with dynamic associations and the calm steady glow of warm friendships. In the 123 convents on both sides of the Atlantic the jubilee was observed for three days[63] in reflective solemnity and thanksgiving to God.

A fresh exposition of the resources of the spirit, blending with the Holy Year's aims for the "great return," was presented to the Congregation in Father Cegielka's treatise on the *Reparatory Mysticism of Nazareth*.[64] The work, developed under the incentive of Sister Neomisia, provincial superior in Philadelphia, was a forerunner of two other ascetical studies by the same author dealing with selected aspects of the Nazareth way, *The Hidden Life of Nazareth* and *Nazareth Spirituality.* [65]

That same year bore a touch of the great Pope's theological depth and vision when he proclaimed and defined the dogma of Mary's Assumption, a belief deeply rooted in both Eastern and Western Churches and observed with popular festivity since the earliest centuries of Christianity. It was by no means a simple expression of his personal piety when he introduced the Age of Mary with the consecration of mankind to her Immaculate Heart. The tragedy of the war then, and the crisis of peace which followed, pointed to the Blessed Virgin as the only hope of the world in its fitful struggles. For this reason he wanted to bring all people under her unfailing protection by designating the year 1954 as Marian Year,[66] and bestowing upon her the title of the Queen of the Universe.[67] He also led the world-wide observance, in 1958, of the one-hundredth anniversary of the apparitions of Mary at Lourdes.

The beginning of the fourth quarter of the century in the life of the Congregation signaled the resuscitation of De Lourdes College in Des Plaines, Illinois. Under its 1927 charter, in-service elementary school teachers received professional preparation, which they subsequently amplified in other colleges and existing universities in major cities. During the somber years of the Great Depression the activities of De Lourdes College were suspended to be revived only in 1951.

Sister Electa Glowienke, reassigned to the Sacred Heart province in 1950, perceived the possibility of reopening the teachers' college, which could easily be staffed by the sisters who had already acquired advanced degrees and were qualified to form the faculty. After consultation with Dr. Roy J. Deferrari, chairman of the Committee on Affiliation and Accreditation at the Catholic University of America, she was aided by a group of colleagues, supremely dedicated sisters, who entered with her into the vision of the new De Lourdes College. For months on end, Sister Micina Arendt invested her professional competence as librarian in revising and updating the library, and Sister Speciosa Luczak contributed her after-school weekends and holidays to secretarial services in establishing the college office files and records.

De Lourdes College was accepted as an affiliate of the Catholic University of America in 1951, in time to commence the first summer session that year with the status of a two-year teachers' college. To Sister Electa, the president, it owned the judicious guidance which gained for it, in May of 1960, the approval to conduct a four-year academic program leading to a Bachelor of Science in Education degree as well as the Illinois State Certification for elementary school teachers.

A historic ripple quietly traced the Congregation's living endorsement of its universal apostolic element with the arrival of the first sisters in Australia in 1952. In a way it paralleled the venture of the first sisters in the United States back in 1885. For Mother Bożena had been approached in Rome by Bishop Gawlina about entering the immense field of boundless potential for the spreading of the Kingdom of God among thousands of displaced Poles and refugees from communism who tried to create in Australia a new life for themselves and their families. The small body of the Missionaries of St. Vincent de Paul had prayed and pleaded for a contingent of apostolic sisters, preferably bilingual, who would generously encompass the broad pastoral needs in family apostolate, child care and education, youth guidance, and the multiple concerns for the sick, the poor, the aged, and the delinquent. It was necessary to fashion and coordinate the religious, welfare, and civic structures with sympathy and understanding in order to save these deeply wounded people from moral deterioration.

In June, 1952, Mother Bożena interrupted her visitation tour of the American convents to proceed to the port of Vancouver in Canada where she embarked on *SS Aorangi* with her traveling companion, Sister Ezechiela. They were joined by the three sisters chosen to begin God's work in the Southern Hemisphere, namely, Sisters Noela Linkowska, Bonosa Siedlecka and Denise Dokurno. After the twenty-five-day trans-Pacific voyage, they landed in Sydney, July 12,[68] and then traveled on to Brisbane where they were met by Father W. Czapla, C.M., spiritual director of the Poles in the state of Queensland, and by Dr. J. Hempel, president of the Queensland Polish Association.

Archbishop James Duhig of Brisbane welcomed the sisters warmly and offered them a vacant convent at 119 Nelson Street in the suburb of Kalinga. Over the next months the building was reconditioned, furnished and equipped to serve a dual purpose: it housed the sisters, and on school days accommodated twenty to thirty Polish girls from the migrant camps. On January 11, 1953, the Archbishop blessed it in public ceremony under the title of Holy Family convent and home.[69]

To the satisfaction of Kalinga's pastor of St. Ann's church, Reverend H. Ryan, the sisters organized a school in his small parish to be attended by local Australian children and the girls from the home. Acceding to the wishes of the girls' parents, Polish language and culture were not neglected in their education, but at the same time the English-language curriculum was ably carried out in the regular classroom sessions. Within the first year of operation under the direction of Sister Bonosa as headmistress, the school merited full recognition following the inspection made by the officials of the Department of Public Instruction of Queensland,[70] and subsequent reports continued to record progress and praise.

Upon the arrival of additional sisters, Nazareth's pioneering efforts began to radiate towards the far removed settlements in Wacol, Enoggera and Darra—at first in adult religion education and the sacramental preparation of children, soon extending to other wholesome contacts in church choirs and glee clubs, cultural recreations and creative crafts, in a shared endeavor to live the Gospel of Christ realistically.

It occurred as an afterthought to the members of the Congregation and to those close to them, that the Australian foundation came into being— without human design—in the year that marked the fiftieth anniversary of the death of Nazareth's revered Foundress. There were also other significant developments. One was the appearance of Mother Mary's biography, *Where There Is Love,* by the noted hagiographer Katherine Burton,[71] whom Sister Neomisia assisted with indispensable research materials and practical insights. In the Vatican, the details towards the beatification advanced another step when the decree of March 2, 1952 affirmed the Validity of the Ordinary and the Apostolic Processes, and a year later, on March 1, 1953, the completed recapitulation, called the *Summarium,* numbering 1,284 pages, was published.

Important to the cause of beatification was the change of the postulator occasioned by the death of Msgr. Bressan. He was succeeded, January 13, 1953, by Father Antonio Ricciardi, O.F.M. Conv., Postulator General of the Friars Minor Conventual, who was also engaged in the investigative work concerning the martyred Father Maximillian Kolbe, ardent apostle of Mary Immaculate, beatified in 1971.

The time was ripe for the act of canonical identification of Mother Mary's remains, and with it rose the hope of having the remains entombed in the chapel of the motherhouse. The preliminaries involved not only compliance with ecclesiastical authorities but also with civic regulations safeguarding public health and sanitation. July 9, 1953 was the date set for the exhumation. Except for the sisters gathered about the Congregation's mausoleum in Campo Verano, no external ceremony accompanied the transfer of the casket with the remains to the convent of the Good Shepherd at Via Machiavelli. While the record of the removal of the casket from the cemetery vault was being drawn up, the sisters returned to the convent to await the retinue.

Chanting the *Salve Regina* and *Laudate Pueri Dominum,* the sisters with lighted candles led the procession to the spacious hall of the Catholic Action in the convent, where white-draped tables had been arranged functionally for the task at hand. Since an exhumation conducted under the auspices of the Church is a private affair, allowing a limited number of witnesses, only the members of the general administration were present besides the Commission of the Sacred Congregation of Rites, a physician and two nurses.

Upon lifting the lid of the casket, a well-preserved rose blossom was found atop the inner coffin. It had been placed there by Mother Lauretta at the time of the translation of the remains to the mausoleum in 1913, when the coffin was inclosed in the external casket. Inside, the disintegrating clothing had spread like a gossamer veil, through which the outlines of the skeletal structure were discernible, but no hint of odor escaped therefrom.

The minute examination and meticulous recording of every detail of the procedure extended until July 24, when all the sisters were permitted to view the remains. The room, now adorned with flowers in affectionate tribute to Mother Foundress, bore a joyous aspect. As they assembled about her relics, the Chancellor of the Sacred Congregation of Rites, Msgr. Orazio Cocchetti, invoked the Blessed Trinity in a prayer of thanksgiving for the successful accomplishment of this stage of the process. On the next day again, the sisters formed a procession to the chapel accompanying the remains which had been arranged and sealed in a metal casket. They were put to rest in a niche built in the wall and covered over with a marble slab.[72]

The impact of this event was experienced across the entire Nazareth Congregation, making the presence of the Foundress felt through the revival of the spirit she had engendered. Even the sisters in Poland were fortunate enough to learn of the recent canonical proceedings, when for the last several years news from outside the Iron Curtain had been conspicuously scarce, diluted and delayed. Though the war for democracy was won, the flay of truce flew but briefly over the suffering land, for world peace had not been secured.

There was a deceptive lull before a rising storm which lashed out in gusts of systematic sovietization and imprisonments of the religious, neither of which spared the Sisters of the Holy Family of Nazareth. To curtail their influence for the good, the sisters were being dismissed from hospitals and schools and from other humanitarian activities where they associated with mentally normal persons. They were allowed to work in institutions for the incurably ill and for mentally disturbed and retarded children. The convents were burdened with progressively increasing taxes and with regulations that infringed on their privacy.

To resolve their economic plight, they were helped to develop the so-called "cottage industry" by sympathetic merchants, business enterprises and local shops, which supplied them with work that could be accomplished within the convent. Small day-care centers, limited by law to nine preschool children of working mothers, were arranged in the convents. The high school in Warsaw was the only Nazareth school allowed to remain in existence, confined as it was to a restricted student enrollment; a large section of the school building had been appropriated by the department of public health under socialized medicine and a wing had been converted into a state-operated school.

On the other hand, as an expression of their evangelical dedication, the sisters carried out parish church activities, catechetical instructions, apostolates of deaf-mutes, tutorial assistance, home nursing of the poor, vigils with the dying, and pastoral ministry in rural areas.

Houses of the Congregation
opened in the years 1947 through 1953:

Year	*Location*	*Convent-Apostolate-First Superior*
1947	ENGLAND Pitsford, Northampton	Our Lady Queen of Peace convent; Holy Family convent school; Sister M. Regina Budzyńska.
1947	UNITED STATES Hollidaysburg, Pa.	St. Ann convent; St. Leonard's Home for senior citizens; Sister Otillia Wiśniewska.
1947	UNITED STATES Sea Cliff, New York	St. Maria Goretti convent; St. Christopher's Home for Children; Sister M. Gracilia Kandyba.
1948	UNITED STATES Menasha, Wisconsin	Immaculate Heart of Mary convent; Maryville, rest and convalescent home for sisters; Sister M. Egidia Kawczyńska.
1948	UNITED STATES Detroit, Michigan	St. Joseph convent; St. Christopher parish school; Sister M. Henrietta Michałowska.
1950	UNITED STATES Hollidaysburg, Pa.	Queen of Peace convent; Villa Nazareth rest home for sisters; Sister M. Eleanore Waszkowska.
1950	UNITED STATES Philadelphia	Holy Spirit convent; faculty house; Sister M. Felixilla Magda.
1951	UNITED STATES Newton Falls, Ohio	Holy Spirit convent; Our Lady of Częstochowa parish school; Sister M. Virgil Gaworska.

Year	*Location*	*Convent-Apostolate-First Superior*

1951   UNITED STATES
      Meadowbrook, Pa.

Holy Family convent;
Villa Nazareth rest home for sisters
    until 1956;
Sister M. Slava Rostkowska.
In 1956, novitiate of the Immaculate
    Conception province; novices trans-
    ferred from Philadelphia.

1951   UNITED STATES
      Neenah, Wisconsin

Merciful Heart of Jesus convent;
St. Margaret Mary parish school;
Sister M. Godwin Zaleska.

1952   UNITED STATES
      Kalinga (Brisbane),
      Queensland

Holy Family convent and home for
    girls;
St. Ann parish school;
Sister M. Noela Linkowska.

1952   UNITED STATES
      Lincoln Park, New Jersey

St. Joseph convent;
St. Joseph parish school;
Sister M. Eustolia Molis.

1953   UNITED STATES
      Allen Park, Michigan

Mary Assumed into Heaven convent;
St. Frances Cabrini parish school;
Sister M. Richard Merman.

1953   UNITED STATES
      Riverhead, New York

Immaculate Conception convent;
Villa Immaculata rest home for sisters;
Sister M. Antonilla Zielińska.

Houses closed:

1947   FRANCE
      Chevreuse, Calvados

St. Therese of the Child Jesus convent
    (1942-1947); pastoral ministry.

1948   UNITED STATES
      Chicago

St. Mary of the Angels convent (1910-
    1948);
St. Francis of Assisi parish school.

1948   UNITED STATES
      Monessen, Pennsylvania

Virgo Fidelis convent (1919-1948);
St. Hyacinth parish school.

1949   UNITED STATES
      DuBois, Pennsylvania

St. Augustine convent (1936-1949);
St. Michael mission center; pastoral
    ministry.

Year	*Location*	*Convent-Apostolate-First Superior*
1950	UNITED STATES Linden, New Jersey	St. Therese convent (1930-1950); St. Therese of the Child Jesus parish school.
1950	UNITED STATES Roundup, Montana	St. Scholastica convent (1939-1950); St. Benedict parish school.
1950	POLAND Wadowice	Our Lady of Consolation convent (1896-1950); municipal general hospital; sisters dismissed by civil authorities.
1953	UNITED STATES Dalhart, Texas	Our Lady of Loreto convent (1929-1953); Loretto Hospital.
1953	FRANCE Potigny, Calvados	St. Michael Archangel convent (1938-1953); pastoral ministry, clinic.

Mother Mary of Jesus the Good Shepherd, according to the portrait by Tade Styka.

Mother M. Lauretta Lubowidzka, Vicar General, 1903-1909; Superior General, 1909-1942.

Mother M. Clare Netkowska, Councilor General, 1913-1920; Assistant General, 1920-1942; Vicar General, 1942-1946.

Mother M. Bozena Staczynska, Superior General, 1946-1959.

Mother M. Neomisia Rutkowska, Superior General, 1959-1971.

Mother M. Neomisia, in 1969, in the modified habit and veil.

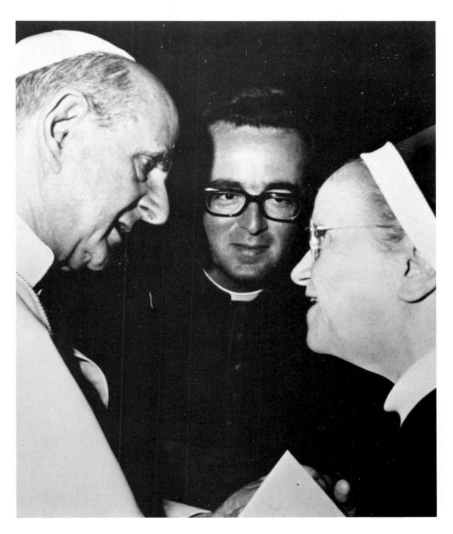

Mother M. Neomisia in the last official conversation with Pope Paul VI, July 14, 1971. Assisting His Holiness was Msgr. Justin Rigali of Los Angeles, California, chaplain to the Holy Father and official of the Vatican Secretariat of State for English-speaking countries.

Mother M. Medarda Synakowska, Superior General, 1971-

4 GREAT IN HOPE

In the strange encounter with destiny, segments of mankind sought to find their level in a massive effort to shake off the wartime hangover of poverty and educational arrest. The immigrants who came to America to escape communism usually settled in large cities, in neighborhoods where they could practice their faith and feel at ease with their culture and language until they would be ready psychologically for assimilation and citizenship. The schools responded to the influx of newcomers by developing special classes for adults and foreign-born children. In tutorial classes the sisters prepared the children to meet with their classmates in study and play, the sooner to overcome their linguistic handicap.

Caught in the wave of transurban migration, the new residents moved in time to other neighborhoods and into the suburbs, and were replaced by other immigrants from abroad and by migrants from parts of the United States and from the south of the border, who formed large ethnic communities in need of the services which God's religious could render. Except in places where Nazareth's apostolate was no longer vital, or where consolidations occurred uniting into one the work of two or three religious orders within a given neighborhood, the sisters continued to function in the old sites, adapting to the changing tenor of life round about them. Where certain districts became densely populated by Spanish-speaking people, Spanish became another language which the sisters acquired to be able to communicate with them intelligently. In one of the more effective programs, called Head Start, culturally deprived children were taught the skills required to make a satisfactory start in school in order to maintain a normal pace in learning.

With the residential and industrial expansion of northeast Philadelphia, the idea of a four-year liberal arts college for women germinated, grew, and at length ripened in 1952 with the approval of Archbishop John O'Hara, C.S.C. The Holy Family Teacher Training School, conducted since 1942 at the provincialate, had been supplying the field of education with Nazareth teachers prepared for the positions which required their immediate services and who were able to advance themselves professionally to satisfy future needs. These needs included teaching in the archdiocesan central high schools of Philadelphia: Hallahan, Little Flower and St. Hubert's, which were staffed jointly by members of several religious congregations. To facilitate a workable religious horarium, coordinated with their class schedule, the sisters appointed to the archdiocesan high schools resided at Holy Spirit convent, which became the Nazareth faculty house.

As the emphasis on education increased and more and more young people entered colleges, it became evident that the Congregation's cultural mission to womanhood in the true Christian tradition could be furthered

253

through the establishment of a college in the recently developing and growing locality of metropolitan Philadelphia. With the full authorization of the general council and the archdiocesan authorities, Sister Neomisia, provincial superior, sought and obtained from the State Council on Education the endorsement of the name "Holy Family College" and, on February 11, 1954, the legal charter which gave the college its corporate existence.

In the capacity of the founding president of the college, she moved at once towards a twofold goal. One was the construction of the college building on the campus of Nazareth Academy for which ground was broken on March 25 the same year; the completed edifice was dedicated the following year, November 21. Another prime concern was the planning for the first full-time academic year, scheduled to open in September, 1954, with classes held temporarily in the upper floor facilities of Nazareth auditorium building and with residence at St. Mary's Hall, the former Tall Oaks estate, acquired for that purpose.

Closely associated with Sister Neomisia in developing the administrative and curricular patterns of the college was Sister Florence Tumasz, who—for the next eighteen years as academic dean—maximized the college's effectiveness with responsive action, prudent choices and foresight. Together with Sisters Aloysius Sabacinska and Florianne (Misaela) Zacharewicz comprising an informed organizational team, they also served as members of the first faculty with one priest, three lay teachers and Sisters Rose Ann (Flaventia) Federowicz, Callista Klos and Gregoria Kozlowska.

Affiliated with the Catholic University of America, the college's liberal arts programs was oriented towards the Bachelor of Arts and the Bachelor of Science degrees. It hinged on the four-year sequences of both theology and philosophy, and for the fields of concentration provided a choice of eight major areas of study. In the third year of its existence, the college was granted the Pennsylvania State certification of its Secondary School Teacher Preparation program.

Traditions—academic, religious, and social—were established with the earliest students, infusing distinct characteristics, some commonly accepted in college life, others typical of Holy Family College, to be continued through the years to come. Charter Day became an annual observance of the founding of the college and for the freshmen—a day remembered with the capping ceremony when they received their academic caps and gowns. The Family Symposium, open to relatives and friends, was presented annually within the octave of the feast of the Holy Family, reviewing different aspects of married and family life in the light of the Holy Family at Nazareth as the model of family living.

For the purpose of giving recognition to the students who merited a position on the dean's list, the Honors Convocation was initiated, imparting an aura of distinction to their sense of achievement. Each year, a charm all its own pervaded the Regina Night, a ceremony with an outdoor candlelight procession in May in honor of Our Lady. Spring concerts and Christmas Rose festivities occasioned the regular expression of artistic interests through religious and classical motifs. With the progress of time and the growth of the student body, the crescendo of college experiences rose in wisdom and beauty.

In consequence of the widespread trend to depart from long-inhabited city centers, a complete array of sociological services had to come into being for the benefit of the people in the new communities they created. The proliferation of new parish schools, then recorded, can be compared with a similar phenomenon noted during the decade prior to the end of the First World War. In St. Joseph province, Sister Emnilda Opps, school supervisor, gave undivided attention to the continuing enrichment of the sisters' academic resources and to directing their performance aimed at excellence in every department of the school program. School administration became an arena for such master teachers as Sisters Angela Iwanicka, Mary Caesar Skrzycka and Sophia Bielewicz, whose initiative and informative leadership shone in the reflected light of teacher and student successes.

Since the expanding national welfare assistance removed the necessity of institutional care for orphans of disadvantaged families, the social character of Holy Family Institute had changed significantly. The children now referred to the Institute were frequently wards of the court or were recommended by protective agencies while home and family conflicts were being resolved. To give the children as favorable and as nearly homelike environment as possible and to adjust the school program to the irregularities of admissions without detriment to progress, Sister Pulcheria Pol exerted her innate energy to assure the total welfare of the young charges. As superior-director, she improved with refined sensitivity and love their dormitory and dining room conditions, and as principal of the Institute's self-contained school she guided its course with due regard for scholastic standards, of which the addition of a school library was but one of her accomplishments. In her efforts to retain a measure of stability despite changing standards and policies, Sister Pulcheria received able and wise cooperation from Sister Amanda Kawalkowska, registrar since 1924, upon whom the Commission of Catholic Charities of the Diocese of Pittsburgh conferred the Scroll of Honor for her services in Catholic social welfare.[78]

While Sister Hyacinth Gorecka supported the unfolding projects in the province to upgrade the sisters' role as educators in the hope of Christian formation of modern society, personally her dominant concern embraced the deepening of spiritual motivation in their apostolic activity—the culture of the soul, which she saw as the soul of culture. Institutes on spirituality for general attendance and seminars for superiors were strongly encouraged for the purpose of enlarging the grasp of basic concepts without substituting feelings for faith. Much care was given to the guidance of newly professed sisters, and a new vitality entered the novitiate under the two successive directors, Sisters Josephine Wąsikowska and Frances Sikorska, who displayed a true understanding of the contemporary novice and of her background.

As a result, Bishop John F. Dearden of Pittsburgh, in discussing the affairs of the province with the provincial superior, summarized his evaluation, saying, "These sisters are not only good teachers, but good religious." With reference to the novitiate, he commented that Sister Frances was the best director of novices in the diocese, and for this reason he advised the directors of other congregations to apply to her for practical orientation.[74]

The tenth general chapter had been expected to convene some time in 1952, but owing to the extended visitations which the superior general undertook in the United States, the convocation of the chapter was postponed until October 19, 1955.[75] To give the chapter a broad base of representative thought emanating from the entire Congregation, the sisters were invited to express in writing their *desiderata* and recommendations to be weighed and acted upon by the capitulants.[76]

In fairness to the special nature of the hospital apostolate, second only in size to the field of education in which Nazareth is engaged, Mother Bożena deemed it expedient to obtain before the chapter a reliable opinion on the state of the hospitals. Sister Geraldine Sledz, registered nurse, science instructor and recognized hospital administrator, was delegated to make a reconnaissance of the Congregation's hospitals in the United States. She held interviews, observed procedures, studied the administrative manuals and records, then offered her appraisals and suggestions. The survey displayed a clear composite of meaning and relevancy of the sisters' presence in hospital work. In a diversity of geographic, social and economic settings, the professional elements of service possessed a cohesive quality which bound the institutions, large and small alike, to a common objective, immaterial but real.[77]

In place of the elected delegates from the two Polish provinces who were denied exit visas to go to the chapter, substitutes were selected from among the sisters residing outside of Poland who were empowered to exercise the prerogatives of delegates. Nineteen capitulants comprised the chapter assembly. After the preliminary formalities and the rendering of reports, the problems shadowing the chapter quite obviously had to do with the drastically altered conditions of life and the questions spurred by growth

—a legitimate grist for the Nazareth mills to grind in a thoughtful dialogue until an enlightened consensus would be reached.

But where current issues were described as new, they were new mostly in outer detail, not in principle; they were extensions of the process of living. There was no intention or necessity of changing or abandoning the fundamental principles of religious life or of the charismatic inspiration of the saintly Foundress. However, since the last general chapter, in 1938, the Holy See had published numerous directives concerning religious congregations which indicated the need for suitable amendments of the Constitutions and the Book of Customs.[78] The editing of both documents in conformity with the decisions of the chapter required considerable length of time, so that the revised and approved Constitutions were published, February 22, 1959, and the new Book of Customs, July 6, 1961.

To reenforce the leadership positions in the maze of conflicting realities in the provinces of Poland, new provincial superiors were appointed, namely, Sister Marguerite Piątkowska to Warsaw, and Sister Lucilline Stelmaszuk to Cracow.

One of the measures put into practice immediately after the chapter was the renovation program made available to the sisters who were perpetually professed for eight to ten years, and at ten-year intervals thereafter. The program was designed to provide for the mature religious a refined interest in the inevitable and transforming operation of grace through expanding Scriptural and ascetical knowledge and to replenish their spiritual intelligence through sustained interior prayer. In an atmosphere of contemplative research each probed and redefined the implications of the Nazareth Constitutions and the teachings of Mother Mary of Jesus the Good Shepherd. The importance of the little virtues to the family spirit in community living was reassessed in shared tasks and exchanged courtesies as well as in communal worship and community recreations.

Another post-capitular event brought to life was the first meeting of the directors of novices with Mother Bożena in Albano, October 9 to 13, 1956, to coordinate the policies of formation and to determine priorities.[79]

In England the three houses emerged from the stream of passing events to the awareness of vigorous new potentials. The formation of a provincial structure for administrative purposes, geographically distinct, was seen as the sound means to growth in dignity and quality in educational endeavors, more so since Pitsford Hall and the Enfield school have already embarked upon building projects. On November 1, 1956, the Holy Family province became a reality with Sister Brigid Callanan as the first provincial superior, maintaining the provincial office at Enfield.

There was an urgency that impelled the superior general to revisit the youngest and most remote foundation in Australia, where an extensive apostolate was nurtured by three convents and a fourth one was in prospect. For an uncaring world there would have been an instant remedy that should have eliminated suffering, despondency and estrangement if the uprooted and displaced people had simply conformed to the power of might. When the Polish exiles came to Australia, they were a heterogeneous multitude of recent migrations, mostly poor, and in turn subjected to the prejudice and discrimination of nativist groups. The anguish of becoming an Australian had all the overtones of nostalgic recollections, mirroring the fundamental values of family, home, education, and country.

The pioneering sisters, though with Polish origins, were Americans by birth and education, but their knowledge of Polish language and customs endeared them at once to the Poles who had been cut adrift from their ancient moorings as if lashed by fate, and helped them to negotiate with hope their transition into the Anglo-Saxon system. Those who volunteered to serve in "the land down under" the tropic of Capricorn were possessed of a kinship with the Foundress who believed that Nazareth's mission was above and beyond frontiers. They were convinced that the culture they had studied, inhaled and treasured was not the property of any one race or class, but that it should be shared and diffused freely.

In the state of New South Wales, the Building Committee of the Polish Children's Home, headed by Father Francis Arciszewski, C.M., had acquired a tract of land and a cottage in Marayong, a sparsely populated locality of wide-open spaces on the outskirts of Sydney. To the first three sisters who arrived there from the United States, August 28, 1954, the cottage became their convent, and to three pre-school boys an emergency home. By January 20, 1957, when the construction of the Holy Family Children's Home, with dormitories and classrooms, was completed and blessed by His Eminence Norman T. Cardinal Gilroy, the Housing Commission had also been active developing the surrounding area and building hundreds of homes that attracted an influx of population, partly Australian and largely the migrant families from barrack-type dwellings.

Meanwhile, January 17, 1956, an arrangement comparable to that at Kalinga was made at neighboring Bowen Hills, Queensland, where the sisters provided a home for Polish parentless boys. They also took charge of the parish school of Our Lady of Victories, attended by these boys together with native Australian children.

Now Mother Bożena was considering the petition of Msgr. Witold Dzięcioł to provide mission-minded sisters to come to Perth in Western Australia, two thousand miles across the continent from Sydney, on the shores of the Indian Ocean. She reviewed the multiplicity of affairs into which the Nazareth group had already been drawn within a relatively short space of time. For the sisters stepped in gently to save the crumbling structure of the Christian family unit that had all but vanished in the homeless wanderings, enforced camp living and barrack-type housing. Children were their first concern, but unavoidably they became immersed in pastoral ministry to adults encompassing the widest range of connotations. Knowing how greatly dependent man is on his environment for his relationship with God in religion, they attempted to introduce ways of enriching the Polish colony as a society living in the spirit of the Gospel. They aimed to establish a respect for social order and a desire to safeguard all human rights, anticipating moral and religious revival to follow.

The superior general decided to give the Australian mission an objective appraisal personally in July of 1957. At the recommendation of Sister Neomisia, provincial superior in Philadelphia, Sister Medarda Synakowska of Wading River, New York, was appointed to join her.[80] The keynote sounded in all the contacts during that visit was found to be integral to the Congregation's family apostolate, the primary service to the people of God. Until they shall have overcome economic insecurity, religious apathy and social ostracism, the work of rehabilitation would continue to make moral demands on the sisters, which Mother Bożena would not curtail and upon which the local hierarchy looked as indispensable ecclesial ministrations.

In Perth, the small scattered clusters of Polish migrants along the coastline were a promising field wide open to initiative and inspiration, and replete with opportunities for sacrifice. That same year, during the Australian summer season, four sisters from the United States made their way across the jade and sapphire Pacific, then across the exotic island continent to a reconditioned bungalow in West Perth, arriving on December 12. At the advice of Archbishop R. Prendiville, they began with a day care center for young children and the supervision of summer camps for older children. They reached out to several small Polish settlements to hold weekly religion classes and to meet the people.

In 1959, they were invited by the Archbishop to staff the parish school of Our Lady of Grace in North Beach, outside of Perth. Until a convent was built for them in North Beach, they were commuting from West Perth where the day nursery continued in operation.

With the end of her term of office in view, Mother Bożena desired to visit the convents in Poland officially at least this one time, before the convocation of the electoral chapter which was due in November, 1958. However, entry regulations governing admissions into Poland, similarly as those controlling exit permits, imposed lingering and unaccountable delays. To enable her to carry out the planned visit, the Sacred Congregation of Religious consented to the deferment of the chapter by six months.[81] Her departure from Rome occurred the latter part of July and her duties occupied all of four months in Poland.[82] When Mother Bożena returned to

Rome, Pope John XXIII had already ascended to the See of Peter, subsequent to the death of Pope Pius XII on October 9, 1958.

Her encounter with the sisters in Poland had been a revealing experience in that she came to know the burdens and risks of the accelerated processes and ideological tactics within the country taxing human endurance and faith. In the cockpit of mixed tensions the sisters had to search for alternatives to counter existing problems and retain their separate identity. In penetrating to the far end of Gethsemane, as it were, they were still able to develop the inner resources that permitted them to come to terms with life. They learned in prayer that no disaster could deprive them of what they had in the realm of the spirit, and their mind was at peace in hope.

The convocation announcement set the date of May 27, 1959 for the beginning of the closed retreat of the capitulants which would immediately precede the opening of the chapter on June 4.[83] All the sisters were encouraged to submit their requests or recommendations which they wished to be placed before the chapter. A total of twenty-three capitulants assembled in Albano, among whom substitute delegates residing outside of Poland were once again authorized to act in the name of those who were unable to leave Poland in order to participate in the chapter deliberations. Following the reports covering the general administration of the Congregation and those submitted by the provincial superiors, the session of elections took place, June 5, in the presence of Bishop Raphael Macario of the diocese of Albano.

Mother M. Neomisia, heretofore the provincial superior of the Immaculate Conception province in Philadelphia, was elected to the office of the superior general.[84] When the results of the ballot were announced and when in the silence of the chapter hall the Bishop in the presence of the capitulants put the question to the superior general-elect, "Do you accept?"—her reply was in the words of the humble Virgin of Nazareth, "Behold the handmaid of the Lord."

Other officers elected to the general administration were: Sister Bożena Staczyńska, assistant general; Sisters Laurence Crowe, Precious Pruszynska and Aloysius Kozlowska, councilors general; Sister Christine Markiewicz, secretary general, and Sister Fides Tomkowicz, elected anew to serve as treasurer general.[85]

Left in abeyance at the previous chapter was the matter of the geographic revision of the American provinces. The subject was now reconsidered according to longitudinal demarcation. The division of the Immaculate Conception province provided for retaining its name and including the houses of Eastern Pennsylvania as far west as Harrisburg, also in the District of Columbia, state of Maryland, Puerto Rico, and the houses from the state of Florida which were to be transferred from the Sacred Heart province.

The houses in the states of New York, New Jersey and in New England, from the Immaculate Conception province, were to comprise the new province under the patronage of the Immaculate Heart of Mary. The houses in the state of Alabama were ceded by the Sacred Heart province to St. Joseph province. These proposals were accepted by the chapter and were approved by the Holy See.[86]

To fill the vacancies created by the termination of office in the American provinces, new provincials were appointed: Sister Getulia Honorowska, Sacred Heart province; Sister Mary Caesar Skrzycka, St. Joseph province; Sister Medarda Synakowska, Immaculate Conception province, and for the new province of the Immaculate Heart of Mary—Sister Albina Kowalkowska.

Among a number of resolutions adopted by this chapter to revise certain practices of long standing was the decision to remove the distinction of apparel between the lay and the choir sisters. The time has passed when social and practical considerations warranted such distinction. Throughout the Congregation the lay sisters were to wear a pleated collar instead of the plain one, and a silver cross with a relic instead of the nickel crucifix.[87]

The act of presiding over the deliberations which were continued after the elections held character-defining moments for Mother Neomisia. She introduced specific points of the agenda with a refreshing absence of pretense and quiet strength, her ideas flowing far and freely ahead of the times. It is true that she had become preeminent in educational policy and was preceded by a reputation for exceptional brilliance. Now she took a large view of the Congregation's problems, pointing to the necessity and propriety of forward motion, while she dealt effortlessly with the details of her new position. The election came as a sign that God could use her; she was henceforth in the ineffable Presence.

Houses of the Congregation
opened in the years 1954 through 1959:

Year	Location	Convent-Apostolate-First Superior
1954	AUSTRALIA Marayong (Sydney), New South Wales	Our Lady Queen of Poland convent; Holy Family Children's Home and School; Sister M. Jolanta Kiczuk.
1954	POLAND Ligota	St. Joseph convent; catechetical center; Sister M. Dobromilla Warchałowska.

Year	*Location*	*Convent-Apostolate-First Superior*
1954	POLAND Marcyporęba	Holy Trinity convent; pastoral ministry; affiliate of the House of Providence, Wadowice.
1954	UNITED STATES Philadelphia	St. Joseph convent (originally: Our Lady of Lourdes); Holy Family College; Sister M. Aloysius Sabacińska.
1954	UNITED STATES Coraopolis, Pennsylvania	St. Pius X convent; St. Malachy parish school; Sister Ann Marie (Adolorata) Lijek.
1955	UNITED STATES Colorado Springs	Regina Mundi convent; El Nido Nazareth retreat and rest home; Sister M. Desolata Niemczyk.
1955	UNITED STATES Miami, Florida	St. Therese of the Child Jesus convent; St. Brendan parish school; Sister M. Christine Luczak.
1955	UNITED STATES Ardsley, Pennsylvania	Queen of Peace convent; Queen of Peace parish school; Sister M. Bonita Naumowicz.
1955	UNITED STATES Romulus, Michigan	Holy Face convent; St. Aloysius parish school; Sister M. Hyacinthe Kaczor
1955	UNITED STATES Library, Pennsylvania	Holy Trinity convent; St. Joan of Arc parish school; Sister M. Eucharia Skibicka.
1955	UNITED STATES Dearborn, Michigan	Mary Queen of the Universe convent; St. Martha parish school; Sister M. Thomasine Stachowicz.
1956	AUSTRALIA Bowen Hills (Brisbane), Queensland	St. Joseph convent and home for boys; Our Lady of Victories parish school; Sister M. Victoria Woźniak.
1956	UNITED STATES Norristown, Pennsylvania	Visitation B.V.M. convent; Visitation B.V.M. parish school; Sister Sophia Marie (Januaria) Karpowicz.
1956	UNITED STATES Irving, Texas	Our Lady of Grace convent; ɔt. Luke parish school; Sister M. Boniface Kunkel.

Year	Location	Convent-Apostolate-First Superior
1957	AUSTRALIA West Perth, Western Australia	Infant Jesus convent; day care center; in 1959, Our Lady of Grace parish school in North Beach (Perth); Sister M. Chrysantha Karasek.
1959	UNITED STATES Dallas, Texas	Our Lady of Victory convent; St. Thomas Aquinas parish school; Sister M. Godwin Zaleska.
1959	UNITED STATES Beaver Falls, Pennsylvania	St. Philomena convent; St. Philomena parish school; Sister M. Benedette Olszewska.
1959	UNITED STATES Philadelphia	Our Lady of Calvary convent; Our Lady of Calvary parish school; Sister M. Louise Huczek.
1959	UNITED STATES Mount Union, Pennsylvania	Our Lady of Grace convent; St. Catherine of Siena parish school; Sister Martha Jane (Marcella) Czerwińska.
1959	FRANCE Sallaumines, Pas-de-Calais	St. Joseph the Worker convent; St. Joseph dispensary; pastoral min- istry; Sister M. Nicette Muszyńska.
1959	UNITED STATES Rosemont, Illinois	St. Anthony convent; Our Lady of Hope parish school; Sister M. Illuminata Karczewska.

Houses closed:

Year	Location	Convent-Apostolate-First Superior
1954	POLAND Ostrzeszów	St. Michael convent (1936-1954); St. Anthony parish kindergarten; closed by civil authority.
1955	UNITED STATES Footedale, Pennsylvania	St. Clare convent (1944-1955); St. Thomas parish school.
1956	UNITED STATES Cambridge, Massachusetts	Queen of Peace convent (1916-1956); St. Hedwig parish school.
1958	UNITED STATES Montgomery, Alabama	St. Jude convent (1938-1958); City of St. Jude: school, pastoral ministry.
1957	POLAND Wróblowice	Our Lady of Perpetual Help convent (1946-1957); catechetical center.

Year	*Location*	*Convent-Apostolate-First Superior*
1959	UNITED STATES Farrell, Pennsylvania	Holy Cross convent (1920-1959); St. Adalbert parish school.
1959	UNITED STATES Pittsburgh	Precious Blood convent (1895-1959); St. Stanislaus Kostka parish school.
1959	UNITED STATES Portage, Pennsylvania	St. Therese of the Child Jesus convent (1924-1959); Sacred Heart parish school.
1959	UNITED STATES Park Ridge, Illinois	Sacred Heart of Jesus convent (1940- 1959); Sacred Heart Villa; house of prayer; retired sisters' residence.

V

Age of Renewal
1959-1975

1 WITHOUT TRUMPETS

It did not take long for Mother Neomisia to discover, in the main-stream of life, a gulf opening between that segment of the membership which remained behind the Iron Curtain and the rest of the Congregation. Cut off from normal interaction with the western world and restricted in their traditional activities—religious, educational and humanitarian, the sisters in Poland hoped to preserve intact their prewar mode of life and work. On the rebound they viewed with reluctance the new demands and pressures, while in all other parts of the world the Congregation, caught up in the general acceleration, saw itself as an integral part within the modern milieu, though not of it.

When the superior general arrived in Poland with Sister Christine, secretary general, August 21, 1959, she felt her way about carefully, doing great things inconspicuously. She sought to revive in the sisters a sense of confidence that would spark renewed enthusiasm in spite of the official policies which militated against the freedom of religion and of religious. What she accomplished in the way of frank dialogue that contributed to a new understanding was to enter fully into the attitudes and doubts of the sisters. With quiet power of mind and heart that lay beneath a gentle and patient manner, Mother Neomisia helped them to adjust their mental focus in an orientation toward innovative steps and to invigorate their faith in the face of the problems that were chiefly the outcome of confusing politics.

By making the Gospel the touchstone of their lives, they could, as authentic Nazareth religious, look upon their mission of building the Kingdom of God under adverse conditions as the early Christians have done, even when the forms of their witnessing should bear little resemblance to the types of services they had performed before.

The key point now was to become open to all possibilities under all circumstances, this being consistent with the outlook often expressed by the Foundress in her exhortations, lest the fear of unknown risks—implied in the absolute surrender to God's will—cause absorbing preoccupations with mere mundane security. It was necessary to reaffirm in no uncertain terms the validity of the statement that corporate unity of goal and effort can thrive despite diversity of means, more so since religious congregations were collectively excluded from the field of education in a policy aimed against the Catholic Church and religion. Probably the greatest challenges for the sisters in Poland arose from the fact that neither precedent nor tradition revealed much that could help them to cope with the dramatic variety of methods by which they would be able to interpret the life of faith to their environment.

Among the earliest decisions of the new administration was the appointment of Sister Frances Sikorska to take charge of the novitiate in Albano. Before occupying her post, however, Sister Frances joined the meeting arranged by the superior general for the newly appointed provincial superiors in the United States in conjunction with the directors of the American novitiates[1] who assembled at the provincialate in Pittsburgh, September 2, 1959.

The discussions, led by Reverend Francis A. Cegielka, elaborated the general ideals of religious life and the specific aspects of Nazareth heritage which were to constitute the cultural essence for the development of young religious and the basis for renovation programs and for continuing formation. It was agreed that a direct link exists between the Eucharist life and the hidden life, both being an expression of the reparatory spirit. An honest appreciation of the spirit of penitence and mortification, as an acknowledgement of human sinfulness, was seen to be closely associated with one's growth toward spiritual maturity. To achieve a rational formation of novices, it was determined that their guidance may not overlook to fashion the qualities of womanliness and refinement in a delicate harmony of grace and nature—for, by virtue of their vocational response, they no longer were merely human, but sought to become new persons, radically changed and living on a new plane of existence.[2]

Another issue of immediate concern for the superior general was the investigation of the tentatively accepted Dispensaire de St. Joseph in France, in the coal mining region of the Department of Pas-de-Calais, at Sallaumines. Irrespective of considerable communist agitation among the miners of Sallaumines and the presence of a communist mayor in power, the Catholic director of local mines acted upon the demand of Catholic families, French, Polish and Italian, to secure a replacement for the French group of the Little Sisters of Catholic Action, who had been recalled after twenty-one years of service. The ordinary of Arras, Bishop Victor-Jean Perrin, approved of inviting the Sisters of the Holy Family of Nazareth into the diocese with the understanding that they will serve all persons without any nationality bias.

Operating a dispensary for ambulatory patients and available on call to make home visits to the sick, the sisters were engaged to render health services to which the miners and their families were entitled as fringe benefits under the terms of mine employment. The director of mines and the local clergy were further concerned for the moral and religious welfare of the people which might be provided prudently, as a collateral activity, escaping communist interference. The apostolic nature of the work which was expected of the sisters who would be assigned there placed upon them certain requisites which they could exercise interchangeably. There was a need for fluency in the three languages dominant in that region, a proficiency in nursing skills acceptable under the French ordinance and—for an effective youth apostolate—a knowledge of catechetical pedagogy and music.

To take on the responsibilities of the superior-director of the dispensary, Sister Nicette Muszynska was summoned from the United States. Her background of nearly fourteen years of European experience, 1932-1946, virtually prepared her for the singular combination of duties at Sallaumines. She had studied at Rome, Warsaw, and Paris, and having completed a standard nursing course in Paris, had become a medical assistant in the health center for the Potigny miners in Normandy, in the Department of Calvados. Upon returning to Rome in 1940, Sister Nicette, with other similarly qualified sisters, had volunteered her services in the hospital of the Dominican Sisters of the Presentation to ease the burdens created by the shortage of nursing personnel and the growing volume of war casualties. After the Italian armistice, she taught in the provisional school in Albano, and when the need arose went to Noci with Sister Josephine Wąsikowska to serve in the army convalescent camp. After a period of reintegration in the contemporary American educational system, she left her teaching assignment at De Lourdes College, February 5, 1960, for the arduous duties that awaited her in Sallaumines.

Ever since the death of the late Pontiff, Pius XII, there had been the open matter of the Cardinal Protector of the Congregation. As secretary of State to Pope Pius XI, Eugenio Cardinal Pacelli had accepted, in 1933, the position of Cardinal Protector of the Sisters of the Holy Family of Nazareth and, six years later, upon his accession to the papacy, had consented to retain the protectorate. Fifteen months following his death, the title and function of the Cardinal Protector fell to His Eminence Amleto Giovanni Cardinal Cicognani, who had only recently returned to the Vatican after serving as the Apostolic Delegate to the United States for twenty-five years, 1933-1958.

His ceremonial ingress at the motherhouse was greeted on January 10, 1960, the day designated in the liturgical calendar that year as the solemnity of the Holy Family. The Cardinal's appointment resumed his association with Nazareth which had commenced during his sojourn in Washington and which obviously the provincial superiors of the Philadelphia province were able to cultivate under favorable conditions. His vast experience through prolonged exposure to a world quivering in the throes of change betokened his perception of Nazareth's possibilities to insert itself tellingly within humanity's evolution and progress without compromising its primary goals. For Mother Neomisia it was a propitious happening, hopefully indicating realistic ways of ecclesial collaboration which she was determined to foster actively, in full, after the manner of Mother Foundress.

Apart from administrative considerations, she was sensitive to the values reposing in the sisters' reciprocal trust solidified through personal contact. To become acquainted with all the members and their particular pursuits, Mother Neomisia timed an early schedule of visits to the convents, and on January 18, 1960 arrived in the United States with Sister Laurence, councilor general.

Sister Aloysius Sabacinska, now president of Holy Family College in Philadelphia, found this occasion opportune for the purpose of finalizing with the board of trustees the plans for the dedication of Lourdes Hall. The building had been under construction since November of 1958 to provide a residence with accommodations for one hundred students. Its dedication was accomplished February 11, 1960 by the Auxiliary Bishop of Philadelphia, the Most Reverend Joseph McShea, with the participation of the superior general.

Another noteworthy episode in the history of the college occurred later that month, when a commission of seven examiners from the Middle Atlantic States Association of Colleges and Secondary Schools conducted an intensive three-day evaluation study of the curriculum, policies, faculty, and performance. The outcome of the evaluation, when communicated formally, announced full accreditation.

In May, Mother Neomisia interrupted the American visits to give her attention to the Congregation's promising development in Australia. It was then that she came to the conclusion that the sisters' dedicated work may become even more fruitful and for them more abounding in grace through unified coordination under a local major superior. This subsequently met with ecclesiastical approval, and the Holy Spirit vice-province was established to encompass the Nazareth apostolate in Australia. Temporarily the convent in Marayong became the seat of the vice-provincial superior, Sister Godwin Zaleska. In Kalinga, again, several applicants to the religious life were housed, and a program of formation, extending through the novitiate, was introduced under the direction of Sister Victoria Wozniak.[3]

From the earliest times, the care of the sick in hospitals has been in Nazareth only second in scope to teaching, for both activities in their multiple ramifications looked to the luminous exemplar of the person of Christ, the incomparable teacher and the compassionate healer. Thus, no service was regarded as demeaning, no person frustrating. While over the years educational and scholarly endeavors received their proper share of emphasis in inter-provincial exchanges in the United States and in Poland, Mother Neomisia felt that the time was ripe to pool, on an inter-provincial basis, the fund of knowledge and experience that was coursing within the Congregation's individual hospitals to benefit all.

Upon returning from Australia, she held a joint hospital conference in Des Plaines, June 3-4, 1960, to which she invited the provincial superiors, local superiors of hospital convents, and hospital administrators. The two days' deliberations climaxed with the appointment by the superior general of three committees to develop guidelines for the hospitals, broad enough to allow for adaptation to varying conditions and specific enough to preserve a familial degree of internal unity. One year later, the committees dealing with hospital policies, administrative practice, and financial management prepared a manual in tentative form which was reviewed at a joint meeting, assembled in Detroit during the Catholic Hospital Association convention. With the approval of the provincial superiors and the consensus of the local superiors present, the guidelines were accepted with revisions to be submitted to Mother Neomisia.[4]

Meanwhile, the provincial administration of the Immaculate Heart of Mary province was facing some organizational setbacks in the first year of its corporate existence, not the least of which was the lack of a central office. Sister Albina Kowalkowska and her councilors had taken residence at Villa Immaculata, situated at Riverhead on Long Island. The villa, a gift of appreciation for the sisters' services, was presented to the Congregation in 1953 by Bishop Thomas E. Molloy of Brooklyn and had since provided facilities for convalescence, rest and vacations.

To advance the orderly functioning of the province in a practical setting, the provincial council was exploring available sites suitable for a provincialate. The investigation ended in the summer of 1962 with the purchase of Trumpeter Estate in Monroe, Connecticut, with a sturdy residence in a scenic location partly screened off by woodland. The house was converted into an interim convent and office building for the officers of the province until other plans would be definitively drafted. The Long Island villa was, in turn, occupied by resident aspirants of the new province with their director.

Acceding to the invitation of the Sacred Heart province, the superior general attended in Des Plaines the seventy-fifth anniversary of the American foundation, July 4, 1960. The celebration of life has always been inseparable from the family spirit of Nazareth community living, for festivity is indigenous to human nature, being ingrained by the prior experience of paradise. In this respect, Mother Mary of Jesus the Good Shepherd had set the pace for her sisters, observing feastdays and holidays with them in an atmosphere of warmth and good humor, knowing that true joy is the gift of the Holy Spirit, compatible with genuine piety. The memoirs of her contemporaries reveal that community recreations at which she was present were usually abounding in light-hearted wit and jovial laughter.

On this occasion radiant with joy, the jubilee was voiced in the Mass of Thanksgiving by exultant chant and worshipful organ accompaniment, and followed by "A Pageant of the American Foundations," displayed with music and song. To the happy amazement of the sisters, Mother Neomisia knew each by name, many of whom she had met but once. Through the succeeding years it became an endless wonder how she continued to remember them all so vividly.

The requirements of the highest superior's office being severe, only an agile, searching and retentive intelligence could be the answer. But there was more. She had absorbed, assimilated and refined the Congregation's educational philosophy built upon the concept of supernatural personalism that lay at the root of Nazareth inspiration. In the uniqueness of each personality, as in a measureless sea, she recognized distinct, individual qualities and potentials that could be made to ascend as a sweet odor before the face of God, and in that recognition exhibited a large capacity for selecting and inspiring persons to the fulfillment of his will on earth.

In many ways she was a prismatic person through whom were refracted the cross-currents of the generation trapped between levels of society, but whose depths—fed at the wellspring of the divine—captured the secret of tranquility. She received as a regular order of things, without exaltation, the announcement of an honor to be conferred upon her by the Catholic University of America. On November 12, 1960, she became the first recipient of the Alumni Association's award created for outstanding achievement in the field of education.

But the philosophy of continuing education permeated the Congregation and its institutions with seriousness and ardor, and maintained contact with the astonishing transformations that took place in the making of a new kind of society in the sixties. At Ohio Valley General Hospital, in McKees Rocks, Sister Noemi Tereszkiewicz of the school of nursing faculty was elected to a lifetime membership in Sigma Theta Tau, a national honor society in nursing, in May, 1961. Next year she became the director of Mercy Hospital school of nursing in Altoona.

Mercy Hospital, furthermore, has made a contribution of professional intangibles and acquisitions to the American Hospital Association by offering to participate in the Association's hospital management review program.[5] The administrator, Sister Geraldine Sledz, unfolded to the researcher the scope of the fundamental management responsibilities as defined and discharged under the policies of Mercy Hospital, and presented to him a portfolio of documentary evidence and basic hospital data to supplement the information.

At Bethania Hospital, in Wichita Falls, there was likewise evidence that virtue does not supplant knowledge, when Sister Electa Trela, noted for and consulted by others in the stewardship of hospital finances, was accorded Fellowship in the American Association of Hospital Accountants. Also at Bethania, Sister Aquinas Muszynska was named for the educational award of the American Pharmaceutical Association.[6] The award represented a national recognition of the strides gained in professional organization of the hospital pharmacy by Sister Aquinas. Associated with these was the successful information service she introduced for the benefit of the physicians of the hospital's medical staff and an educational series for nursing and paramedical personnel, by which she disseminated the latest reports on new drugs, their uses, effects, and pharmacologic qualities.

With man's mastery of energy and matter, the dazzling prospects for biological sciences, chemistry and physics cast their light over the discoveries in medical research. To the extent that scientific advances penetrated into the unknown, technology deepened its insights; then medicine and health care reaped equivalent gains from their application. Not only did higher standards spiral a demand for increasing improvements in hospital care, but also broader medical insurance made comprehensive care available to greater numbers. Determined to equal achievement with achievement and quality with quality, the hospitals of Nazareth were rededicated to follow their course with intimate concern.

In their healing mission they had to provide incentives and versatility through growth and innovation which required long-range planning for the education of personnel in new techniques, departmental renovation and remodeling, and architectural expansion to live up to the expectations of the many persons who hoped to find cure and recovery in a climate ennobled by the charity of Christ. "There is nothing like material satisfaction for convincing a people that material satisfaction is not enough."[7] But the accredited standing of the hospitals and the level of services for which they were known spared the sisters the onus of making alone the sacrifices they were prepared to shoulder. Government grants joined in the partnership of charity with voluntary pledges of local citizens supported the building of new hospital units, which were legally inscribed, as in the past, in the corporate ownership and under the management of the Sisters of the Holy Family of Nazareth.

With the approval of religious and civic authorities significant developments were accomplished after months, and even years, of judicious planning in order to embody new hospital concepts in the additions built during this period:

Bethania Hospital, Wichita Falls, Texas—third addition: west wing encompassing hospital rooms and facilities, 1959;

Mercy Hospital, Altoona, Pennsylvania—third addition: four-story new wing comprising nursing units, clinical departments and administrative offices, 1962;

Mother Frances Hospital, Tyler, Texas—second addition: four-story wing which increased the patient capacity by 130 beds, 1965; and an expanded intensive care unit, 1968;

Nazareth Hospital, Philadelphia, Pennsylvania—third addition: new nine-story structure, proclaimed by experts "the hospital of the future," incorporating bombproof provisions to safeguard vital services against the interference that might arise from possible above-ground catastrophes, 1963;

Ohio Valley General Hospital, McKees Rocks, Pennsylvania—third addition: new west wing containing ancillary, administrative and service areas, 1965.

At the time when the existing hospitals were entering new dimensions and productivity by the unceasing process of self-renewal and progress, a project for an entirely new hospital began to germinate in Chicago's northwestern suburb of Des Plaines.[8] Skirting Lions Woods on Des Plaines River, the Sacred Heart provincialate was situated there since 1908, a place of great peace, with its adjunct departments for religious formation, education, and administration. Unacclaimed, its invisible functions were benefiting countless individuals across and outside the United States, whose lives were touched by the Nazareth religious who had been prepared within its confines for the life of service.

By the middle of the twentieth century, Des Plaines became well-populated and—together with a cluster of new municipalities round about —in need of hospital accommodations and of the care that modern science made possible. Sister Aloysius Kozlowska, then provincial superior, announced the plans for the establishment of Holy Family Hospital, for which ground was broken, June 20, 1959, facing the convent across River Road. Two years later, the hospital was dedicated by Albert Cardinal Meyer, Archbishop of Chicago, on June 9, and was immediately put into operation. No time was lost in laying the designs for continuing construction, namely, to erect a convent addition for the sisters engaged in the hospital, which was completed in 1963. By 1965, a full-height extension at the south end of the building enlarged the diagnostic and service areas and satisfied in a measure the critical need for increased patient capacity.

In the unfolding of this historical inventory of the emergence of the Sisters of the Holy Family of Nazareth at various outposts and of their withdrawal in time, it must be remarked that sociological shifts of enormous complexity have been largely responsible for throwing into eclipse some of the Congregation's hospitals. The decisions to withdraw were not arbitrary, for there were elsewhere in the Church and in the world other social and pastoral obligations which did not permit the indefinite continuance of human and material investment at the rate of diminishing returns. The reasons to withdraw were decidedly other than purely financial ones.

As recorded earlier, the sisters withdrew from Loretto Hospital, Dalhart, Texas, in 1953, and soon afterwards two other withdrawals occurred: from St. Joseph Hospital, Clayton, New Mexico, in 1962, and Christ the King Hospital, Vernon, Texas, in 1964. For many years these small havens of hope and solicitude served the small communities at great personal sacrifices, when the absence of employable lay personnel repeatedly placed the tasks involving long, unrelieved hours of work upon the limited strength of the same few sisters. The comforting thought remained that none of the towns was deprived of hospital facilities by the departure of the sisters. In Dalhart and Clayton, respectively, the buildings were acquired by boards of wealthy investors who pledged themselves to the health interests of the people. In Vernon, furthermore, there was in operation one other local hospital, and for health problems of greater magnitude Bethania Hospital in Wichita Falls could be reached without inconvenience.

A side effect of the departure from St. Joseph Hospital was the concern expressed by Mother Neomisia for the graves of nine sisters who were buried in the little cemetery in Clayton. It was decided to transfer their remains to the Sacred Heart cemetery in Wichita Falls, which procedure took the best part of four days. The remains of a tenth sister of another order were also exhumed and transferred, so that although unidentified and unclaimed, she could in death share the glory of witnessing Christ in the silent company of others whose lives have also been vowed to him alone.

After the Holy Sacrifice of the Mass, offered in the chapel of Bethania Hospital for the repose of the souls of the ten sisters, October 22, 1962, the entourage representing Nazareth's southern hospitals proceeded to the cemetery under dignified police escort. There, Reverend Gerard Groeneger, chaplain of Bethania Hospital, presided at the graveside services and led the prayers.[9]

2 WISDOM BUILT A HOUSE

Over the years, the regular visitation of convents by major superiors, provincial and general, was regarded by them as a moral obligation under the Constitutions and has been discharged with zeal and love. Although freedom of communicating with higher superiors at any time, whether in person or by correspondence, has been upheld as the sisters' inalienable prerogative, visitations provided those human intervals when private interviews and communal dialogues on location ranked with life's impressive moments. Summaries of the observations and recommendations inscribed by visiting superiors in the respective visitation records were preserved in each convent for periodic review and the edification of local sisters.

The expanding geographic range and apostolic variety in the Congregation placed increasing demands upon the persons of the superiors general. Only the careful budgeting of time enabled Mother Neomisia to maintain a laborious circuit of travel and visitations, correspondence and meetings without seeming to be weighed down or hurried. Her entries in the visitation records carried flashes of discernment and direction for keeping alive the Nazareth principles in their purity and for investing them in new ways. To this end she approved new projects and advocated the enrichment and diligent use of convent libraries. Repeatedly, whenever in the United States, she met in conference with the provincial superiors in a body, not only for the purpose of coordinating common endeavors, but also to scan the influence of rapidly changing conditions and to form a united front, responsive to the Church's contemporary needs. For the same reason she held inter-provincial meetings with formation directors.

Of paramount interest everywhere was the decision of Pope John XXIII to call the twenty-first Ecumenical Council.[10] The implications for Nazareth's ecclesial tradition—"to live with the Church"—were overwhelming. For the Holy Father hoped "to bring the attention of the whole world the ancient truth reflected in new forms," emphasizing that "the Church is alive and is not the custodian of a museum. Though the Church has great respect for what is ancient, beautiful and good, her first concern is souls."[11] In essence, these were the sisters' aspirations verbalized. It was in this direction that their prayers and sacrifices were oriented during the four years of exhaustive preparations for the Second Vatican Council, which opened on October 11, 1962, and throughout the period of the four sessions of the Council, as their attention was keyed to the issues emanating from conciliar deliberations.

This period again registered a rise in the enrollment at parish elementary schools and in the private and parochial high schools. Revived eagerness for special religion classes called for expanded programming by which the sisters gave added hours of instruction to public school children and adolescents and to questioning adults. Saturday and summer missions in outlying places were still very much in demand.

With the growth of the liturgical movement and the revised Code of Rubrics,[12] the desire of the faithful quickened to participate actively in the Sacrifice of the Mass. An intimate acquaintance with this supreme act of worship and sanctification was largely fostered through the intelligent use of popular daily missals, published bilingually, in Latin and the vernacular. As a direct consequence, the dialogue Mass became widespread, making it possible for the congregations to render the usual responses in Latin and to pray in Latin the *Gloria, Credo,* and *Pater noster* in unison with the celebrant.

Through parish and diocesan activity, the building of schools has been going forward at a rapid pace and new school buildings were replacing the older ones in order to facilitate the introducing of progressive methods by the teaching sisters and by the lay personnel that became allied in ever greater numbers with the staff of Catholic schools. Cooperative endeavors between home and school brought the sisters and the laity into closer interaction through parish groups, such as Mother's Clubs, Women's Aid Societies, Fathers' Guilds and Parent-Teacher Associations. These groups took pride in having a share in the total Catholic education apostolate by way of their interest, support and volunteer services. Local civic organizations have, in turn, contributed learning incentives to the students by sponsoring educational contests, tours and recognitions.

At the vanguard of education stood the provincial school supervisors who, alert to the trends signified by state and diocesan school boards, promoted fresh approaches to education by means of assemblies and symposia, evaluations and experience charts and, invariably, by formal courses. In this exuberant age there arose newly developed concepts in mathematics which revolutionized the entire methodology of teaching this subject from the beginners' level onward. In all grades, moreover, physical sciences were receiving a broad emphasis.

To identify and overcome reading disabilities of children, diagnostic and remedial procedures were introduced under the direction of specialists in remedial instruction, outstandingly represented by Sisters Clarisse Wojtyczka and DeLourdes Zdrojewska. The widening utilization of audio-visual media in the classroom amplified the teaching techniques to enhance the learners' grasp of experiential knowledge. Cultural readership among primary school children was motivated by the "Great Books Program" as a fascinating extracurricular project, which became more or less responsible for the general development of elementary school libraries and the proportionate interest among the sisters in library science as a profession.

Besides the systematic aim to achieve excellence in educational practice as a whole, school supervisors concentrated usually upon a select area of importance. At this time, Sisters Louise Kondek and Edith Wierzbowska demonstrated their forte in language arts—written, oral and creative. Social studies were a strong point in the work of Sister Tarsitia Rymsza, while school music was elevated to major significance by Sister Infanta Kurcz and Sister Simplicia Grochocka.

The drive toward the self-improvement of students was advancing dramatically. In a very true sense the teaching sisters viewed themselves as the architects of tomorrow's society. They were acutely aware that, as such, they would have to know not only the quality of the materials they had, but also the conditions and climate in which they had to work. The enormous intelligence of the people at one pole and the stinging aridity at the other called for a many-sided variety of virtue and skill. Nazareth principals and teachers developed close relations with the administrators and faculties of public schools and other parish schools for a meeting of the minds on matters of education. Rich in learning and deep in understanding they collaborated with leading educators in specific fields, served on regional and national committees, and wrote articles for school journals.

On the high school level, Sisters Rodricia Gonsiorowska and Leonette Wilczynska achieved gratifying results in the performances of student bands, orchestras and choral groups, while teacher growth in music was stimulated through the interest and efforts of Sisters Eulalia Wisniewska, Cecilia Ciuzycka and Patricia Pilarska. Art instructors, Sisters Damien Grondziowska and Jolanta Polak, whose own productions had been accorded creative merit, gave continuous impetus to their students to find self-expression in graphic art. At Holy Family College, the psychological subtlety of Sister Martina Banach was exhibited in a lavish range of art forms and media, by which she was capable of evoking the individuality of student talent. Art as a subject constituted a major field for those who had the inspiration and the initiative. One of Sister Martina's originals was a palette knife oil painting entitled *The Holy Family at the Crossroads of Time and Eternity.*

In a class by itself, though not isolated from modern science and human implications, was the impact of aerospace exploits which uncovered new vistas of educational opportunities to prepare youth for responsible citizenship in the space age. Sister Veronica Grzelak drew the inference that education for space age and the expanding horizons for women in aerospace demanded practical integration in curriculum planning. As a certified pilot with actual flight experiences, she undertook to interest her Latin high school students in acquiring space age knowledge. The unique and imaginative Latin reader, published by her, was used as a supplementary classroom text treating of air space subjects in twenty-four simple lessons.[13] In 1963, she guided the students in the project of compiling a dictionary of aerospace terms, identifying their Latin origins and tracing their etymology.[14]

To illustrate the possibilities of education for space age, specifically for the intellectual development of young women in aerospace careers, Sister Veronica held lecture demonstrations for live audiences, as well as radio addresses and television appearances. She formed an all-girl cadet unit of Civil Air Patrol at Nazareth Academy, composed entirely of students in the school, which she named Our Lady of Space Squadron, an auxiliary of the U. S. Air Force.

In the presence of ranking Air Force officers and Msgr. Edward T. Hughes, Philadelphia superintendent of schools, she received the squadron charter on March 31, 1963. At the same ceremony, Pennsylvania State Representative Vincent F. Scarcelli presented her with the National Aerospace Education Leadership Award, of which she was the first recipient. On November 30, 1964, the Freedom Foundation awarded her the Valley Forge Teachers Medal and citation scroll in recogition of her personal contribution to the patriotic understanding of the American way of life by young people.

At Holy Family College, the positive strides made and sustained during the first decade of its existence projected an image of strong academic and physical developments. All that the so-called knowledge explosion meant in terms of expensive equipment, expanding curriculm and the diversity of qualified faculty confronted the president, Sister Aloysius Sabacinska, and her board of trustees. They have seen the new dimensions, the great and growing responsibilities that the Catholic college must take to fulfill its mission, and they saw that mission, predominantly, as culminating in the students' experience of God—alike in nature as in historical events, in the Scriptures and in the teaching Church, and in the liturgy. Since both domestic and foreign students presented a profile of high scholastic quality, it was not surprising that they would increasingly propound serious inquiries into the order of life. Though "to do" and "to serve" were still the objectives, they needed a forum for thinking, analyzing and empathizing. Their inquiries have properly become the basis for religious and philosophical debate, a part of the educational dialogue.

The one-hundred-years-old La Salle College for men in Philadelphia took note of the dynamic upswing in educational services at Holy Family College, and on the occasion of its centenary awarded Sister Aloysius the honorary degree of Doctor of Pedagogy for recognized leadership and dedication to the advancement of learning.[15] Perhaps the most copious source of the intellectual stimulus experienced by the student body and the faculty was provided by the scholarly environment of the library, where annual additions to holdings promoted constant growth in the process of satisfying research activity.[16] A separate library building on the campus was proposed, planned and at length realized in 1967, as also a progressive elementary school for supervised experimental and training purposes of student-teachers from the education department of the college.

The chairman of the college board of trustees, Sister Medarda, being the provincial superior, lent a general tenor to the life of the sisters in their capacity of educators and religious—more precisely, as religious who were also educators. Herself a firm believer in academic freedom, she supported their scholastic pursuits and added strength and beauty by providing for them the balancing ingredient of spiritual fare essential to attain the full stature of women consecrated in spirit and in truth.

Sister Rose Szczesna of Pittsburgh was in the meantime tracing a rich and productive career out of the resources of her mind and experience. After several years of membership on the faculty of St. John's Teachers College in Cleveland, she gained an affiliate status at Duquesne University and at Mount Mercy College as an instructor in psychology. Following a vigorous five-year period in school supervision, she entered the field of social service with an eventual apointment to Holy Family Institute.

In Chicago, adjacent to the Holy Family Academy, Gordon Technical High School had been vacated and stood available to an acceptable bidder. With a view to the future, the Nazareth Congregation gave serious thought to the repossessing of the property, which had originally been known as Holy Family Orphanage.[17] Another practical consideration was the need to obviate the possibility of an undesirable enterprise from becoming entrenched next to the academy. The property was therefore acquired from the Congregation of the Resurrection, June 24, 1961, and the building, unsafe for occupancy, was demolished on August 29, 1963. Plans for the utilization of the property were temporarily suspended due to the sociological and educational cross currents prevalent in the immediate environs surrounding the Holy Family Academy.

The trends of the age have been steadily reshaping the organizational policies of the homes for dependent children, specifically at Wading River, Ambler and Emsworth. As a matter of fact, the latter, the Holy Family Institute, found that the suburb of Emsworth where it was situated had been incorporated into the City of Pittsburgh and, as a result, no longer referred to its former suburban location.

Taking due notice of the psychological components that were affecting the development of youth in the homes, within the context of social realities, the sisters were firmly supported by local ordinaries and enjoyed full cooperation of the respective diocesan Catholic Charities. Homelike units, each placed in charge of one sister as the cottage mother, accommodated small groups of children. To conduct the schools on the premises there were separate staffs of teachers, while the processing of the details of intake and placement of the children was coordinated by a professional corps of social workers.

The Little Flower House of Providence at Wading River, the largest child-care agency in Suffolk County, New York, saw the realization of its new office building, October 3, 1963, for the establishment of its foster-home department and diagnostic center. The modernization of children's dormitories has been accomplished here, as at Holy Family Institute, with love, imagination and a sense of organization.

At St. Mary's Home in Ambler a major expansion project was undertaken with the groundbreaking on March 19, 1964, and completed two years later. On the grounds, a suitable chapel was built to replace the provisional one; a spacious building housing both the cafeteria and the gymnasium solved the many day-to-day problems arising from the increased institutional population; and a quasi-apartment building with family-type units was designed for children who came from the same families.

In the interest of historical clarity it must be remarked here that the Sacred Heart Vicariate in the United States, established in 1938 as an administrative entity for Texas and New Mexico, was suppressed in 1951. It became apparent in the years that followed that—considering the dominant regional characteristics—some subsidiary form of administration in the southwestern area was expedient. A vice-province was therefore erected, August 30, 1962, with the temporary seat at Bethania Hospital in Wichita Falls, Texas, and Sister Reginella Grodecka as the vice-provincial superior.

Experimentally, the same year, three Italian sisters from Rome were sent to open a center for Catholic Action in northern Italy, in the province of Udine. By way of pastoral ministry they hoped to impregnate the idea that one's faith must enter one's ordinary daily life and be shared with others. Their efforts brought them into contacts with children, youth and adults, but despite their missionary determination the apostolic sense somehow eluded the local population and the experiment was terminated after ten months.

The ecumenical dimension in Nazareth's spiritual and temporal concerns signified that the time has come to insure the proficiency of the Congregation's central administration. It was also necessary to further the efficacy of those functions which the generalates of religious in Rome have been customarily called upon to perform and which have increased proportionately. Heeding the implications of Pope John's call to *aggiornamento,* Mother Neomisia advanced the idea of a new generalate and prayerfully committed its fruition to the Holy Family's unfailing provider,

St. Joseph. The Second Vatican Council had entered the second month of its first session when, on November 21, 1962, Stefan Cardinal Wyszynski, Primate of Poland, blessed the thirteen-acre terrain[18] for the construction of Nazareth's new headquarters and symbolically turned a shovelful of soil.

The convent site, located west of the Vatican, stretched along the ancient Via d'Acquafredda, later renamed Via Nazareth, which joined two active arteries of Roman traffic, Via Aurelia Nuova and Via Boccea. The date of the groundbreaking recalled the anniversary of the death of Mother Mary of Jesus the Good Shepherd who, having lived in the days of the First Vatican Council, experienced strong sentiments and impressions that confirmed her in the affection and loyalty for the Church and the Supreme Pontiff.

Quite unawares, in 1962, the first decade slipped up upon the Nazareth mission activity in Australia in the course of its laying a sound foundation. Approaching a position of prestige, it became the leaven for a concerted growth toward Christian maturity among the migrants and the nativists alike. With gradual assimilation the newcomers not only became a part of the Australian social and civic life, but—what was psychologically more important—they were able to rebuild their self-esteem and the pride in their ethnic heritage. Gradually they were moving out of the camp-type settlements in their own homes, the backbone of a strong family structure.

This circumstance accounted for the rapid societal transformations in Bowen Hills and Kalinga, so that with the disappearance of the barrack community the sisters have relocated from these way stations to other points for a new beginning.

The Australian anniversary was sealed in progress by the completion of a substantial school building in Marayong, representing one phase of the total plan for the development of the Holy Family Children's Home complex. Besides providing the educational needs of the children cared for at the Home, the school eased the problem of overcrowded schools in the vicinity. The same year, the hopes and prayers of the people of Stafford, Queensland, appeared to have been answered in the consent given by the Congregation to staff the school erected by Queen of the Apostles parish, which had remained unoccupied for one year due to the lack of qualified teachers. The first decade in Australia also saw the first Australian novice preparing for the life of a Nazareth religious.

During the visitation of the Australian Vice-Province in 1963, Mother Neomisia decided to remedy the time-consuming and inefficient arrangement arising from the fact that the sisters who taught at Our Lady of Grace school in North Beach had to travel daily to the home originally assigned them in West Perth. The day nursery in West Perth had been discontinued in 1962, while the enrollment of Our Lady of Grace increased from year to year. To eliminate the problems a convent was built close to the school, on one of the highest points of North Beach, with a commanding view of the Indian Ocean less than a quarter of a mile away. Blessed by Archbishop Prendiville, April 19, 1964, the convent accommodated not only the sisters from Our Lady of Grace school, but also those who in the following year staffed the nearby school of Our Lady of Good Counsel.

In the year 1964, the 600th anniversary of the Jagellonian University of Cracow presented a favorable opportunity for visits to Poland. Welcomed to the official celebration were scholars and scientists from all over the world as well as the University's alumni. Mother Neomisia, accompanied by Sister Olympia Nowakowska, both former students of the university in the prewar years, arrived on May 2 and remained in the country for four weeks, during which time it was possible to visit the sisters at their convents. Though external pressures and limitations were still unrelieved, the unfolding of Nazareth's numerous occupations in Poland allowed them to reach the needs of various segments of the population hitherto untapped and unmet.

A religious philosophy of life, however, was not of itself profitable, atheism being one of the basic beliefs of professed communists. Consequently, when the communists took control of eastern Europe's eight governments after World War II, they aimed to stamp out religious belief. Poland alone remained predominantly Catholic, for in the face of evident risks the outspokenness of its Church leaders won for religion the right of peaceful coexistence.

The sisters' attitudes, springing from the profounder elements of faith, were wisely encouraged by the provincial superiors, Sister Inez Strzałkowska, Warsaw, and Sister Thomas Michalunio, Cracow, both appointed in January, 1962. These superiors were, in turn, supported by the Office for the Affairs of the Religious, established by Cardinal Wyszynski and placed under the direction of Bishop Bronisław Dąbrowski, Auxiliary Bishop of Warsaw. One of the functions of the Office was to sponsor inter-community courses of practical and cultural value to the sisters. With increasing frequency they then prepared to qualify for admission to the Catholic University of Lublin, pursued higher studies and engaged in scholarly investigations on graduate level.

Several deaths in that period touched Nazareth at close range, including that of Pope John XXIII, June 3, 1963, and of the United States President John F. Kennedy, assassinated November 22, 1963; and in the general administration: Sister Fides Tomkowicz, treasurer general, who died April 4, 1964, and Sister Bożena Staczyńska, assistant general, October 1, 1964.

Death had also taken toll of the life of Sister Electa Glowienke, first president of De Lourdes College in Des Plaines, September 21, 1963, creating a vacancy which was filled the following August by the appointment of Sister Canisia Majewska to that position. Sister Canisia, a member of De Lourdes faculty since 1952 as instructor in mathematics, was dean of studies at the college at the time of her appointment. With a strong faculty, religious and lay, and a warm, supportive board of trustees, she was able to move consistently towards broader objectives. The character of De Lourdes was changing from a strictly Sister Formation College to a teachers' college for women, and subsequently to a non-restrictive college admitting male and female students alike, who aimed to qualify in the field of education.

A new apostolic venture opened in 1965 with Nazareth's entrance upon the South American continent. The preliminaries were kindled by the insistent call of Pope Paul VI who, like his predecessor, saw the need for priests, brothers, sisters and lay volunteers to aid the Latin American Church there in solving the religious, social and economic problems. Bishop Walter W. Curtis of Bridgeport, Connecticut, who had adopted the mission of Santa Cruz in Peru, invited the Sisters of the Holy Family of Nazareth to work with his priests in the mission.

In February, 1964, Mother Neomisia and the provincial superior from Monroe, Connecticut, Sister Albina, proceeded to Peru to study the local conditions. Santa Cruz was reached by way of Chiclayo, along the rugged, serpentine road up the precipitous slopes of the Andes. The inhabitants of the mission, mostly of Indian origin, recommended themselves by their poverty and ignorance. It was obvious that the sisters who would be sent to work there should be adequately equipped with the knowledge of Spanish, an orientation in missiology, and a general acquaintance with the culture and the customs of the people. With this object in view they have taken up an intensive program of missionary formation and were ready to assume their work in January of 1965.

To pursue to the ultimate conclusion the action of the chapter of 1959, by which the differences in apparel of the choir and the lay sisters were removed,[19] the general administration sought an indult from the Sacred Congregation of Religious to abrogate the article of the Constitutions which provided for the existence of two categories of sisters. The indult was issued, January 20, 1965, and became effective throughout the Congregation on March 9. This measure preceded by nine months the directive of the Second Vatican Council contained in the *Decree on Religious Renewal and Appropriate Adaptation,* generally known by the opening words of the *Decree,* "Perfectae Caritatis."[20]

With every return to Rome after a visitation tour in any of the provinces, Mother Neomisia concerned herself with the progress of the construction of the new generalate. On March 24, 1965, members of the general administration and a number of sisters, designated to reside there, were able to move in. The novitiate from Albano was also transferred and occupied a reserved section of the building. Sister Alodia Zapolska, superior of the Albano convent, was appointed the first superior at the generalate which became known as the convent of the Holy Family. Holy Mass was celebrated for the first time at the new convent on the feast of the Annunciation, March 25, and formal dedication with blessing by Amleto Giovanni Cardinal Cicognani, the Cardinal Protector, took place the following month, April 26, on the day commemorating Our Blessed Lady under the title of the Mother of Good Counsel.

The establishment of a new central house called for some practical reorganization, including the alienation of property for which there appeared no immediate effective use under Nazareth management. The building and the land in Albano were purchased by the Missionary Sisters of the Most Sacred Heart who found the property suited for their purposes. Three sections of the building at Via Machiavelli were acquired by the Fathers of the Holy Spirit, while the two sections which had been in the possession of the Congregation since the days of the Foundress were completely sealed off. This then, the initial motherhouse of the Good Shepherd, remained a memorial to the early years of Nazareth's foundation and to the presence of Mother Mary of Jesus the Good Shepherd. Here a three-step nursery school for young children of working mothers was arranged and conducted according to prescribed standards.

That year, the province of the Immaculate Heart of Mary was authorized to open a novitiate[21] in the provincialate building dedicated in Monroe, Connecticut. In a master plan, the building encompassed a formation center for all levels of religious of the province and the Marian Heights Academy for girls.

Another novitiate, approved for the Holy Name of Mary province[22] was officially established in Częstochowa in the existing convent of the Patronage of Our Lady, since until then one novitiate alone served the two provinces in Poland. In the American province of the Sacred Heart the construction of a novitiate unit was undertaken as a result of the expanding programs of De Lourdes College which required additional space in the main building of the provincialate. The novitiate, structurally attached to the chapel wing of the provincialate, was afforded the measure of privacy requisite for the effectiveness of its specific purpose in religious formation.

Normally, the general chapter would have convened in 1965, were it not for the expectation of definitive instructions from the Second Vatican Council for religious congregations, which might have been included in the chapter agenda. Already the Council's pivotal document, *Dogmatic Constitution on the Church,* promulgated November 21, 1964, subjected to a searching review the persons of religious and their canonical status.[23] When on October 28, 1965 the Council issued the *Decree on Religious Renewal and Appropriate Adaptation,* dealing with the life and rules of the religious, it seemed feasible to convoke the chapter of affairs without further delay and to discuss incidentally the questions stimulated by the two conciliar documents, pending the issuance of the norms of implementation by the Holy See.

*Houses of the Congregation
opened in the years 1960 through 1965:*

Year	Location	Convent-Apostolate-First Superior
1960	UNITED STATES Mott, North Dakota	Queen of Peace convent; St. Vincent de Paul parish school; Sister M. Timothy Ćwik.
1960	UNITED STATES Hickory Hills, Illinois	Mother of the Sacred Heart convent; St. Patricia parish school; Sister M. Mariella Witek.
1960	UNITED STATES Plantation, Florida	St. Michael Archangel convent; St. Gregory parish school; Sister M. Romuald Burakiewicz.
1961	POLAND Blachownia	St. Joseph the Worker convent; pastoral ministry; affiliate of Patronage of St. Joseph convent, Częstochowa.
1961	UNITED STATES Des Plaines, Ill.	Divine Providence convent; Holy Family Hospital; Sister M. DeSales Antczak.
1961	UNITED STATES Philadelphia	St. Katherine of Siena convent; St. Katherine of Siena parish school; Sister M. Bonita Naumowicz.
1961	UNITED STATES Allen Park, Michigan	St. Frances Cabrini convent; Cabrini High School; Sister M. Virgilyn Lukaszewicz.
1962	AUSTRALIA Stafford (Brisbane), Queensland	Our Lady Queen of Apostles convent; Our Lady Queen of Apostles parish school; Sister M. Adria Wijas.

Year	*Location*	*Convent-Apostolate-First Superior*
1962	UNITED STATES Mt. Prospect, Illinois	St. Michael Archangel convent; St. Emily parish school (school opened in 1961); Sister M. Valentine Maraczewska.
1962	UNITED STATES Monroe, Connecticut	Immaculate Heart of Mary convent; provincialate; scholasticate and novitiate, 1965; Sister M. Antolia Jachimowicz.
1962	UNITED STATES Riverhead, New York	Guardian Angels convent; St. Isidore parish school; Sister M. Frances Lotko.
1962	UNITED STATES Southampton, New York	Regina Mundi convent; Our Lady Queen of Poland parish school; Sister M. Clare Lewandowska.
1962	ITALY Torreano di Cividale, Udine	Santa Lucia convent;* Catholic Action; Sister M. Immacolata Marinelli.
1963	UNITED STATES Fort Worth, Texas	St. Andrew the Apostle convent; St. Andrew the Apostle parish school; Sister M. Colette Muszynska.
1964	UNITED STATES Trumbull, Connecticut	Precious Blood convent; Precious Blood parish school; Sister M. Josephine (Alphonsilla) Zane.
1964	UNITED STATES Stratford, Connecticut	St. Mark convent; St. Mark parish school; Sister M. Antonia Zdrodowska.
1965	ITALY Rome	Holy Family of Nazareth convent; generalate; novitiate (transferred from Albano); day care center; Sister M. Alodia Zapolska.
1965	PERU Santa Cruz via Chiclayo	Holy Family convent; catechetical and clinical services; Santa Lucia high school; Sister M. Euphemia Franiak, superior-principal; Sister M. DeChantal Krysinska, clinic director.

Year	*Location*	*Convent-Apostolate-First Superior*
1965	UNITED STATES Philadelphia	Bl. John Neuman convent; Bl. John Neuman diocesan nursing home; Sister M. Auxencia Polakowska.
1965	UNITED STATES Pottsville, Pennsylvania	Holy Family in Bethlehem convent; Nativity BVM diocesan high school; Sister Helen Marie Kosciuszko.
1965	UNITED STATES Irving, Texas	Patronage of the Holy Family convent; Holy Family of Nazareth parish school; Sister M. Loretta Ludtka.

Houses closed:

1960	UNITED STATES Hollidaysburg, Pa.	Queen of Peace convent (1950-1960); Villa Nazareth rest home for sisters.
1960	UNITED STATES South Heart, N.D.	Queen of Peace convent (1941-1960); South Heart public school.
1960	UNITED STATES Chicago	St. Frances of Rome convent (1933-1960); St. Joseph mission school.
1962	UNITED STATES Clayton, New Mexico	Patronage of St. Joseph convent (1921-1962); St. Joseph hospital.
*1963	ITALY Torreano di Cividale, Udine	Santa Lucia convent; Catholic Action.
1965	UNITED STATES Vernon, Texas	Christ the King convent (1937-1965); Christ the King hospital.
1965	ITALY Albano-Ariccia	Patronage of St. Joseph convent (1906-1965); novitiate; transferred to the generalate.
1965	AUSTRALIA Bowen Hills, Queensland	St. Joseph convent and home for boys (1956-1965); Our Lady of Victories parish school.
1965	UNITED STATES Washington, D.C.	Mother of Divine Love convent (1921-1965); Nazareth house of studies (sold to the Missionaries of Our Lady of La-Salette).

3   HIS COVENANT FOREVER

The fourth and final session of the Second Vatican Council was concluded ceremonially by Pope Paul VI, on December 8, 1965, with a concelebrated Mass in St. Peter's Square. One month later, on January 13, even with the commemoration of the Baptism of Christ, the millennium observance of Poland's Christianity was opened in Rome by Bishop Ladislaus Rubin, Episcopal Delegate of Cardinal Wyszynski to the Polish emigrants, in the presence of the Holy Father, the hierarchy and the diplomatic corps. Numerous groups of tourists, prevented by adverse circumstances from making a pilgrimage of piety to Poland, participated in Rome in the manifestations associated with the nation's historic anniversary of faith and fidelity.

In the United States, the chapel of Our Lady of Częstochowa at the National Shrine of the Immaculate Conception in Washington was built around a replica of the painting of the Madonna in Częstochowa, as a monument to the conversion of Poland in 966. In Australia, the War Memorial Shrine of Our Lady of Częstochowa was erected in Marayong in honor of the millennium by the efforts of the emigrant Poles and was dedicated with great festivity, December 27, 1966, by Norman Cardinal Gilroy. The custody of the shrine was entrusted to the Sisters at the Holy Family Children's Home.

The outpourings of light and grace that spread during the Council to the farthest reaches of the Church activated the noblest energies in the Nazareth Congregation. Conscious of their identity and responsibility as members of one of the Church's religious families, the sisters projected constructive proposals for the twelfth general chapter which was to open June 1, 1966.

Thirty participants assembled in the new generalate, including the provincial superiors and elected delegates from Poland for whom elaborate exit applications had been executed far in advance to insure their arrival. Sister Catherine (Berchmans) Hickey, provincial superior in England since 1963, and Sister Gloria Madura in like capacity in the Sacred Heart province, Des Plaines, since 1965, were the most recent appointees in the ex-officio group of capitulants. On the second day of the chapter, the assembly was visited by His Eminence Ildebrando Cardinal Antoniutti, Prefect of the Sacred Congregation of Religious. In his address he emphasized the permanence of the essentials which constitute the fullness of religious life and warned against a hasty drive for changes in disregard of the spirit of the Foundress and the instructions of the Church.

Six working committees consisting of the capitulants examined the proposals which had been submitted under the headings of: spiritual life, community practices, religious formation, apostolate, government, and financial management. Two weeks were devoted exclusively to committee meetings for the purpose of preparing objective studies of the proposals to be reported at the plenary sessions which followed. It was decided to retain, in principle, the Constitutions which were currently in force, eliminating only those matters which were obsolete and confirming the measures which had been previously adopted.[24] The consensus was strongly in favor of wisely directing the attention of the sisters to a deeper understanding of the spirit of the Council by carefully pondering its documents. Experimental revisions and directives relating to specific practices and procedures were made part of the Decrees of the Twelfth General Chapter.

Vacancies in the general administration, occasioned by death, were filled by elections conducted in the chapter. Sister M. Hilary Bortkiewicz was elected general councilor and, from among the councilors, Sister Laurence Crowe was chosen for the position of assistant general. Tentatively, since the death of Sister Fides, Sister Frances Sikorska had been attending to the affairs of the treasurer general, while Sister Maria-Teresa Jasionowicz succeeded her as the director of novices. Now, the general chapter voted in favor of retaining Sister Frances in the capacity of the treasurer to coincide with the remainder of the term of the superior general.

On the closing day of the chapter, July 6, Mother Neomisia addressed the capitulants on the subject of the true nature of renewal and adaptation, commenting on the necessity of continuing self-renewal. She traced a vision of the Nazareth way of religious life in the post-conciliar age and summed up the dominant thoughts of Mother Mary of Jesus the Good Shepherd in their relation to the message of the Council. In the souvenir brochure of the chapter, entitled *Virtues*,[25] she compiled under nine brief headings the counsels extracted from the writings and recorded dialogues of the Foundress in an attempt to articulate the manner of living the characteristic virtues of Nazareth spirituality. For, the spirit of strong and flourishing religious orders has always mirrored the persons of the founder or foundress as expressed in their personalities and attitudes.

The chapter accepted the recommendation of the financial audit commission, Sisters Alphonsina Stachowicz, Chrysantha Karasek and Berchmans Hejnowska, to hold a financial management workshop in September of 1966 at the provincialate in Des Plaines. Sister Frances, treasurer general, and the representatives from Europe and Australia joined the officers of the American provinces and other sisters from the local levels of administration to survey the total fiscal situation in the light of progressive methods, simplification and functional coordination of records and reports. The workshop was conducted by Sister M. Gerald Hartney, treasurer general of the Sisters of the Holy Cross. The upshot of the discussions was the formation of a task force to develop a simple and forthright accounting system to facilitate the process of accumulating and interpreting financial data.

The chapter has also expressed full accord for the translation of the remains of Mother Mary of Jesus the Good Shepherd from the motherhouse at Via Machiavelli to the chapel of the generalate. The ceremony of translation was accomplished, September 29, 1966, according to the ritual of the Sacred Congregation of Rites.

Before departure from Rome after the chapter, Sister Mary Caesar made known her resignation from the office of the provincial superior in St. Joseph province. The crowning accomplishment of her tenure was the realization of the Holy Family Manor[26] on the grounds of the provincialate, a convent planned with those sisters in mind who for reasons of failing health or advancing age were obliged to curtail their activity or withdraw entirely from their former duties. Sister Louise Kondek succeeded Sister Caesar as the provincial.

A new horizon opened up during the early months of 1966 when the Christian Brothers of Ireland applied to Sister Catherine Hickey, provincial superior in England, for four sisters to be assigned to their ninety-six-years-old Artane Industrial School in Dublin. It was a protective home for orphaned and destitute boys, ranging between the ages of eight and fifteen years. The brothers prepared the boys to take their place in society, provided them with education, sound knowledge of religion, and offered an apprenticeship in a variety of trades and crafts. Special emphasis was always placed on music education, so that in later years the school became known for the Artane Boys' Band, which gave recitals and concerts in many countries of the world.

With changing sociological approaches towards the institutional care of children, the brothers were prompted to invite the sisters to act as housemothers for a total, psychologically balanced personality development of their charges. One of the sisters, a professional nurse, was responsible for the boys' infirmary. The sisters took up their residence in a section set apart for them in the infirmary, which was in a separate building.

At Nazareth Catholic Mission in Montgomery, Alabama, the sisters had joined forces with the Resurrectionist Fathers since 1943. Even when at first they had to travel daily from the City of St. Jude to teach in the primary school and care for spastic children, they engaged in a varied pastoral ministry defined by need. These services brought to their attention the intimate social problems of the negro community whom they were eager to help regardless of the controversy surrounding the racial question. By 1966, Resurrection Catholic Center replaced the earlier Nazareth Mission when the director, Father Walter Mikosz, C.R., planned the functional layout including the Resurrection Church, rectory, convent, parish school, and a clinic with therapeutic facilities and specially equipped classrooms for children afflicted with cerebral palsy. The new Resurrection Center has crystallized out of years of experience in this apostolate in the south and out of the profound compassion of Father Mikosz. Death claimed him, however, before the completion of the center, and the clinic was named in his honor as "Father Walter Memorial." The sisters continue to staff and operate the school and the clinic in the new setting.

In Marayong, Australia, St. Andrew parish school, established in 1966, drew upon Nazareth's teaching religious for personnel. The children from the Holy Family Home were then transferred to the parish school for their classes, and the schoolroom facilities at the Home were remodeled and reorganized to be used for the new Holy Family High School. With financial assistance from the American provinces, supplemented by a government grant, a science block and the library addition were provided and furnished. In January, 1967, Sister Clare Ann Rusk, principal, admitted the first class of students to the high school. Four years later, a favorable report from the panel of secondary school inspectors was borne out by the Certificate of Registration granted the school by the Department of Education.

A benefactor of the Holy Family Children's Home, Henry Liszewski, bequeathed to the sisters his property in Gosford, facing the brilliant waters of Copacabana Bay. The bequest became known after his death which occurred in a fatal street accident, June 24, 1967. The house on the property lends itself to holiday and retreat purposes and is used at various times of the year by the sisters and the children interchangeably.

Acting under expert advice, Mother Neomisia saw reasonable advantages for the Congregation's future in Australia by becoming established within the Australian Capital Territory. There were easily accessible opportunities for higher learning and a proximity to the Sisters' Formation Center. Archbishop Eris O'Brien of Canberra was pleased to have the sisters staff the schools of Sts. Peter and Paul in Garran, beginning January, 1968, although temporarily they had to live in neighboring Mawson. Meanwhile plans were being laid for a convent in Garran which became the seat of the vice-provincialate and housed the teaching religious from Sts. Peter and Paul school. Holy Mass in the convent chapel was offered for the first time on the baptismal feastday of the Foundress, March 9, 1971, and on April 12, the building was blessed with liturgical solemnity by Archbishop Thomas V. Cahill.

In England, the school in Enfield was granted the rank of a state school, for which it became eligible after pursuing a plan of reorganization under state rights. Professional advancement in methods and content and in the scholarly caliber of the faculty gained the full approval of the Department of Education and Science, April 8, 1967, for a Four-Form

Entry in the upper school. Corresponding with its new status, the school was allowed to expand its facilities by using leased premises of the Bush Hill Park County School as an integral unit of the Holy Family School.

In Monroe, Connecticut, Marian Heights Academy began to function by offering, at first, high school courses to small classes on an affiliate basis for a few seasons, until in September, 1968, the secondary school program was formally inaugurated by the principal, Sister Tarsitia Rymsza. She came to this post with a rich background of past experience in education and high school administration, and gained state approval for the school's college-preparatory curriculum. The students who sought admission to the academy arrived from surrounding towns and generally represented parental concern for both the quality of instruction and the moral reputation of the school.

A second Peruvian mission with convent and school was opened in 1968, in Trujillo. The sisters were responsible for teaching in the elementary grades at Escuela Santa Maria and for multiple missionary services; additionally, they held classes in English and Religion in the secondary school conducted by Marianist Brothers. Their presence slowly sensitized the people to the mission dimension of faith and emphasized the role of the Christian as a missionary. The people began to realize in time that the mission apostolate is not at the outer rim of the Church, but is really at the very heart of the Church.

At Inver Grove Heights, Minnesota, four sisters became the coordinating staff at the Confraternity School of Christian Doctrine in 1968. Religious education, as a full-time program outside the conventional scholastic timetable, was organized through the initiative of two Franciscan Fathers at St. Patrick's parish with the cooperative effort of forty-eight teachers of the parish laity. The first year, fifteen hundred public school students of elementary and secondary levels enrolled for daily instructions that were staggered for their convenience over the late afternoon and the evening hours, with the exception of the youngest children for whom classes were arranged during Saturday mornings. The aims defined in the program were to communicate to them the entire authentic Christian message, while presenting it in a manner adapted to the needs of the times, by employing methods compatible with the learners' stages of psychological development in order to inspire and confirm a conscious and active faith.

The first hospital of the Congregation, St. Mary of Nazareth in Chicago, in existence since 1894, took a bold step forward by providing the near northwest segment of the metropolis with new hope through rounded out total health care. The addition of mental health services on an ambulatory basis was conceived from the standpoint of keeping families intact during psychiatric therapy and the rehabilitation process, so that those in need of help could remain in the community, working and living as useful citizens and family members. In 1968, St. Mary's Mental Health Center stemmed from extensive consultation with local civic leaders, mental health directors and related agencies to mitigate the growing incidence of emotional difficulties and drug and alcohol addiction among the residents. For children, appropriate diagnostic and treatment services were established to deal effectively with retardation and organic brain problems.

Planning for the future in truly human terms, a complete new St. Mary of Nazareth Health Center was envisioned, including expanded mental care services for patients who may require continuing care in the hospital. The construction of the health center, on the site of the former Lutheran Deaconess Hospital facing St. Mary's, was begun with ground-breaking ceremony on February 2, 1972. The new hospital rising from its foundations held the promise of a concentration of skills and the last word in technology for comprehensive care available within the community.

That same year, the school of nursing at St. Mary's radically revised its syllabus of theory and practice for student nurses. Without sacrificing the content and scope of instruction, the three-year program was condensed to one of two years' duration by eliminating holiday periods from the school's calendar.

Ever since the general chapter of 1966, the provinces and convents have turned to an intensified study of the documents of the Second Vatican Council. There was an open desire to prepare intelligently for the new relationships introduced by the Council and the new goals of the Church in the modern world. Especially pertinent to the religious life were chapters 5 and 6 of the *Dogmatic Constitution on the Church* and the *Decree on Religious Renewal and Appropriate Adaptation*. Additional insights concerning religious life were derived from the exhortation of Pope John XXIII to women religious in 1962,[27] and the two addresses of Cardinal Antoniutti delivered to the major superiors in 1967[28] and 1968.[29]

Reflections upon these matters with concrete reference to the norms of implementation, which were issued in the Apostolic Letter of Pope Paul VI, August 6, 1966, and made effective on October 11 of that year,[30] became an indispensable preliminary to the anticipated special general chapter stipulated in the norms. To enlist the input of the entire membership, all the sisters were expected to give free expression in writing to their views concerning all the areas of Nazareth's religious life and the Constitutions. In each province the responses were channeled to pertinent committees of sisters to formulate follow-up questionnaires and draw up well substantiated proposals based on research.

When the convocation letter announced the opening of the special general chapter as of May 8, 1969,[31] an atmosphere of expectancy and preparedness has already pervaded the convents of the Congregation. In another letter, dated September 21, 1968, Mother Neomisia suggested that particular consideration be given to the subject of community living and the various ramifications of love in the context of community living. This suggestion yielded a wealth of position papers supplementing in depth the previous contributions made by the sisters towards a fresh concept of community as related to the Nazareth ideal contained in the teaching of Mother Mary of Jesus the Good Shepherd.

The abundant material thus accumulated became available to the Central Commission for the Revision of the Constitutions,[32] appointed by Mother Neomisia on November 27, 1968. The commission assembled at the Holy Family Manor in Pittsburgh for three months of exhaustive work, revising the Constitutions and formulating the Statutes. The latter were designed to be an extension and an interpretation of the Constitutions, replacing the Book of Customs. To preserve the spirit and the intent of the Foundress, the original Constitutions of 1887 were researched thoroughly in the light of Mother Mary's writings, since fidelity to the specific intention of the Foundress and to the traditions of the Congregation are confided to those living here and now.

The aim of the commission was to prepare a working text as the point of departure for the deliberations of the special general chapter. As commission chairman, Sister Laurence, assistant general, shared a commonalty with the members of the commission and expedited the progress of the work by imparting to them the evolving orientations concerning the future of religious life. Together with the superior general, she had participated, in Rome, in the conferences and discussions conducted for the International Union of Major Superiors under the leadership of outstanding theologians and representatives of the Sacred Congregation of Religious. Furthermore, to avoid errors, the commission likewise consulted theologians and canonists during the course of its work. Mother Neomisia was present at the commission's opening and, in February of 1969, upon completing a visitation tour, she returned for a résumé of the work accomplished.[33]

Three successive drafts of proposed revisions were mailed to all the sisters, and their recommended additions, deletions and suggestions were seriously considered by the Central Commission in each subsequent editing of the text. Continuing delays in mail deliveries in Poland, however, necessitated a separate revisional project to be undertaken by the two provinces of that country, operating along similar lines as the one in Pittsburgh.[34] Unfortunately, a splinter group within the Holy Name of Mary province, motivated by misguided zeal, gave rise to internal disharmony and opposition. To avert undesirable consequences of a divisive state of affairs, the general council decided upon a corrective action which included transfers of several persons. This affected the position of the provincial superior who was replaced by Sister M. Presentia Góral in 1968. On the other hand, to promote the coordination of endeavors of the two provinces, Sister Marguerite Piątkowska was named the delegate of the superior general for the Congregation in Poland. In token of Nazareth unity, the Central Commission forwarded to Poland its tentative text of revisions in translation.

The opening of the thirteenth general chapter, May 8, 1969, convoked as the special chapter, was preceded by a concelebrated Mass at the generalate, at which the principal celebrant was the former secretary of the Sacred Congregation of Religious, Archbishop Antonio Mauro. In his address to the forty-five capitulants, the Archbishop impressed the assembly with the importance of discovering the presence of the Holy Spirit over and above the modern ferment with its components of conflict and frustration. He inveighed against the dangers of rash and unwarranted change, and counseled the chapter to consider inevitable changes as an evangelical renewal, a rediscovery of the Gospel and a new and fresh discovery of the meaning of Christ in order to make God known, loved and served, and to restore the human hope in the existence of a vibrant, moving, compassionate society.

Mother Neomisia also directed words of prudence to the capitulants, advising them to approach the mystery of a religious congregation and the mystery of a religious vocation with deep reverence and love. She warned against the presumption which might claim a superior perception above that of Mother Foundress and may venture to reduce her inspiration to one's own limitations.

The members of the chapter were assigned to five commissions. After methodical scrutiny they presented at plenary sessions the results of their editing labors on the Constitutions and the Statutes. Voting with the use of electronic equipment began on July 7 and continued until July 18. The new format of the rule of life, comprising two parts—the Constitutions and the Statutes, was given the title *Covenant of Love,* recalling the reference Mother Mary had made to the first Constitutions,[35] as being founded on the messsage of Christ and affirming his principles of life.

Admitting the need for change and progress, the *Covenant of Love* did not give license to deviate from the purposeful direction essential to the Nazareth way. Identification with the essentials faced the complex problems of the so-called "riot years," generated by the mood of a rootless society in a ruined world. But the historical sense with which some of the aspects of the Congregation had to be assessed reflected upon its enduring vocation in the Church. As each person is endowed with distinct physical features and character traits, and each saint becomes noted for a particular virtue exercised in life, similarly each religious congregation, through its members, is called to represent in a pronounced and unique manner some facet of the life or doctrine of the Church. The Nazareth charisma derives from the spirit of the Holy Family, primarily by an immersion of all the aims, concerns, and experiences in the supreme will of God, and by acts of reparation performed for the liberation of the world from sin and the consequences of sin.

In its summons to a total renewal in the faith, the *Covenant of Love* sounded again the pledge of fidelity to the Church and its teaching magisterium, and endorsed again the readiness to carry out ecclesial services for the benefit of mankind. The tradition of reverence and respect for the Sovereign Pontiff, honored in the Congregation since the days of Mother Mary of Jesus the Good Shepherd, was guarded by the superiors general and kept alive until the most recent times by Mother Neomisia, who personally met with Pope Paul VI on several occasions important to the Congregation. Confirmed also was the attitude of respect and reverence ingrained by the Foundress toward members of the clergy, who were in union with the Holy See, in recognition of their sacred ministry of salvation to souls.

In the revised text of the Constitutions, the permanence and validity of religious vows were given a positive expression of their lasting values. Presented in the perspective of faith and love, they were shown to open the path to a fullness of personal integrity that is capable of going beyond self and beyond time. Contrary to the critics of permanent, lifelong choice, the chapter on the Gospel counsels justified the crucial truth that each person has the power to make final decisions which are binding for life. However, the insidious denial of this quality of loyalty unto death has not been without its baleful influence upon the religious who were persuaded to renounce their vows in a gust of rationalizations in Nazareth and in the Church, generally.

Community life, not sought as a goal in itself, but as an ever developing lifestyle, cultivated on supernatural principles, was described as a striving "for unity of mind, heart and purpose, respecting diversity of age, character, personality, and natural gifts."[36] Drawing upon the Holy Family for inspiration, the family spirit in community living was acknowledged to be the source of mutual support and encouragement, of caring for each and sharing with all, and ultimately as a means to spiritual and psychological maturity.

The leading themes of the life of prayer focused upon the primacy of liturgical celebration and the breviary, and emphasized the unifying element of communal prayer in Nazareth for the building and maintaining of community, both personal—where the sisters live, and functional—where they work. The full weight of the obligation to foster continual growth in prayer devolved upon each sister as her personal responsibility.

Without placing restrictions upon future developments, the *Covenant of Love* identified the services by which the sisters have been participating actively in the mission of the Church to bring about an improvement in the human condition, for the apostolates to which the Congregation devotes its energies and personnel are the work of the Church. From a strictly human standpoint, the ability of the Congregation to perpetuate itself by maintaining current membership and gaining new members was correlated with the impact of the sisters' image among those whom they serve and upon their willingness to continue accepting the sisters for their influence, service and leadership.

The articles dealing with government at various levels introduced a broad-based framework for fruitful dialogue and decisive action to achieve goals. Participative obedience shaped the policies for the new structures of house assembly, provincial conference and general advisory conference, and aligned the norms for administrative procedures. The wide interests of the Congregation were thereby intended to become a vital part of the concerns of the sisters at large whose contribution of competence would be at the service of all.

It was uncommon to have achieved an overwhelming degree of unity among the participants of the chapter whose opinions were initially characterized by sharp differences of viewpoint. The individual members proved to their lasting credit that they possessed within themselves the genuine resources for building up timeless ideas into the reality of contemporary needs. They spoke with the full freedom that agitated emerging concepts into a living spark which fused judgment and learning with experience and piety. Throughout the longest chapter gathering in the history of the Congregation Mother Neomisia presided over the deliberative body with rare comprehension of human nature. Her ability and tact were put to test on occasion, but she responded more fully as greater demands were made upon her.

The closing of the special general chapter coincided with the first lunar landing of the American spacecraft *Apollo 11,* July 19, 1969. After adjournment, the sisters from Poland learned of the appointment of Sister Bernarda Krzeczkowska to the office of the provincial superior in Cracow in consideration of the general welfare of that province and its members.

As soon as the *Covenant of Love* was published and distributed, the implementation of its provisions was begun under the leadership of the respective major superiors. Group study days, scheduled over the ensuing months, reached all the sisters in an orientation undertaken for a deeper understanding of the newer formulations in which the original Nazareth spirit was embodied. To be useful, experimentation, whenever proposed, had to comply with evaluative criteria and stipulated controls. Apart from dropping obsolete customs and adopting certain practical modifications in the externals of daily living, the really important outcome was a more vigorous rebound in dedication. The obvious conclusion to be drawn was that the Congregation was not inclined to tolerate mediocrity; this clearly engendered the seeds of stability and continuity.

Houses of the Congregation
opened in the years 1966 through 1969:

Year	Location	Convent-Apostolate-First Superior
1966	EIRE Artane (Dublin)	Mater Dei convent; Artane Industrial School for Boys; Sister Mary James O'Hara.
1966	UNITED STATES Glen Head, New York	St. Hyacinth convent; St. Hyacinth parish school; Sister M. Ernestine Szpiegowska.
1966	UNITED STATES Grand Prairie, Texas	Immaculate Conception convent; Immaculate Conception parish school; Sister M. Gracilia Krukowska.
1966	UNITED STATES Pittsburgh, Pennsylvania	Our Lady of Loreto convent; Holy Family Manor for retired sisters; Sister M. Adrianne Pelkowska.
1967	AUSTRALIA Marayong (Sydney), New South Wales	St. Andrew convent; St. Andrew parish school (school opened in 1966); Sister M. Cassilda Kukla.
1967	AUSTRALIA Copacabana (Gosford), New South Wales	St. John convent; holiday home; affiliate of Holy Family Children's Home.
1967	POLAND Boguszyce	St. Mary of Nazareth convent; pastoral ministry; affiliate of Warsaw provincialate.
1967	POLAND Tursko	Holy Family convent; pastoral ministry; affiliate of Warsaw provincialate.
1967	UNITED STATES Belfield, North Dakota	Christ the King convent; St. Bernard parish school; Sister M. Timothy Cwik.
1968	UNITED STATES Inver Grove Heights, Minnesota	Sacred Heart of Jesus convent; St. Patrick Confraternity School; Sister M. Priscilla Zaremba.

Year	*Location*	*Convent-Apostolate-First Superior*
1968	AUSTRALIA Mawson (Canberra), A.C.T.	Sts. Peter and Paul convent; Sts. Peter and Paul parish school; temporary vice-provincialate; Sister M. Irmina Paszkiewicz.
1968	PERU Trujillo	Santa Maria convent; Santa Maria school; Sister M. Euphemia Franiak.

Houses closed:

1966	POLAND Ligota	St. Joseph convent (1954-1966); catechetical center.
1966	UNITED STATES Pittsburgh	Mary Mother of God convent (1931-1966); St. Hyacinth parish school.
1966	UNITED STATES Mt. Union, Pennsylvania	Our Lady of Grace convent (1959-1966); St. Catherine of Siena parish school.
1966	UNITED STATES Gallitzin, Pennsylvania	Queen of the Sacred Heart convent (1913-1966); Our Lady of Częstochowa parish school.
1966	UNITED STATES Mobile, Alabama	Infant of Prague convent (1943-1966); Zimmer Memorial Home for Children.
1967	UNITED STATES Springfield, Massachusetts	Our Lady of Consolation convent (1919-1967); Our Lady of the Rosary parish school.
1967	UNITED STATES Kankakee, Illinois	Our Lady the Good Shepherdess convent (1910-1967); St. Stanislaus parish school.
1968	UNITED STATES Mineral Wells, Texas	Holy Family convent (1931-1968); Nazareth Hospital.
1968	AUSTRALIA Kalinga (Brisbane), Queensland	Holy Family convent and home for girls (1952-1968); St. Ann parish school.
1969	UNITED STATES Cicero, Illinois	Our Lady of Lourdes convent (1912-1969); St. Valentine parish school.
1969	UNITED STATES Taos, New Mexico	Holy Cross convent (1937-1969); Holy Cross Hospital.

4 HOUSE ON A ROCK

Social concerns in Nazareth have always been associated with its two major corporate apostolates, education and health care. The Congregation was engaged in these concerns not purely out of humanistic motivations, since even unbelievers devote themselves to socio-economic welfare and charitable activity, but because social and charitable activities are the channel for the goodness of the Lord to reach those in need through the ministrations of the sisters who have come to experience transcendent values in their way of life. The individuals they met were seen as persons loved and redeemed by God, deserving to be aided in their quest for what is true, good and beautiful.

As in the early years of the Congregation, renewed emphasis was placed upon the family, the focal unit of society, to help restore its dignity and integrity through positive orientation to the cardinal moral issues of human life. Family days, conducted by the sisters, provided the means to establish contacts with instructive social and religious overtones. Visits to the families, on the other hand, introduced opportunities to become acquainted with existing problems, material and otherwise, and—where indicated—opened the avenues to family reconciliation and stability.

Among the social ills of the latter third of the twentieth century, crime and addiction to drugs and alcohol were caused largely by the deterioration of the moral fiber of the family, or else contributed to the family's breakdown. Sisters qualified by competence and inspired by compassion visited penal institutions and rehabilitation centers to assist the inmates to regain self-respect and to revive their confidence in God and man, the first step to decency and responsibility.

Sister Rita Kathryn Sperka, as social worker at the Catholic Family and Community Services of the Diocese of Bridgeport in Connecticut, has spread her enthusiasm and charity beyond the requirements of her position. In the diocesan office she dealt with parent-child problems, marital difficulties, unwed mothers in distress, and held consultations with adoptive parents, but allocating with circumspection whatever time she had at her disposal, she also took interest in the girls of minority groups, residing in a low socio-economic area, to help them acquire a constructive outlook on life while developing variety of practical skills that would enable them to improve their condition.

In a school known for its heavy quota of students with social and learning disabilities, Sister Rita Kathryn offered individual and group counseling on regular basis. These and other services brought her to the attention of the Outstanding Young Women of America Awards Program, in 1971, to be given recognition for her efforts towards the betterment of community, country and profession. Subsequently, when she received the appointment to the faculty of Holy Family College in the Department of

Sociology, she brought to the teaching position, besides specialized theoretical knowledge, the desirable assets of broad experience and dedication.

Another phase of family-directed concern arose out of the plan to organize religion instructions for mentally retarded children and adolescents. With the volunteers who responded to Sister Christella Gacek, the program came into being in the Diocese of Rockville Center, New York. It aimed to impart basic doctrinal information to educable children in a manner easily understood by them and to prepare them for the sacraments of the Eucharist and Confirmation. Under the auspicies of the Diocesan Department of Special Education, an association of the parents of these exceptional children was underway. By acquainting the parents with the course of their children's spiritual growth, a common ground was established whereby they shared the joy which the children experienced in the knowledge of the eternal truths.

At the homes for dependent children, staffed by the Nazareth religious, well-timed occasions were utilized for the exploration of familial relationships and Christian family living. The parents of the children who were at these homes and the personnel alike stood in need of a supportive network of assistance to assimilate the spirit of the Holy Family and dispel the confusion of what was going on in both secular and religious aspects of family life. To secure for the children the optimum benefit from the residential care and education which they received, help and guidance were offered discreetly to the parents by means of family therapy and the identification of religious, social and psychological factors in child rehabilitation.

Since the Second Vatican Council, ecumenical attitudes in the Church gained momentum on the strength of the Gospel. In like manner, the spirit of ecumenism, which had been Nazareth's hallmark right along, became reinvigorated and diffused its influence in countless ways. It reached out in human brotherhood by the new evolutionary trends that entered education and health care administration, building communities of faith of the schools and hospitals conducted by the Sisters of the Holy Family of Nazareth. As a community within the Church, the sisters accepted cultural pluralism as a fact of life. Over the years increasing numbers of persons of deep faith, who were not themselves Catholics, have joined the staffs and faculties of Nazareth institutions and by their efforts added luster to the achievements of these institutions.

The state of flux in education called upon educators, primarily upon educators of future teachers, to become completely conversant with the unfolding new techniques. Combining the flexibility of new procedures with the structure of the old, the students majoring in elementary school education were prepared at Holy Family College, Philadelphia, to create an enriched environment for each learning situation. They were given the basics in pedagogical disciplines, educational research and behavioral sciences to implement individually guided instructions. With the use of outlined materials they were equipped to develop a continuum of skills for each child, allowing him to move at his own pace, whether he needed remedial assistance or had the capacity for accelerated growth. And equally, if not even more important, these techniques pointed up to the teachers-in-training that their own learning efforts must necessarily be an unending, lifelong process.

At De Lourdes College, Des Plaines, the curriculum was geared to the needs of mature students whose educations had been interrupted at some earlier date for economic or family reasons. As time and opportunity became available, their desire for intellectual development found satisfaction in the peaceful atmosphere of De Lourdes College, where they preferred to pursue their studies without the distractions of youth's multiple extra-curricular interests usually present in residential colleges. In this way numerous capable persons were salvaged for the teaching profession, guided by Sister Canisia Majewska in the choice of qualifying courses.

Similarly, experienced employed teachers, who had to comply with the newer requirements for state certification, were given in-service opportunities under the supervision of Sister Lenore Truszkowska, director of student teaching. In this capacity she has been directing the first- and second-year internships of undergraduate students in elementary school education and helped to expand the curriculum of the college by initiating advanced courses in contemporary progressive methods for career teachers, who were desirous of continuing their self-improvement.

In a long-considered move by the governing boards of two hospitals, St. Mary of Nazareth in Chicago and Holy Family in Des Plaines, a corporate form of management went into effect in each. In the rapidly changing social and technological trends, instinctive good judgment was no longer sufficient. The forces of change significantly affected the management process, and the higher educational level of employees altered the patterns of motivation, so that the concern had to be not so much how things are done but how things might be done better. The patient and his family have learned to depend upon the hospital for more services and to call upon these services more frequently.

To insure a constant high degree of quality in all patient care services, a larger number of persons, religious and lay, were needed who truly understood the hospital culture, the nature of health care environment, and the art of administration. Through the expansion and realignment of management personnel positions, a more refined mode of administrative control has been established. The corporate management teams of the two hospitals, headed by Sister Stella Louise Slomka and Sister Amata Sweeney, respectively, supplied broader human resources for greater operational efficiency and a more factual accountability. By blending convention and consensus, the internal management principles were those of influence and deference, rationality and civility, and a generous atmosphere of reciprocity.

The management function, moreover, is a field of action concerned not only with the knowledge of commodities, tactics and procedures, but embraces attitudes and abilities. Because the persons in managerial positions are chiefly the product of their religious, moral and philosophical training and exposure, they tend to make decisions, in a large measure, in the light of their own ethics and sense of values. Through the corporate organization the managerial personnel at Holy Family Hospital recognized their responsibility to be the formation of employees in their respective departments. To develop enlightened insights into this responsibility, they were assisted by means of monthly discourses led by Father Regis N. Barwig, theologian and scholar. As prior of the Community of Our Lady, founded in the illustrious tradition of St. Benedict, ascetic and contemplative in spirit, he was given to the works of salvation and to the cause of Christian unity.

For the hospital officers Father Barwig correlated the professional aspects of administration with the teaching of the Gospel, applying the conclusions to the actual situations they encountered. Out of these sessions the members of the management team derived additionally an introduction into the philosophy of Mother Mary of Jesus the Good Shepherd. For Father Barwig, having edited the English translation of her conferences[37] and translated from the Italian the biography written by the postulator of her cause of beatification,[38] was able to excerpt from her conferences and correspondence the principles which she imparted to the major and local superiors in their administration of convents and in the guidance of sisters. Though enunciated in a previous century, these principles bore surprising similarity to contemporary professional ideas in spite of a difference in terminology.

Alongside the vigorous apostolic developments of the latter years, the vitality of the Congregation's religious objectives has not diminished. Efforts at spiritual renewal, it was found, were in fact bringing about a renewal particularly through the study of the original inspiration of the Foundress. Acting within its prerogatives as a discretionary society, Nazareth rejected the tentative theologies that had proliferated during the post-conciliar decade and which—deviating from the fundamental character of religious life—had advocated substituting the concern for the Kingdom of God with the concern for the welfare of man and displacing genuine prayer with programmed sensitivity.

But, generally speaking, religious congregations, in their attempts to recapture the immutable fundamentals in an honest renewal, had to contend with a noxious crop of mistaken notions. Not only have such opinions tended to undermine the wholesome work of renewal, but moreover, they purported justification in the documents of the Council. A statement by John Cardinal Krol, Archbishop of Philadelphia and President of the National Conference of Catholic Bishops in the United States, dispelled whatever doubt may have existed. The Cardinal, who had personally participated in the deliberations of the Vatican Council, declared,

> Many things said about the Second Vatican Council were not said in the Council, and many things said in the Council were not said by the Council. The sixteen Conciliar documents promulgated by the Holy Father contain the record of what was said by the Council.[39]

In the midst of the agitation stirred by confusing ideas, some of Nazareth's members chose to be dispensed from their vows, while religious of good will regarded this time as the age of the second creation when, in the darkness of faith, the hovering Spirit of God would lead them into the light of reaffirmed conviction in the reality of their vocation.

Almost too soon, it seemed, the Congregation was alerted to the forthcoming fourteenth general chapter. By the convocation letter of June 27, 1970, Mother Neomisia announced the meeting of the chapter to take place a year hence.[40] Though it would be predominantly electoral in character, the chapter would consider and act upon the current general affairs of the Congregation.

Accordingly, provincial chapters met in special session with the capitulants from their particular provinces to research and study the existing problems and imminent developments in preparation for the general chapter. At Rome, Mother Neomisia appointed, in March, 1971, a Preparatory Commission[41] to develop the agenda for the chapter. The preliminary draft of the agenda was forwarded to all the delegates to acquaint them in advance with the questions to be discussed at length.

Before the departure of the delegates for the chapter, Holy Family College in Philadelphia conferred upon Sister Medarda the honorary degree of Doctor of Humane Letters during the 1971 commencement exercises. The award was made in recognition of the outstanding services she had rendered in promoting religious, educational, social and health care endeavors throughout the twelve-year tenure as provincial superior of the Immaculate Conception province.

Several major superiors who were coming to the chapter decided to bring with them the details for significant provincial undertakings which they and their councils had under serious consideration for some time. The occasion to consult directly with the general council warranted a much fuller understanding of the implications involved than could be accomplished by correspondence alone.

Sister Gloria, from the Sacred Heart province, carried with her the architectural designs for a home to accommodate those sisters who would be retiring from active participation in their lifetime apostolates. The projected specifications proposed such facilities which were deemed essential to the physical and psychological well-being in conditions associated with infirmity and aging.[42]

Plans of another nature were brought to Rome by Sister Reginella, vice-provincial superior for the Texas region, namely, the latest data pertaining to the construction of the administration building of the vice-provincialate to be erected on the land purchased in 1965 in Grand Prairie, Texas.[43] Sister Reginella also presented a condensed report on the expansion in progress at Bethania Hospital, Wichita Falls, which when completed was to increase the hospital capacity by 100 beds for patients.[44]

From Monroe, Connecticut, Sister Albina gave an account of the opening of the house of prayer at the Villa Immaculata in Riverhead on Long Island. Acting upon the recommendation of the Special General Chapter of 1969,[45] the Immaculate Heart of Mary province had studied the possibilities of realizing the recurring wish of Mother Mary of Jesus the Good Shepherd to establish a house of prayer. The program was under experimentation since February, 1971, and was given the blessing of Bishop Walter P. Kellenberg of Rockville Center.[46] An experience in the house of prayer was intended to aid individual sisters to deepen their spirituality and arrive at a greater union with God through recollection and prayer, as well as reflection and dialogue, and to become the source of constant renewal in the entire religious family.

Developments surrounding the institutional care of normal children in Ireland affected the Artane Industrial School in a process of phasing out, since it was no longer fulfilling the role for which it had been originally established. Sister Catherine Hickey of the Holy Family province, which comprised the Congregation's apostolates in England and Ireland, acquainted the general council with the concluding particulars with regard to the sisters' finishing their work at Artane officially in July and taking up a totally new type of work in Shankill, at the Shanaganagh Castle.

The castle, a massive Edwardian edifice, was converted into a hotel over thirty years earlier and, in 1968, it was acquired by the Department of Justice to be transformed into an open prison for youthful offenders between the ages of 16 and 21. As a progressive experiment in penal reform, the liberal environment of the castle provided a kind of boarding school existence to first offenders, where their privacy was assured, freedom of movement in the building and on the grounds was allowed, and no prison uniform required. Basic training in a variety of trades and skills enabled the boys to become rehabilitated to take a place in society as responsible citizens. Because of a consistent percentage of illiteracy and backwardness, the sisters were entrusted with the standard education of the inmates.

The steps in preparation to change an existing apostolate in St. Joseph province, Pittsburgh, were related by Sister Louise, the provincial superior. They encompassed the discontinuance of the 44-year old Mount Nazareth Academy in the face of declining student enrollment and the presence of other high schools which were more easily accessible by public transportation. To utilize the physical resources of the school, a full-time day care center was planned for pre-school children under the supervision of Sister Florence Therese Sarnowska to serve the needs of families and children alike.

The change of name from Mount Nazareth Academy to Mount Nazareth Center signified the anticipation of a complex of other activities to be housed within these quarters, pertaining chiefly to family services in the immediate neighborhood community. The library of the former academy, listing books which ranged from the elementary through the adult reading level, were made available to the general public under the regular policies of a circulating library, maintained professionally by Sister Secundilla Kniszek.

The provincials from Poland, Sisters Inez and Bernarda, recounted the many-sided aspects which continued to affect the sisters' activities under the existing political restrictions and indoctrination. The types of services in which they engaged extended all over the apostolic spectrum accessible to them in behalf of the Church and society. The subversive elements at work throughout the country militated against morality and religion, and, consequently, emphasized the urgency of salvaging family life from destruction and retrieving youth from the tentacles of atheism and depravity. Pastoral ministry in all its ramifications sprang from these interests or was related to them in some degree, though the material returns were utterly insignificant due to the poverty of the parishes, and the facilities for catechetical instruction inadequate for the same reason.

The fourteenth general chapter, assembled at the generalate of the Congregation in Rome, opened June 28, 1971. It was preceded by three days of recollection and prayer when the delegates received timely guidelines in precapitular conferences, in English by Father Barnabas Ahern, C.P., and in Polish by Msgr. Andrew Deskur. Both conference masters commended highly the Constitutions and Statutes in the *Covenant of Love,* and advised the chapter to devote its attention at this time, primarily, to consolidating the ranks of the members by conveying assurance to the sisters and guaranteeing their spiritual and temporal security through the preservation of organic unity. A note of warning was sounded against diluting the spirit of prayer and minimizing the inspiration of the Foundress.

A total of forty-nine capitulants met at the opening session, but Sister M. Precious Pruszynska, councilor general, has been present only then, being unable to attend the succeeding sessions because of progressively failing health. She was obliged to leave Rome before the conclusion of the chapter to undergo special medical treatment in the United States.[47]

Mother Neomisia, as chapter president, appointed the capitulants to six commissions to study the proposals on the agenda, and named Sister Geraldine Sledz the chapter coordinator. In a detailed 35-page report of the religious and apostolic life of the Congregation, the superior general covered the period since the twelfth general chapter of affairs. Her report was followed by the statistical report of the secretary general and the financial report of the treasurer general.

Inasmuch as it was agreed that the *Covenant of Love* has been in effect too briefly to attempt a conclusive evaluation, the chapter decided that the entire Congregation be encouraged to continue the thorough study and application of its articles in relation to the teachings of Mother Mary of Jesus the Good Shepherd and the pronouncements of the Holy See. Providentially, along these lines, Pope Paul VI issued an apostolic exhortation *On the Renewal of Religious Life (Evangelica Testificatio),* June 29, 1971,[48] copies of which were distributed among the capitulants.

The chapter has taken for one of its objectives the safeguarding of the essentials of religious life and has accordingly developed specific instructions dealing with seven sensitive areas: prayer life, religious formation, community life, religious habit, authority and obedience, religious poverty, and the apostolate.[49] The deliberations concerned with the life of the Congregation were completed on July 21, and the next day was designated for the election of the superior general.

Bishop Ladislaus Rubin, secretary general of the World Synod of Bishops, presided at the electoral session, and after the votes were cast, verified, and tallied, he announced the election of Mother M. Medarda Synakowska[50] to the office of the superior general. Voting for the members of the general administration was scheduled to take place the day after, on July 23, when the following were elected: Sister M. Geraldine Sledz, assistant general; Sisters Albina Kowalkowska, Aloysius Sabacinska and Maria-Teresa Jasionowicz, councilors general; Sister M. Benedicta Nowakowska, secretary general, and Sister M. Electa Trela, treasurer general. On July 24, after the capitulants had signed the minutes of the proceedings, Mother Medarda declared the fourteenth general chapter officially closed.

Among the first acts of the new administration was the appointment of provincial superiors where vacancies occurred, namely, Sister M. Agnes Grynkiewicz to Immaculate Heart of Mary province; Sister Mary Rose Gumienna to Immaculate Conception province, and Sister M. Alexandra Budzinska to the Sacred Heart province.

Adhering consistently to clearly defined principles, Sister Neomisia at once renounced the title reserved now to the superior general solely during her term of office, similarly as she declined to be induced to accept any position in the general administration, in keeping with the statement she had made to that effect in the convocation letter.[51] Retreating from great affairs, literally into the veiled existence of the hidden life, she also relinquished an office of prestige for the development of Holy Family College, the institution she had founded in 1954, but willingly joined the faculty of the college in the Department of Modern Languages.

Houses of the Congregation
opened in the years 1970 through 1971:

Year	Location	Convent-Apostolate-First Superior
1971	AUSTRALIA Garran (Canberra) A. C. T.	Holy Spirit convent; Vice-provincialate, replacing the temporary convent in Mawson; Sts. Peter and Paul parish school in Mawson; Sister M. Irmina Paszkiewicz.
1971	EIRE Shankill, Co. Dublin	Mater Dei convent; penal reform home for adolescent boys; Sister Mary James O'Hara.

Houses closed:

1970	UNITED STATES Colorado Springs	Regina Mundi convent (1955-1970); El Nido Nazareth retreat and rest home.
1971	UNITED STATES South Bend, Indiana	St. Dominic convent (1904-1971); St. Stanislaus parish school.
1971	AUSTRALIA Mawson (Canberra) A. C. T.	Sts. Peter and Paul convent (1968-1971); temporary vice-provincialate.
1971	EIRE Artane (Dublin)	Mater Dei convent (1966-1971); Artane Industrial School for boys.

5   A NEW CHAPTER

As soon as was feasible after her election, Mother Medarda undertook the tour of acquaintance of the Congregation, beginning at Loreto on September 7, 1971. There she not only wanted to meet the sisters, but— moved by the example of Mother Mary of Jesus the Good Shepherd— wished to pray at the shrine of the Annunication and Incarnation for guidance in her work and for Nazareth everywhere.

Into the highest leadership position, Mother Medarda necessarily had to integrate her own distinctive gifts when building on the foundations which had been laid before her. She realized without a doubt, as one possessed of the social consciousness of the times, that if the Congregation were to enrich the outside culture, it first must be internally strong. Nazareth unity, she was aware, could never be convincing or truly human, unless it succeeded to gather together individuals who were different in many ways and kept them living, praying and working harmoniously for the same goals despite their differences. Change being an ever present condition of human life, it was important to maintain balance in the midst of change. This was the initial message she conveyed to the sisters with an air of simplicity and confidence.

To further the sense of internal unity within each province and, more-over, between provinces, regular provincial newsletters were encouraged and began to be published by staffs of sisters for intra-community circula-tion. The Australian newsletter was given the title *Nazareth Communiqué*; Sacred Heart province—*The Bond*; Immaculate Conception province— *The Link*; St. Joseph province—*Intercom*; Immaculate Heart of Mary province—*In-Sight;* Holy Name of Jesus province—*Nazaret;* Holy Name of Mary province—*Fiat*; and the generalate issued its newsletter under the name of *Nazareth Unity*.

While making the first general visit to the United States, Mother Medarda was accompanied by Sister Aloysius, who then had the occasion to witness the inauguration of the four-year nursing program at Holy Family College, towards which end plans and preparations were in progress during her tenure as president of the college. As a result of her election to the general council of the Congregation, Sister Aloysius was succeeded in the college presidency by Sister M. Lillian Budny, recognized scientist, who held the rank of associate professor in the Department of Biology.

The new program leading to the degree of Bachelor of Science in Nursing was designed to provide a curriculum of required sciences and an affiliation with approved hospitals for the students' clinical experience in nursing. Another hospital-based program of long standing at Holy Family College, which was acceptable to the American Society of Clinical Pathologists, has been awarding the degree of Bachelor of Science in Medical Technology.

Concurrently with Mother Medarda's visits to the convents, two councilors, Sisters Albina and Maria-Teresa, proceeded to the houses of Nazareth's religious formation in the capacity of consultants. Their background of knowledge and experience in the guidance of beginners in the religious life and of young religious gave the formation directors an opportunity to evaluate and raise the quality of their own efforts. A second, and farther reaching, objective of the consultants was to survey the actual state of religious formation in order to supply their findings to the Sacred Congregation for Religious and Secular Institutes, Nazareth being one of the selected participants of the study. The purpose of the survey was to accumulate factual material for an international symposium, to make an impartial analysis, and ultimately, to determine an appropriate mode of action in terms of the contemporary situations, viewed in relation to the immutable bases of religious life.

Other services of the general administration planned for a later date[52] were the meetings in Dallas, Texas, for provincial secretaries with Sister Benedicta, secretary general, and in Wichita Falls, Texas, for provincial treasurers conducted by Sister Electa, treasurer general.

In response to the Third World Synod of Bishops, assembled in Rome, October, 1971, the religious congregations of men and women introduced the observance of *The Year of Peace through Justice* and, with it, the serious consideration of the role of religious in witnessing to justice by promoting it through education and by international action for justice. Sisters Geraldine and Electa represented the generalate at the seminars which dealt with these burning questions of the moment, and were joined by Sister M. Lucy Golon, director of education in the Sacred Heart province.

In the Church's aims for world peace through justice, educators were in a particularly strong position. Using educational processes to reach all those who came under their influence, they were able to achieve education for justice, for the liberation of the human person, and for the protection of human dignity. Thus, Nazareth's ecclesial character was reenforced by the apostolic understanding of witness in its full, demanding and boundless extension.

The keynote for these considerations had been touched repeatedly by Pope Paul, and occurred recently in the apostolic exhortation.[53] It led Sister Reginella to contemplate surrendering the ownership of the Nazareth Hospital property in Mineral Wells, Texas. Since the operations of the hospital had been discontinued on April 2, 1968, and no alternatives for its utilization by the Congregation were in evidence, the general council was in favor of donating the buildings and grounds to the diocese of Fort Worth, for which the approval of the Apostolic Delegate was secured.[54] The Diocesan Social Action Department of the Catholic Charities enlisted the cooperation of the county and city social services to convert the hospital plant into a local service building, where various social agencies would be housed at the one location.

In Italy, at the request of the Oblates of St. Joseph three sisters entered upon the works of pastoral ministry among the rural population of Ceglie del Campo in the province of Bari. From the beginning, October 2, 1972, their efforts centered around youth apostolate, including kindergarten, tutorial assistance, religion classes, and the development of aptitudes in arts and crafts. Early and continued contacts with the sisters tended to awaken an interest in the religious and priestly vocations which, in turn, the Oblates in the parish supported by their zeal and fervor.

Two weeks after the opening of the mission in Bari, Pitsford Hall in England marked the expansion of its school, October 15, 1972, simultaneously with the twenty-fifth anniversary of its establishment. The daughters of Polish immigrant families have found within the precincts of the school the solace of a homelike atmosphere and the education which respected their lineage, conditioning them at the same time toward confident integration into the country of their adoption. Since the school attracted also girls of British and other ancestries, the social exchanges among the students had a broadly formative impact.

It was through the generosity of an Englishman, G. M. Reeves, that a wing to the main building was realized. Named "the Queen Hedwig Annex," it became the arts and crafts center where the cutural and practical programs of the school could be enlarged and individual talents encouraged. The dedication and opening of the annex were honored by the presence of Bishop Rubin from Rome who officiated at the religious functions.

But in the apostolic life the sisters recognized that human satisfaction must be subservient to evangelical fidelity, and thus it was that the withdrawal from Santa Cruz mission in Peru was accepted by the sisters at the termination of their mission contract. They have helped the people to help themselves in the pursuit of true humanity and their eternal destiny. The testimony of the people was a proof of what they had gained, as they expressed their gratitude in countless little ways. They remembered with love and sorrow the mission nurse, Sister M. DeChantal Krysinska, who lost her life following an automobile accident.[55] They recalled also the comfort and encouragement they had received from the sisters when the earthquake and landslide in a nearby district[56] filled them with terror and apprehension. The sisters who returned to the United States with the joy and the memory of their missionary experiences became confirmed apostles of the pilgrim Church in the underdeveloped region of the Andes, stimulating others to help uplift their brothers and sisters who lived in want in distant lands.

Meanwhile, an apostolic awareness among the very young prompted in 1957 by Sister M. Donata Gracyalny, director of the medical records department of Nazareth Hospital in Philadelphia, continued to flourish uninterruptedly. Girls ranging in age from 9 to 14, known as "Little Miriams of Nazareth Hospital," enjoyed visible distinction among their peers. Guided by Sister Donata in numerous charitable interests, in Christian social living, and in the appreciation of religion, they have been contributing of their allowance and leisure time to bring moments of happiness to the patients and participated in the hospital's benefit activities.

This, however, in no way impeded Sister Donata's professional commitment. In fact, she merited, in 1972, a citation by the Temple University College of Allied Health Professions. The university's Department of Medical Records Science granted her the rank of clinical instructor in recognition of her services to Temple University students who pursued their practice requirements under her direction in the medical records department of Nazareth Hospital.

Recognition in another domain was earned by Sister M. Grace Kuzawa, chairman of the Department of Mathematics at Holy Family College. Her doctoral dissertation, published under the title of *Modern Mathematics: The Genesis of a School in Poland*,[57] won acclaim from mathematicians and professors of mathematics, in the United States and abroad, as a perceptive contribution to the history and sociology of mathematics. Several scholarly listings, including *Who's Who among American Women, American Men of Science,* and the *International Scholars Directory,* noted Sister Grace and her work in their entries.

In a field by itself was a project of lasting value to Nazareth, initiated by Sister M. Jane Menżeńska, director of Library Services at Holy Family College. She compiled a one-hundredth years' bibliography entitled *Guide to Nazareth Literature, 1873-1973: Works by and about the Congregation of the Sisters of the Holy Family of Nazareth.*

The expiration of the terms of office in major positions, in 1972, necessitated new appointments to the duties of leadership and trust. In Warsaw, Sister M. Raphael Wielgut assumed the responsibilities of the provincial superior; in Pittsburgh, a comparable office was entrusted to Sister M. Edward Lijek; and in Australia, Sister M. Bernice Dudek was designated the vice-provincial superior.

Houses of the Congregation
opened in the year 1972:

Year	*Location*	*Convent-Apostolate-First Superior*
1972	ITALY Ceglie del Campo (Bari)	Our Lady of Mercy convent; youth apostolate, tutorial assistance, religious guidance, kindergarten; Sister M. Eletta Ridolfi, director

Houses closed:

1972	UNITED STATES Chicago	St. Augustine convent (1931-1972); Holy Rosary parish school.
1972	UNITED STATES Dearborn, Michigan	Our Lady Queen of Heaven convent 1955-1972); St. Martha parish school; (teaching sisters reside at Sacred Heart convent, St. Barbara parish in the same city).
1972	PERU Santa Cruz via Chiclayo	Holy Family convent (1965-1972); catechetical and clinical services; Santa Lucia high school.

* * *

The year 1973 was an early forerunner of the centenary of the foundation of the Sisters of the Holy Family of Nazareth. For, on March 9, 1873, Frances Siedliska, the future Foundress, was assured of her religious vocation, and on Easter Sunday, April 13, she learned that she was destined to establish a new religious congregation within the Church. On the advice of her spiritual director, Father Leander Lendzian, O.F.M.Cap., she made her religious profession, July 2, 1873, taking the name of Mary as her religious name. The same year, on October 2, she was granted a private audience with Pope Pius IX and received his approval and guidance for the congregation she was to establish.

But it was two years later, on her subsequent return to Rome, that the Congregation began its existence. The date indicated by her for the observance of this event was to coincide each year with the First Sunday of Advent in union with the Church's beginning of the liturgical year.

The Nazareth Congregation has been peopled by uncommon personalities of every description in asceticism. There were the disciples and the apostles, the Good Samaritan women of Christian service, and the contemplatives, penitents and victim souls. In all these, the Nazareth way remained lifelike, but—like the Master of Nazareth himself—seldom attained acclaim. In recent years the tremendous resurgence of prayer and penitential life was an obvious evidence that increasing numbers choose to avoid the naturalistic ingredient of life to be able to reach for the larger-than-life concepts recognized in the light of divine will and love.

With the age of renewal and rediscovered horizons, a new chapter opened upon Nazareth's new century in 1975, even as the Holy Year of Reconciliation converged on Rome in worldwide initiatives that had the common purpose of Christian unity and peace.

NOTES AND REFERENCES

PART I
(Pages 1-26)

1. Wallace K. Ferguson and Geoffrey Bruun, *A Survey of European Civilization* (Boston: Houghton Mifflin Co., 1952), p. 652.

2. André Maurois, *A History of France* (New York: Farrar, Straus and Cudahy, 1956), pp. 365-432 *passim*.

3. Rachel Challice, *History of the Court of Spain: 1802-1906* (New York: D. Appleton & Co., 1909), pp. 149-223.

4. Oscar Halecki, *The Millennium of Europe* (Notre Dame, Ind.: Notre Dame University Press, 1963), p. 316.

5. Ferguson and Brunn, *loc. cit.*, p. 676.

6. *Ibid.*, pp. 669-674.

7. *Ibid.*, p. 647.

8. Carlton J. Hayes, Marshall Whithed Baldwin and Charles Woolsey Cole, *History of Western Civilization* (New York: Macmillan Co., 1967), pp. 630-631.

9. Denis Mack Smith, *Italy: A Modern History* (Ann Arbor: University of Michigan Press, 1959), pp. 27-37.

10. Koppel S. Pinson, *Modern Germany: Its History and Civilization* (New York: Macmillan Co., 1954), pp. 156-163.

11. John F. Kennedy, *A Nation of Immigrants* (New York: Harper and Row, 1964), p. 133.

12. Warren Bartlett Walsh, *Russia and the Soviet Union: A Modern History* (Ann Arbor: University of Michigan Press, 1958), pp. 246-264 *passim*.

13. Manfred Kridl, *Polska Myśl Demokratyczna w Ciągu Wieków* (New York: Gascony Printing Co., 1945), pp. 68-69.

14. *Ibid.*

15. Halecki, *op. cit.*, pp. 285-286, 305.

16. Lillian Parker Wallace, *The Papacy and Eastern Diplomacy* (Chapel Hill, N. C.: University of Carolina Press, 1948), pp. 147, 187.

17. Carlton J. Hayes, *A Political and Cultural History of Modern Europe* (New York: Macmillan Co., 1937), Vol. II, p. 604.

18. Agaton Giller, *Historia Powstania Narodu Polskiego* (Paryż: Księgarnia Luksemburska, 1870), Vol. III, p. 63.

19. *Ibid.*, p. 63: "Under date of April 20, 1832, the czar dispatched a note to the pope by his envoy in Rome, Prince Ivan Sergejevitch Gagarin, accusing the Polish uprising of Jacobin policies and subversive tendencies, and the clergy of collaboration, leadership in combat, and directing revolutionary operations—all of which was untrue . . . The pope was constantly deceived about the real conditions in Poland." Prince Gagarin became a convert to Catholicism in 1842 and entered the Society of Jesus (*Catholic Encyclopedia,* New York: Robert Appleton Co., 1909).

20. Ladislas Zamoyski, "Memoire sûr le Prince Adam Czartoryski," *Sacrum Poloniae Millennium* (Rzym: Typis Pontificiae Universitatis Gregorianae, 1955), Vol. II, pp. 193-203.

21. Giller, *op. cit.*, p. 64.

22. *Ibid.*, p. 67.

23. Sophie Olszamowska-Skowrońska, "Documents Pontificaux," *Sacrum Poloniae Millennium* (Rzym: Typis Pontificiae Universitatis Gregorianae, 1966), Vol. XII, pp. 403-435.

24. Józef Białynia Chołodecki, *Księga Pamiątkowa w 40stą Rocznicę Powstania 1863-1864* (Lwów: Piller i Spólka, 1904), p. 275: "Ladislas Sas Kulczycki, chamberlain of His Holiness Pius IX, cavalier of the Papal Order of the Golden Spur, commander of the Portuguese Order of the Immaculate Conception, officer of the Order of Megiddo, served as the secretary of the Polish diplomatic agency at the Holy See and subsequently became the accredited representative of Poland to the Holy See."

25. Andrew Beck, "Pius IX, Russia and Poland," *The Clergy Review*, XVIII (May, 1940), 416.

26. Hayes, Baldwin and Cole, *op. cit.*, pp. 619, 642.

27. Record of Birth and Baptism, No. 508, *Civil Register of St. Andrew Parish in Warsaw*, preserved in the national archives of the city of Warsaw.

28. *Ibid.*

29. Krzycki-Minasowicz, *Encyklopedyja Powszechna S. Orgelbranda* (Warszawa: Nakład. Druk i Własność S. Orgelbranda Synów, 1884), Vol. VII.

30. Giller, *op. cit.*, pp. 195-196.

31. Wincenty Sardi i Karol Sica, *Zywot Sługi Bożej Marji Franciszki Siedliskiej* (Kraków: Drukarnia "Glos Narodu," 1924), pp. 15-16.

32. S. M. Rozaria Bakanowicz, CSFN, "Okruchy Wspomnień z Rodzinnego Parku Matki Franciszki Siedliskiej w Żdżarach" (unpublished manuscript).

33. Stanisław Lencewicz, *Geografia Fizyczna Polski* (Warszawa: Państwowe Wydawnictwo Naukowe, 1955), p. 232.

34. Aleksander Janowski, *Warszawa (Poznań: Wydawnictwo Polskie,* 1946), p. 32.

35. Polish National Committee of America, *General Demography of Poland* (Geneva, Switzerland: Atar Ltd., 1921), p. 119.

36. Sardi-Sica, *op. cit.*, p. 16.

37. Wojciech Bryndza, *Kronika Parafii Żdżary: 1848-1875* (unpublished chronicle of the parish of Żdżary).

38. *Ibid.* The inscription on the plaque reads: "Dedicated by son-in-law to the memory of Joseph Morawski, privy councilor and founder of this church, who died on August 17, 1855. Pious mementos requested."

39. L'Abbé V. Kurtz, S.J., *Livre d'Or du Collège Saint-Clément* (Metz, Moselle, 1927). Adam Siedliski, as a former student of Collège du Saint-Clément, is listed in this publication with his date of birth.

40. Kasper Niesiecki, S.J., Herbarz Polski (Lipsk: Breitkopf i Haertel, 1841), Vol. VII, p. 331. "SIEDLISKI: armorial device 'Ostoja' (mainstay) consists of a crimson escutcheon with a silver sword centrally

placed in a vertical position with the hilt uppermost; the sword is flanked by two golden crescents with their convex edges lateral to the blade and their concave edges opening outward. The helmet over the escutcheon bears a coronet, adorned with five ostrich plumes. This coat of arms dates back to the reign of Boleslas the Bold."

41. Zbigniew Leszczyc, *Herby Szlachty Polskiej* (Poznań: Antoni Fiedler, 1908), Vol. II. Several collateral families by the name of MORAWSKI have the same essential heraldic insignia, only the embellishments differ. The armorial device of Cecilia's line of ancestors was " 'Dabrówka' (oakwood), represented in the azure field of the escutcheon by a silver horsehoe with the opening placed downward and three cavalier crosses, one surmounting the highest convex edge of the horseshoe, the other two extending outward from the ends of the horseshoe. The eschutcheon is embellished by a helmet with a coronet from which a lion rises carrying a battle-ax. The entire coat of arms is surrounded by oak leaves."

42. Amand von Schweiger Lerchenfeld, *Życie Kobiet na Ziemi*, Polish translation by L. Kaczyński (Warszawa: Redakcja "Przeglądu Tygodniowego," 1882), p. 444.

43. Mother Mary of Jesus the Good Shepherd, *Journal: 1842-1873* (unpublished manuscript).

44. Giller, *op. cit.,* p. 196.

45. Karolina Beylin, *Tajemnice Warszawy* (Warszawa: Państwowy Instytut Wydawniczy, 1956), 150.

46. Sardi-Sica, *op. cit.,* p. 86.

47. Mother Mary, *op. cit.*

48. *Ibid.* Frances recorded the religious apathy of her parents in this period, saying: "God did not reign in our home." As a matter of fact, Jan Dobraczyński, in his psychological treatise *Lepsza Cząstka* (Chicago: Stanek Press, 1949), pp. 26-27, concludes that the Siedliskis were not worse than their milieu, that undoubtedly they were better. Frances, however, writing her *Journal* between the years 1884 and 1887, as a mature religious and foundress, viewed her early home life from the exalted heights she had attained through union with God and extraordinary graces. From this perspective her early home life suffers by comparison.

49. X. A. M. (Tow. Krzyża św.), *Droga do Pozyskania Spokojności Sumienia i Wiekuistego Szczęścia w Niebie* (Warszawa: Nakładem i drukiem XX. Misjonarzy św. Krzyża, 1860), pp. 440. This is but one example of the type of exegetical works in Catholic doctrine and Christian living that began proliferating in this period in Poland for the instruction of the laity at all levels. Besides works written in the vernacular, pious books by reputable foreign authors were imported and widely read, many of which were also translated into Polish to meet a newly created demand.

50. Jan Bystroń, *Warszawa* (Warszawa: Wydawnictwo Józefa Kubickiego, 1953), pp. 203-204. The author quotes a newspaper article of 1857: "It is uncommon for a city of almost two hundred thousand population to be given to piety with such unanimity and honesty. Each Sunday

and holiday all the churches in Warsaw are crowded to capacity. The elite of the capital worship particularly at the Capuchins, at the Canonesses of St. Augustine, and at the church of St. Alexander; the churches of the Bernardines and the Franciscans are also densely attended, as are the churches of the nuns of the Visitation and of the Blessed Sacrament."

51. *Ibid.,* pp. 55, 158.

52. Giller, *op. cit.,* p. 120.

53. Sardi-Sica, *op. cit.,* pp. 20-21, 22, 29-30.

54. Zofia Kossak-Szczucka, *Rok Polski: Obyczaj i Wiara* (Londyn: Biblioteka Polska, 1955), pp. 144-149.

55. Sardi-Sica, *op. cit.,* p. 16.

56. Mother Mary, *op. cit.*

57. *Ibid.*

58. *Ibid.*

59. Sardi-Sica, *op. cit.,* p. 22.

60. Mother Mary, *op. cit.*

61. Sardi-Sica, *op. cit.,* p. 23.

62. Mother Mary, *op. cit.*

63. *Ibid.*

64. Sardi-Sica, *op. cit.,* p. 30.

65. S. M. Augustine Pietrzykowska, CSFN, "Reminiscences from the Life of Mother Mary of Jesus the Good Shepherd" (unpublished manuscript).

66. Mother Mary, *op. cit.* [The church and the statue in the church square are still in existence.]

67. S. M. Augustine, *op. cit.*

68. Mother Mary, *op. cit.*

69. Death Record No. 15, *Parish Death Register of Żdżary for the year 1855.*

70. Mother Mary, *op. cit.*

71. *Ibid.*

72. Sardi-Sica, *op. cit.,* p. 41.

73. Mother Mary, *op. cit.*

74. *Ibid.*

75. Sardi-Sica, *op. cit.,* p. 49.

76. Mother Mary, *op. cit.*

77. Sardi-Sica, *op. cit.,* pp. 62-63, 64.

78. Mother Mary, *op. cit.*

79. *Ibid.*

80. Sardi-Sica, *op. cit.,* p. 69.

81. Mother Mary, *op. cit.*

82. *Ibid.*

83. *Ibid.*

84. Sardi-Sica, *op. cit.,* p. 64.

85. Mother Mary, *op. cit.*

86. Sardi-Sica, *op. cit.,* pp. 74-77.

87. Jan Dobraczyński, *Lepsza Cząstka* (Chicago: Stanek Press, 1949), p. 32.

88. Chołodecki, *op. cit.,* p. 77.

89. Edmund Oppman, *Wodzowie Polski* (Warszawa: Instytut Propagandy Państwowo-Twórczej, 1935), p. 302.

90. H. Sutherland Edwards, *The Private History of a Polish Insurrection* (London: Saunders, Otley & Co., 1865), Vol. I, pp. 44-45, 47, 48, 53-55. Referring to the first visit of Alexander II in 1856, Edwards comments that the czar ". . . insulted the Poles: 'Above all, no dreams. I shall know how to restrain those who give themselves up to them. . . What my father [Nicholas I] did, was well done, and I shall maintain it. My reign will be a continuation of his.' This language chilled the hearts of every Pole who heard it. They reflected now that the reign of Alexander II was to be the continuation of the odious reign of Nicholas I."

91. Mother Mary, *op. cit.* This is confirmed by l'Abbe V. Kurtz, S.J., in his letter to Mother Lauretta, Superior General of the Sisters of the Holy Family of Nazareth, dated January 15, 1927 at Collège Saint-Clément, 28 rue du Pontiffroy, Metz (Moselle), France: "J'ai dans mes fiches: *'Adam Siedliski,* né le 27 octobre 1846, a Varsovie, élève a Saint Clément 1860-1864.' "

92. Mother Mary, *op. cit.*

93. *Ibid.*

94. *Ibid.*

95. *Ibid.*

96. *Ibid.*

97. Sardi-Sica, *op. cit.,* p. 88.

98. Chołodecki, *op. cit.,* p. 18.

99. *Ibid.,* p. 28: "For security reasons, civilian and military leaders used assumed names; their identity was known to the inner circle of higher ranking officials. Frequently the same name was used by more than one person for additional protection."

100. Sardi-Sica, *op. cit.,* pp. 87-88.

101. Mother M. Gabriel Lubowidzka and Mother M. Joanne Ziętkiewicz, "Memoirs" (unpublished manuscripts).

102. Sardi-Sica, *op. cit.,* p. 89.

103. Walsh, *op. cit.,* p. 269.

104. Mother Mary, op. cit.

105. Chołodecki, *op. cit.,* pp. 72, 73.

106. Stanisław Grzegorzewski, *Wspomnienia Osobiste z Powstania 1863 r.* (Lwów: Tow. Wydawnicze, 1903), pp. 188-200.

107. Sardi-Sica, *op. cit.,* p. 86.

108. Mother Mary, *op. cit.*

109. *Ibid.*

110. Sardi-Sica, *op. cit.,* p. 93.

111. Joseph Hube, C.R. (1805-1891): professor of Roman Law at the University of Warsaw; in 1838 studied theology in Rome; in 1842 ordained to the priesthood; 1845-1857 second Superior General of the

Congregation of the Resurrection. In an entry for 1856, Mother Mary mentions in her *Journal* having read his book on frequent Holy Communion. *O Częstej Komunii św.* (Roma: Propaganda Fide, 1855).

112. Mother Mary, *op. cit.*

113. Sardi-Sica, *op. cit.*, p. 104.

114. Arthur H. Douthwaite, M.D., ed., *French's Index of Differential Diagnosis* (Baltimore: Williams and Wilkins Co., 1967), ninth edition, p. 91.

115. Paul B. Beeson, M.D. and Walsh McDermott, M.D., ed., *Cecil-Loeb Textbook of Medicine* (Philadelphia and London: W. B. Saunders Co., 1967), twelfth edition, p. 274.

116. J. S. Speed, M.D. and Robert A. Knight, M.D., ed., *Campbell's Operative Orthopaedics* (St. Louis: C. V. Mosby Co., 1956), pp. 1203-1204.

117. W. A. Newman Dorland, M.D., *Illustrated Medical Dictionary* (Philadelphia and London: W. B. Saunders Co., 1957), twenty-third edition.

118. Father Lucas of St. Joseph, O.C.D., *The Secret of Sanctity of St. John of the Cross* (Milwaukee: Bruce Publishing Co., 1962), pp. 125-126.

119. Dom Hubert Van Zeller, O.S.B., *Suffering in Other Words* (Springfield, Ill.: Templegate Publishers, 1964), pp. 20, 24.

120. Sardi-Sica, *op. cit.*, p. 105.

121. Mother M. Raphael Lubowidzka, "Ojciec Leander Lendzian, Kapucyn" (unpublished manuscript, 1913): Father Leander was known in civilian life as Leopold Lendzian; born in 1816 in Pułtusk, Poland; died in 1890 in Cracow. He served on the staff of the National Treasury Commission in Warsaw; in 1841 he was imprisoned in the citadel for alleged subversive activities; upon release, he entered the Capuchin Order in 1848 and was ordained to the priesthood in 1851.

122. Sardi-Sica, *op. cit.*, p. 105.

123. *Ibid.*, p. 106.

124. *Ibid.*, pp. 110-11.

125. Mother Mary, *op. cit.*

126. Sister M. Augustine, *op. cit.*

127. The mausoleum is still in existence at the cemetery in Żdżary. Four caskets are in the crypt, including that of Adam Siedliski who died in 1893. The inscription above the chapel entrance reads: "Grób Rodziny Siedliskich (Tomb of the Siedliski Family)" and within there is a plaque stating: "Adolfowi Siedliskiemu—Matka, Żona i Dzieci, 1870 (To the memory of Adolphe Siedliski—Mother, Wife and Children, 1870)."

128. Mother Mary, *op. cit.*

129. *Ibid.*

130. Sardi-Sica, *op. cit.* pp. 114-115, 127-128.

131. Beeson and McDermott, *op. cit.*, p. 274. These procedures were much employed prior to the antimicrobial era, but have now been discarded.

132. Sardi-Sica, *op. cit.,* pp. 118-119.

133. Mother Mary, *op. cit.*

134. Mother M. Gabriel Lubowidzka and Mother M. Raphael Lubo-widzka, "Życiorys Świątobliwej Matki Marii Franciszki Siedliskiej" (un-published manuscript, 1912).

135. *Ibid.*

136. *Ibid.*

137. *Ibid.*

138. *Ibid.*

139. Sardi-Sica, *op. cit.,* pp. 125-126.

140. Mother Mary, *op. cit.*

141. *Ibid.*

142. *Ibid.*

143. *Ibid.*

144. *Ibid.*

145. Mothers Gabriel and Raphael, *op. cit.*

146. Mother Mary of Jesus the Good Shepherd, "Report to the First General Chapter of the Sisters of the Holy Family of Nazareth, held in Chaville, France, from August 25 to September 5, 1895" (unpublished manuscript).

147. Mother Mary, *Journal.*

148. J. A. Birkhaeuser, *History of the Church* (New York and Cin-cinnati: Pustet, 1893), pp. 711-712: "Diplomatic stipulations proved no bar to Russian intolerance and the Catholics of the conquered districts [of Poland] were subjected to fierce and constant persecution on the part of the imperial government . . . All possible means that fanaticism and brutal force could devise were employed by the Moscovite Government to separate them from Rome."

149. *Ibid.,* pp. 692-694: "May Laws of 1873 aimed at the complete dissolution of the Catholic Church in Prussia . . . The next act of tyranny was the expulsion of some nine thousand religious, about eight thousand of whom were women, in accordance with the law which suppressed all existing religious orders and congregations and interdicted all future foundations of the same in Prussia. These laws were enforced in Prussian-dominated section of Poland with equal severity."

150. Sardi-Sica, *op. cit.,* p. 136.

151. J. B. Goetstouwers, S.J., *Synopsis Historiae Societatis Jesu* (Lovanii: Typis ad Sancti Alphonsi, 1950). Joseph Laurençot, S.J. (1824-1899).

152. Sister M. Augustine, *op. cit.*

153. Mère Marie de Jésus (Countess Emilie d'Oultremont, widow of Baron d'Hooghvorst) founded in France, in 1857, the Society of Mary Reparatrix whose aim is to offer atonement to God, in union with the Blessed Virgin Mary, through perpetual adoration of the Blessed Sacra-ment. Its apostolate includes catechetical instructions and retreats for laywomen. She died in Florence in 1878.

154. Under date of September 26, 1873, Mother Mary of Jesus the

Good Shepherd compiled a series of notes entitled, "Du Noviciat Mystique," which are preserved in original manuscript in the archives of the Generalate of the Sisters of the Holy Family of Nazareth.

155. Sister M. Augustine, *op. cit.*
156. *Ibid.*
157. Joseph Burnichon, S.J., *Vie du P. Fr.-X. Gautrelet, S.J.* (Paris: Retaux, 1896). Father Gautrelet (1807-1886) was also the author of *Nature et Obligations de l'état Religieux* and of *Nouveau Mois du Sacré Coeur de Jésus.*
158. Sister M. Augustine, *op. cit.*

PART II
(Pages 27-129)

1. Mother Mary of Jesus the Good Shepherd, "Report to the First General Chapter of the Sisters of the Holy Family of Nazareth, held in Chaville, France, from August 25 to September 5, 1895" (unpublished manuscript).
2. Louis Lescoeur, Père de l'Oratoire, *L'Eglise Catholique en Pologne sous le Gouvernement Russe depuis le Premier Partage jusqu'à nos jours: 1772-1875* (Paris: Plon, 1876), vol. II, p. 170.
3. When the aged archbishop Fijałkowski died, his successor to the see of Warsaw was archbishop Sigismond Felix Feliński (1882-1895), consecrated January 14, 1862. One year later he was condemned to a twenty-year exile into Russia for conducting correspondence with the pope. At his liberation he was required by the Russian government to renounce his claim to the see of Warsaw and to remain outside its confines. Pius IX named him titular archbishop of Tarsus. His cause of beatification is in progress.
4. Lescoeur, *loc. cit.*
5. Mother M. Raphael Lubowidzka, "Ojciec Leander Lendzian, Kapucyn" (unpublished manuscript, 1913).
6. Mother M. Gabriel Lubowidzka and Mother M. Raphael Lubowidzka, "Życiorys Świątobliwej Matki Marii Franciszki Siedliskiej" (unpublished manuscript, 1912).
7. J. A. Birkhaeuser, *History of the Church* (New York and Cincinnati: Pustet, 1893), p. 674.
8. Karolina Beylin, *Jeden Rok Warszawy: 1875* (Warszawa: Polski Instytut Wydawniczy, 1959), p. 253.
9. Mothers Gabriel and Raphael, *op. cit.*
10. *Ibid.*
11. Anthony Ricciardi, O.F.M. Conv., postulator for the beatification of Mother Mary of Jesus the Good Shepherd, in a conference on her virtue of faith, delivered at the Generalate in Rome, January 21, 1968, stated: "If your motherhouse is in Rome, it is not for the same reason as that for which many religious communities are here, that is for practical purposes, to have easier contact with the Holy See and with the

Roman Curia. Your motherhouse is here because of your Foundress's attachment to the Church. She wanted to begin the work of founding her community with the Holy Father's blessing. Your community was born in Rome because of the love of your Mother Foundress for the Church and for the Holy Father. This is a very important point when the sanctity of a founder or foundress is being considered."

12. Marie Cuny; she withdrew after one year.

13. Following the death of Victor Emmanuel II, who was proclaimed the first king of united Italy (reigning 1861-1878), a large space—now the hub of Rome known as Piazza Venezia—was cleared for the erection of a huge impressive monument of white marble to his honor. It was being built between 1885 and 1911. In the process of construction a number of old streets, including Via Giulio Romano, disappeared from this district, although other landmarks like the church of Santa Maria d'Aracoeli remained intact.

14. Peter Semeneńko, C.R. (1814-1886) maintained a *Diary* from June, 1851 until his death. It is a source of abundant information and contains numerous references to Mother Mary of Jesus the Good Shepherd and her congregation for the period between April, 1875 and April, 1885.

15. After the Second Vatican Council the title of "Sacred Congregation of the Holy Office" was changed to "Sacred Congregation for the Doctrine of the Faith."

16. Semeneńko, *Diary*.

17. Mother Mary of Jesus the Good Shepherd, letter to Peter Semeneńko, C.R., Rome, September 19, 1875.

18. Mothers Gabriel and Raphael, *op. cit.*

19. *Ibid.*

20. Semeneńko, *Diary*.

21. Mothers Gabriel and Raphael, *op. cit.*

22. Semeneńko, *Diary*.

23. Mothers Gabriel and Raphael, *op. cit.*

24. Mother Mary of Jesus the Good Shepherd, letter to Peter Semeneńko, C.R., Rome, August 28, 1875.

25. Semeneńko, *Diary*.

26. Mothers Gabriel and Raphael, *op. cit.*

27. Mother Mary of Jesus the Good Shepherd, letter to Peter Semeneńko, C.R., Rome, August 13, 1875.

28. Mother Mary of Jesus the Good Shepherd, letter to Peter Semeneńko, C.R., Rome, October 24, 1875.

29. Semeneńko, *Diary*.

30. Eleonore Rembiszewska, Sister M. Josepha of the Seven Dolors of Our Lady (1852-1932).

31. Mothers Gabriel and Raphael, *op. cit.*

32. *Ibid.*

33. Mother Mary of Jesus the Good Shepherd, letter to Peter Semeneńko, C.R., Lyons, September 9, 1876.

34. Mother of Mary of Jesus the Good Shepherd, letters to Peter

Semeneńko, C.R., St. Germain, September 24 and October 10, 1876.

35. Mother Mary of Jesus the Good Shepherd, letter to Peter Semeneńko, C.R., Lourdes, November 18, 1876.

36. Eliza Müller; she withdrew after one year.

37. Mother Mary, "Report to the First General Chapter."

38. Thecla Lubowidzka (1862-1942), later became Mother M. Lauretta of the Nativity of Our Lord and the superior general succeeding Mother Mary.

39. Mathilda Sosińska, who was named Sister M. Salomea, withdrew in 1880.

40. Kenneth MacGowan, *The House of Loreto* (Dublin: Kamac Publications, 1964), pp. 3-9 *passim*.

41. Fr. Eugene, O.F.M.Cap., *Guide to Loreto* (Loreto: Congregazione Universale della S. Casa, 1965), pp. 11-13.

42. Mother Mary of Jesus the Good Shepherd, "On Simplicity in Exterior Conduct," *Conferences* (Rome, 1968), pp. 88-95 *passim*.

43. Mother Mary, "Report to the First General Chapter."

44. Mother Mary of Jesus the Good Shepherd, letter dated August 27, 1877.

45. Mother Mary, "On the Order of Daily Duties," *Conferences*, pp. 71-76 *passim*.

46. Mother Gabriel Lubowidzka, "Chronicle: 1877-1880" (unpublished manuscript).

47. *Ibid.*

48. *Ibid.*

49. Wanda Lubowidzka, Mother M. Michael of the Blessed Sacrament (1844-1886); Laura Lubowidzka, Mother M. Gabriel of the Infant Jesus (1847-1927); Felicia Lubowidzka, Mother M. Raphael of the Sacred Heart of Jesus (1850-1921).

50. Mothers Gabriel and Raphael, *op. cit.*

51. *Ibid.*

52. Mother Mary, "On Christ's Hidden Life in Nazareth," *Conferences*, pp. 26-28 *passim*.

53. Mother Mary, "On the Religious Vows," *Conferences*, pp. 109-119 *passim*.

54. Mother Gabriel Lubowidzka, "Chronicle: 1879-1881" (unpublished manuscript).

55. Mary I. M. Bell, *A Short History of the Papacy to 1903* (New York: Dodd, Mead and Co., 1921), p. 383.

56. Mother Gabriel, "Chronicle: 1877-1880" (unpublished manuscript).

57. Semeneńko, *Diary.*

58. Mother Mary of Jesus the Good Shepherd, *Notes Journalieres: Année 1878* (unpublished manuscript).

59. *Ibid.*

60. Charles J. O'Malley, ed., *The Great White Shepherd of Christendom* (Chicago: J. S. Hyland & Company, 1903), pp. 212-224 *passim*.

61. Francis T. Furey, *Life of Leo XIII and History of His Pontificate* (New York and Philadelphia: Catholic Educational Company, 1903), p. 338.

62. Mother Gabriel, *op. cit.*

63. Liberata Lanciotti, Sister M. Luigia of the Resurrection of Christ (1852-1919): entered October 7, 1878.

64. Mother Gabriel, *op. cit.*

65. *Ibid.*

66. Mother Mary of Jesus the Good Shepherd, letter to Mother Gabriel Lubowidzka, August 16, 1879.

67. Mother Mary of Jesus the Good Shepherd, letter to Mother Raphael Lubowidzka, August, 1879.

68. Mother Gabriel, *op. cit.*

69. Reisswitz sisters: Hedwig (Sister M. Assumpta) and Wanda (Sister M. Immaculata); admitted April 2, 1879; dismissed September 24, 1879.

70. Mother Mary of Jesus the Good Shepherd, joint letter to Father Leander and Brother Stephen, Rome, April 17, 1884.

71. *Ibid.*

72. Mother Gabriel, *op. cit.*

73. Mother Mary, joint letter to Father Leander and Brother Stephen.

74. Mother Mary of Jesus the Good Shepherd, *Notes Journalieres: Année 1880* (unpublished manuscript).

75. Furey, *op. cit.*, p. 195.

76. *Plan Abrégé de l'Institut de Marie á Nazareth.*

77. Mother Gabriel, *op. cit.*

78. Mother Mary of Jesus the Good Shepherd, letter to Mother Raphael, September 21, 1880.

79. Mother Gabriel, "Fundacja w Krakowie (Foundation in Cracow): 1880-1883" (unpublished manuscript).

80. Mother Gabriel, "Chronicle: 1877-1880."

81. Maria Ziętkiewicz, originally named Alcantara; later her name was changed to Joanne of the Cross (1847-1915).

82. Alodia Malentynowicz, originally named Bernardina; later her name was changed to Bernarda of the Nativity of the Blessed Virgin Mary (1856-1936).

83. Hedwig Zatorska, Sister M. Antonine, novice (1848-1881).

84. Mother Gabriel, "Chronicle," *op. cit.*

85. Mother Gabriel, "Fundacja w Krakowie."

86. Mother M. Bernarda Malentynowicz, "Chronicle: 1883-1884."

87. Semeneńko, *Diary.*

88. Mother M. Joanne Ziętkiewicz, "Notatki z dziejów naszego ukochanego Nazaretu (Memoirs): 1880-1913" (unpublished manuscript).

89. Mother Gabriel, "Fundacja w Krakowie."

90. *Ibid.*

91. *Ibid.*

92. Mother Joanne, *op. cit.*

93. Mother Gabriel, "Rok Łaski (Year of Grace): 1883-1884" (unpublished manuscript).

94. Mother Gabriel, "Fundacja w Krakowie."

95. Mother M. Columba Trzewiczek, "Chronicle: 1882-1884" (unpublished manuscript).

96. Brother William J. Kiefer, S.M., *Leo XIII: A Light from Heaven* (Milwaukee: Bruce Publishing Company, 1961), pp. 169-173.

97. Mother Bernarda, *op. cit.*

98. Furey, *op. cit.,* p. 103.

99. Mother Columba, *op.* cit.

100. Mother Bernarda, *op. cit.*

101. Mother Gabriel, "Rok Łaski."

102. Josepha Łuszczewska, Sister M. Baptista, admitted November 8, 1882, dismissed August 18, 1884; readmitted September 21, 1884, dismissed second time February 16, 1885.

103. Mother Gabriel, "Rok Łaski."

104. *Ibid.*

105. Mother Mary of Jesus the Good Shepherd, letter to Father Anthony M. Lechert, January 7, 1884.

106. Mother Columba, *op. cit.*

107. Mother Gabriel, "Rok Łaski."

108. Semeneńko, *Diary.*

109. Mother Gabriel, "Rok Łaski."

110. *Ibid.*

111. Mother Bernarda, *op. cit.*

112. *Ibid.*

113. Anthony Lechert, "Alcune date della mia vita, 1845-1906" (unpublished manuscript): 1874, laurea utriusque juris; 1885, laurea in S. Theologia.

114. *Ibid.*

115. Mother Gabriel, "Rok Łaski."

116. Thecla Trzewiczek, Sister M. Columba of the Presentation of Our Lord in the Temple (1863-1914); she received the permanent title "Mother" in 1890.

117. Janine Czoppe, Sister M. Angela of the Holy Trinity; originally she was named Benedicta, but the name was changed to Angela on the day of her first profession, March 25, 1884. She withdrew from the Congregation in 1899.

118. Mother Bernarda, *op. cit.*

119. Mother Mary of Jesus the Good Shepherd, letter to the sisters in Cracow, Poland, written in Rome, May 2, 1884.

120. Mother Columba, *op. cit.*

121. Mother Gabriel, "Rok Łaski."

122. *Ibid.*

123. *Ibid.*

124. Mother Mary of Jesus the Good Shepherd, "Report to the First General Chapter."

125. Mother Gabriel, "Rok Łaski."

126. Anna Parzyk, Sister M. Philomena (1862-1885); the first sister who died in the United States.

127. Mother Mary of Jesus the Good Shepherd, "Report to the First General Chapter."

128. Mother Gabriel, "Journal of the house in Rome: 1885" (unpublished manuscript).

129. Mother Raphael and Mother Bernarda, "Chronicle of the house in Cracow: 1883-1886" (unpublished manuscript).

130. *Ibid.*

131. *Ibid.*

132. Mother M. Lauretta, "Początki Pracy Misyjnej Nazaretu w Ameryce (The Beginnings of Nazareth Mission in America): 1885" (unpublished manuscript).

133. *Ibid.*

134. Kiefer, *op. cit.,* p. 157.

135. Msgr. John Tracy Ellis, *American Catholicism* (Chicago: University of Chicago Press, 1956), p. 101.

136. Furey, *op. cit.,* p. 357.

137. Ellis, *op. cit.,* p. 102.

138. Allen S. Will, *Life of James Cardinal Gibbons* (Baltimore and New York: John Murphy Company, 1911), p. 107.

139. Vincent Michael Barzyński, C.R., letter to Father Anthony Lechert, Chicago, October 13, 1884.

140. John Iwicki, C.R., *Resurrectionist Studies: The First One Hundred Years, 1866-1966* (Rome: Gregorian University Press, 1966), pp. 28-61, *passim.*

141. James Washington Sheahan, *The Great Conflagration* (Philadelphia: Union Publishing Co., 1871).

142. Iwicki, *op. cit.,* pp. 61-62.

143. Barzyński, *op. cit.*

144. Mother Gabriel, "Journal of the House in Rome: 1885."

145. Mother Lauretta, *op. cit.*

146. Mother Mary of Jesus the Good Shepherd, diary, July 9, 1885.

147. Mother Lauretta, *op. cit.*

148. *Ibid.*

149. *Ibid.*

150. Mother Mary of Jesus the Good Shepherd, letter to Mother Joanne, Chicago, July 12, 1885.

151. Mother Mary of Jesus the Good Shepherd, diary, July 27, 1885.

152. Mother Mary of Jesus the Good Shepherd, *Rozmowy z Panem Jezusem,* unpublished manuscript (*Dialogues with Jesus*); entries in this intimate record of her reflections lay bare her soul before the sight of God with rare openness and sensitivity to the demands of faith.

153. Mother Mary of Jesus the Good Shepherd, diary, July 27, 1885.

154. Sister M. Theresa Czermińska, "Kronika Fundacji w Ameryce przy parafii św. Józafata: 13. VI—4. X. 1885" (Chronicle of the American Foundation in St. Josaphat Parish: June 13 to October 4, 1885), unpublished manuscript).

155. Mother Mary of Jesus the Good Shepherd, letter to Mother Gabriel, Chicago, September 2, 1885.

156. Mother Lauretta, *op. cit.*

157. Sister Theresa, *op. cit.*

158. Albertina Szopińska, Sister M. Martina of the Assumption of Our Lady (1862-1928).

159. Balbina Dańczyk, Sister M. Rose of Divine Love (1870-1954).

160. Christina Konior, Sister M. Hedwig of the Patronage of St. Joseph (1864-1937).

161. Mother Mary of Jesus the Good Shepherd, letter to Mother Gabriel, Chicago, September 2, 1885.

162. Mother Lauretta, *op. cit.*

163. Archdiocese of Chicago, Doc. #4, 1885.

164. Mother Lauretta, *op. cit.*

165. Sister M. Paula Czarnowska, "Kronika Domu Najśw. Maryi Panny przy parafii św. Wojciecha: 1885-1886" (Chronicle of the Convent of the Blessed Virgin Mary in St. Adalbert Parish: 1885-1886), unpublished manuscript.

166. Sister Theresa, *op. cit.*

167. Mother M. Raphael Lubowidzka, "Kronika Domu św. Józefa, od 9 marca 1886 do 18 maja 1888" (Chronicle of St. Joseph Convent: March 9, 1886 to May 18, 1888), unpublished manuscript.

168. Mother Mary of Jesus the Good Shepherd, letter to Mother Joanne, Paris, October 19, 1885.

169. Mother Mary of Jesus the Good Shepherd, letter to Mother Joanne, Loreto, October 30, 1885.

170. Mother Mary of Jesus the Good Shepherd, letter to Mother Joanne, Rome, December 21, 1885.

171. Mother Mary of Jesus the Good Shepherd, letter to Mother Joanne, Rome, June 21, 1886.

172. Mother Mary of Jesus the Good Shepherd, letter to Mother Raphael, Rome, March 10, 1886.

173. Mother M. Raphael Lubowidzka, letter to Mother Mary of Jesus the Good Shepherd, Chicago, March 9, 1886.

174. Mother Mary of Jesus the Good Shepherd, letter to Mother Raphael, Rome, February 3, 1886.

175. Mother M. Raphael, letter to Mother Mary of Jesus the Good Shepherd, Chicago, March 19, 1886.

176. Mother Mary of Jesus the Good Shepherd, diary, January 1, 1886.

177. Mother M. Raphael, letter to Mother Mary of Jesus the Good Shepherd, Chicago, May 17, 1886.

178. Mother M. Raphael, letter to Mother Mary of Jesus the Good Shepherd, Chicago, November 17, 1887.

179. Lechert, *op. cit.,* July 9, 1886.

180. Mother Mary of Jesus the Good Shepherd, letter to Mother Michael, Rome, August 15, 1884.

181. November 18, 1886.

182. Rev. John Radziejewski, letter to Father Lechert, Chicago, November 11, 1886.

183. Mother M. Bernarda, "Chronicle, Rome: 1886-1887" (unpublished manuscript).

184. Massimo Salvadori, *Italy* (Englewood Cliffs, New Jersey: Prentice-Hall, Inc., 1965), pp. 113-115.

185. Mother M. Gabriel, "Rok Opieki Bożej (Year of Divine Protection): 1887 (unpublished manuscript).

186. Mother Bernarda, *op. cit.*

187. Furey, *op. cit.,* p. 252.

188. Mother Bernarda, *op. cit.*

189. "This Congregation of the Daughters of the Holy Family of Nazareth shall always acknowledge Our Lord Jesus Christ, who called them by his divine love, as their Founder, Master and King and shall be totally consecrated to his service and love," Original *Constitutions,* Part I, Chapter I, Article 1.

190. Mother Mary of Jesus the Good Shepherd, letter to Mother Raphael, Rome, November 23, 1887.

191. Mother Mary of Jesus the Good Shepherd, letter to Sister Columba, Rome, August 24, 1887.

192. Mother Mary of Jesus the Good Shepherd, "Chronique de la Maison-Mère, 1889" (unpublished manuscript).

193. Mother Bernarda, *op. cit.*

194. Furey, *op. cit.,* pp. 258-272 *passim.*

195. Mother Mary of Jesus the Good Shepherd, letter to Mother Joanne, Rome, September 24, 1887.

196. Mother Mary of Jesus the Good Shepherd, letter to Mother Joanne, Rome, November 18, 1887.

197. The name of St. Petersburg was changed in 1914 to Petrograd, and in 1924 to Leningrad. In 1918 the capital of Russia was moved to Moscow.

198. Franciszek Rutkowski, *Arcybiskup Jan Cieplak* (Warszawa: Drukarnia Archidiecezjalna, 1934), pp. 214-266 *passim.* Father Cieplak was the future Archbishop of Vilna and confessor-martyr under the Bolshevik regime.

199. Mother Mary of Jesus the Good Shepherd, letter to Sister Lauretta, Rome, January 2, 1889.

200. Mother Mary of Jesus the Good Shepherd, letter to Father Lechert, August 16, 1888.

201. Mother Mary of Jesus the Good Shepherd, letter to Mother Joanne, Rome, February 2, 1888.

202. Mother Mary of Jesus the Good Shepherd, letter to Mother Joanne, Rome, July 30, 1886.

203. Mother Mary of Jesus the Good Shepherd, letter to Sister Lauretta, Rome, July 11, 1888.

204. Mother Mary of Jesus the Good Shepherd, letter to Sister Lauretta, Rome, June 6, 1888.

205. Mother Mary of Jesus the Good Shepherd, letter to Sister Lauretta, Rome, June 20, 1888.

206. *Kronika Domu Najśw. Panny* (Chronicle of the Convent of Our Lady) Chicago: 1885-1895 (unpublished manuscript).

207. Mother Mary of Jesus the Good Shepherd, "Report to the First General Chapter."

208. Mother Mary of Jesus the Good Shepherd, letter to Sister Lauretta, Albano, October 4, 1888.

209. Mother Mary of Jesus the Good Shepherd, letter to Sister Lauretta, Rome, January 2, 1889.

210. Mother Raphael letter to Mother Gabriel, Albano, September 24, 1888.

211. Iwicki, *op. cit.,* p. 79.

212. Sister Lauretta, letter to Mother Mary of Jesus the Good Shepherd, Chicago, January 9, 1889.

213. Mother Mary of Jesus the Good Shepherd, letter to Sister Lauretta, Rome, November 28, 1888.

214. Mother Mary of Jesus the Good Shepherd, letter to Sister Lauretta, Rome, February 6, 1889.

215. Lechert, *op. cit.*

216. Sister Lauretta, letter to Mother Raphael, Chicago, December 30, 1888.

217. Sister Lauretta, letter to Mother Mary of Jesus the Good Shepherd, Chicago, August 5, 1888.

218. Mother Mary of Jesus the Good Shepherd, letter to Sister Lauretta, Rome, January 17, 1889.

219. Mother Mary of Jesus the Good Shepherd, letter to Sister Lauretta, Rome, April 24, 1889.

220. Mother Mary of Jesus the Good Shepherd, letter to Sister Lauretta, Rome, May 8, 1889.

221. Mother of Mary of Jesus the Good Shepherd, "Report to the First General Chapter."

222. Anna Grudzińska, Sister M. Bronislaus of the Holy Face (1866-1939).

223. Angela Kulawik, Sister M. Sophia of Jesus in Gethsemane (1864-1943).

224. Maria Keyha, Sister M. Leontine of the Transfiguration (1858-1917).

225. Mother Mary of Jesus the Good Shepherd, "Report to the First General Chapter."

226. Sister Lauretta, letter to Mother Mary of Jesus the Good Shepherd, Chicago, April 7, 1889.

227. *Diamond Jubilee Memoir of Sacred Hearts of Jesus and Mary Parish, Scranton, Pa., 1885-1960.*

228. Anthony Lechert, open letter to the sisters in the United States, Rome, June 15, 1889.

229. Mother Mary, "On the Spirit of Sacrifice and Mortification," *Conferences.* pp. 304-307 *passim.*

230. Mother Mary, "On the Goal of the Congregation," *Conferences,* pp. 12-15 *passim.*

231. Mother Mary, "On Interior Relationship with Our Divine Lord," *Conferences,* pp. 220-223 *passim.*

232. Mother Mary, "On the Spirit of Nazareth," *Conferences,* pp. 17-20.

233. *Ibid.,* pp. 20-22.

234. Mother Mary of Jesus the Good Shepherd, letter to Father Lechert, Chicago, September 7, 1889.

235. Mother Mary of Jesus the Good Shepherd, "Report to the First General Chapter."

236. Reverend Adolphe Śnigurski, letter to Father Lechert, Scranton, July 18, 1889.

237. *Wiara i Ojczyzna* (Faith and Fatherland), August 7, 1889.

238. Rome, July 16, 1889.

239. Rome, July 17, 1889.

240. The contents of the cornerstone cassette were examined by the author after the razing of the building which was accomplished on February 5, 1964.

241. Mother Mary of Jesus the Good Shepherd, letter to Father Lechert, Chicago, August 5, 1889.

242. Mother Mary, "On Interior Relationship with Our Divine Lord," *Conferences,* p. 222.

243. *Kronika Domu Najśw. Panny.*

244. Maria Czarnowska, Sister M. Paula of the Blessed Sacrament (1851-1913).

245. Emma Morgenstern, Sister M. Frances of the Holy Spirit (1865-1946). Throughout her lifetime her actual surname was not generally known. It was necessary to eliminate possible clues leading to her person and to protect her against the threatened pursuit by members of her family who objected vehemently to her becoming a Catholic and a religious.

246. Josepha Sierpińska, Sister M. Stanislaus of the Immaculate Heart of Mary (1863-1912).

247. Sister M. Theresa Czermińska, letter to Mother Joanne, Chicago, September 2, 1889.

248. *Constitutions* (original), Part II, Chapter I, Article 3.

249. *Drogą Ukrycia i Ofiary* (Rome: privately published, 1951), p. 65.

250. Mother Lauretta, letter to Mother Mary of Jesus the Good Shepherd, Scranton, September 12, 1889.

251. Mother Mary of Jesus the Good Shepherd, letters to Father Lechert, Chicago, September 13 and 17, 1889.

252. Mother Mary of Jesus the Good Shepherd, letter to Father Lechert, Chicago, September 23, 1889, ". . . de votre courage, que vous n'avez pas cédé à cette foule; il ne faut jamais descendre à leur niveau, mais se tenit au dessus d'eux, et quoique avoir bonté et charité, mais les gouverner et ne pas leur céder."

253. *Ibid.*

254. *St. Josaphat's Diamond Jubilee Memoir, 1884-1959.*

255. Mother Mary of Jesus the Good Shepherd, "Report to the First General Chapter."

256. Mother Mary of Jesus the Good Shepherd, "Report of the Visitation in the United States, 1889-1890."

257. *Ibid.*

258. Mother Mary of Jesus the Good Shepherd, letter to Mother Gabriel, Chicago, October 24, 1889.

259. O'Malley, *op. cit.*, pp. 282-283.

260. Mother Mary of Jesus the Good Shepherd, "Report to the First General Chapter," as also "Report of the Visitation in the United States, 1889-1890;" and Mother M. Lauretta, "Provincial Report to the First General Chapter."

261. *Ibid.*

262. Mother Mary of Jesus the Good Shepherd, letter to Mother Lauretta, Albano, September 17, 1890.

263. Mother Lauretta, letter to Mother Mary of Jesus the Good Shepherd, Chicago, August 13, 1890.

264. The School Sisters of Notre Dame conducted Holy Family Orphanage, until July, 1899, at which time the children were transferred to St. Joseph's Home in charge of the Franciscan Sisters of Bl. Kunegunda. The Holy Family Orphange building became St. Stanislaus College for boys, conducted by the Resurrectionist Fathers; in 1930 it was renamed Weber High School, and in 1952 it was reorganized as Gordon Technical High School.

On August 11, 1961, the Congregation of the Resurrection sold the property to the Sisters of the Holy Family of Nazareth, whereupon the building was razed upon the recommendation of building consultants and the Chicago Fire Department.

265. Mother Mary of Jesus the Good Shepherd, letter to Mother Lauretta, Albano, August 29, 1890.

266. Mother Lauretta, letter to Mother Mary of Jesus the Good Shepherd, Chicago, August 30, 1890.

267. Mother Lauretta, letters to Mother Mary of Jesus the Good Shepherd, Chicago, September 14 and 24, and November 7, 1890.

268. Mother Lauretta, letters to Mother Mary of Jesus the Good Shepherd, September 24 and November 16, 1890, as also Mother Mary's letter to Mother Lauretta, Cracow, October 20, 1890. This project never materialized. Later developments proved it impractical to establish a novitiate in Scranton. The land was sold in 1916.

269. Mother Lauretta, letter to Mother Mary of Jesus the Good Shepherd, Chicago, December 7, 1890.

270. Mother Mary of Jesus the Good Shepherd, "Report to the First General Chapter."

271. Mother Mary of Jesus the Good Shepherd, letter to Father Lechert, Cracow, October 26, 1890.

272. Mother Mary of Jesus the Good Shepherd, letter to Father Lechert, Cracow, November 2, 1890.

273. S. Irene Marianowska, "Chronicle: Cracow, 1890-1894" (unpublished manuscript).

274. Countess Hortense Tyszkiewicz, Mother Joseph-Teresa of the Immaculate Conception (1836-1911). By a rescript of the Holy See, dated November 12, 1902, permission was granted for her transfer to the Sisters of the Holy Family of Nazareth. Owing to the terminal illness of Mother Foundress, this act was not carried out until May 21, 1903, when Mother Joseph-Teresa received the Nazareth habit and pronounced the religious vows according to Nazareth Constitutions; her perpetual profession in the Congregation was consummated on December 8, 1903.

275. Mother Mary of Jesus the Good Shepherd, letters to Mother Lauretta, Rome, May 12 and November 24, 1892; also letter to Mother Joanne, Rome, December 23, 1892.

276. Mother Mary of Jesus the Good Shepherd, letter to Mother Lauretta, Albano, September 20, 1890.

277. Mother Mary of Jesus the Good Shepherd, "Report to the First General Chapter."

278. Mother Mary of Jesus the Good Shepherd, letter to Mother Lauretta, Paris, September 28, 1891.

279. Mother Mary of Jesus the Good Shepherd, letter to Mother Lauretta, Paris, January 4, 1892.

280. Mother Mary of Jesus the Good Shepherd, "Kronika (Chronicle): 1892" (unpublished manuscript).

281. S. Irene Marianowska, *op. cit.*

282. Josephine Marianowska, Sister M. Irene of the Blessed Trinity (1864-1938).

283. May 15, 1891.

284. S. Irene Marianowska, *op. cit.*

285. Casimira Królikowska, Sister M. Laurence of the Most Sacred Body and Blood of Christ (1867-1931); received the permanent title of Mother in 1895.

286. Mother M. Joanne Ziętkiewicz. "Kronika Początków Domu we Lwowie (The Beginnings of the Foundation in Lemberg): 1892-1893; unpublished manuscript.

287. Emily Gukala, Sister M. Faustina of the Sorrowful Mother (1867-1950).

288. Mother Lauretta to Mother Mary of Jesus the Good Shepherd, letters, Chicago, November 4, 1891 and January 1, 1892, also Philadelphia, January 10, 1892.

289. Mother Lauretta to Mother Mary of Jesus the Good Shepherd, letter, Chicago, January 1, 1892.

290. Mother Lauretta to Mother Mary of Jesus the Good Shepherd, letters, Chicago, March 24, also August 14 and 24, 1892.

291. Mother Lauretta to Mother Mary of Jesus the Good Shepherd, letters, Chicago, December 4, 1891 and March 24, 1892.

292. Mother Lauretta to Mother Mary of Jesus the Good Shepherd, letter, Chicago, December 22, 1891.

293. Mother Lauretta to Mother Mary of Jesus the Good Shepherd, letter, Chicago, April 27, 1892. The original street address of this building, before the allocation of new house numbers, was 258 W. Division St. The Holy Family Academy site, now bearing the address 1444 W. Division Street, was initially 130 W. Division Street.

294. Mother Lauretta to Mother Mary of Jesus the Good Shepherd, letter, Chicago, May 5, 1892. The chapel with the adjoining parlor, the choir, and Mother Mary's room are preserved as memorials. Original items of furniture in Mother Mary's room and various articles which she used during her stay in Chicago are carefully kept.

295. *Dziennik Chicagoski* (The Chicago Polish Daily News), August 1, 1892, p. 4.

296. Leo XIII, Apostolic Letter to the Bishops of Spain, Italy and the two Americas, June 16, 1892.

297. Furey, *op. cit.*, pp. 367-369 *passim*.

298. Leo XIII, Apostolic Brief *Neminem Fugit*.

299. Mother Mary of Jesus the Good Shepherd, "Report to the First General Chapter."

300. Historical Archives of the Vicariate of Rome, 1892, fol. 574v.

301. Mother Mary of Jesus the Good Shepherd, "Kronika: 1892."

302. *Ibid.*

303. *Ibid.* During the interview on October 31, 1892, Cardinal Parocchi said among other things, "Je pleure avec vous, je souffre avec vous, je compatis à vos peines."

304. Mother Mary of Jesus the Good Shepherd, letters to Cardinal Verga, Prefect of the Sacred Congregation of Bishops and Regulars, Rome, November 19 and 24, 1892.

305. Father Lechert to Mother Lauretta, letter, Rome, December 14, 1892.

306. Historical Archives of the Vicariate of Rome, 1892, fol. 1045v.

307. Mother Mary of Jesus the Good Shepherd, letter to Mother Lauretta, Rome, December 10, 1892; also Father Lechert to Mother Joanne, letter, Rome, December 20, 1892.

308. Mother Mary of Jesus the Good Shepherd, "Report to the First General Chapter."

309. Father Lechert to Mother Joanne, letter, Rome, December 20, 1892.

310. Lechert, "Alcune date della mia vita, 1845-1906."

311. Mariano Cardinal Rampolla del Tindaro, Papal Secretary of State, letter No. 11810, Vatican, April 19, 1893.

312. Mother Mary of Jesus the Good Shepherd, "Report to the First General Chapter."

313. Mother Mary of Jesus the Good Shepherd to Father Lechert, letter, Rome, January 19, 1893.

314. Mother Mary of Jesus the Good Shepherd, "Report to the First General Chapter."

315. Mother Mary of Jesus the Good Shepherd letter to Father Lechert, Lemberg, May 28, 1893.

316. S. Irene, *op. cit.*

317. Mother Mary of Jesus the Good Shepherd to Father Lechert, letter, Rome, April 13, 1898.

318. Mother Mary of Jesus the Good Shepherd to Father Lechert, letter, Lemberg, June 16, 1893.

319. Sheila Sherlock, M.D., *Diseases of the Liver and Biliary System,* third edition (Philadelphia: F. A. Davis Co., 1963), pp. 109-111 *passim.*

320. Mother Mary of Jesus the Good Shepherd, "Report to the First General Chapter."

321. Mother Bernarda, "Kronika Domu w Paryżu (Chronicle of the Foundation in Paris): 1893-1896;" unpublished manuscript.

322. *Regulamin* (Poznań: Drukarnia Kuryera Poznańskiego, 1894). The imprimatur was granted February 28, 1894.

323. Mother Mary of Jesus the Good Shepherd, "Report to the First General Chapter."

324. Lechert, *op. cit.*

325. Mother Mary of Jesus the Good Shepherd, "Report to the First General Chapter."

326. *Ibid.*

327. Father Lechert to Mother Lauretta, letter, Sèvres, June 14, 1894.

328. Mother Lauretta to Mother Mary of Jesus the Good Shepherd, letter, Chicago, November 7, 1890.

329. Mother Lauretta to Mother Mary of Jesus the Good Shepherd, letter, Chicago, October 25, 1893.

330. Mother Lauretta to Mother Mary of Jesus the Good Shepherd, letters, Chicago, November 3 and 27, 1893.

331. Mother Lauretta to Mother Mary of Jesus the Good Shepherd, letter, Chicago, February 28, 1894.

332. Mother Lauretta to Mother Mary of Jesus the Good Shepherd, letter, Chicago, May 9, 1894.

333. Apollonia Dahlke, Sister M. Euphemia of the Humble Heart of Jesus (1876-1962).

334. "Kronika Domu św. Józefa (Chronicle of St. Joseph Convent): 1894-1895;" unpublished manuscript.

335. *Ibid.*

336. Brother Maximus, C.S.C., *Pamiątka Złotego Jubileuszu Kapłaństwa Ks. Kazimierza S. Sztuczki, C.S.C., Proboszcza Parafii św. Trójcy* (Chicago, 1941), A Souvenir of the Golden Jubilee of Priesthood of the Reverend Casimir S. Sztuczko, C.S.C., Pastor of Holy Trinity Parish, p. 30.

337. Mother Lauretta to Mother Mary of Jesus the Good Shepherd, letter, Chicago, January 30, 1889.

338. Martha Fatz, Sister M. Victoria of the Heart of the Sorrowful Mother (1871-1936).

339. Mother Lauretta, "Provincial Report to the First General Chapter."

340. Letter to Mother Lauretta, Paris, January 16, 1895. By more than forty years Mother Mary antedated the conclusion of Paul E. Campbell, Litt. D., in *Parish School Problems* (New York City: Joseph F. Wagner, 1941), pp. 67-68: "Nothing contributes to the distinctive atmosphere of the Catholic school as does the religious teaching sister . . . made over from the child of the world into a child of God [she is] fitted to teach others how to live a life instinct with religious principles. The work assigned to her must be done in the very best manner possible, not because of any temporal reward, but out of a sense of devotion to the cause of the Master, who has bidden her."

341. Stephanie Staeubli, Sister M. Gertrude of Our Lady of Sorrows (1859-1915).

342. "Kronika Domu św. Józefa" (Chronicle of St. Joseph Convent).

343. Elizabeth Sadowska, Mother M. Cecilia of the Five Holy Wounds, (1854-1925).

344. Mother Mary of Jesus the Good Shepherd to M. Gabriel, letter, London, August 14, 1894.

345. Mother Mary of Jesus the Good Shepherd to Father Lechert, London, August 19, 1894.

346. Mother Mary of Jesus the Good Shepherd to Mother Lauretta, letter, September 14, 1894.

347. Mother Mary of Jesus the Good Shepherd, "Report to the First General Chapter."

348. Mother Lauretta to Mother Mary of Jesus the Good Shepherd, letter, Chicago, March 7, 1895.

349. Mother Lauretta to Mother Mary of Jesus the Good Shepherd, letter, Chicago, March 20, 1895.

350. Mother Lauretta, "Provincial Report to the First General Chapter."

351. Mother Stanislaus Sierpińska, "Kronika Domu Przenajdr. Krwi P. J. (Chronicle of the convent of the Most Precious Blood): 1895," unpublished manuscript.

352. Mother Mary of Jesus the Good Shepherd to Father Lechert, letter, Rome, June 22, 1895.

353. Proceedings of the First General Chapter of the Sisters of the Holy Family of Nazareth, Chaville, France, August 25-September 5, 1895.

354. Mother Bernarda, *op cit.*

355. Mother Mary of Jesus the Good Shepherd to Mother Columba, letter, Paris, September 6, 1895.

356. Mother Mary of Jesus the Good Shepherd to Mother Columba, letter, Paris, September 13, 1895.

357. Mother Mary of Jesus the Good Shepherd, "Report to the

Second General Chapter for the period from September, 1895 to March, 1899."

358. Helen Targońska, Sister M. Thecla of the Love of the Eternal Father, 1866-1956.

359. Mother Bernarda, *op. cit.*

360. Mother Mary of Jesus the Good Shepherd, "Report to the Second General Chapter."

361. Mother Bernarda, *op. cit.*

362. Father Lechert, "Alcune date della mia vita, 1845-1906."

363. Cecilia Leggett, Sister M. Alphonsus of the Glory of God, 1870-1953. She was the first British-born sister who discovered Nazareth while she was in Paris in 1892, prior to the opening of the mission in London.

364. Mother Mary of Jesus the Good Shepherd to Father Lechert, letter, London, January 10, 1896.

365. Mother Bernarda, *op. cit.*

366. Mother Lauretta to Mother Mary of Jesus the Good Shepherd, letter, Cracow, September 12, 1895.

367. Letter to Mother Gabriel, Cracow, November 12, 1895.

368. Mother Lauretta to Mother Mary of Jesus the Good Shepherd, letter, Cracow, March 26, 1896.

369. Mother Raphael to Mother Gabriel, letter, Cracow, April 16, 1896.

370. Mother Lauretta to Mother Mary of Jesus the Good Shepherd, letter, Cracow, September 15, 1895.

371. Mother Lauretta to Mother Mary of Jesus the Good Shepherd, letter, Cracow, April 14, 1896.

372. S. Irene, "Kronika Domu Lwowskiego (Chronicle: Lemberg): 1894-1896;" unpublished manuscript.

373. Mother Lauretta to Mother Mary of Jesus the Good Shepherd, letters, Lemberg, November 17, and Cracow, December 20, 1895.

374. Mother Lauretta to Mother Mary of Jesus the Good Shepherd, letters, Wadowice, February 15, also March 5, 13 and 26, and April 14, 1896.

375. Mother Lauretta to Mother Mary of Jesus the Good Shepherd, letters, March 26 and April 14, 1896.

376. S. Irene, *op. cit.*

377. Mother Lauretta to Mother Mary of Jesus the Good Shepherd, letters, Cracow, December 30, 1895 and March 26, 1896.

378. Mother Mary of Jesus the Good Shepherd, "Report to the Second General Chapter."

379. "Kronika Domu św. Józefa" (Chronicle of St. Joseph Convent).

380. "Kronika Domu Najśw. Panny" (Chronicle of the Convent of Our Lady).

381. Ursula Łęga, Sister M. Joachim of the Immaculate Heart of Mary, 1875-1921.

382. Josephine Wdzięczkowska, Sister M. Gregoria of the Immaculate Conception, 1876-1958.

383. Antoinette Zielińska, Sister M. Leocadia of the Love of the Infant Jesus, 1878-1960.

384. Leocadia Ruszkowska, Sister M. Margaret of the Prisoner of Love, 1879-1967.

385. Marcella Kapcia, Sister M. Valentine of the Immaculate Conception, 1869-1937.

386. Theophila Bartkowska, Sister M. Bridget of Our Lady of Nazareth, 1873-1954.

387. Josephine Rogalska, Sister M. Vincent of the Holy Family, 1868-1904.

388. Mother Columba to Mother Mary of Jesus the Good Shepherd, note of New Year greetings, Rome, January 1, 1902.

389. Maria Menge, Sister M. Amata of the Mother of Good Counsel, 1874-1940.

390. Mother Mary of Jesus the Good Shepherd to Father Lechert, letter, Chicago, August 28, 1896.

391. Mother Mary of Jesus the Good Shepherd, "Report to the Second General Chapter."

392. Mother Frances to Mother Mary of Jesus the Good Shepherd, letter, Rome, September 9, 1896.

393. This incident is recorded in the chronicles of the Immaculate Conception Province by Sister M. Celestine of Jesus of Nazareth (Balbina Piekarska, 1872-1942), who happened to be traveling with Mother Mary and Mother Lauretta on the occasion described, and witnessed the conversation.

394. Mother Mary of Jesus the Good Shepherd to Father Lechert, letter, Philadelphia, October 6, 1896.

395. Mother Lauretta to Mother Mary of Jesus the Good Shepherd, letters, Philadelphia, November 22 and 27, 1896, also February 21, 1900.

396. Mother Lauretta to Mother Mary of Jesus the Good Shepherd, letter, Chicago, May 19, 1892.

397. Mother Lauretta to Mother Mary of Jesus the Good Shepherd, letter, Chicago, October 5, 1898. In this letter Mother Lauretta referred to the intention the Foundress had expressed during the visitation in 1896-1897, namely, to take action along these lines in the spring of 1899, when she planned to come again to the United States. Unforeseen developments, however, prevented Mother Mary from making another visit to the American houses, and the proposed division of the province was tabled.

398. Mother Mary of Jesus the Good Shepherd to Father Lechert, letter, Chicago, February 28, 1897.

399. Mother Mary of Jesus the Good Shepherd to Father Lechert, letters, Chicago, May 26 and June 7, 1897.

400. Mother Mary of Jesus the Good Shepherd to Father Lechert, letter, Chicago, June 7, 1897.

401. Anna Bielecka, Sister M. Lucille of the Immaculate Conception, 1868-1916.

402. Sisters of St. Francis of the Providence of God, *Dievo Apvaizdai Déka:* 1922-1932 (Pittsburgh, 1932), tenth anniversary memoir in Lithu-

anian, published privately by the Sisters of St. Francis, Mount Providence Pittsburgh, Pennsylvania.

403. Mary Dahlke, Sister M. Ladislaus of the Holy House of Nazareth, 1870-1947.

404. Mother Mary of Jesus the Good Shepherd to Father Lechert, letter, Pittsburgh, June 10, 1897.

405. Mother Mary of Jesus the Good Shepherd to Father Lechert, letter, Pittsburgh, June 14, 1897.

406. Mother Mary of Jesus the Good Shepherd, "Report to the Second General Chapter."

407. Naturalization took place in the Superior Court at Chicago, Illinois, and is recorded in V-54, P-467. The file copy of the naturalization certificate was viewed by the author in the archives of the Superior Court, on December 16, 1971. It bears the authentic original signature "Marie Françoise de Siedliska."

408. November 23, 1896.

409. Father Lechert, "Alcune date."

410. Mother Mary of Jesus the Good Shepherd to Mother Lauretta, letter, London, September 21, 1897.

411. Frances Danisch, Sister M. Antonia of Our Lady the Good Shepherdess, 1875-1943.

412. Mother Mary of Jesus the Good Shepherd, "Report to the Second General Chapter."

413. Mother Mary of Jesus the Good Shepherd to Father Lechert, letter, Chicago, March 3, 1897. Numerous similar acknowledgments are present in Mother Mary's correspondence and in her private journals.

414. Father Lechert to Mother Mary of Jesus the Good Shepherd, letter, Sèvres, September 8, 1896.

415. A. Trombetta, Pro-Secretarius S. Congregatio Episcoporum et Regularium, "Animadversiones in Constitutiones Sororum Sacrae Familiae a Nazareth," Rome, September 1, 1896.

416. *Ibid.*

417. *Ibid.*

418. Mother Mary of Jesus the Good Shepherd to Mother Lauretta, letters, October 20, and November 3, 1897.

419. Mother Mary of Jesus the Good Shepherd to Father Lechert, letters, Lemberg, July 19 and August 2, 1898.

420. Marie Gostomska, Sister M. Jerome of the Will of God, 1860-1940.

421. Mother Raphael, "Kronika Domu Najśw. Serca Pana Jezusa (Chronicle of the Sacred Heart Convent): 1898;" unpublished manuscript.

422. Mother Mary of Jesus the Good Shepherd to Mother Theresa Czermińska, letters, Lemberg, July 10 and 19, 1898, also Cracow, October 3, 1898.

423. Mother Mary of Jesus the Good Shepherd, "Report to the Second General Chapter."

424. Mother Mary of Jesus the Good Shepherd to Father Lechert, letter, Paris, January 7, 1899.

425. Mother Raphael to Mother Mary of Jesus the Good Shepherd, letter, Cracow, February 9, 1899.

426. Mother Frances to Mother Mary of Jesus the Good Shepherd, letter, Rome, January 8, 1897.

427. Anna Wesołek, Sister M. Alexis of the Immaculate Heart of Mary, 1878-1959.

428. Furey, *op. cit.,* pp. 515-517.

429. Mother Mary of Jesus the Good Shepherd to Mother Lauretta, letters, London, October 6 and November 24, 1899.

430. Mother Mary of Jesus the Good Shepherd to Father Lechert, letters, Rome, April 3 and 15, 1899; also to Mother Paula, Rome, May 30, 1899.

431. Therese Whitehurst, Sister M. Reginald of Divine Providence, 1863-1947.

432. Catherine Whelton, Sister M. Scholastica of the Blessed Trinity, 1863-1919.

433. Mother Mary of Jesus the Good Shepherd to Mother Lauretta, letters, London, July 12, 1899 and January 10, 1900.

434. Mother Mary of Jesus the Good Shepherd to Mother Lauretta, letter, London, January 2, 1900.

435. Father Lechert, "Alcune date."

436. Adam Karczewski to Mother Mary of Jesus the Good Shepherd, letter, Kowanówko, September 6, 1899.

437. Mother Mary of Jesus the Good Shepherd to Mother Lauretta, letter, London, September 8, 1899.

438. Mother Gabriel to Mother Mary of Jesus the Good Shepherd, letters, Paris, August 23, 1899, also January 1 and 29, 1900.

439. Mother Joanne, "Mała Kronika Domu Macierzystego (Little Chronicle of the Motherhouse): 1900-1901;" unpublished manuscript.

440. Mother Mary of Jesus the Good Shepherd to Mother Lauretta, letters, Rome, February 7 and 21, also March 14, 1900.

441. Mother Mary of Jesus the Good Shepherd to Father Lechert, letter, Rome, May 6, 1900.

442. Mother Mary of Jesus the Good Shepherd to Mother Lauretta, letter, Rome, April 4, 1900.

443. Mother Mary of Jesus the Good Shepherd to Mother Lauretta, letter, Rome, April 25, 1900; also letter to Father Lechert, Rome, August 2, 1900.

444. Sophia Waśkiewicz, Sister M. Kunegunda of Mary Queen of Poland, 1860-1938.

445. Antoinette Waśkiewicz, Sister Maria-Josepha of Jesus Crucified, 1862-1955.

446. Mother Mary of Jesus the Good Shepherd to Mother Joanne, letter, Rome, June 23, 1900.

447. Mother Joanne, *op. cit.*

448. Holy Family Institute, *Golden Jubilee Memoir, 1900-1950 (The Pittsburgher:* Pittsburgh, 1950), p. 13.

449. Mother Lauretta to Mother Mary of Jesus the Good Shepherd, letter, Chicago, February 28, 1900; also letter of Mother Mary of Jesus the Good Shepherd to Mother Lauretta, Rome, March 28, 1900.

450. Mother Lauretta to Mother Mary of Jesus the Good Shepherd, letters, Chicago, September 19 and 26, 1900.

451. Mother Mary of Jesus the Good Shepherd to Mother Lauretta, letter, Paris, November 9, 1900; also letter of Mother Lauretta to Mother Mary of Jesus the Good Shepherd, Chicago, November 20, 1900.

452. Mother Mary of Jesus the Good Shepherd to Mother Lauretta, letter, Paris, June 12, 1901.

453. Mother Mary of Jesus the Good Shepherd to Mother Lauretta, letter, Paris, November 23, 1900.

454. Mother Gabriel to Mother Mary of Jesus the Good Shepherd, letters, Paris, August 12 and 23, 1900.

455. Mother Mary of Jesus the Good Shepherd to Mother Joanne, letters, Paris, November 22, also December 14 and 29, 1900.

456. Marie Siefert, Sister M. Redempta of the Immaculate Conception, 1870-1960.

457. Mother Mary of Jesus the Good Shepherd to Mother Lauretta, letter, Paris, February 9, 1901.

458. Mother Joanne, *op. cit.*

459. Mother Mary of Jesus the Good Shepherd to Mother Lauretta, letter, Rome, May 8, 1901.

460. Mother Lauretta to Mother Mary of Jesus the Good Shepherd, letter, Chicago, March 12, 1901.

461. Mother Lauretta to Mother Mary of Jesus the Good Shepherd, letters, Chicago, April 10 and May 6, 1901.

462. Mother Mary of Jesus the Good Shepherd to Mother Lauretta, letter, Rome, May 3, 1901.

463. Mother Gabriel, "Rok z naszą Jedyną Matką (The Year with our Mother): 1901;" unpublished manuscript.

464. Mother Lauretta to Mother Mary of Jesus the Good Shepherd, letters, Brooklyn, July 31, also Chicago, August 27, 1901.

465. Mother Gabriel, *op. cit.*

466. Theodosia Mindak, Sister M. Donata of the Mother of Good Counsel, 1874-1918.

467. Mother Lauretta to Mother Mary of Jesus the Good Shepherd, letter, Brooklyn, October 9, 1901.

468. Mother Mary of Jesus the Good Shepherd to Mother Lauretta, letters, Rome, December 25, 1901, also January 8, 1902.

469. Mother Mary of Jesus the Good Shepherd to Mother Lauretta, letter, Rome, February 5, 1902.

470. Mother Frances to Mother Mary of Jesus the Good Shepherd, letters, London, April 16 and Enfield, August 27, 1902.

471. The original address of the hospital's new location was 545 North

Leavitt Street; in 1909 the city numbering system was changed, and the hospital's address became 1120 N. Leavitt Street.

472. Mother Mary of Jesus the Good Shepherd to Mother Lauretta, letter, Rome, Wednesday of Holy Week, 1902.

473. Mother Lauretta to Mother Mary of Jesus the Good Shepherd, letter, Chicago, March 25, 1902.

474. Mother Lauretta to Mother Mary of Jesus the Good Shepherd, letter, Chicago, April 8, 1902.

475. Mother Lauretta to Mother Mary of Jesus the Good Shepherd, letter, Chicago, May 15, 1902.

476. Mother Lauretta to Mother Mary of Jesus the Good Shepherd, letters, Chicago, December 2, 1901 and April 8, 1902; also letter of Mother Mary of Jesus the Good Shepherd to Mother Lauretta, Rome, January 12, 1902.

477. Mother Mary of Jesus the Good Shepherd, request to Lucido Cardinal Parocchi and his endorsement affixed thereto, Rome, February 8, 1902.

478. Mother Mary of Jesus the Good Shepherd to Father Lechert, letter, Rome, August 20, 1900; also letter to Mother Lauretta, Rome, November 12, 1902.

479. Mother Mary of Jesus the Good Shepherd to Father Lechert, letter, Rome, June 29, 1902.

480. Mother Bernarda, "Notes and Reminiscences;" unpublished manuscript.

481. Mother Mary of Jesus the Good Shepherd to Mother Lauretta, letter, Rome, March 12, 1902.

482. Mother Mary of Jesus the Good Shepherd to Mother Lauretta, letters, Rome, April 2, 16 and 30, 1902; also letter to Mother Laurence, Rome, June 20, 1902.

483. July 12, 1902.

484. Mother Mary of Jesus the Good Shepherd to Mother Paula, letter, Rome, October 23, 1902.

485. Mother Mary of Jesus the Good Shepherd to Mother Lauretta, letters, Subiaco, September 30, also Rome, October 22, 1902.

486. Mother Mary of Jesus the Good Shepherd to Mother Lauretta, letter, Rome, October 22, 1902. In this letter Mother Mary quoted Father Cormier's statement, "Faites bien mûrir les choses; il faut réfléchir et prier avant de donner les choses aux soeurs; car après, s'il faut changer, cela monte les esprits."

487. Mother Mary of Jesus the Good Shepherd to Mother Lauretta, letter, Rome, November 12, 1902.

488. Arthur H. Douthwaite, M.D., ed., *French's Index of Differential Diagnosis,* ninth edition (Baltimore: Williams and Wilkins Co., 1967), pp. 3, 92, 176, 686 *passim.* "The diagnosis of peritonitis in most cases means immediate operation . . . For acute general peritonitis, due to ruptured appendicular abscess, urgent laparotomy is needed. Pyrexia ceases as a rule when the pus obtains free drainage . . . When the temperature falls, the pulse becomes small and rapid, rising progressively;

these signs are the indications of approaching death."

489. Father Lechert to Mother Lauretta, letter, Rome, November 23, 1902.

490. Alfred F. Havighurst, *Twentieth Century Britain* (Evanston, Illinois: Row, Peterson and Company, 1962), p. 69.

491. C. S. Peel, *A Hundred Wonderful Years: 1820-1920* (New York: Dodd, Mead and Company, 1927), p. 66.

492. Father Lechert, *op. cit.*

493. Mother Cecilia, "Notes on the last illness and death of Mother Mary of Jesus the Good Shepherd;" unpublished manuscript. Mother Cecilia, as the infirmarian, attended Mother Foundress in her illness.

PART III
(Pages 131-213)

1. Chronicle of the Good Shepherd convent, Rome, 1903; unpublished manuscript.

2. Sacred Congregation of Bishops and Regulars, Decree No. 2602/15, Rome, March 24, 1903.

3. Mother Raphael to Mother Lauretta, letter, Cracow, April 3, 1903.

4. *Drogą Ukrycia i Ofiary* (Rome: privately published, 1951), p. 98.

5. Mother Mary of Jesus the Good Shepherd to Mother Lauretta, letter, Rome, January 31, 1900.

6. This suburb was then known as Feehansville.

7. Power of Attorney from Mother Mary Lauretta Lubowidzka to Mother Mary Sophia Kulawik, November 27, 1903, notarized by Frank A. Kwasigroch, Notary Public, Chicago, Cook County, Illinois.

8. Decree of the Court of Common Pleas, Allegheny County, State of Pennsylvania, December 3, 1904, Charter Book, vol. 37, p. 140.

9. The flight occurred at Kitty Hawk, North Carolina, December 17, 1903.

10. S. Irene Marianowska, "Chronicle of Wadowice Hospital, 1906-1912;" unpublished manuscript.

11. *Op. cit.*

12. S. Maria-Josepha Waśkiewicz, "First Foundations in the Kingdom of Poland under Russian occupation, 1902-1918;" unpublished manuscript.

13. *Op. cit.*

14. *Op. cit.*

15. Articles of Incorporation of the Missionaries of the Divine Love of Jesus, Washington, D.C., March 15, 1909.

16. Anthony Lechert, "Missionaries of the Divine Love of Jesus in the United States;" unpublished manuscript.

17. Anthony Lechert, "Alcune date della mia vita;" personal memoranda.

18. Mother Gabriel to Mother Lauretta, letter, Rome, Easter Monday, 1910.

19. Anthony Lechert to Mother Lauretta, letters, Rome, February 2 and 6, 1906.

20. Mother Joanne Ziętkiewicz, "Kroniczka Fundacji Domu w Wiedniu (A Little Chronicle of the Viennese Foundation), 1908;" unpublished manuscript.

21. *Nazaret,* Vol. V, No. 7, p. 394; the Congregation's periodical publication privately printed.

22. *Ibid.,* pp. 391-395 *passim.*

23. J. E. Quigley, Archbishop of Chicago, to Mother Lauretta, letter, Chicago, January 28, 1908.

24. Translation from the French of the decree dated January 1, 1909, promulgated by Fr. Hyacinth M. Cormier, M.G., O.P., delegated by Pietro Cardinal Respighi.

25. A photograph of St. Pope Pius X with the inscribed invocation and signature, dated July 14, 1907, is preserved at the generalate of the Congregation in Rome.

26. Decree signed by I. C. Cardinal Vives, prefect of the Sacred Congregation of Religious. In the reorganization introduced by Pius X in 1908, the Sacred Congregation of Religious was formed to attend to all matters concerning orders and congregations while the problems of bishops were turned over to the new Consistorial Congregation. These two curial Congregations comprised formerly the Sacred Congregation of Bishops and Religious.

27. Wilhelm Cardinal Van Rossum, "Word portrait of the Servant of God Mother Mary of Jesus the Good Shepherd," Rome, February 28, 1905; unpublished manuscript.

28. Proceedings of the Fifth General Chapter of the Sisters of the Holy Family of Nazareth, Albano, Italy, August 11-15, 1909; unpublished manuscript.

29. *Chicago Sunday Tribune,* November 14, 1909.

30. *Chicago Daily News,* November 15, 1909.

31. *Chicago Daily News,* November 19 and 20, 1909.

32. Program of the Testimonial Concert in honor of the Sisters of the Holy Family of Nazareth on the occasion of the Silver Jubilee of their coming to America, Sunday, July 3, 1910; St. Stanislaus Auditorium, Chicago.

33. Mother M. Sophia, circular issued to the sisters in the American province, January 21, 1912.

34. Cardinal Vives to Cardinal Respighi. The decision contained in this decree was later reversed (Mother Lauretta, circular, Rome, January 29, 1919), so that all superiors, major and local, were referred to as "Mother."

The most recent action of the Special General Chapter of 1969, abrogated this practice entirely, except for the person of the superior general and that only during the term of office.

To avoid confusing the identity of persons over the years, the title

"Mother" is used in this work from here on with reference to the superior general alone and to those sisters who were so named by the Foundress.

35. In 1913, the surviving eleven were: M. Lauretta Lubowidzka, M. Gabriel Lubowidzka, M. Raphael Lubowidzka, M. Joanne Ziętkiewicz, M. Columba Trzewiczek, M. Cecilia Sadowska, M. Bernarda Malentynowicz, M. Frances Morgenstern, M. Laurence Królikowska, M. Gertrude Staeubli, and M. Sophia Kulawik.

36. M. Lauretta, circular, Rome, May 18, 1913.

37. *Ibid.*

38. Anna Netkowska, Sister M. Clare of the Five Holy Wounds, 1878-1959.

39. Maria Szeligowska, Sister Mary Magdalene of Jesus Crucified, 1870-1970.

40. M. Lauretta, *op. cit.*

41. Novitiate Chronicle, Des Plaines, Illinois, entries for August 14 and 30, 1913; unpublished manuscript.

42. Mother Gabriel, letter to Mother Raphael, Rome, 19, 1915, written in the name of Mother Lauretta, confirming the delegation.

43. S. Maria-Josepha, *op. cit.*

44. Mother Raphel, wartime correspondence with Mother Lauretta, 1914-1918.

45. Mother Lauretta, circular to the sisters in the United States, Rome, December 12, 1915.

46. Sister M. Alma Sebowicz, "Kronika domu Opieki Najśw. Rodziny w Szwajcarii (Chronicle of the house in Switzerland);" unpublished manuscript.

47. Anthony Lechert, letter to Mother Gabriel, Washington, February 3, 1917.

48. July 10, 1915.

49. The first apparition occurred on May 13, 1917; the final, with the wondrous phenomenon of the sky, on October 13, 1917. In October of 1930, the apparitions and the message were authenticated by the Church.

50. Chronicle of the Good Shepherd convent, Rome, 1917; unpublished manuscript.

51. Sister Maria-Josepha Waśkiewicz, "Nowa Fundacja w Kaliszu (The New Foundation in Kalisz), 1918-1921;" unpublished manuscript.

52. *Drogą Ukrycia i Ofiary*, p. 132.

53. C. J. Alger, chairman, Institutional Relations, Corn Products Refining Company, letter to Sister M. Antonia, provincial superior, Chicago, February 5, 1920.

54. Mother Lauretta, circular, Rome, April 7, 1915.

55. Mother Lauretta, circular, Rome, November 21, 1917.

56. Mother Lauretta, another circular bearing the same date as above.

57. Promulgated May 27, 1917.

58. Mother Lauretta, circular, Rome, July 2, 1918.

59. (a) Sacred Congregation of Religious, rescript dated July 18,

1918; (b) Wilhelm Cardinal Van Rossum, letter to the Sisters of the Holy Family of Nazareth in the United States, Rome, July 30, 1918; (c) Mother Lauretta, circular, Rome, August 2, 1918.

60. Andrew Ignasiak, to Mother Lauretta, letters, Erie, Pa., July 26 and October 19, 1917, also February 14, 1918.

61. Louis Pinderski to Mother Lauretta, report, Chicago, November 16, 1918.

62. Francis Retka, C.S.Sp., to Mother Lauretta, letter, Emsworth, Pa., June 6, 1919.

63. Anna Czarnowska, Sister M. Valeria of the Hearts of Jesus, Mary and Joseph, 1878-1945.

64. Sister M. Tarsicia Bzowska, "Kronika Domu w Rabce (Chronicle of Rabka Foundation), 1905-1921;" unpublished manuscript.

65. *Op. cit.*

66. Mother Gabriel to Mother Raphael, letter, Rome, May 9, 1920.

67. Proceedings of the Sixth General Chapter of the Sisters of the Holy Family of Nazareth, Albano, June 5 to 18, 1920; unpublished manuscript.

68. *Op. cit.*

69. *Op. cit.*

70. Sister M. DeChantal, "The Lithuanian Question," unpublished monograph, Des Plaines, Ill., 1965.

71. Proceedings of the Sixth General Chapter.

72. *Op. cit.*

73. *Op. cit.*

74. Sister M. Thecla Targońska, "Pamiętnik z Czasów Inwazji Bolszewickiej w Grodnie (Journal of the Bolshevik Invasion in Grodno);" unpublished manuscript, two notebooks.

75. *Op. cit.*

76. *Op. cit.*

77. *Nazaret,* Vol. XXII, June, 1939, pp. 173-174.

78. *Vita della Serva di Dio Maria Francesca De Siedliska, Fondatrice della Congregazione della Sacra Famiglia di Nazareth,* Opera postuma, Grottaferrata, Scuola tipografica Italo-Orientale "S. Nilo," 1921, 530 pp.

79. *Żywot Sługi Bożej Marji Franciszki Siedliskiej od Pana Jezusa Dobrego Pasterza* (Cracow: Głos Narodu, 1924), 512 pp.; translated by Msgr. Władysław Chotkowski.

80. *La Servante de Dieu Mère Marie Françoise De Siedliska* (Rome: Ecole Typographique Pie X, 1926), 468 pp.; adapted in French by Msgr. H.

81. Pietro Cardinal Gasparri to Father Lechert, cablegram, Vatican City, August 15, 1921.

82. Father Lechert to Mother Lauretta, letter, Rome, February 6, 1906.

83. Sister M. Antonia Danisch, circular to the sisters in the Sacred Heart Province, Des Plaines, January 15, 1921.

84. Sister M. Antonia to Mother Lauretta, letter, Des Plaines, November 2, 1921.

85. Purchase accomplished October 8, 1924.

86. Cracow: Polonia, 1910; 464 pp.; Nazareth meditations.

87. Cracow: Koziański Publishers, 1913; 213 pp.; spiritual exercises based on the Holy Scripture, under the *imprimatur* of Archbishop Adam Sapieha.

88. Cracow: Alliance Publishers under the management of A. Szyjewski, 1916; 224 pp.; thoughts for days of monthly recollection based on the Holy Scripture, under the *imprimatur* of Archbishop Adam Sapieha.

89. Poznań: Drukarnia św. Wojciecha, 1920; 612 pp,; Scriptural reflections for visits to the Blessed Sacrament.

90. "The Lithuanian Question."

91. Sacred Congregation of Religious, Decree No. 7852-R. 37:21, Rome, June 4, 1923.

92. Proceedings of the Seventh General Chapter of the Sisters of the Holy Family of Nazareth, Albano, Italy, July 17 to 27, 1925.

93. *La Congregazione della Sacra Famiglia di Nazareth nel primo cinquantenario della sua fondazione—1875-1925* (Roma: Tipografia Poliglotta Vaticana, 1925), 78 pp.

94. Encyclical *Quas Primas,* December 11, 1925.

95. Mother Mary of Jesus the Good Shepherd, First Constitutions, 1887; conferences; letters.

96. Mother Lauretta, circular, Volosca, October 28, 1926.

97. Mother Lauretta, appeals, June 26, 1921, March 3, 1924, undated 1925, and May 1930.

98. Reports to the Eighth and Ninth General Chapters, 1932 and 1938, respectively.

99. Report to the Eighth General Chapter, 1932.

100. Reports to the Eighth and Ninth General Chapters, 1932 and 1938.

101. Report to the Eighth General Chapter, 1932.

102. Rescript of the Sacred Congregation of Religious, June 30, 1931.

103. Mother Lauretta to Sister Antonia Danisch, letter, Rome, October 7, 1929.

104. When Mother Frances Morgenstern left England for France in 1928, she was succeeded by Sister Electa Wright as superior in Enfield. For reasons of health, Sister Electa was relieved in 1929 and was replaced by Sister Antonia Danisch.

105. Chronicle of the Good Shepherd convent, Rome; entries under dates of March 7, 9 and 29, 1927.

106. The term *foyer,* meaning hearth, home, center, is applied in France to homelike establishments for students who are away from their own homes, particularly those from outside their countries.

107. Mother Lauretta, circular, Rome, August 30, 1926. *Nazaret,* published privately by the Sisters of the Holy Family of Nazareth, was

discontinued in 1940 due to active enemy operations in and around Albano during World War II.

108. Mother Lauretta, circular, Rome, December 2, 1928.

109. *Zwyczajnik,* Part I (Rome, 1928), 543 pp.; Part II (Rome, 1929), 182 pp. Over the years the *Book of Customs* underwent several revisions and was also published in English and Italian.

110. The novitiate of St. Joseph province, Pittsburgh, Pennsylvania, was canonically erected by a rescript of the Sacred Congregation of Religious, dated, June 13, 1927.

111. The novitiate of the Immaculate Conception province, Philadelphia, Pennsylvania, was canonically erected by a rescript of the Sacred Congregation of Religious, June 18, 1928.

112. Sister M. Idalia to Mother Lauretta, letter, Torresdale, February 6, 1929.

113. *The De Paulia,* De Paul University publication, Chicago, November 7, 1935.

114. John Kenneth Galbraith, *The Affluent Society* (Boston: Houghton Mifflin Co., 1958), pp. 44-46.

115. Proceedings of the Eighth General Chapter of the Sisters of the Holy Family of Nazareth, Albano, Italy, June 2 to 16, 1932.

116. New *Code of Canon Law,* Canon 505, par. 3.

117. Proceedings of the Eighth General Chapter.

118. *Ibid.*

119. Encyclical *Miserentissimus Redemptor,* May 8, 1928.

120. Encyclical *Mens Nostra,* December 20, 1929.

121. Encyclical *Caritate Christi Compulsi,* May 3, 1932.

122. Encyclical *Divini Illius Magistri,* December 31, 1929.

123. Encyclical *Non Abbiamo Bisogno,* June 29, 1931.

124. *Nazaret,* Vol. 6, June, 1932, pp. 21-22. Cardinal Van Rossum was a native of Holland, whose last cardinal had been created four centuries earlier, in 1522. When a pilgrimage from Holland came to Rome in 1911 to thank Pius X for creating Father Van Rossum a cardinal, the Pope replied, "Do not thank me, but thank His Eminence that he was selected for his virtue and merits. It is not Father Van Rossum who is honored by the College of Cardinals, but rather the College is honored in having him."

125. Mother Lauretta, circular, Rome, September 1, 1932.

126. The journal is the official publication of the Polish American Historical Society, published biennially by the Orchard Lake Schools, Orchard Lake, Michigan.

127. The scholarship students were: in 1936-1937, Sisters Noela Linkowska, Desolata Machan, Sulpicia Niewiadoma and Conceptia Niemet; in 1937-1938, Sisters Liliosa Melerska, Honorata Tabaka, Palmaria Durlak, Theobald Jaskulska, Loyola Kościuszko and Henrietta Michałowska; in 1938-1939, Sisters Severine Jakubowska, Laurenta Okray, Eleutheria Pociask and Clarisse Siudowska.

128. *Śpiewnik dla Dzieci Szkolnych, Część I, dla klas niższych* and *Zbiór Typowych Melodii Polskich, Część II, dla klas wyższych* (Rapid

Copy Service: Chicago, 1946)—*Children's Songbook,* part I, for the lower grades, *Collection of Typical Polish Melodies,* part II, for the upper grades. The art work for both volumes was done by Harry Scully.

129. Sister Ignatius Romanowska, letter to Mother Lauretta, Torresdale, December 28, 1935.

130. Our Lady of Częstochowa parish; convent of Our Lady of Victory.

131. St. Michael the Archangel parish; convent of the Holy Spirit.

132. St. Ann parish; convent of St. Ann.

133. Proceedings of the Ninth General Chapter of the Sisters of the Holy Family of Nazareth, Albano, Italy, May 28 to June 11, 1938.

134. *Ibid.*

135. Mother Lauretta, circular, Rome, July 10, 1938.

136. March 2, 1939.

137. (a) Luigi Cardinal Maglione, Papal Secretary of State, to Mother Lauretta, letter, Vatican City, May 19, 1939; (b) Mother Lauretta, circular, Rome, May 21, 1939.

138. *Academy Review,* Vol. VI, June, 1939, student publication of Mount Nazareth Academy, Pittsburgh, Pennsylvania.

139. Annual Convention, Catholic Hospital Association, St. Louis, Missouri, June 18, 1940.

140. Mother Lauretta, letters to provincial superiors: Sister M. Richard Rutkowska (Sacred Heart), Sister M. Electa Glowienke (Immaculate Conception), and Sister M. Ignatius Romanowska (St. Joseph), Rome, October 3, 1940.

141. *Pierwszy Zjazd Naukowo-Pedagogiczny Sióstr Nauczycielek Zgrom. Najśw. Rodziny z Nazaretu* (Chicago: Stanek Press, 1941). The second conference was held in Philadelphia, 1942, after which wartime restrictions in travel made it necessary to suspend further meetings for the duration. The conferences were resumed in 1956 with a meeting in Philadelphia, followed in 1958 in Pittsburgh, then again in Chicago in 1961 and in Philadelphia in 1963.

142. *Gazetka* (Newsletter), issued in Rome and privately circulated among the houses of the Congregation. Pertinent information is contained under dates: (a) October 13, 1939; (b) October 25, 1939; (c) November 15, 1939; (d) January 4, 1940; (e) January 31, 1940; (f) February 21, 1940; (g) March 12, 1940; (h) May 1, 1940; (i) May 28, 1940; (j) May 1941-June 1942; (k) June-July 1942.

143. Sister M. Veritas Piątkowska to Mother M. Clare, letter, Rongai, Kenya, June 17, 1945.

144. *Op. cit.*

145. Florian Piskorski, delegate of the Polish-American Relief Council, to Sister M. Richard Rutkowska, letter, Lisbon, July 25, 1942.

146. Sister M. Veritas, *op. cit.*

147. *Nazaret,* Vol. XIV, December, 1939, p. 214.

148. The Papal decree initiating the Apostolic Process is dated December 4, 1940 and is attested to by Carlo Cardinal Salotti, prefect of the Sacred Congregation of Rites.

PART IV
(Pages 215-264)

1. Obituary files, Generalate of the Sisters of the Holy Family of Nazareth, Rome, Italy. Mother M. Clare (Anna Netkowska) died in Philadelphia, Pa. October 2, 1959.

2. Pope Pius XII, letter to Mother Clare, Vatican City, August 24, 1942.

3. Msgr. Swanstrom became Auxiliary Bishop of New York, consecrated October 28, 1960.

4. Sister M. Deodata Markiewicz to Sister M. Richard Rutkowska, letter, Coburg, Germany, August 2, 1945.

5. *Op. cit.*

6. *Academian,* Holy Family Academy students' yearbook (Niles, Ill.: St. Hedwig's Printery, 1943).

7. Sister M. Veritas Piątkowska to Mother Clare, letter, Rongai, Kenya, June 17, 1945.

8. *Op. cit.*

9. Sister M. Electa Glowienke to Mother Clare, letters, Philadelphia, November 17, 1943; November 24, 1944; June 13 and October 7, 1945; January 15, February 4, September 15, October 30, and November 17, 1946; also to Mother Bożena Staczyńska, March 17, 1947.

10. Sister M. Bożena Staczyńska to Mother Clare, letter, Cracow, August 22, 1945.

11. *Gazetka* (Newsletter), Rome, May 1, 1941-June 1, 1942.

12. Proceedings of the First General Chapter of the Sisters of the Holy Family of Nazareth, Chaville, France, August 25-September 5, 1895, Art. XII, par. 2.

13. Sister Electa to Mother Clare, letter, Philadelphia, August 12, 1942.

14. Sister M. Cordia Skonieczna, Chronicle of the Scholasticate, Des Plaines, June 21 to August 16, 1943; unpublished manuscript.

15. Sister Electa to Mother Clare, letter, Philadelphia, November 11, 1942.

16. Rev. Aleksander Zienkiewicz, *No Greater Love* (Pulaski, Wisconsin: Franciscan Publishers, 1968), pp. 24-25.

17. *Op. cit.,* pp. 25-26.

18. *Op. cit.,* pp. 40-41.

19. This account of the chaplain's was prepared on the twenty-fifth anniversary of the massacre; it appeared also in Polish and in Italian.

20. *Gazetka* (Newsletter), Albano, 1943-1944.

21. *Ibid.,* Albano-Rome, February, 1944.

22. Sister Adela was killed October 13, 1944.

23. Sister Jucundine was killed July 16, 1944.

24. Sister Notburga died suddenly September 4, 1944.

25. Winston S. Churchill, *The Second World War: Triumph and Tragedy,* Vol. VI (Cambridge, Mass.: Houghton Mifflin Co., 1953), pp. 128-145.

26. *Gazetka,* Rome, March 15, 1945.

27. *Ibid.,* Rome 1944-1945.

28. Mother Clare to Sister Richard Rutkowska, letter, Rome, February 5, 1945.

29. *Gazetka,* Rome, March 15, 1945.

30. *Ibid.*

31. Mother Clare, circular to the sisters in the American provinces, Rome, December 1, 1944.

32. Sacred Congregation of Religious, Prot. No. 3207/45, Rome, August 13, 1945, signed by Archbishop S. M. Pasetto, secretary.

33. Mother Mary of Jesus the Good Shepherd to Mother Gabriel, letter, Cracow, September 30, 1880.

34. Sister Berchmans died in Grodno, April 17, 1970.

35. Zienkiewicz, *op. cit.,* pp. 45-46.

36. Reverend M. Krzywicki to Mother M. Neomisia Rutkowska, letter, Nowogródek, May 4, 1966.

37. Sister Deodata Markiewicz to Sister Richard Rutkowska, letter, Coburg, July 2, 1945.

38. Sister Deodata Markiewicz to the sisters in Africa, letter, Rome, December 15, 1945.

39. *Nazaret,* Vol. II, January, 1928, pp. 64-65.

40. *Ibid.,* Vol. VII, October, 1933, pp. 139-144.

41. *Ibid.,* Vol. XI, December, 1937, pp. 806-807.

42. *Ibid.,* Vol. XII, June, 1938, 18-20.

43. *Ibid.,* Vol. XII, December, 1938, pp. 84-85.

44. *Gazetka,* Rome, Advent, 1945.

45. Churchill, *op. cit.,* pp. 85-86.

46. Mother Clare, circular to the sisters in the United States, Rome, March 30, 1946.

47. *Ibid.*

48. Sister Theobald became the secretary general following the death of the incumbent, Sister Antonina Kalicka, August 9, 1940. Subsequently, in the United States, she served as superior in the house of studies in Washington and as provincial secretary in Philadelphia.

49. Sister Frances entered the religious life in St. Joseph province and made her novitiate in Albano. After profession she studied in Warsaw, Paris and Rome, and held the position of director of scholastics in Albano, 1939-1942. In the United States she became the director of novices in the Sacred Heart province, 1947-1953, and in St. Joseph province, 1953-1958, then—upon returning to Europe—in Albano, 1959-1964. Following the death of the treasurer general, Sister Fides Tomkowicz in 1964, she assumed the duties of this office.

50. Sister Josephine joined the Sisters of the Holy Family of Nazareth in the Immaculate Conception province. After her novitiate in Albano and profession, she continued her studies in Europe until the outbreak of World War II. In the United States she became the director of novices in St. Joseph province, 1947-1953. Thereupon, she was appointed superior to Queen of Peace convent, Pitsford, England, 1953-

1959, and to Holy Family convent in Enfield, 1959-1965; then bursar in Pitsford, 1965-1968. More recently she became the buyer and bursar at the generalate in Rome.

51. Novitiate chronicle, Karczew-Ostrzeszów, 1943-1947; unpublished manuscript.

52. Sacred Congregation of Religious, Prot. No. 9416/46, signed by Al. Card. Lavitrano, prefect, and Archb. S. M. Pasetto, secretary.

53. Janine Staczyńska, Mother M. Bożena of Jesus in the Sacred Host, 1883-1964.

54. *Gazetka,* Rome, December, 1946.

55. Mother Clare, letter, Chicago, January 24, 1947.

56. Mother Clare, to Sister Antonia Danisch, letter, Rome, August 26, 1921.

57. *Gazetka,* Rome, January-February, 1947.

58. *Gazetka,* Rome, October-November, 1948.

59. Novitiate chronicle, Karczew-Ostrzeszów, 1943-1947.

60. Mother Bożena, circulars to the provinces in the United States, Chicago, August 16, 1947.

61. Rider to the decree of the Sacred Congregation for Religious which had been issued November 25, 1946, Prot. N. 9416/46; the rider bears the same file number.

62. May, 1949, Vol. 8, No. 9.

63. Mother Bożena, Circular, Rome, August 16, 1950.

64. Star Printers: Philadelphia, 1951; published also in Polish, under the title *Wynagrodzicielska Mistyka Nazaretu;* English translation by Sister M. Florence Tumasz.

65. *The Hidden Life of Nazareth* (Philadelphia: Star Printers, 1954), and *Nazareth Spirituality* (Milwaukee: Bruce Publishing Company, 1966).

66. Encyclical, *Fulgens Corona,* September 8, 1953. The year 1954 also marked the 100th anniversary of the proclamation of the dogma of the Immaculate Conception of the Blessed Virgin Mary by Pope Pius IX.

67. Encyclical, *Ad Coeli Reginam,* October 11, 1953.

68. *Gazetka,* Chicago, June-July, 1952.

69. W. Sojka, C.M., "Brisbane-Sydney-Perth: Trzy Nowe Pola Pracy Sióstr Nazaretanek," *Skarb Rodziny* (The Family Treasure), Vol. 46, No. 2, March-April, 1963, published by the Missionary Fathers of St. Vincent de Paul, Erie, Pennsylvania. The entire issue of this publication was dedicated to the Sisters of the Holy Family of Nazareth on the tenth anniversary of the Australian foundation.

70. Report of Inspection of the Holy Family Convent School, Kalinga, November 6, 1953.

71. New York: P. J. Kenedy and Sons, 1951.

72. *Gazetka,* Rome, July 9-25, 1953.

73. The Scroll of Honor, signed by Bishop John J. Wright of Pittsburgh, was presented on the occasion of the Commission's fiftieth anniversary in April of 1960.

74. Both observations were quoted to the author, April 16, 1963, by Sister Hyacinth Górecka whose term of office had expired in 1959.

75. Mother Bożena, circular, Rome, February 26, 1955. Although the circular assigned the date of October 10 for the opening of the chapter, it did not begin until October 19.

76. *Ibid.*

77. Sister Geraldine Sledz, letters to Sisters Hyacinth, Neomisia and Aloysius, provincial superiors; Pittsburgh, August 6, 1955.

78. Proceedings of the Tenth General Chapter of the Sisters of the Holy Family of Nazareth, Albano, October 19 to November 3, 1955.

79. Present were: S. Ezechiela Szupenko (Albano), S. Adele Wajda (Des Plaines), S. Albina Kowalkowska (Philadelphia), and S. Frances Sikorska (Pittsburgh); absent: S. Bernarda Krzeczkowska who was unable to come from Poland.

80. Mother Bożena, circular, Rome, June 1, 1957.

81. Mother Bożena, circular, Rome, April 14, 1958.

82. Mother Bożena, circular, Rome, December 1, 1958.

83. Mother Bożena, circular, Rome, December 12, 1958.

84. Josephine Rutkowska, Mother M. Neomisia of the Mother of Perpetual Help, 1892-   .

85. Proceedings of the Eleventh General Chapter of the Sisters of the Holy Family of Nazareth, Albano, June 4 to 12, 1959.

86. Rescript of the Sacred Congregation of Religious, N. 15715/59, July 22, 1959.

87. Proceedings of the Eleventh General Chapter.

PART V
(Pages 265-315)

1. Directors of novices appointed in 1959 were: Sister Ancilla Zebrowska, Meadowbrook, Pennsylvania, and Sister Richard Merman, Pittsburgh. Continuing in office at that time was Sister Adele Wajda, Des Plaines.

2. The proceedings of this meeting were recorded by Sister Mercedes Zelczak, provincial secretary in Pittsburgh. The concepts referred to are incorporated in *Spiritual Theology for Novices,* by Rev. Francis A. Cegielka (published privately by Immaculate Conception College: Lodi, New Jersey, 1961).

3. Rescript of the Sacred Congregation of Religious, November 1, 1960.

4. *Management Guide for Hospitals conducted by the Sisters of the Holy Family of Nazareth,* Detroit, Michigan, June 12, 1961; unpublished typescript sent to Mother M. Neomisia, superior general, and copies to the incumbent provincial superiors.

5. Richard L. Johnson, Director, Hospital Counseling Program, American Hospital Association, to Sister M. Geraldine, letter, Chicago, March 25, 1963.

6. Presented at the annual convention of the American Pharmaceutical Association, New York City, August 4-7, 1964.

7. *America in the Sixties,* by editors of *Fortune* (Harper & Brothers: New York, 1960), p. xvi.

8. Already on October 15, 1926, an editorial in the *Park Ridge Herald,* entitled "A Hospital an Imperative Need for Des Plaines," stated, "Des Plaines, a prosperous city approaching the 10,000 total of residents, the center of an area of farming and real estate wealth, with costly modern show houses, is woefully in need of a hospital." Park Ridge is one of the suburbs near Des Plaines.

9. Report of the exhumation, translation and reinterment of the remains of ten sisters from Clayton, New Mexico to Wichita Falls, Texas, dated November 21, 1962, from the files of Bethania Hospital, Wichita Falls, Texas. The names and dates of death of the sisters are as follows:

Sister M. Paula (surname and order unknown), November 16, 1916

Sister M. Benedict Renko, C.S.F.N., December 9, 1922

Sister M. Tryphona Witkowska, C.S.F.N., July 6, 1929

Sister M. Nestoria Radwan, C.S.F.N;., November 1, 1929

Sister M. Sancia Wąsikowska, C.S.F.N., March 18, 1930

Sister M. Pius Szpejnowska, C.S.F.N., November 8, 1930

Sister M. Priscilla Brahland, C.S.F.N., November 5, 1931

Sister M. Gemma Chrostowska, C.S.F.N., December 4, 1938

Sister M. Wolfganga Radek, C.S.F.N., October 2, 1943

Sister M. Simeona Kopek, C.S.F.N., June 12, 1946

10. Pope John made the announcement unexpectedly, on January 25, 1959, in the presence of 17 cardinals assembled at the Benedictine monastery adjoining the Ostian Basilica of St. Paul Outside the Walls, following the Pontifical Mass offered there for persecuted Catholics.

11. Zsolt Aradi, Msgr. James I. Tucek and James C. O'Neill, *Pope John XXIII* (Farrar, Straus and Cudahy, Inc.: New York, 1959), pp. 319-320.

12. Promulgated July 26, 1960.

13. *Latina in Era Spatio* (Latin in the Space Age), published privately by Nazareth Academy, Philadelphia, 1962.

14. "Potesne Aetatis Spatii Linguam Dicere?" (Can you speak the language of the air space age?)—presented in typescript and commended by the United States Air Force Educational Division of Wright-Patterson Air Force Base, August 12, 1963.

15. The presentation was made on June 5, 1962.

16. A Progress Report of Holy Family College, October, 1963; typescript.

17. Notes and References, Part II, No. 264.

18. According to conversion tables, 2.471 hectares of land = one acre; the tract of land measured 5.37 hectares.

19. Refer to page 261 herein.

20. The *Decree* was promulgated October 28, 1965.

21. Indult of the Sacred Congregation of Religious, January 8, 1965.

22. Indult of the Sacred Congregation of Religious, July 16, 1965.

23. Chapter VI in the *Dogmatic Constitution on the Church.*

24. Edited version of the Constitutions, "Pro Manuscripto," Rome, 1966.

25. Published privately, "Pro Manuscripto," Rome, 1966.

26. Dedicated October 16, 1966 by Bishop John J. Wright of Pittsburgh.

27. *Il Tempio Massimo,* subtitle "Letter to Women Religious" (Washington: National Catholic Welfare Conference, 1962), 14 p.

28. *Religious Life in the Post-Conciliar Period* (Rome: Scuola Grafica Salesiana Pio XI, 1967), 31 pp.

29. *Guidance to Religious on Adaptation and Renewal* (Boston: Daughters of St. Paul, 1968), 16 pp.

30. *Ecclesiae Sanctae* (Boston: Daughters of St. Paul, 1966), 45 pp.

31. Mother M. Neomisia, circular No. 39 to the convents of the Congregation, Rome, September 12, 1968.

32. Chairman, Sister Laurence Crowe; members: Sisters Angela Kuzia, Theodosette Lewandowska, DeChantal Dylewska, Electa Trela and Eugene Klaniecka.

33. Sister M. Edward Lijek, *The History of the Special General Chapter* (Rome; privately published, 1969), pp. 23-27, *passim.*

34. *Ibid.*

35. Mother Mary of Jesus the Good Shepherd, letter to Mother Raphael, Rome, November 23, 1887.

36. *Covenant of Love* (Rome; privately published, 1969).

37. Mother Mary of Jesus the Good Shepherd, *Conferences of Our Mother Foundress,* translated by Sister M. Theophame Ruszkowska (Rome: privately published, 1968).

38. Antonio Ricciardi, O.F.M.Conv., *Francesca Siedliska* (Edizioni Agiografiche, Rome, 1970), published in English under the title *His Will Alone* (Oshkosh, Wisconsin: Castle-Pierce Press, 1971).

39. This frequently quoted statement was an indisputable refutation of fallacies under similar recurring circumstances. It was cited, among others, in *Our Sunday Visitor,* October 10, 1971, published in Huntington, Indiana.

40. *The Acts of the Fourteenth General Chapter* (Rome: privately published, 1971), pp. 47-50.

41. *Ibid.,* p. 51.

42. Groundbreaking for the sisters' retirement home in Des Plaines, on the grounds facing the provincialate, took place on Saturday, November 20, 1971.

43. Groundbreaking ceremony for the vice-provincialate was held on May 28, 1972.

44. Dedication, religious and civic, of the West Wing Tower and adjunct facilities of Bethania Hospital was concluded on May 7, 1972.

45. Recommendation #2 of the Special General Chapter: "That a committee be appointed to investigate the possibilities of establishing a house of prayer in the Congregation; [and] that a report of its findings be presented to the superior general and her council."

46. Letter, October 19, 1971.

47. Sister M. Precious died in Pittsburgh, Pennsylvania, June 25, 1972.

48. Rome: Typis Polyglottis Vaticanis, 1971.

49. *The Acts of the Fourteenth General Chapter*, pp. 12-40.

50. Monica Synakowska, Mother M. Medarda of the Immaculate Conception, 1914-   .

51. *The Acts of the Fourteenth General Chapter*, pp. 49-50.

52. October, 1972.

53. *On the Renewal of Religious Life (Evangelica Testificatio)*, 18.

54. Archbishop Luigi Raimondi, Protocol No. 95/72,, Washington, D.C., February 5, 1972.

55. The accident occurred on March 1, 1966, when she sustained the loss of one eye and a leg fracture. After surgery, she developed an embolism which caused her death on March 14, 1966.

56. May 31, 1970.

57. New Haven, Connecticut: College and University Press, 1968, 143 pp. The book is based on Sister Grace's dissertation for the doctorate, submitted to the New York University in 1966 under the title, *The Origin and the Development of the Polish School of Mathematics*.

BIBLIOGRAPHY

I. GENERAL WORKS

Aradi, Zsolt; Tucek, Msgr. James I. and O'Neill, James C. *Pope John XXIII* (New York: Farrar, Straus and Cudahy, Inc., 1959).

Beck, Andrew. "Pius IX and Poland," *The Clergy Review,* XVIII (May, 1940).

Beeson, Paul B., M.D., and McDermott, Walsh, M.D., ed. *Cecil-Loeb Textbook of Medicine,* twelfth edition (Philadelphia and London: W. B. Saunders Co., 1967), 2 vols.

Bell, Mary I. M. *A Short History of the Papacy* (New York: Dodd, Mead and Company, 1921).

Beylin, Karolina. *Jeden Rok Warszawy: 1875* (Warszawa: Polski Instytut Wydawniczy, 1959).

―――― *Tajemnice Warszawy* (Warszawa: Państwowy Instytut Wydawniczy, 1956).

Birkhaeuser, J. A., Rev. *History of the Church* (New York and Cincinnati: Fr. Pustet & Co., 1893).

Burnichon, Joseph, S.J. *Vie du P. Fr.-X. Gautrelet, S.J.* (Paris: Retaux, 1896).

Bystron, Jan. *Warszawa* (Warszawa: Wydawnictwo Józefa Kubickiego, 1953).

Campbell, Paul E. *Parish School Problems* (New York: Joseph F. Wagner, 1941).

Challice, Rachel. *History of the Court of Spain, 1802-1906* (New York: D. Appleton & Co., 1909).

Chołodecki, Józef Bialynia. *Księga Pamiątkowa w 40stą Rocznicę Powstania r. 1863-1864* (Lwów: Piller i Spółka, 1904).

Churchill, Winston S. *The Second World War* (Cambridge, Mass.: Houghton Mifflin Co., 1953), 6 vols.

Dorland, W. A. Newman, M.D. *Illustrated Medical Dictionary* (Philadelphia and London: W. B. Saunders Co., 1957).

Douthwaite, Arthur H., M.D., ed. *French's Index of Differential Diagnosis,* ninth edition (Baltimore: Williams and Wilkins Co., 1967).

Edwards, H. Sutherland. *The Private History of a Polish Insurrection* (London: Saunders, Otley & Co., 1865).

Ellis, John Tracy, Msgr. *American Catholicism* (Chicago: University of Chicago Press, 1956).

Eugene, Fr., O.F.M.Cap. *Guide to Loreto* (Loreto: Congregazione Universale della S. Casa, 1965).

Ferguson, Wallace K. and Brunn, Geoffrey. *A Survey of European Civilization* (Boston: Houghton Mifflin Co., 1952).

Fortune, Editors of. *America in the Sixties* (New York: Harper & Brothers, 1958).

Furey, Francis T. *Life of Leo XIII and History of His Pontificate* (New York and Philadelphia: Catholic Educational Co., 1903).

Galbraith, John Kenneth. *The Affluent Society* (Boston: Houghton Mifflin Co., 1958).

Giller, Agaton. *Historia Powstania Narodu Polskiego w 1861-64 r.* (Paris: Księgarnia Luksemburska, 1867-71), 4 vols.

Goetstouwers, J. B., S.J. *Synopsis Historiae Societatis Jesu* (Lovenii: Typis ad Sancti Alphonsi, 1950).

Grzegorzewski, Stanisław. *Wspomnienia Osobiste z Powstania 1863 r.* (Lwów: Tow. Wydawnicze, 1903).

Halecki, Oscar. *The Millennium of Europe* (Notre Dame, Ind.: Notre Dame University Press, 1963.)

Havighurst, Alfred F. *Twentieth Century Britain* (Evanston, Ill.: Row, Peterson and Company, 1962.)

Hayes, Carlton J.; Baldwin, Marshall Whithed and Cole, Charles Woolsey. *History of Western Civilization* (New York: Macmillan Co., 1967).

Iwicki, John, C.R. *Resurrectionist Studies: The First One Hundred Years, 1866-1966* (Rome: Gregorian University Press, 1966).

Kennedy, John F. *A Nation of Immigrants* (New York: Harper and Row, 1964).

Kiefer, Brother William J., S.M. *Leo XIII: A Light from Heaven* (Milwaukee: Bruce Publishing Co., 1961).

Kossak-Szczucka, Zofia. *Rok Polski: Obyczaj i Wiara* (Londyn: Biblioteka Polska, 1955).

Kridl, Manfred. *Polska Myśl Demokratyczna w Ciągu Wieków* (New York: Gascony Printing Co., 1945).

Lencewicz, Stanisław. *Geografia Fizyczna Polski* (Warszawa: Wydawnictwo Naukowe, 1955).

Lerchenfeld, Amand von Schweiger. *Życie Kobiet na Ziemi* (Warszawa: Redakcja Przeglądu Tygodniowego, 1882).

Lescouer, Louis. *L'Eglise Catholique en Pologne sous le Gouvernement Russe depuis le Premier Partage jusqu'à nos Jours, 1772-1875* (Paris: Plon, 1876).

Leszczyc, Zbigniew. *Herby Szlachty Polskiej* (Poznań: Antoni Fiedler, 1908).

Lucas, Father, of St. Joseph, O.C.D. *The Secret of Sanctity of St. John of the Cross* (Milwaukee: Bruce Publishing Co., 1962).

MacGowan, Kenneth. *The House of Loreto* (Dublin: Kamac Publications, 1964).

Maurois, André. *A History of France* (New York: Farrar, Straus and Cudahy, 1956).

Niesiecki, Kasper, S.J. *Herbarz Polski* (Lipsk: Breitkopf i Haertel, 1841).

O'Malley, Charles J., ed. *The Great White Shepherd of Christendom* (Chicago: J. S. Hyland & Co., 1903).

Oppman, Edmund. *Wodzowie Polski* (Warszawa: Instytut Propagandy Państwowo-Twórczej, 1935).

Peel, C. S. *A Hundred Wonderful Years: 1820-1920* (New York: Dodd, Mead and Company, 1927).

Pinson, Koppel S. *Modern Germany: Its History and Civilization* (New York: Macmillan Co., 1954).

Polish National Committee of America. *General Demography of Poland,* vol. II of *Polish Encyclopaedia* (Geneva, Switzerland: Atar Ltd., 1921).

Rutkowski, Franciszek, *Arcybiskup Jan Cieplak* (Warszawa: Drukarnia Archidiecezjalna, 1934).

Salvadori, Massimo. *Italy* (Englewood Cliffs, N. J.: Prentice-Hall, Inc., 1965).

Sheahon, James Washington. *The Great Conflagration* (Philadelphia: Union Publishing Co., 1871).

Sherlock, Sheila, M.D. *Disease of the Liver and Biliary System,* third edition (Philadelphia: F. A. Davis Co., 1963).

Smith, Denis Mack. *Italy: A Modern History* (Ann Arbor: The University of Michigan Press, 1959).

Speed, J. S., M.D., and Knight, Robert A., M.D., editors. *Campbell's Operative Orthopaedics* (St. Louis: C. V. Mosby Co., 1956), 2 vols.

Van Zeller, Dom Hubert. *Suffering in Other Words* (Springfield, Ill.: Templegate Publishers, 1964).

Wallace, Lillian Parker. *The Papacy and Eastern Diplomacy* (Chapel Hill, N.C.: University of Carolina Press, 1948).

Walsh, Warren Bartlett. *Russia and the Soviet Union: A Modern History* (Ann Arbor: The University of Michigan Press, 1958).

Will, Allen S. *Life of James Cardinal Gibbons* (Baltimore and New York: John Murphy Company, 1911).

X. A. M. K. S. T. *Droga do Pozyskania Spokojności Sumienia i Wiekuistego Szczęścia w Niebie* (Warszawa: XX. Misjonarze u św. Krzyża, 1860).

II. HISTORICAL AND BIOGRAPHICAL SOURCES
pertinent to the Congregation of the Sisters of

the Holy Family of Nazareth

Book of Customs of the Sisters of the Holy Family of Nazareth, first edition, Rome, 1928; second edition, Rome, 1958.

Burton, Katherine. *Where there is Love* (New York: P. J. Kenedy & Sons, 1951).

Constitutions of the Congregation of the Sisters of the Holy Family of Nazareth, (a) original text, manuscript, 1887; (b) text definitively approved, June 4, 1923; (c) second edition, revised and approved, June 19, 1956; (d) proposed adaptations, 1966; (e) interim Constitutions with Statutes, published under the one title, *Covenant of Love,* Rome, 1969.

Dobraczyński, Jan. *Lepsza Cząstka* (Chicago: Stanek Press, 1949).

Drogą Ukrycia i Ofiary (Rome: privately published, 1951).

Gazetka (newsletter), issued in Rome and privately circulated mong the houses of the Congregation at different intervals, 1933-1959.

Kurtz, V., S.J. *Livre d'Or du Collège Saint-Clément* (Metz, Moselle, 1927).

La Congregazione della Sacra Famiglia di Nazareth nel primo cinquantenario della sua fondazione, 1875-1925 (Roma: Tipografia Poliglotta Vaticana, 1925), also translated into English and Polish.

Lubowidzka, Mother M. Gabriel, and Lubowidzka, Mother M. Raphael. *Życiorys Świątobliwej Matki Marii Franciszki Siedliskiej* (unpublished manuscript, 1912).

Lubowidzka, Mother M. Raphael. *Ojciec Leander Lendzian, Kapucyn* (unpublished manuscript, 1913).

Mary, Mother, of Jesus the Good Shepherd (Frances Siedliska). *Conferences* (Rome: privately published, 1968).

Nazaret, the Congregation's periodical publication privately printed in Rome, from May, 1927 to June, 1942, for internal distribution.

Pierwszy Zjazd Naukowo-Pedagogiczny Sióstr Nauczycielek Zgrom. Najśw. Rodziny z Nazaretu (Chicago: Stanek Press, 1941). Proceedings of the first educational conference of the Sisters of the Holy Family of Nazareth in the United States.

Progress Report of Holy Family College (Philadelphia: unpublished typescript, 1963).

Regulamin (Poznań: Kuryer Poznański, 1894). A directory for the Sisters of the Holy Family of Nazareth.

Ricciardi, Antonio. *Francesca Siedliska* (Roma: Edizioni Agiografiche, 1970), translated into English by Regis N. Barwig under the title, *His Will Alone* (Oshkosh, Wisconsin: Castle-Pierce Press, 1971).

Sardi, Vincenzo, and Sica, Carlo. *Vita della Serva di Dio Maria Francesca De Siedliska, Fondatrice della Congregazione della Sacra Famiglia di Nazareth* (Grottaferrata: Scuola Tipografica Italo-Orientale "S. Nilo." 1921). Translated into Polish by Msgr. Władysław Chotkowski under the title, *Żywot Sługi Bożej Marji Franciszki Siedliskiej od Pana Jezusa Dobrego Pasterza* (Kraków: Głos Narodu, 1924); adapted in the French by Msgr. H. under the title, *La Servante de Dieu Mère Marie Françoise De Siedliska* (Rome: Ecole Typographique Pie X, 1926).

Zienkiewicz, Aleksander. *No Greater Love* (Pulaski, Wisconsin: Franciscan Publishers, 1968); translated from the Polish, *Ofiara Przyjęta* (Rome: privately published, 1968).

III. ARCHIVES

Archival materials, preserved at the generalate of the Sisters of the Holy Family of Nazareth in Rome, consisted of the following:

1. chronicles
2. personal notes and memoirs
3. journals and diaries
4. correspondence and circulars
5. newsletters

6. obituary files
7. administrative records
8. proceedings of general chapters
9. civil documents
10. decrees of the Holy See

INDEX OF PERSONS

INDEX OF PLACES